WITHDRAWAL

Developmental Psychology and Social Change

What is the unique mission of developmental psychology? How has it evolved historically? What are its current challenges? The chapters in this collection present the view that research, history, and policy are essential and interlocking components of a mature developmental psychology. Patterns of human development differ markedly across historical epochs, cultures, and social circumstances. Major societal changes examined by contributing authors – the advent of universal compulsory schooling, the adoption of a one-child policy in China, U.S. policy shifts in healthcare, welfare and child care – present "natural experiments" in social design. Authors challenge the idea of a clear distinction between basic and applied developmental research. In sharp contrast with the view that science is value-neutral, developmental psychologists have from the outset pursued the betterment of children and families through educational, child-care, and health initiatives. An historical perspective reveals the beneficial, if sometimes contentious, interplay between empirical research and social programs and policies.

David B. Pillemer is the Dr. Samuel E. Paul Professor of Developmental Psychology at the University of New Hampshire. His research specialty is autobiographical memory across the life span. He has studied memory development in children, memories of adolescence, "flashbulb" memories of momentous events, and memories of educational experiences.

Sheldon H. White is John Lindsey Professor of Psychology Emeritus at Harvard University. A developmental psychologist, he has done research on children's learning, attention, and memory. He has chaired committees concerned with the development of a research program for Head Start. He also has been chair of the Board on Children and Families of the National Research Council.

Cambridge Studies in Social and Emotional Development

General Editor: Carolyn Shantz, *Wayne State University*

Advisory Board: Nancy Eisenberg, Robert N. Emde, Willard W. Hartup, Lois W. Hoffman, Franz J. Mönks, Ross D. Parke, Michael Rutter, and Carolyn Zahn-Waxler

Recent books in the series:

Developmental Psychology and Social Change

Research, History and Policy

Edited by

DAVID B. PILLEMER
University of New Hampshire

SHELDON H. WHITE
Harvard University

CAMBRIDGE
UNIVERSITY PRESS

CAMBRIDGE UNIVERSITY PRESS

Cambridge, New York, Melbourne, Madrid, Cape Town, Singapore, São Paulo

Cambridge University Press
40 West 20th Street, New York, NY 10011-4211, USA

www.cambridge.org
Information on this title: www.cambridge.org/9780521826181

© Cambridge University Press 2005

First published 2005

Printed in the United States of America

A catalog record for this publication is available from the British Library.

Library of Congress Cataloging in Publication Data
Developmental psychology and social change : research, history and policy / edited by
David B. Pillemer, Sheldon H. White.
    p.   cm. – (Cambridge studies in social and emotional development.)
    Includes bibliographical references and index.
    ISBN 0-521-82618-7 – ISBN 0-521-53360-0 (pbk.)
    1. Social change.   2. Developmental psychology.   I. Pillemer, David B., 1950–
II. White, Sheldon Harold, 1928–   III. Title.   IV. Series.
    HM831.D48   2005
    303.4 – dc22   2004018272

ISBN-13   978-0-521-82618-1 hardback
ISBN-10   0-521-82618-7 hardback

ISBN-13   978-0-521-53360-7 paperback
ISBN-10   0-521-53360-0 paperback

March 9, 2006

Contents

Preface

As Professor Sheldon (Shep) White approached retirement from his position as William James Professor of Psychology at Harvard University, his colleagues and students began organizing an event in his honor. Barbara Rogoff and Alex Siegel were especially active in pursuing this idea. When I approached Shep for his input, he stated clearly that he did not want a traditional festschrift. Rather, he preferred to co-organize a lively, substantive conference and to co-edit an accompanying book that would concentrate on the three main foci of his life work: research, history, and policy in developmental psychology, and especially their intersections. The conference, titled *Developmental Psychology and the Social Changes of Our Time*, was held at Wellesley College, June 20–22, 2002. We adopted the more personal title, "Three Faces of Shep Conference," because Shep has represented and promoted each and all of these faces – research, history, policy – throughout his career. Connections between the three faces of his work provide the foundation for a new way of thinking about developmental psychology and the lives of children. Contributors were asked to write chapters that addressed the intersection of at least two of the three faces.

In addition to the chapter authors, conference participants included Alex Siegel, Edward Zigler, Emily Cahan, Jack Shonkoff, Tami Katzir, Robert Lawler, Julia Hough, Ruby Takanishi, and Bob Granger. Conference assistants Susan Camuti and Kate Collins were invaluable to this project. We are deeply grateful to the Foundation for Child Development and the William T. Grant Foundation for financial assistance, and to Cambridge University Press for producing an excellent book. Special thanks to Rachel Gooze and Zorana Ircevic for editorial assistance, to Julia Hough and Phil Laughlin at Cambridge for editorial advice and support, to Doug English at TechBooks for technical help, to Jane Pillemer for creating the imaginative conference program design, and to Barbara White and family for their interest and support.

David B. Pillemer

Contributors

Barbara Beatty
Department of Education
Wellesley College
Wellesley, MA

Stephen L. Buka
Department of Maternal and Child
  Health
Harvard School of Public Health
Cambridge, MA

Michael Cole
Laboratory of Comparative Human
  Cognition
University of California, San Diego

Maricela Correa-Chávez
Department of Psychology
University of California,
  Santa Cruz

Marta Navichoc Cotuc
Department of Psychology
University of California,
  Santa Cruz

Wolfgang Edelstein
Max Planck Institute for Human
  Development
Berlin, Germany

Ron Haskins
Brookings Institution
Washington, DC

Aletha C. Huston
Department of Human Ecology
University of Texas at Austin

Alex Kozulin
International Center for the
  Enhancement of Learning
  Potential and Hebrew University
Jerusalem, Israel

Michelle D. Leichtman
Department of Psychology
University of New Hampshire

Lewis P. Lipsitt
Department of Psychology
Brown University
Providence, RI

Kathleen McCartney
Harvard Graduate School of
  Education
Cambridge, MA

Deborah Phillips
Department of Psychology
Georgetown University
Washington, DC

David B. Pillemer
Department of Psychology
University of New Hampshire
Durham, NH

Barbara Rogoff
Department of Psychology
University of California, Santa Cruz

William McKinley Runyan
School of Social Welfare
University of California, Berkeley

Sidney Strauss
School of Education
Tel Aviv University
Israel

Charles M. Super
School of Family Studies
Division of Health and Human
    Development
University of Connecticut
Storrs, CT

Jaan Valsiner
Department of Psychology
Clark University
Worcester, MA

Qi Wang
Department of Human Development
Cornell University
Ithaca, NY

Sheldon H. White
Department of Psychology
Harvard University
Cambridge, MA

Introduction: What Kind of Science Is Developmental Psychology?

Sheldon H. White and David B. Pillemer

What is the mission of developmental psychology? What is its role in history and society? Traditional philosophical models asserted the doctrine of the unity of science, with the natural sciences providing the model for all scientific endeavors. In this view, conceptual definitions, procedures, and methodologies of the "less mature" human sciences ought to be patterned after those of experimental physics, as a "mature" science. In the Age of Theory, Sigmund Koch's (1964) term for the period of theoretical behaviorism spanning the 1930s and 1940s, a vision of psychology as an "immature physics" was set forth.

Today, psychology continues to use many concepts, procedures, and definitions of "good science" borrowed from the natural sciences, although many aspects of developmental research are unlike those of experimental physics. The full range of children's thought and behavior is not captured easily by simple laws, numerical equations, or mathematical models. What, then, holds the natural-science model of developmental psychology in place? One factor is a set of institutional structures built up during the great growth period immediately after World War II, in the 1940s and the 1950s. During this era, much of the cooperative architecture of contemporary science was established – granting agencies, journals, norms and values of graduate education, definitions of appropriate methodology, and so forth. This institutional architecture implicitly enforces a traditional view of what science is and ought to be.

The architecture was designed primarily to fit the needs of the natural sciences and medicine, and it succeeds, to a degree, for developmental psychology. Unquestioningly, interesting and significant knowledge about human development is being produced under its support. However, we struggle to deal with patterns of phenomena that stretch the boundaries of traditional

1

physical science models:

- We rarely deal with universal laws or phenomena that are invariant across time and place. Patterns of human development differ across historical epochs, cultures, and social strata of a large and complex world society.
- The path of development is determined in part by active human design: options, choices, schedules, and tradeoffs created by members of society.
- The environment in which a child grows up is largely a human creation. There is human intelligence, human contrivance, and human intentionality buried in that environment. As a child develops, he or she must deal not only with the traditional invariant Kantian modalities – space, time, causation, number – but with the changeable vicissitudes of social influence.
- The developing child's continuing life task is not only to adapt to his or her environment, but also to construct it, manage it, build it, and rebuild it. Consider, for example, the famous question of whether children's play is or is not serious business. We posit that through play children are learning how to invent and manage environments.
- Developmental psychologists do not deal with a naïve or ignorant laity. People outside of academic psychology have important practical knowledge about human behavior and development and have significant responsibilities for predicting and managing it.
- There exists a strong demand for practical knowledge among developmental psychology's audience, and a corresponding profusion of "offshore knowledge" to meet this demand. Any commercial bookstore contains one or more floor-to-ceiling bookshelves on child psychology. The sometimes disparaging view within universities is that this body of writing represents only "popular psychology," watered-down and sometimes opportunistic translations of basic research. Yet, offshore books on childhood represent a variety of practical concerns of utmost importance to parents and educators, and these concerns demand our attention and respect.
- Developmental psychology departs from traditional views of basic scientific discovery because it deals explicitly with values. We have the peculiar spectacle of a supposedly "value-free" discipline addressing qualities of "good" or "bad" parenting, good or bad schooling, good or bad child-care arrangements, good or bad media influences, and good or bad social programs. Distinguished commentators,

including Dewey, Kohlberg, and Habermas, have argued that values are a necessary and important part of the mission of disciplines like developmental psychology. If one looks carefully at evaluations of government programs for children, it is not hard to discern a thinly concealed process through which social scientists help to define program goals and values.

From the Past toward the Future: Historical Analysis of Developmental Psychology

Philosophers of science in the 1930s discussed the practices and goals of psychology by aligning it with the history of experimental physics. Although developmental psychology is not physics-like, an historical approach to the field is a fundamental and perhaps essential way to think about its nature. How is developmental psychology an expression of the societies in which it exists? What does it do for such societies? How has it changed over time? What should its rightful goals and values be? What are the possible dangers, or side effects, associated with the practical application of developmental research? We look to the past to identify trends, processes, influences, or constraints. The early adventures of the discipline are, in effect, a series of transformational experiments that reveal important aspects of its construction. Historical perspective broadens our view of what possibilities exist for developmental psychology in the future.

Historical analysis illuminates the flow of questions, ideas, and practices back and forth between developmental psychology and the society surrounding it. Chapters in this volume explore connections between developmental psychology (and its philosophical ancestors) and child care and welfare (Phillips & McCartney; Huston; Haskins), nursery-school education (Beatty), design and management of educational systems and programs (Rogoff, Correa-Chávez, & Cotuc; Strauss), intelligence testing (Kozulin), healthcare for children (Buka; Lipsitt), and adolescent behavior problems (Edelstein). With an immediacy that transcends academic departments and research laboratories, developmental psychology participates in the life of the society surrounding it. In the beginning, not quite by coincidence, the rise of developmental psychology was associated with liberal, progressive forces in American politics. But now liberals and conservatives alike use the data of developmental psychology to build programs and strengthen their positions (Haskins).

In its earliest years, developmental psychology tended to dwell on the primitive in human nature, inspired in part by Darwin's evolutionary theory.

Developmental studies centered on questions of how the growing child's mind departs from the animal mind. The theorizing of those early years often pictured human infants as primitive, savage, amoral, egocentric, narcissistic, and living in a world of formless experience.

At the turn of the 20th century, G. Stanley Hall struggled to link Darwinian views of developmental psychology to the problems of children, parents, and professionals living in the institutional web of a modern society. Generations of developmental researchers have made the struggle after him and gradually the substance and modalities of their science have changed. A network of "applied" researchers now connects the university to communities of practitioners, professionals, and policymakers. Some romantic images projected by 19th century evolutionism have been set aside. Humans do not develop in a world of "nature red in fang and claw." From the very beginning, they grow up in an environment impregnated with human intelligence, in the midst of objects and activity patterns designed by humans for human purposes. As everyday environments change, patterns of human growth change, and developmental psychologists participate actively in the design processes of a changing, experimenting society. Ever more closely approaching the forefront of scientific inquiry is a cultural-historical perspective on both human development and the scientific work of developmental psychology.

Enlarging Developmental Psychology's Perspective: Some Modest Proposals

How can developmental psychology construct an identity that fully encompasses its historical, applied, and research faces? Some modest changes in undergraduate and graduate education, and in the programs and priorities of universities and funding agencies, would provide a good start. We propose the following changes:

- Graduate students in developmental psychology take a required course on the scholarly and social history of their discipline. The scholarly history will trace the emergence of ideas and methods used by contemporary developmental psychologists out of scientific and philosophical traditions of the 18th, 19th, and early 20th centuries. At the same time, the course will trace the increasing scholarly interest in child study alongside the emergence of modern societies and welfare states in the late 19th and early 20th centuries.
- Undergraduate and graduate students in developmental psychology have available to them a course on the organization of professions,

social services, and institutions dealing with families and children, and the role played by psychologists in their formation.

- Universities recognize that developmental psychology is a pluralistic field, which requires a variety of approaches and levels of inquiry. The pluralistic perspective will extend across faculties, disciplines, professions, and field sites.
- Universities and funding agencies recognize and give high priority to developmental psychology's agency as a science of design – as a cooperative human endeavor that has enduring ties and particular relevance to the problems and needs of contemporary society.

We believe that the chapters in this volume will contribute to a framework for achieving these goals.

Organization of This Book

Authors were invited to contribute to this book because they have done significant work in developmental psychology, and their work crosses traditional boundaries of research, historical scholarship, and policy analysis. For their chosen topics, we asked authors to address the intersection of at least two of these three domains: research, history, and policy. All of the chapters fulfill this request, and several advance developmental science in all three domains.

The chapters all challenge the idea of a sharp or meaningful distinction between "basic" and "applied" research. Applications to everyday social problems have not evolved secondarily, as add-ons to extended programs of theoretically driven "pure" research. Rather, developmental psychology has been connected to practical concerns from the outset. Nevertheless, the relationship between research and policy has been uneasy, with cooperation appearing to be much stronger in some domains than in others.

One prominent focus of developmental psychology since its inception is the betterment of children and families. Barbara Beatty shows how the rise of American nursery schools was tied directly to research movements in colleges, universities, and training institutes. Practical issues driving research included the question of whether nursery-school education could support women's career pursuits without impairing their children's healthy development, and if in fact early schooling could enhance successful socialization. In contrast, Deborah Phillips and Kathleen McCartney identify a general "disconnect" between research and policy on child care, compared to a much closer connection for Head Start enrichment programs. The authors pinpoint a number of reasons why child-care research and policy have largely developed side-by-side rather than hand-in-hand. Ron Haskins also discusses the long and complex history of developmental science's relationship to child-care programs, but from the perspective of a policy analyst and Washington insider. Aletha Huston shows not only how research examining the effects of poverty on child development may inform public policy, but also how issues raised by the politics of welfare reform have enriched developmental science.

Education has long been a prominent point of intersection between research and practice. Barbara Rogoff, Maricela Correa-Chávez, and Maria Navichoc Cotuc chart the emergence of compulsory schooling in the United States and Guatemala. They show how some "naturalized" conceptions of child development, such as the linking of chronological age with standards of test performance, originally grew out of practical concerns. Even the developmental psychologist's essential independent variable – age – became an organizing principle for research on intelligence and achievement in large part because of its utility in solving bureaucratic problems relating to social sorting and educational placement. Alex Kozulin describes how the assessment of children's cognitive capacities, whether by IQ testing or other procedures, was tied "from the very beginning" to applied issues – predicting learning ability and school performance. Michael Cole and Jaan Valsiner illustrate the intimate connection between basic and applied agendas with their creative application of Vygotsky's theoretical construct "zone of proximal development" to children's failures to learn to read. Similarly, Sidney Strauss's original theoretical work on teaching as a "natural cognitive ability" carries with it important implications for the classroom and for teacher education.

In the domain of health policy, Steven Buka's sophisticated model of "developmental epidemiology" and Lewis Lipsitt's critical examination of research on the problem of crib death both illustrate how developmental research can make an invaluable contribution to effective policymaking. Buka presents stunning examples of how early life events may have a profound and lasting impact on health and well being. Lipsitt's analysis underscores the potential losses for society if critical research is overlooked or if "acceptable" research paradigms are defined too narrowly.

Several chapters capitalize on "natural experiments" in social design. Wolfgang Edelstein explores developmental explanations for a surge of neo-Nazi activity among East German adolescents following the collapse of the Berlin Wall and German reunification. He examines why these ideas are especially appealing to young people, and why adolescents are particularly vulnerable to their destructive influence. Michelle Leichtman and Qi Wang compellingly show how culture influences the ways that children and adults talk, write, and, ultimately, think about the personal past. They demonstrate that governmental policies dictating family structure in China (the one-child policy) and governmental solicitation of certain types of autobiographical writing in China and the Soviet Union are reflected in the personal memory styles of individual citizens. Although Westerners accept compulsory schooling as a long-standing and unquestioned governmental policy, Rogoff and colleagues focus on its historical emergence in the United States and in Guatemala. When introduced, this dramatic social change had a profound impact on family life and the child's place in society.

Psychologists not only analyze the effects of societal change on children's development, but also effect change by linking their research insights to policy initiatives. Historical shifts in welfare policy (Huston), child care policy (Phillips & McCartney; Haskins), and healthcare policy (Buka; Lipsitt) also offer natural experiments in social design that are prime targets for psychological analysis and policy recommendations. But psychologists may help to shape the future even in areas that are a step removed from pressing policy considerations. Edelstein's perceptive analysis of the social consequences of the collapse of the Berlin Wall for East German society may suggest interventions directed to problem adolescents. Rogoff and colleagues' cultural-historical perspective portrays compulsory education not as a given, but as a changing societal characteristic, with good and bad qualities. This frees us to think creatively about the role of compulsory schooling in contemporary society, and what its role could and should be in the future.

Two chapters in particular help to set the tone for the entire volume. Charles Super presents a far-reaching, interpretive historical account of cross-cultural studies within developmental psychology, and he identifies a slow but important trend to "globalize" the field of human development. William Runyan offers a personal analysis and appreciation of Shep White's central role in establishing the history of developmental psychology as a prominent field of inquiry. Runyan's account of his own encounters with White, face-to-face and in print, provides a unique assessment of the value of an historical approach to human development.

To borrow a term from Runyan, we hope that this volume will contribute to a better and more adequate "story" of human development in its full historical, cultural, and political context.

Reference

Koch, S. (1964). Psychology and emerging conceptions of knowledge as unitary. In T. W. Mann (Ed.), *Behaviorism and Phenomenology* (pp. 1–41). Chicago: University of Chicago Press.

PART ONE

The Developing Child

Global and Historical Perspectives

1   The Globalization of Developmental Psychology

Charles M. Super

> Near the end of the first millennium of the Common Era, it is said, Khaldi, a
> goat herd living in the Horn of Africa, noticed that his animals were
> particularly frisky after consuming the red berries of a particular bush. The
> first hot beverage of "kahva" (meaning 'against sleep') was devised shortly
> thereafter either by monks, who learned of the beans from Khaldi, or by a
> Muslim dervish who, banished and starving, tried to soften the berries in
> water upon instructions from God (Starbucks, 2004; Anonymous, 2004).
> Soon Yemeni traders were exporting coffee beans from the port of
> Al-Mukha (hence: mocha), under a carefully protected monopoly.
>
> (Tchibo, nd)

In 1875 in Leipzig, Germany, Wilhelm Wundt established a laboratory for
using the experimental method of physics to isolate and measure what were
presumed to be the elements of sensation, perception, and ultimately the
functioning of the psyche. His goal was to "mark out a new domain of science"
(Wundt, 1874, cited in Schultz, 1975, p. 53). In this historical moment, it is
said, lies the origin of modern psychology – scientific, empirical psychology,
beyond the mere logic of the philosopher (Boring, 1950). In 1879, Leipzig
University incorporated Wundt's laboratory, and in recognition of that event
100 years later, the American Psychological Association (APA) declared the
centenary of the field itself. The APA was actually formed in 1892, with
G. Stanley Hall presiding over a membership of 42 persons who were engaged
in the advancement of psychology as a science (American Psychological
Association, 2003).

Frans Boas, the founder of American anthropology, studied briefly in
Wundt's experimental laboratory, but he eventually concluded that "even
'elementary' sensations were conditioned by their contexts of occurrence"
(Laboratory of Comparative Human Cognition, 1983, p. 297). Thus he set
out for North America to see more of humanity's contexts. Boas's lifetime

of field work among the Kwakiutl and other native American groups, and the intellectual line that descended from this project, defined a new, systematic ethnography focused on how cultural features shape human experience (Harris, 1968). The work of this tradition became housed in departments of anthropology, and the American Anthropological Association (AAA) was founded in 1902, with an initial membership of 175 (American Anthropological Association, 2000).

Sociology – a term originated in 1838 by the French philosopher Auguste Comte to encompass the cultural, political, and economic evolution of Western society (Scharff, 1995) – had firmer disciplinary roots in Europe than did either psychology or cultural anthropology, but a distinctly American version was evident by the time the American Sociological Association (ASA) was formed in 1905. The founders noted both that several European nations already had established associations devoted to the scientific study of society and its improvements, and that it was highly desirable to create a new American group "separate and independent" from existing organizations (e.g., the American Economics Society), as otherwise it would have a "subordinate position, and, what is worse, would seem to indicate that sociology is a branch of either history, political science, economics, or anthropology" (F. W. Blackmar, cited in Rhoades, 1981, p. 3). At the first Annual Meeting, in Providence, Rhode Island, members of the society numbered 115, including those with both theoretical and "practical" interests (Rhoades, 1981).

> During the reign of Süleyman the Magnificent (1520–1566), coffee was introduced to the Ottoman empire either by two Syrian traders, Hükm and Shems, or, according to another story, by the Ethiopian governor Özdemir Pasha. Although initially opposed by the empire's clerics as evil and narcotic, coffee quickly became popular and 600 coffeehouses had been established in Istanbul alone within a generation. The coffeehouses served there, as they have everywhere else since, as places of refreshment, news, and debate; by 1683 they had become central to the cultural and social functioning of the Ottoman empire. The Dutch by this time had successfully transplanted the coffee plant to their colonies in Java. (Kocaturk, nd; Vienna CC, 1998)

Thus psychology, anthropology, and sociology, like siblings separated in infancy, grew in their own directions. Their central energy was devoted to developing their own institutional architecture. Academic degrees and departments were established to carry the disciplinary names as early as 1878 (the Ph.D. in "Philosophy and Psychology" at Harvard). Disciplinary journals were adopted to communicate new findings and to reflect on the nature of the field of inquiry (the *American Anthropologist* in 1888; the *American Journal of Sociology* in 1895; the *American Journal of Psychology* in 1897). Mechanisms to fund research were established by the professional societies and private foundations, and, much later, Federal funding was called forth with disciplinary guidance. Membership grew exponentially, to 10,000 currently for the AAA, 13,000 for the ASA, and 85,000 for the APA. The criteria for membership in the professional organizations were debated and tightened, increasing the associations' functioning as professional guilds. This was most evident in psychology, where credentialing for the therapeutic practice of psychology dominated discussion for much of the 20th century, but all three associations sought boundaries of one sort or another on their membership to ensure their integrity. ("The undersigned members," wrote M. Parmelee in a memorandum circulated at the 1931 Annual Meeting of the American Sociological Association, "animated by an ideal of scientific quality rather than of heterogeneous quality, wish to prune the Society of its excrescences [in applied sociology]"; cited in Rhoades, 1981, p. 24.) In the process, each profession constructed its own history, its "mythic origin story" to shape the understanding of what the discipline, and its disciples, ought to be (White, 1977).

Although the press toward a prototype for each discipline pulled away from ideas at the interstices, there have always been countervailing forces, primarily the integrated nature of reality. In the early period, it was perhaps more likely that a single scholar would roam freely across the intellectual fields. Wundt was indeed revolutionary in his determined efforts to apply the experimental rigor of physics to workings of the mind, but he later developed a much broader view of understanding human nature. His largest single project was a ten-volume, descriptive analysis of *Volkerpsychologie* ("ethnic psychology"), focusing on cultural and historical products of the human mind in particular times and places. He believed, as Blumenthal wrote in a centennial review (1979, p. 550), "that naturalistic observation, the study of development, evolution, and history, as well as the study of logic, linguistics and cultural products were equal and, in his later years, even more important methods (than experimentation)." Similarly, one can note that W. H. R. Rivers, sometimes considered the father of British anthropology, but also known for his psychiatric work with "shell-shocked" soldiers in World War I, served as president of the Anthropology section of the British Association for the Advancement of Science (1911) and was a founding member of the British Psychological Society in 1901 (Matisoo-Smith, 2002; Steinberg, 1961).

As the study of human behavior and society grew in size and in its own social structure, the boundaries became more established and the very institutions that created them made efforts to communicate across them. Sociology was perhaps the most energetic field in this regard, led by visions such as that of Albion Small, who in 1907 declared "that all the social sciences are unscientific in the degree in which they attempt to hold themselves separate from each other, and to constitute closed systems of abstractions" (Small, cited in Rhoades, 1981, p. 6). In the first decades of the 20th century, the ASA became directly involved in a variety of projects to promote the social sciences in general. One of its first collaborations was the founding of the Social Science Research Council, along with the national associations for Political Science, Economics, History, Statistics, Psychology, and Anthropology. Shortly thereafter, sociology was part of another interdisciplinary collaborative project of particular relevance here – founding of the Society for Research in Child Development. The key individuals in this case were Margaret Mead (anthropology), Myrtle McGraw (psychology), Arnold Gesell (pediatrics), Robert S. Lynd (sociology), and T. Wingate Todd (anatomy).

In light of this ever-evolving interplay of discipline and interdiscipline, the birth and death of "Social Relations" is particularly interesting. The concept, born in the mid-20th century, attempts to recognize the social structuring of human relations, the cultural frame for such structuring, and the role of personal psychology as both consequence and antecedent of these structures. One of the major instantiations of this interdisciplinary concept took place at Harvard University in 1946, when Gordon Allport, Talcott Parsons, Clyde Kluckhohn, and Henry Murray formed the Department of Social Relations from the social, developmental, personality, and clinical fields of psychology, along with sociology and social anthropology; this left experimental and physiological psychology in its own department, and likewise physical and linguistic, and archeological anthropology. That arrangement lasted 25 years, at which point the faculty reverted to the traditional structure of psychology (inclusive), sociology, and anthropology (Patullo, 1999). A similar innovation had taken place at Johns Hopkins in the interim, but it lasted no longer; and at Lehigh University, where it now is also an historical footnote. Today, the term remains important – as judged by an internet search – at Rikkyo University (Japan); the University of California, Riverside (as a program, not a department), Keele University (England), and Eastern Nazerene College (Massachusetts).

> Late in the afternoon of 12 September 1683, 20,000 Polish cavalry, led by the warrior-king Jan Sobieski, descended unexpectedly out of the foothills near Vienna and charged straight into the camp of the 200,000 Turks and Tartars who had besieged the desperate city for months. By

nightfall the Ottoman siege of Vienna was broken, the western surge of Islam had been stopped short, and a victorious Sobieski entered the tents, now abandoned, of the Grand Vizier. There he found, along with gold and weapons, bags of small dark beans, rumored to be the source of "kahve." These sacks ultimately were given as reward to Georg Franz Kolscitsky, a Pole who had worked for a Turkish trading company, knew the language and traditions, and had spied for the Viennese. In 1686 he opened what was long considered Vienna's first coffeehouse. By the early 18th century there were four such establishments; these grew to well over 600 at the height of the Austro-Hungarian empire toward the end of the 19th century. Today, even though their number has declined to about 200, coffeehouses and Vienna are still considered quintessential of each other to tourist guidebooks and to the Western mind more generally. (Vienna CC, 1998)

The systematic study of children in North America and Western Europe has a variety of roots, academic and applied, professional and interdisciplinary, which by the late 20th century had joined into a recognizable if not unitary entity (Siegel & White, 1982). The study of children outside the "Western world" has a more motley history, as it has been taken up from time to time for various purposes by the diverging disciplines (Harkness & Super, 1987). It was an elementary observation, even among philosophers such as Rousseau who preceded the emergence of the social sciences, that a true understanding of humanity must include the study of humans whose social world lies outside Western society, and that consideration of "the child" is essential. In 1900, Alexander Francis Chamberlain, an instructor in Anthropology at Clark University (where G. Stanley Hall, the founding developmentalist, served as president), published a monograph whose basic premise was reflective of the times and is still heard in the modern literature. Overstating the empirical base, perhaps, he nevertheless declared: "There is abundant evidence to show that the children of primitive peoples, whatever the condition of adults may be, are quite as well endowed mentally as the children of civilised [sic] peoples, the great difference between them existing in the greater number of learnable things which the environment of the latter provides, and the care and trouble which the community takes to make the acquisition of these things possible. Not the minds so much as the schools of the two stages of human evolution differ" (Chamberlain, 1900, p. 457f).

Anthropological interest in child development – at least nominally present in the earliest, classical ethnographies – flourished from the 1930s through the 1950s, as the "culture and personality" school considered enculturation to be a key theoretical construct (Harkness, 1992). With the decline of that framework, however, social anthropology has generally taken up other topics, and the study of children has been marginalized in the discipline. It is noteworthy in this regard that contemporary anthropologists who retain developmental interests now tend to work in interdisciplinary settings, publish in cross-disciplinary journals, and increasingly either collect data within the U.S. or orient their publications to contemporary U.S. concerns (Harkness, Super & Keefer, 1992; LeVine et al., 1994; Weisner & Garnier, 1992).

Within psychology, the speciality of development has struggled both for a legitimate place in the discipline and for an adequate framework to address the natural environments of development. In the late 1950s and early 1960s, "child study" was transformed into "developmental psychology," linguistically marked as a subdiscipline of psychology (Cairns, 1983). It emerged with a strong dependence on experimental techniques to study changes over age in perception, learning, and social behavior. Two decades later, however, concern with aspects of human development not so easily modeled in the laboratory led to a surge of basic research in the familial, social, and historical context of child development (Bronfenbrenner, 1979; Kessen, 1979; McCall, 1977). Curiously, the cultural dimension was still neglected. Even Bronfenbrenner, whose innovative ecological model was highly influential in moving developmental psychology out from the laboratory into "the real world," dismissed the cross-cultural literature as scientifically weak and "limited to variations that presently exist or have occurred in the past" (Bronfenbrenner, 1979, p. 40). More recently, recognition of the historical origins of contemporary diversity within the United States has widened psychologists' vision further (Garcia-Coll & Garrido, 2000; Greenfield & Cocking, 1994).

> When the Duke of York seized the Dutch colonies in North America in 1664, Garrit van Swearingen, a Dutchman who had worked for the East India Trading Company and was then employed by a settlement owned by the City of Amsterdam on the Delaware River, migrated to St. Mary's City, Maryland. There he established an inn and around 1685 opened what is sometimes claimed to be the first coffee house in North America. Less than a century later coffee was an immensely popular drink in America, and "coffee houses" – more like taverns than the Viennese establishments – had become a standard location for the delivery of postal services. Coffee became even more popular in colonial America following the Boston Tea Party. (Anonymous, 2004; Marr, 2004)

In the interdisciplinary context of the Social Relations department at Harvard, where laboratory developmentalists, policy gurus, and field anthropologists were all appropriate mentors and role models, it seemed relatively straightforward for a student to pursue a line of research that would provide more information about the development of non-Western children than was available to Chamberlain seven decades earlier, or in the contemporary literature of the late 1960s. Other psychologists, too, were beginning to focus their efforts in this direction (Cole, Gay, Glick, & Sharp, 1971; Dasen, 1976; Munroe & Munroe, 1971). Of particular interest to this student was the set of changes in cognition that have been found to occur around age 6 years, in the U.S.-based literature. Chamberlain made an extended comparison of young (Euro-American) children with the "feeble-minded," criminals, and the unschooled children of "savages," observing both similarities and differences. This line of analysis was taken up in greater detail half a century later by Heinz Werner (1948), also at Clark University. His conclusion – that particularly human kinds of higher order thinking develop in humans only during middle childhood, do not develop in lower animals, and are vulnerable to many kinds of mental disorder – provides a theoretical background for what came to be known as the "five-to-seven shift" (White, 1965; Sameroff & Haith, 1996).

White (1965, 1970), in particular, assembling diverse strands of evidence, noted that in all major theories of development the period around age 6 years assumes particular importance. Piaget and his associates located the beginnings of rational, operational thought at this time (Inhelder & Piaget, 1964). Similarly, Soviet psychologists emphasized that higher order processes overlay the mechanisms of classical conditioning beginning around 6 years of age (Luria, 1961; Vygotsky, 1962). American mediation theorists, in their expansion of traditional learning theory, pointed to a similar process in the sixth year, as language comes to play an increasing role in conceptual learning (Kendler, 1963). Even Freud, for whom cognition was not a central concern, saw in the resolution of the Oedipal conflict the emergence of inhibitory systems in the superego, and thus a new level of cognitive control. For each theorist, in different languages and from different data, the period around 5 to 7 years old is seen as the beginning of a dramatically more mature organization of the mind, the beginning of a new stage of development. Fischer and Silvern (1985), setting strict criteria for what can be considered nonlinear, developmental stage shifts, concluded that changes at age 6 or 7 years fulfill the definition completely. One must note, however, that this is also the age at which Western children typically begin formal didactic instruction. Thus, it cannot easily be discerned whether the introduction of schooling causes or reflects this profound change in mentation. One might hope, given all the evidence accumulated and reviewed, that psychologists had succeeded in learning something fundamental about the development of human children,

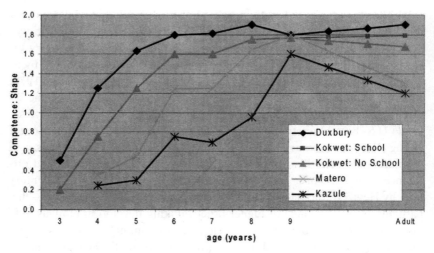

Figure 1.1. Age-related competence in copying shape.

not simply of schooled Euro-Americans; but only studies outside of Western cultures and Western schooling can truly address this question.

Therefore, two related field projects were undertaken, the first a pilot study in Zambia (Super, 1972) and the second a broader investigation in rural Kenya (Super, 1991; Super & Harkness, 1986). The Kenyan project took place in Kokwet, a rural farming area of Kipsigis-speaking people in the Western Highlands, where few children went to school at the time the data were collected in the mid-1970s. The Zambian data were collected in 1968 from two sites: Matero, a working-class housing development in Lusaka, populated by immigrants from many rural areas of the country; and Kazule, a farming area of Chewa people, more isolated and less prosperous than Kokwet. Additional data were collected for comparative purposes in Duxbury, Massachusetts, the second oldest European settlement in New England, now a prosperous, distant suburb of Boston. In the figures that follow, each data-point represents about 10–15 individuals.

Figure 1.1 shows the percent of persons at each age from each sample who correctly copied from sight "Figure A" of the Bender Gestalt test (Bender, 1938). This classic test has had wide use for the assessment of neurological functioning in children and in adult clinical patients. The greatest improvement in performance is observed prior to school entry in U.S. samples, according to Koppitz (1960). Responses here were scored according to a variation of her system, yielding a three-point scale for accuracy in shape and in internal orientation (rotation). The test figure consisted of a circle and a diamond

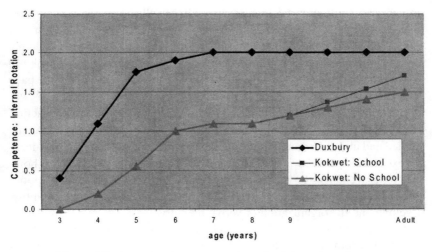

Figure 1.2. Age-related competence in maintaining orientation.

(square rotated 45 degrees) placed next to each other and just touching, drawn in black ink on a 5″ × 7″ white card. Children's common errors in copying the shapes include extra or missing angles in the diamond, and failure to close the circle. Placement of the two parts of the figure relative to each other is the feature of responses coded as internal orientation; in the model, one point of the diamond touches the circle such that a projection of the diamond's axis is horizontal for the viewer and would pass through the circle's center point – a deviation of 45 degrees or greater is scored as an error. In both cases, the scores shown here are for competence or the absence of errors.

Figure 1.1 presents the results for competence in copying the shape of the two subfigures. The most striking similarity among all the samples is the timing of reduction in distortions of shape, being very rapid in the first few years; and there is a curious pause in all samples between ages 6 and 7 years. Overall, analysis of variance using ages 3 to 9 years indicates that both the Age and the Sample effects are highly significant ($p < 0.0001$). There is no formal Interaction effect, and it is evident that the more urban and educated the group – thus, the more exposed to writing and graphical representation – the earlier full competence is achieved. By age nine, virtually all the children perform well, regardless of experience. The adult cohorts differ in expectable ways, given their histories, and all but the closest means are statistically different from each other ($p < 0.05$).

Figure 1.2, showing competence in copying the two subfigures in their original relationship to each other, reveals a somewhat similar but more pronounced configuration. In this case, almost all the improvement takes place before age 7. In Duxbury, all the children perform perfectly at this point. In Kokwet, this graphic convention is virtually absent in the children's environment and overall competence is only half as great. What is striking, however, is that progress before age 7 is quite rapid – indeed at the same pace as in Duxbury – and then it too levels off.

In summary, these two measures of basic graphic analysis and reproduction reveal a striking similarity in the timing of growth across all the environments studied and also differences in the degree to which these emerging potentials are exercised and elaborated. The argument for a "five-to-seven shift," however, aims at changes far more pervasive than a single modality of perception. A second set of tasks, therefore, assessed changes in a classic area of cognitive development, the organization of verbal memory.

There is a general contrast in psychological theories of cognitive development that compares organization based on abstracted, structural categories on the one hand and on the other, organization based on physical features or practical function. The more formal and abstract method is usually considered the more "mature" and "normal" for adult humans (Werner, 1948). In the literature on word associations tasks, category-based paradigmatic responses given by adults – such as *cat* with *dog* – are contrasted with the syntagmatic responses more typical of children, such as *dog–bark* or *dog–brown* (Brown & Berko, 1960; Nelson, 1977). A related task, the one used here, examines the way subjects actively, but not necessarily consciously, restructure words presented for memorization. For example, given the list *orange – ax – knife – tree*, a subject might later recall them as *ax* and *knife, tree* and *orange*, putting together the two tools and then the two plant items. Or, the response might be *ax* and *tree, orange* and *knife*, making two functional pairs. Use of the more abstract and categorical form is a central distinction in the Piagetian tradition (Inhelder & Piaget, 1964) as well as in U.S. intelligence tests (Wechsler, 1944). The developmental literature generally marks age 6 years as the turning point.

In the present study two lists were prepared, one with functional pairs (e.g., *food–eat*) and one with categorically related pairs (e.g., *come–go*), following the procedure used by Denney and Ziobrowski (1972). Each list was read to the subject in a pseudo-random order (no paired words adjacent), and after the child recalled as many as possible the full list was repeated two more times with a different order of words. Individual scores were computed as the conditional probability of listing the second word of a pair immediately following the first, if the first was recalled (or vice-versa). The results indicate first that older subjects use both kinds of implicit structure in the word lists more than

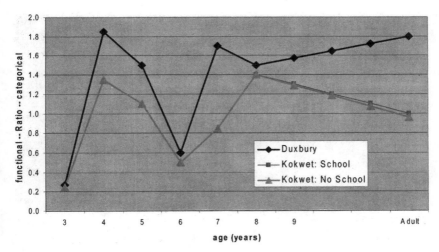

Figure 1.3. Age-related changes in the organization of recalled words.

younger ones; that is, their conditional probability of sequentially pairing the matched words – regardless of the basis of pairing – is generally greater than that for the younger subjects. In addition, however, the results also reveal that the use of each kind of pairing relative to the other shifts considerably from age to age, and that the shape of this year-to-year change in the categorical: functional ratio is remarkably similar in the two samples (Figure 1.3). The initial growth in category-based clustering is suddenly reversed at age 6 in both samples, and then it recovers. The age trends are highly significant, whereas there are no significant differences by group during childhood. In adulthood, culturally based preferences are more evident (Super, Harkness, & Baldwin, 1977).

A third point of comparison between the children in Duxbury and Kokwet relates to self-concept, or consciousness of the self as an independent agent in the world. David Foulkes (Foulkes, 1982; Foulkes, 1999) has summarized an extensive set of data on children's dreams to argue that there is an "intimate relationship between consciousness and the development of self-identity" (Foulkes, 1999, pp. 150–151). This is exquisitely revealed, he indicates, in the surprisingly late appearance of dreaming (during the late preschool years), and by the actual content of recorded dreams. Young children, under 4 or 5 years, do not usually appear in their own dreams; rather, the dreamscape is as one might see through one's own eyes. Around age 6, Foulkes reports, children begin to report their own presence in their dreams, first as passive observers of the ongoing events, then finally as active participants. The differences

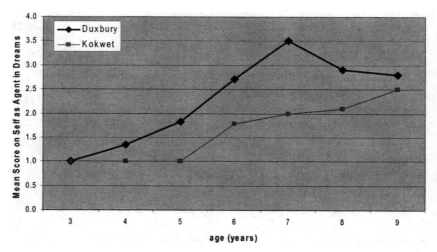

Figure 1.4. Age-related changes in representation of the self in dreams.

are captured in (1) "There was a lion," (2) "I was standing there and a lion appeared," (3) "I was being chased by a lion, and (4) "I was chased by a lion, but I ran home and locked myself in." Scoring of responses in the present study used a 4-point scale, corresponding to these four presentations.

Dream stories were somewhat more difficult to collect than drawings or memory tests, especially at the youngest ages, but a sufficient number of children succeeded in recounting a recent dream to produce reliable results, presented in Figure 1.4. In both sites, there is considerable growth in the presentation of the self as an active agent in dreams during the years 5 to 7, with a slightly earlier start and peak in Duxbury, where verbal commentary about oneself, and reflective engagement with young children are much more common. (The group differences are marginally different, $p < 0.07$, age $p < 0.001$.)

One outcome of extended fieldwork – living with the people one studies – is that many of the unstated assumptions and practices become evident. In all the figures shown here, there is a relative lag in the African children's performance in the early years. Some of these group differences may reflect true differences in competence, as there is such different emphasis on the particular skills assessed here in these two niches of childhood. The distinction between competence and performance is important to highlight here, however, as there is also a dramatic difference between samples in the children's familiarity with the testing situation. In the more traditional, rural African samples

(Kokwet and Kazule), it is an unprecedented and no doubt anxiety-arousing social context. Never have these young children sat down alone, facing an adult, to be asked questions to which the adult knew the answer, or to be asked to perform arbitrary and unfamiliar tasks. Rather, obedient silence in the presence of elders and the parallel modeling of behaviors were the norms for relating and learning (Harkness & Super, 1977; Harkness, 1988). The social act of being evaluated in this way, in other words, is itself a culturally constructed and differentially familiar test. Short of testing silent obedience, sibling care, and animal tending, therefore, it is not surprising that the African children generally score below Americans – these are American tests used here.

In light of this observation, it is all the more striking to see such parallels in the rate of growth in competencies related to the 5-to-7 shift. In the diverse domains of visual analysis and construction, memory organization, and self-concept, the children of Kokwet and Duxbury undergo rapid growth in a surprisingly similar manner, in several instances with nearly identical non-linear shifts (Figures 1.2 and 1.3).

Cross-cultural comparisons are often framed as investigations into which aspects of human behavior are universal and which are culturally specific. The developmental perspective offered here suggests that all human behaviors are both: They are culturally specific instantiations of universally emerging potentials. According to this view, healthy children everywhere undergo very similar developments and transformations in their mental functioning, according to a sequence and general timing that is characteristic of our species. Directing the emerging competencies to particular tasks in specific contexts, and managing their refinement, is what cultures do. The more redundant – across time, across scale, and across context – are the particular demands in the culturally structured developmental niche, the more fundamental to that culture is the ultimate behavioral skill (Super & Harkness, 1999).

> Coffee was introduced as a crop in the New World in the early 18th century by Gabriel Mathieu de Clieu, a young naval officer posted to Martinique who, refused a cutting of this wonderful plant from the Royal Botanical Garden in Paris (a gift to Louis XIV from the mayor of Amsterdam), simply stole it. Coffee production in the French Caribbean became plentiful and profitable. The French, like the Arabs and Dutch before them, tried to protect their local monopoly. But in 1727 Lt. Col. Francisco de Melo Palheta, sent to French Guiana by the Emperor of Brazil, seduced the wife of the French governor while mediating a border dispute. At the state dinner for the Brazilian's departure,

the governor's wife presented him with a grand bouquet, and deep inside the floral arrangement was a sampling of coffee seeds. A century
later, Brazil emerged as the largest producer of coffee in the world, a
distinction it still holds today. (Anonymous, 2004)

The roots of psychology, like those of coffee, are in the Old World. In both
cases, the New World variety has prospered in its climate and it has grown
to dominate the world market. Knowledge of human development, however,
is a different commodity. Brazilian coffee is just as flavorful and warming in
Reykjavik as it is in Rio di Janero, but knowledge of North American children
is less useful in either of those places than it is where it was grown, in North
America. For reasons of distance, time, and money, as well as discipline-
centric research, we have only the beginning of a science of human children,
even more than a century after Chamberlain. In trade, finance, technology,
and media, the pace of globalization has increased asymptotically in the past
decade. There is some reason to believe the same is beginning to happen in
the study of children, as evidenced by two related trends.

The first reflects the fact that we are now a full academic generation beyond the creation of developmental psychology in the late 1950s. In that
time Europe has rebuilt from the trauma and destruction of World War II,
Cold War barriers have fallen, and all but the most impoverished and isolated
countries of the Third World have at least started to develop their own academic strength in the social and behavioral sciences. A century ago it was
still the case that Americans went to England, Germany, or France for advanced education in the social and psychological sciences. Half a century ago,
the production of knowledge shifted its center of gravity to North America,
and a quarter a century ago the flow of students had reversed as well. Now
many of those students who studied in North America have returned to their
homeland and have carried with them the seeds of knowledge garnered in
their New World doctoral education. This is true both generally and specifically in developmental science. To cite one example, 1989 marked the first
non-American to win the American Psychological Association's Dissertation
Award in Developmental Psychology; Dymphna van den Boom, the recipient,
is now Professor at the University of Amsterdam. (Interestingly, it was also in
1989 that the APA first gave its G. Stanley Hall award to a non-American, to
Jacqueline Goodnow – save to Piaget, when the award was first begun.) The
increasing contribution of developmentalists based outside the United States
can be seen in Figures 1.5 and 1.6, which show, respectively, the locality
of the institutional base for published authors in two leading journals,
Developmental Psychology and *Child Development* (both of which are

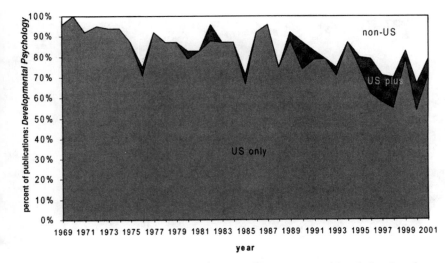

Figure 1.5. Trends in global location of *Developmental Psychology's* authors.

published by U.S. professional organizations, the APA and SRCD respectively). We examined four randomly chosen, empirical reports per issue and found that although the vast majority of reports continue to be from scientists at U.S. institutions, there is nevertheless a significant trend to publish work

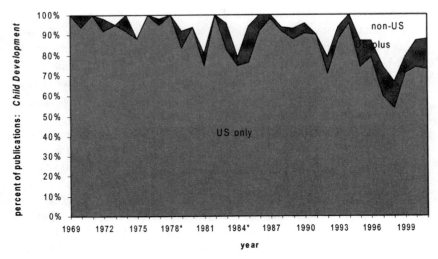

Figure 1.6. Trends in global location of *Child Development's* authors.

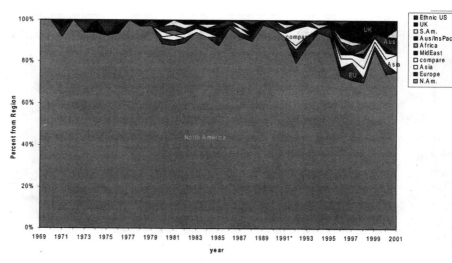

Figure 1.7. Trends in global location of children studied.

by researchers from other parts of the world, sometimes in collaboration with U.S. researchers, but primarily in their own right.

The second, related, trend is that the children whose development is reported are increasingly more likely to be living outside of North America. Figure 1.7 illustrates this finding, summed across both journals. It is still the case that 80% of the literature is based on mainstream U.S. children, but there is a distinct trend toward a more global sampling. Limiting the effectiveness of this trend, however, the number of reports about children who are not embedded in a predominantly European cultural context (that is, Europe, North America, and Australia) remains quite small. Further, the number of studies that are directly comparative in their design, and thus uniquely powerful in their conclusions, are a scattered few.

Despite the small presence, even now, of non-U.S. children in the primary developmental literature, the issue of cultural processes and representation has come to loom relatively large in the current phase of developmental science. Almost all introductory textbooks for child development are now explicit in their claim to include cross-cultural findings, and in 1995 "culture" was for the first time the most frequently indexed term in papers presented at the annual meetings of the Society for Research in Child Development. There is an emerging recognition that traditional developmental theory is so fundamentally based on North American children that it is of limited value in understanding human development around the world (Rubin, 1998; Super & Harkness, 1999).

> In December 2001, Starbucks of Seattle, USA, opened a coffeehouse on Karntner Strasse in Vienna, directly opposite the Sacher Hotel, home of the Sachertorte, and around the corner from the Café Mozart. This global reach of the American corporate empire back to a mythic origin of the Old World coffeehouse was noteworthy for both its business and symbolic significance. Despite dire predictions of cultural resistence by the proud and conservative Viennese, Starbucks has thrived there. (Erlanger, 2002)

Brief histories, recounted for a purpose, are almost always "mythic," as White intended the term. The stories presented here are like that, even the fable of Kolscitsky and his coffeehouse: Johannes Diodato, a Greek resident of Vienna, actually opened a coffeehouse a year before Kolscitsky (Augustin, 2003). A proper history of science goes beyond the mythic, beyond a statement of dates and recounting of who did what. It is necessarily an intellectual history also. It tells us something about the sequential elaboration of human knowledge over generations, and thus it also tells us about the human mind in aggregate as well as in the individual. "The historical approach to understanding of scientific fact is what differentiates the scholar in science from the mere experimenter" (Boring, 1961).

Among the many interesting thematic observations derived by Heinz Werner in his examination of mental development was the "orthogenic principle," which states that development proceeds by alternating periods of differentiation and integration (Werner, 1948). He was speaking of the individual child, from embryology through cognition, but a similar pattern can be seen in the emergence of a truly interdisciplinary science of development. There have been, to date, two complete orthogenic cycles. In the beginning – as with the fertilized ovum – there is differentiation from a unitary if complex origin. Here, the basic social scientific disciplines emerged around the turn of the 20th century, and they worked to distinguish themselves both from each other and from applications of their accumulating knowledge. After some decades, the press for integrating the now-established knowledge bases grew strong enough for institutional recognition, and the 1920s and 1930s were witness to such efforts as the National Research Council's Committee on Child Development and the founding of the Society for Research in Child Development (Smuts, 1985). There was at the same time a deliberate effort to integrate academic science with reform and educational efforts in society at large (Schlossman, 1983).

The second cycle began with differentiation of subdisciplines within psychology and the other social and behavioral sciences, part of the dramatic increase in the scientific enterprise that emerged in the 1950s. It is during this period, for example, that the American Psychological Association added many of its now 53 official divisions, marking specialities within the profession. The subsequent revolution in applying the lessons of developmental psychology, and in breaking free of the restrictive experimental paradigm, began the integration phase of this second cycle. The inauguration of the national Head Start program in 1965 (whose first director, Edward Zigler, is a developmental psychologist) brought together narrow developmental perspectives with more sociological, medical, and nutritional ones, as well as concerns with families and eventually even adult development. Shortly thereafter, as noted above, standing paradigms of developmental research were called into question by a number of authors (Bronfenbrenner, 1979; Kessen, 1979; McCall, 1977). At the same time, several new scholarly associations were formed deliberately to cut across disciplinary boundaries: the International Society for the Study of Behavioral Development in 1969, the International Association for Cross-Cultural Psychology and the Society for Cross-Cultural Research in 1972, and the Society for Psychological Anthropology in 1977.

With this last period of integration has come, even if slowly, the realization that some aspects of development may proceed with different trajectories in different environments, and that relationships once taken to be directly causal may reflect as much about the larger organization of the social and cultural environment as about the universal nature of human development. The cultural anthropologist A. F. C. Wallace (Wallace, 1961) once pointed out that cultures organize the variation within themselves. Because the niche of human development is organized and dynamically regulated by culture (Super & Harkness, 1999), individual features such as sex or temperament will have different meanings, different settings to exploit, and thus different developmental consequences in, for example, North America and China (Chen, Rubin, & Li, 1995; Ember, 1981; Super & Harkness, 1993). Similarly, specific child-rearing behaviors may have variable effects, depending on other aspects of the developmental environment such as local meaning systems and relationship structures. Hess and his colleagues found this for the effect of maternal socialization style on cognitive development, comparing Japanese and mainstream U.S. samples (Hess & Azuma, 1990), as did Deater-Deckard and colleagues regarding the effect of parental punishment style on childhood aggression, comparing ethnic groups within the United States (Deater-Deckard, Dodge, Bates, & Pettit, 1996). As findings we once considered to reflect fixed causality are subjected to replication in varying contexts, we are finding that environment-development relationships can themselves be variable.

The failure to see the relationship between variables as itself a variable has been noted elsewhere in psychology (Posner, 1978), and probably reflects our incomplete growth as a science. Piaget (1950) made a similar observation regarding the development of mathematical understanding at the level of both the individual and aggregate history. The first historical stage, he noted, was classical arithmetic and Euclidean systems, which emphasize the description of attributes. Later, algebra and analytic geometry emerged in the 17th century, with a focus on operations and processes. Finally, in the late 19th and early 20th centuries new approaches came to consider functions and families of functions as units of description, that is, to consider relationships as variables, and to extrapolate to unseen possibilities and dimensions. These disciplinary stages, Piaget proposed, correspond to individual sequences in the construction of knowledge: preoperational, concrete operational, and formal operational thought. Perhaps the study of child development has grown from a preoperational period prior to 1950, through a concrete operational epistemology in the later half of the 20th century, and is now beginning to utilize formal operational thinking to recognize context-development relationships as variable. When this process of theoretical-cognitive growth is fully mature, developmental psychology will be truly global.

There are currently six Starbucks outlets in Istanbul, and nearly 100 on the Arabian peninsula.

References

American Anthropological Association. (2000). A brief history of the American Anthropological Association. http://www.aaanet.org/history.htm.

American Psychological Association. (2003). Directory of Annual Meetings of the American Psychological Association, 1892–2000. http://www.apa.org/archives/dirintro.html.

Anonymous. (2004). The history of coffee. http://www.realcoffee.co.uk/Article.asp?Cat=History.

Augustin, A. (2003). The most famous hotels in the world. http://www.famoushotels.org/famoushotels/ARCHIVES/COFFEE_HISTORY/coffeehtm/cenviehist.htm.

Bender, L. (1938). A visual motor Gestalt test and its clinical use. *Research Monographs of the American Orthopsychiatric Association* No. 3:xi 176.

Blumenthal, A. L. (1979). The founding father we never knew. *Contemporary Psychology 24*, 547–550.

Boring, E. G. (1950). *A history of experimental psychology.* (2nd ed.). New York: Appleton-Century-Crofts.

Boring, E. G. (1961). Archives of the American Psychological Association. http://www. apa.org/archives.

Bronfenbrenner, U. (1979). *The Ecology of Human Development.* Cambridge, MA: Harvard University Press.

Brown, R., & Berko, J. (1960). Word association and the acquisition of grammar. *Child Development 31*, 1–14.

Cairns, R. B. (1983). The emergence of developmental psychology. In P. Mussen (Ed.), *Handbook of Child Psychology, Vol. 1: History, Theory, and Methods.* W. Kessen (vol. ed.) (pp. 41–102). New York: Wiley.

Chamberlain, A. F. (1900). *The Child: A Study in the Evolution of Man.* New York: Scribner.

Chen, X., Rubin, K. H., & Li, Z.-Y. (1995). Social functioning and adjustment in Chinese children: A longitudinal study. *Developmental Psychology 31*, 4, 531–540.

Cole, M., Gay, J., Glick, J. S., & Sharp, D. W. (1971). *The Cultural Context of Learning and Thinking.* New York: Basic Books.

Dasen, P. (Ed.). (1976). *Piagetian Psychology: Cross-Cultural Research.* New York: Gardner Press.

Deater-Deckard, K., Dodge, K. A., Bates, J. E., & Pettit, G. S. (1996). Physical discipline among African American and European American mothers: Links to children's externalizing behaviors. *Developmental Psychology 32*, 6, 1065–1072.

Denney, N. W., & Ziobrowski, M. (1972). Developmental changes in clustering criteria. *Journal of Experimental Psychology 13*, 275–282.

Ember, C. (1981). A cross-cultural perspective on sex differences. In R. H. Munroe, R. L. Munroe & B. B. Whiting (Eds.), *Handbook of Cross-Cultural Human Development* (pp. 531–580). New York: Garland.

Erlanger, S. (2002). An American coffeehouse (or 4) in Vienna. *New York Times*, June 1, sec. A, p. 1, col. 5.

Fischer, K. W., & Silvern, L. (1985). Stages and individual differences in cognitive development. *Annual Review of Psychology 36*, 613–648.

Foulkes, D. (1982). *Children's Dreams: Longitudinal Studies.* New York: Wiley.

Foulkes, D. (1999). *Children's Dreaming and the Development of Consciousness.* Cambridge, MA: Harvard University Press.

Garcia-Coll, C., & Garrido, M. (2000). Minorities in the United States: Sociocultural context for mental health and development. In A. J. Sameroff & M. Lewis (Eds.), *Handbook of Developmental Psychopathology* (2nd ed.) (pp. 177–195). New York: Kluver.

Greenfield, P. M., & Cocking, R. R. (1994). In P. M. Greenfield & R. R. Cocking, (Eds.), *Cross-Cultural Roots of Minority Child Development.* Hillsdale, NJ: Lawrence Erlbaum.

Harkness, S. (1988). The cultural construction of semantic contingency in mother-child speech. *Language Sciences 10*, 1, 53–67.

Harkness, S. (1992). Human development in psychological anthropology. In T. Schwartz, G. M. White, & C. A. Lutz (Eds.), *New Directions in Psychological Anthropology* (pp. 102–121). New York: Cambridge University Press.

Harkness, S., & Super, C. M. (1977). Why African children are so hard to test. In L. L. Adler (Ed.), *Cross-Cultural Research at Issue* (pp. 145–152). New York: Academic Press.

Harkness, S., & Super, C. M. (1987). The uses of cross-cultural research in child development. *Annals of Child Development 4*, 209–244.

Harkness, S., Super, C. M., & Keefer, C. H. (1992). Culture and ethnicity. In M. D. Levine, W. B. Carey, & A. C. Crocker (Eds.), *Developmental-Behavioral Pediatrics* (2nd ed.) (pp. 103–108). Philadelphia: Harcourt Brace Jovanovich.

Harris, M. (1968). *The Rise of Anthropological Theory*. New York: Thomas Y. Crowell.

Hess, R. D., & Azuma, H. (1990). Cultural support for schooling: Contrasts between Japan and the United States. *Educational Researcher 20*, 9, 265–288.

Inhelder, B., & Piaget, J. (1964). *The Early Growth of Logic in the Child*. London: Routledge & Kegan Paul.

Kendler, T. S. (1963). Development of mediating responses in children. In J. C. Wright & J. Kagan (Eds.), *Basic Cognitive Processes in Children. Monographs of the Society for Research in Child Development 28*, 2, 33–51.

Kessen, W. (1979). The American child and other cultural inventions. *American Psychologist 34*, 815–820.

Kocaturk, H. (nd). Turkish coffee. http://www.turkishpeople.com/food/coffee/coffee.html.

Koppitz, E. M. (1960). The Bender Gestalt test for children, a normative study. *Journal of Clinical Psychology 16*, 432–435.

Laboratory of Comparative Human Cognition. (1983). Culture and cognitive development. In P. Mussen (Ed.), *Handbook of Child Psychology, Vol. 1: History, Theory, and Methods*. W. Kessen (vol. ed.) (pp. 295–356). New York: Wiley.

LeVine, R. A., Dixon, S., LeVine, Richman, A., Leiderman, P. H., Keefer, C. H., & Brazelton, T. B. (1994). *Child Care and Culture: Lessons from Africa*. New York: Cambridge University Press.

Luria, A. R. (1961). *The Role of Speech in the Regulation of Normal and Abnormal Behavior*. New York: Liveright.

Marr, E. (2004). Historical Correspondence: The first coffee house in Colonial North America. http://www.blackapollo.demon.co.uk/first.html.

Matisoo-Smith, E. (2002). William Halse Rivers. http://www.arts.auckland.ac.nz/ant/Lisa%20Matisoo-Smith/Courses/300/WHR%20Rivers-LIFE.htm.

McCall, R. B. (1977). Challenges to a science of developmental psychology. *Child Development 48*, 333–344.

Munroe, R. H., & Munroe, R. L. (1971). Household density and infant care in an East African society. *Journal of Social Psychology 83*, 1, 3–13.

Nelson, K. (1977). The syntagmatic-paradigmatic shift revisited: A review of research and theory. *Psychological Bulletin 84*, 4, 93–116.

Patullo, P. (1999). Department history. http://www.wjh.harvard.edu/psych/history.html.

Piaget, J. (1950). *Introduction: l'Épistemologie Génetique, Vol. 1 (Introduction to Genetic Epistomology)*. Paris: Presses Universitaires de France.

Posner, J. I. (1978). *Chronometric Explorations of the Mind*. Hillsdale, NJ: Lawrence Erlbaum.

Rhoades, L. J. (1981). *A History of the American Sociological Association, 1905–1980*. Washington, DC: American Sociological Association.

Rubin, K. H. (1998). Social and emotional development from a cultural perspective. *Developmental Psychology 34*, 4, 611–615.

Sameroff, A. J., & Haith, M. M. (Eds.) (1996). *The Five to Seven Year Shift: The Age of Reason and Responsibility*. Chicago: University of Chicago Press.

Scharff, R. C. (1995). *Comte After Positivism*. New York: Cambridge University Press.

Schlossman, S. L. (1983). The formative era in American parent education: Overview and interpretation. In R. Haskins & D. Adams (Eds.), *Parent Education and Public Policy* (pp. 7–39). Norwood, NJ: Ablex.

Schultz, D. (1975). *A History of Modern Psychology*. New York: Academic Press.

Siegel, A. W., & White, S. H. (1982). The child development movement: Early growth and development of the symbolicized child. In H. W. Reese (Ed.), *Advances in Child Development and Behavior (Vol. 17)* (pp. 233–285). Orlando: Academic Press.

Smuts, A. (1985). The National Research Council Committee on Child Development and the founding of the Society for Research in Child Development, 1925–1933. In A. Smuts & J. Hagen (Eds.), *History and Research in Child Development. Monographs of the Society for Research in Child Development 50, 3–4, Serial No. 211*. Chicago: University of Chicago Press.

Starbucks. (2004). History of coffee. http://www.starbucks.com/ourcoffees/coffee_edu2.asp.

Steinberg, H. (1961). *The British Psychological Society, 1901–1961*. Leicester, UK: British Psychological Society.

Super, C. M. (1972). *HDRU Reports No. 22*. Lusaka, Zambia: University of Zambia.

Super, C. M. (1991). Developmental transitions of cognitive functioning in rural Kenya and metropolitan America. In K. Gibson, M. Konner, & J. Lancaster (Eds.), *The Brain and Behavioral Development: Biosocial Dimensions* (pp. 225–257). Hawthorne, NY: Aldine.

Super, C. M., & Harkness, S. (1986). The developmental niche: A conceptualization at the interface of child and culture. *International Journal of Behavioral Development 9*, 545–569.

Super, C. M., & Harkness, S. (1993). Temperament and the developmental niche. In W. B. Carey & S. A. McDevitt (Eds.), *Prevention and Early Intervention: Individual Differences as Risk Factors for the Mental Health of Children–A Festschrift for Stella Chess and Alexander Thomas*. New York: Brunner/Mazel.

Super, C. M., & Harkness, S. (1999). The environment as culture in developmental research. In T. Wachs & S. Friedman (Eds.), *Measurement of the Environment in Developmental Research* (pp. 279–323). Washington, DC: American Psychological Association.

Super, C. M., Harkness, S., & Baldwin, L. (1977). Category behavior in natural ecologies and in cognitive tests. *The Quarterly Newsletter of the Institute for Comparative Human Development 1*, 4–7.

Tchibo. (nd). Coffee through the ages. http://company.tchibo.de/concepts/tccom_302.jsp.

Vienna CC. (1998). Coffeehouse. http://www.vienna.cc/ekaffeeh.htm.

Vygotsky, L. S. (1962). *Thought and Language*. Cambridge, MA: MIT Press.

Wallace, A. F. C. (1961). *Culture and Personality*. New York: Random House.

Wechsler, D. (1944). *The Measurement of Adult Intelligence* (3rd ed.). Baltimore, MD: Williams & Wilkins.

Weisner, T. S., & Garnier, H. (1992). Nonconventional family life-styles and school achievement: A 12-year longitudinal study. *American Educational Research Journal* *29*, 3, 605–632.

Werner, H. (1948). *Comparative Psychology of Mental Development*. New York: International Universities Press.

White, S. H. (1965). Evidence for a hierarchical arrangement in learning processes. In L. P. Lipsitt & C. C. Spiker (Eds.), *Advances in Child Development and Behavior* (pp. 187–220). New York: Academic Press.

White, S. H. (1970). Some general outlines of the matrix of developmental change between five and seven years. *Bulletin of the Orton Society 20*, 41–57.

White, S. H. (1977, August). *Psychology in All Sorts of Places*. Presented at the Conference on Research Perspectives in the Ecology of Human Development. Ithaca, NY.

Wundt, W. (1874). *Principles of Physiological Psychology*. Leipzig: Engelmann.

2   A Socio-historical Perspective on Autobiographical Memory Development

Michelle D. Leichtman and Qi Wang

Introspection leaves the impression that personal event memories are private, self-generated products of an individual's experience in the world. When we reflect on the past, "we can accept with little question that biography or the lifetime is the appropriate or 'natural' frame for individual memory" (Schudson, 1995, p. 346). Historically, investigations of memory processes have resided at this phenomenologically justified level of analysis. For example, early studies focused on the nature of adults' childhood memories with limited reference to the particulars of history or other contextual factors situated outside the individual (e.g., Dudycha & Dudycha, 1941; Sheingold & Tenney, 1982; Waldfogel, 1948).

In the past several decades, memory researchers have gained an increasingly sophisticated perspective on context. Autobiographical memory offers a rich platform from which to view contextual effects, and research on the topic has benefited from this perspective. Currently, theory and burgeoning empirical evidence support the notion that both proximal and distal influences have the potential to shape autobiographical remembering in complex ways (Bronfenbrenner, 1979; Ceci & Leichtman, 1992; Leichtman, Wang, & Pillemer, 2003; Wang, 2003).

In the present chapter, we consider context through an exceptionally broad lens. Our overarching goal is to identify the possible roles that socio-historical factors, including government policies and culturally shaped aspects of the social environment, play in shaping the personal event memories of individuals. Researchers have only recently begun to consider connections between such macro-level environmental elements and the personal sphere of autobiographical memory; thus, some of the ideas that follow are speculative. Nevertheless, we can draw on extensive recent work in developmental and cultural psychology to evaluate the impact that specific aspects of the larger environment are likely to wield on how people remember autobiographical events.

34

We set the stage for our discussion with a review of factors in the proximal environment that research has indicated affect autobiographical recollection. These factors are important to discern, because proximal influences may mediate the relationship between more distal influences and event memory outcomes. We then turn to our central question: How might factors in the distal environment – namely, socio-political and cultural factors – affect personal event memory? We treat this question in two major sections. In the first section, we discuss the potential role of government policies, highlighting some relevant examples from the historical archives. We focus on the diverse examples of government-directed autobiographical writing and policies affecting family structure. We also acknowledge the importance of historical timing or cohort effects on the way that individuals think about personally experienced past events. In the second section, we treat culturally shaped dimensions of the social environment that influence autobiographical memory. Here, we focus on relevant differences across cultures and across urban/rural environments.

Proximal Influences on Autobiographical Memory

To understand how the proximal environment might influence autobiographical memory, it is useful to begin with some examples. The following conversation was recorded in the home of a 3-year-old Euro-American child and his mother, while they sat at their dining room table making invitations to the child's fourth birthday party.

Mother: How about putting another one because if Julia gets a lizard and then Heather doesn't get a lizard on hers because you ran out of lizards they'll be upset. I think they're pretty cool.

Patrick: I don't care. They're girls.

Mother: You have a lot of girlfriends. Your best friend is Elizabeth who lives right next door to you.

Patrick: I just like Elizabeth.

Mother: And you don't like any of the other girls?

Patrick: Nope.

Mother: You don't like Erica?

Patrick: No.

Mother: And you don't like Emily?

Patrick: No.

Mother: And you don't like Claire?

Patrick: No. I don't like all the girls. I just like boys.

Mother: Well I thought you played with a lot of girls in your class . . .

Patrick: No.

Mother: . . . and you told me that you like Erica and Emily a lot. And I
have a picture of you during the Valentine's book story with
your hand around Emily. Your arm was around Emily. You were
giving her a hug.
Patrick: No, she just did that to me when she was in the hall.
Mother: I have a picture of it.
Patrick: Two times.
Mother: Two times? Did she hug you? Did you hug her back? It's ok you
hug mommy back, you hug Lu-Lu back, you hug Agner back?
Patrick: Oooh.

In this short conversation, the mother used memories of past events in several different ways. She called Patrick's attention to a general or routine set of past behaviors that he had frequently engaged in (playing with girls). She referred to a specific past event (hugging a girl) and she inspired Patrick to elaborate on that event with further details ("two times"). She then questioned her son about what happened in the past event, probing for more specific information ("Did you hug her back?"). Notably, she also referred to a photograph of the event in question, which served as a reminder of the details. Throughout the conversation, the mother evaluated and followed up on her son's responses to engage him in the joint activity of memory sharing.

Each of these conversational characteristics is frequently apparent in the memory talk of modern, Euro-American mothers and their children. The conversation illustrates a high-elaborative style, in which mothers speak frequently about the past with their children, provide rich descriptive information, and encourage children to talk about the past in detail. Mothers who adopt a high-elaborative style tend to ask many open-ended questions about past events and provide immediate feedback on children's responses to keep the conversation going (Fivush & Fromhoff, 1988; Reese, Haden, & Fivush, 1993; Pillemer, 1998). In contrast, some mothers speak less frequently about the past, provide fewer details about what happened, and often pose pointed questions with single well-defined correct answers when questioning their children. These mothers also tend to repeat their own questions when they do not receive the desired information from children, rarely letting the conversation flow in the direction of the child's comments. Researchers have referred to this second style of memory talk as low-elaborative or paradigmatic (Fivush & Fromhoff, 1988; Reese, Haden, & Fivush, 1993). While this low-elaborative style is also frequently evident in Euro-American homes, it appears to be more predominant in memory conversations between Asian parents and their children (Wang, Leichtman, & Davies, 2000; Wang, 2001a). This is nicely exemplified by the conversation below, recorded in a home in rural India. In this example, the mother questioned her sons about their nourishment the day before and was satisfied once her direct questions had been briefly answered.

Mother: Play quietly. You will dislocate your wrist. You should sing properly.

Mother: Don't pull it, it will fall down. Santosha, what did you eat last night?

Santosha: *Ragi* balls and chutney.

Mother: What chutney?

Santosha: Coconut chutney.

Mother: How many glasses of coffee did you both have?

Krishna: This much.

Mother: Go and play hopscotch with him. How do you play this game? Say it properly.

A number of studies have illustrated that the relative styles of parents' memory talk remain consistent over time and that children of relatively more elaborative parents come to remember the past in more elaborate detail themselves (e.g., Reese, Haden, & Fivush, 1993; Haden, 1998). The difference between high- and low-elaborative styles of memory talk is particularly important because the way in which such talk is carried out affects children's memory reports. Children with high-elaborative mothers tend to provide longer and more detailed reports of past events than children with low-elaborative mothers, even over time (e.g., McCabe & Peterson, 1991; Reese et al., 1993). Most striking is that the event details children remember appear to be in part a function of how parents talk with them about the events.

This latter point was underscored in a recent study that focused on parent–child conversations with preschoolers (Leichtman, Pillemer, Wang, Koreishi, & Han, 2000). Children experienced a surprise event in their preschool classroom, in which their former teacher brought her newborn baby to the school after 3 months of maternity leave. During this visit, a series of scripted activities occurred. On the same day, mothers interviewed their children individually about the event. Mothers had not been present during the event and had no details about it; they were told to question their children in whatever way was natural to them. Three weeks later, a researcher interviewed each child individually. The researcher had not been present during the event and had no information about the content of the parent–child interviews. The researcher asked each child the same set of open-ended and direct questions about the event. The findings showed that mothers who conducted more elaborative interviews had children who provided richer answers during the initial mother–child interviews, and also in the researcher–child interviews three weeks later. For example, mother–child conversations influenced the number of correct details children recalled and the number of descriptive terms they used to explain their memories three weeks after the event. Mother–child conversations also influenced children's recall of the specific objects that had been present during the event. Intriguingly, 83% of the items that children recalled during the researcher–child interview had been initially discussed between children and their mothers.

One possible interpretation for the above findings is that children's language ability was responsible for both the degree of mothers' elaborativeness and the amount that children remembered in the researcher–child interview. A follow-up study with a similar methodology examined this notion, adding a Mean Length of Utterance (MLU) measure of children's language. The findings indicated that both children's language status and the degree of mothers' elaborativeness made separate, significant contributions to children's memory reports during a researcher–child interview after a long delay (Leichtman, Holmes, & Pillemer, 2003). Harley and Reese (1999) also demonstrated in their longitudinal study that maternal reminiscing style uniquely predicted children's shared memory reports across time, independent of their initial language ability. Thus, talking about events with parents has the potential to affect the number and type of details that children remember regardless of their level of language. These findings are consistent with the idea of "co-construction," in which children learn how to construct stories about their lives and share them with other people in the context of joint conversations with their parents (Nelson, 1992).

In addition to the specific style of parent–child conversations, an important related dimension of the proximal environment is the beliefs about memory that those around children convey to them. Beliefs about the significance of remembering the personal past vary among individuals, and such beliefs can be expected to affect the degree to which individuals reflect upon, share, and ultimately sustain access to the details of event memories. Individual differences in the style of memory talk may be associated with variations in beliefs about the importance of remembering the personal past. To the extent that individuals value autobiographical events as an integral part of their own identities, they may talk about such events with frequency and elaboration. Data hinting at this possibility come from a set of studies of American and rural Indian populations (Leichtman, Bhogle, Sankaranarayanan, & Hobeika, 2003). Researchers interviewed adults about various aspects of their memory practices and recollections. The majority of Indian participants indicated that reflecting on the past was not important to them, while the majority of American participants indicated that it was. Only 12% of rural Indian adults reported conversing about past events in their daily lives, whereas 90% of American adults did so. Accordingly, when prompted for memories of childhood, 14% of the Indian sample provided a specific, one-point-in-time memory, while 69% of the American sample did so. Video recordings of the daily home lives of separate samples of individuals from the same populations indicated that parents in the American population tended to have a much more elaborative style of talking about the personal past with their children. Thus, differences in explicit beliefs may be associated with different practices of memory talk.

Beliefs about the importance of the personal past, independent of the language used to revisit events, may be reflected in artifacts used to capture events of significance in the lives of children and families. For example, consider the photograph that Patrick's mother referred to in the previous example of elaborative conversation. Even without language, such a picture could have memory-enhancing effects. A photograph might remind a child of particular details of experience (e.g., the favors given out at a party), highlight specific moments of importance (e.g., the blowing out of candles on a birthday cake), underscore the significance of a culturally valued event (e.g., a birthday), or stress a child's connection to a particular set of individuals and places that define his world. Drawings, paintings, and journals recording specific past events could have similar influences on autobiographical memory. Several programs for the education of young children, such as the currently popular "Reggio Emilia" method, have stressed the uses of such "documentation," encouraging children to review specific past events in connection with present educational goals (Caldwell, 2002). Even without talk about the personal past, the presence of this kind of documentation conveys to children the value of remembering the details of their own past experiences.

One other aspect of the proximal environment deserves mention as a potential influence on autobiographical memory. This is the degree to which the environment emphasizes an orientation toward the self. A number of social psychological explorations have documented variations in the degree to which individuals focus on themselves and their own unique traits, as opposed to those of other people or the community around them. The immediate social environments in which children grow up may be an important source of such variation (Fiske, Kitayama, Markus, & Nisbett, 1998; Wang, Leichtman, & White, 1998). For example, parents who emphasize the value of their children's distinctive personal qualities and talents and who encourage independent thinking and behavior may produce more self-oriented offspring. Given that a primary feature of autobiographical memory is self-relevance, the predominant view of self in children's proximal environments – often conveyed by parents and significant others – is bound to impact upon their personal event memories over the long term.

Kuhn and McPartland's (1954) Twenty Statements Test (TST) has been a widely used index of the organization of self-related information. The task elicits self-descriptions, asking participants to fill in the blank after 20 statements phrased "I am ___." TST responses are typically scored as belonging to three categories: private, collective, or public self-descriptions. *Private* self-descriptions focus on personal traits, states, or behaviors (e.g., "I am intelligent"), *collective* self-descriptions focus on group membership (e.g., "I am a Buddhist"), and public self-descriptions focus on relationships with others (e.g., "I am a person who helps my neighbors"). Numerous studies have documented individual variation in the percentage of responses that fall into each of these three categories (e.g., Greenwald & Pratkanis, 1984; Triandis, 1989).

TST measures of self-description and the characteristics of autobiographical memory are theoretically connected. To the extent that the environment supports the tendency to think about the self as an independent, well-bounded entity with unique characteristics, individuals will be likely to access private self-descriptions more frequently than public or collective ones. At the same time, this kind of focus on the private self is likely to raise the value of remembering and sharing the details of personally experienced past events. In this self-oriented context, it is paramount to retain personal event memories as part of the process of defining and asserting one's identity. Supporting the connection between self-description and autobiographical memory, several studies of large samples of American, Chinese, and French young adults have indicated an association between TST responses and characteristics of memory reports (Kassoff & Wang, 2002; Wang, Leichtman, & White, 1998; Wang, 2001b). For example, Wang, Leichtman, and White (1998) found that private self-description scores were positively related to the length and specificity of childhood memories, while collective self-description scores were negatively related. Variations in self-focus scores are directly reflected in the content of memory conversations between parents and children across cultures, which we will discuss in a later section (Leichtman, Bhogle, Sankaranarayanan, & Hobeika, 2003; Mullen & Yi, 1995; Wang, Leichtman, & Davies, 2000; Wang, 2001a).

In summary, three dimensions conveyed in children's proximal environments stand out as making important contributions to autobiographical memory. These include the ways in which parents talk with their children about past events, the explicit beliefs about the value of memory that the people and artifacts around children convey, and the degree to which children's environments encourage focus on the self as a distinct entity. These influences in children's proximal environments interface with more distal factors.

Socio-Political Contexts

Research psychologists have rarely examined the effects of specific socio-political contexts on individual-level cognitive and social processes. Yet elements of the socio-political environment such as government policies could indeed trickle down, shaping some elements of cognition. Certainly, contextual models suggest the potential for this to occur. For example, Bronfenbrenner's (1979) model posits that government policies are part of an exosystem that indirectly, and in synergy with other environmental factors, affects children's behavior and cognition. Similarly, Super and Harkness's (2002) model implies a connection between the messages conveyed in the environment – which could be shaped by government policies – and outcomes related to particular cognitive processes. Nonetheless, in practice it is not always readily apparent how to empirically capture such influences on cognition.

In the case of autobiographical memory, investigators have not typically considered the potential impact of government policies. Yet, government policies affect a wide spectrum of lifestyle issues that may be related to autobiographical memory. We speculate that under special circumstances government policies may have the potential to quite directly influence how individuals remember autobiographical events. Government-directed autobiographical writing is a case in point.

Government-Directed Autobiographical Writing

A provocative example of the role that government can play in shaping autobiographical recollection comes from the period of the Russian Revolution. Beginning in this period, the Soviet regime encouraged and even required autobiographical writing in a wide array of situations, extracting autobiographical accounts for political purposes. For example, in the trenches of their military camps, soldiers of the Soviet revolutionary army were encouraged to write personal diaries. In the small "Red Army notebooks" provided them, soldiers recorded the ammunition, food, and clothing supplies they received. In addition to space for these practical records, the notebooks contained writing space with the following instructions: "If possible, keep a diary of your service in the Workers' and Peasants' Red Army" (Hellbeck, 2001, p. 343).

As Hellbeck (2001) describes, the extraction of such accounts from military forces was only the beginning of the Soviet regime's interest in autobiographical writing. Following the revolution, individuals throughout Soviet society were required to write "autobiografia," or short accounts of their own lives and the formation of their personalities, as a qualification for entry into party institutions. This model of screening then extended to institutions outside the strict dominion of the ruling party, including to universities and organs of state administration. In addition, "during the first decades of Soviet power, state and party agencies . . . poured considerable energy into the production of large-scale autobiographical projects involving thousands of Soviet citizens" (Hellbeck, 2001, p. 343).

From the Soviet perspective, there were multiple reasons to assign these autobiographical writing exercises during and after the events of 1917. In autobiographical reflection, citizens could glorify the years of the revolution and solidify their sense of intrinsic connection to the regime and the larger context of history (Hellbeck, 2001). As Hellbeck describes it, they could also undergo

> the full trajectory of self-transformation, from "human weed" or "bad raw material," living in a similarly unformed or polluted social environment (before the revolution) to conscious, self-disciplined beings residing in the well-ordered socialist garden created to an extent by themselves. (Hellbeck, 2001, p. 343)

In other words, citizens could revisit in memory their own practices and go forward with renewed dedication to the Soviet cause.

Most germane to the present discussion, Soviet policies encouraging the use of autobiographical accounts apparently resulted in a remarkable explosion of autobiographical writing, across all levels of Soviet society and for many years after the revolution. It is clear that not all of this writing served to strengthen the cause of the Soviet leadership, and in fact Soviet police seized with vigor clandestine diaries containing anti-Soviet interpretations of the personal past (Hellbeck, 2001). Nonetheless, an analysis of diaries from the period of the 1930s indicates a "distinctly Soviet" way of writing about autobiographical experiences (Hellbeck, 2001), and one that squares nicely with the goals of the regime. With regularity, diaries stressed themes of work on the self, social utility and integration, and historical orientation as they recounted personally experienced events and reflections (Hellbeck, 2001). Strikingly, direct encouragement and in some cases requirements of the government to write autobiographical accounts appears to have been taken over by the citizenry, producing normative changes in the tendency to record the details of specific past events. There is no record of the extent to which this bled over into the tendency to speak about or think about the personal past. However, it is quite likely that the concentrated time spent writing and reflecting on autobiographical experiences influenced how individuals remembered them over the long term.

A second example of government-directed autobiographical writing seems to have been somewhat different in origin. During the years of China's Cultural Revolution, the Maoist government sought to strictly monitor citizens' fidelity to Communist party ideals (Solomon, 1971). One of many channels through which this was achieved was the practice of soliciting autobiographical accounts from citizens, beginning at an early age. Unlike in the Soviet case, in which the foremost goal of government-directed autobiographical writing was often to enhance the writer's belief in the cause, the Chinese government appeared to have used autobiographical accounts primarily for political monitoring. Vogel (1966) offered a contemporaneous account of this practice.

> Several times during their school years, students are expected to write autobiographies, which begin from the age of eight. All cadres, all people of importance, and all people under serious suspicions must also write autobiographies. Some people are called on to write annual reports of their activities. . . . In school, children are called upon incidentally to tell about things at home . . . a teacher would be expected to pass on any reports that do create serious doubts about certain families.
>
> Not only contacts, but even incidental details may create risks if reported. For example, any information about dress or house furnishings or eating habits, no matter how innocuous it may seem to the reporter, might be taken to mean that a person is not truly a member of the peasant or proletariat class. (Vogel, 1966, p. 410)

Compared with the Soviet case, it appears that this Chinese practice of soliciting autobiographical accounts was more limited in scope. There is no evidence that the government requirement to submit regular autobiographies was adopted with zeal by individuals and incorporated into their regular practices at home. Nonetheless, it is interesting to recognize that the government was able to use accounts of specific personally experienced past events to influence citizens' lives. These personal writings may be different from a regular sense of autobiography and were often referred to as "self-evaluation" or "self-criticism." They appeared to originate from Confucian teachings that emphasize one's learning from the past (Wang, 2003), but were enacted by the government in service of its political purpose. Vogel (1966) argued that this practice changed the nature of friendships, and particularly the boundaries of the information that was shared between friends, because of the risks that friends might leak jeopardizing information. In this sense, government policy influenced the web of social relations and talk about the personal past that would normally sustain specific autobiographical memories.

Government Policies on Family Structure

In addition to direct government elicitation of autobiographical accounts, more general government policies may play an important indirect role in shaping autobiographical memory. Government policies that affect family structure are one example.

Wang, Leichtman, and White's (1998) study of only-child and sibling Chinese documented the effects of such a policy on autobiographical memory. This study took advantage of modern day China as a sort of natural laboratory in which to study how family structure can affect autobiographical memory. In 1979 the Chinese government enacted the one-child policy, which encouraged all couples to produce only one child in order to curtail population growth. Ever since, Chinese observers have worried about the effects on children of growing up without siblings, in families different from those of traditional Chinese society.

Some observers have suggested that the only-child family structure provides an environment antithetical to traditional Chinese values (Fan, 1994). One view has been that in place of a traditional emphasis on interdependence, interpersonal harmony, and concern with others, the only-child family structure emphasizes the individual interests of the child. The notion of a "4-2-1 syndrome," in which four grandparents and two parents focus excessively on a single child is a case in point (Lee, 1992). Reports have described only-children as "little emperors" who are self-centered, egocentric, and undisciplined in comparison with sibling children (Fan, 1994; Jiao, Ji, & Jing, 1986). Thus, Wang, Leichtman, and White (1998) were motivated to see whether potential differences in the degree of self-focus among only children and children with siblings were associated with differences in the characteristics of their autobiographical memories.

Wang, Leichtman, and White's (1998) study was conducted in Beijing with a sample of 99 only-child participants and 156 sibling participants of high-school and college age. Each participant filled out two questionnaires in Chinese. The first questionnaire asked participants to describe and date their earliest autobiographical memory, and then to do the same for three other childhood memories. The second questionnaire was a shortened version of Kuhn & McPartland's (1954) Twenty Statements Test (TST), in which participants filled in the blank after 10 statements phrased "I am ___."

The results of the study showed differences between only children and children with siblings on a number of memory and self-description measures. All of the results were consistent with the notion that only children were more self-focused and correspondingly more attuned to self-focused personal event memories. In terms of memories, only-child Chinese reported a greater number of specific memories referring to one-point-in-time events. They reported earliest memories that dated on average from the time they were 39 months old, while sibling Chinese reported earliest memories from almost 9 months later. Compared to children with siblings, only-child Chinese reported fewer memories focused on social interactions and on family, while they reported more memories focused on personal experiences and feelings and on themselves alone. Only-child Chinese participants' memories contained a lower ratio of other/self mentions, indicating a relatively greater focus on their own roles in the past event as opposed to those of others.

In this study, responses to the TST fell into the two primary scoring categories described earlier: private self-descriptions focused on personal traits or behaviors and collective self-descriptions focused on group membership. As predicted, only-child Chinese reported relatively more private self-descriptions, while children with siblings reported relatively more collective self-descriptions. Across the entire sample, participants' scores on the self-description questionnaire were directly related to several autobiographical memory variables. Private self-description scores were positively related to narrative length, mentions of the self, and memory specificity, whereas collective self-description scores were negatively related to these measures.

In summary, these data suggest that the Chinese government's only-child policy affected autobiographical memory outcomes. The policy resulted in a situation in which large numbers of Chinese youth grew up with more individually oriented self-constructs and autobiographical memories than would have been the case had the policy not gone into effect. Wang, Leichtman, and White (1998) theorized that the locus of the effects they documented was in the environments of participants' family homes during childhood, consistent with observations of home-environment differences from Chinese researchers (e.g., Lee, 1992; Fan, 1994). The fact that samples of only-children and children with siblings grew up side-by-side in the same larger communities and schools enhanced the viability of this explanation. More recent cross-cultural data, which we discuss later in the chapter, support the impression that self and memory outcomes are formed early within family contexts affected by the cultural-political-historical factors in the larger society.

Cohort Effects

Although little psychological research has been directed at evaluating cohort differences in autobiographical expression, across the generations in any given society there are likely to be marked cohort differences as a function of changes in the socio-political and normative cultural climates in which individuals are raised. For example, returning to the case of China, it is possible to imagine that if the one-child policy were to stay in place for many generations, over time the normative modes of autobiographical expression might shift. Stylistically, individuals might become more likely to focus on one-point-in-time events, expression might become more elaborative, and the normative timing of the earliest autobiographical memory might shift downward to an earlier age. Such changes across cohorts are of course likely to be a function not only of shifts in government policies, but also of more general cultural mores.

From the point of view of content, it is easy to see how autobiographical memories might shift across generations as a function of changes in the larger social climate. Brumberg's (1998) sampling of the private diaries of American adolescent girls from 1830 through the present day serves as a relevant example. Brumberg's analysis revealed that the diaries of early and later cohorts focused on starkly different aspects of experience, representing a shift in values from "good works" to "good looks." Early-to-mid-19th century girls reflected on personally experienced past events that were relevant to improving upon virtues such as charity and kindness. In contrast, contemporary girls more often focused on personally experienced past events that were relevant to improving physical appearance. For example, these girls reviewed in detail their recent eating, exercise, and grooming behaviors. Brumberg (1998) suggested that a confluence of social and economic transformations, including changes in hygiene, medical care, middle-class parenting practices, and the availability of mirrors, that occurred between the earlier and later historical periods served as a catalyst for the differences in girls' attitudes that these diaries reflected. What is clear from the perspective of autobiographical memory research is that the different foci of the earlier and later diaries are likely to reflect larger differences in the contents of autobiographical memories.

Another relevant example is the historical transformations in "egodocuments," including diaries, autobiographies, and other forms of personal records, in Holland from the Golden Age to Romanticism (Dekker, 2000). Dekker observed that the traditional model of autobiography before 1800 contains extensive descriptions of one's family background, with the individual primarily seen as a link in a family lineage. A new type of autobiography emerged around 1800 and gradually developed into a distinct literary genre, in which the author dwells on his or her childhood and youth and the self becomes the center of the text. Egodocuments also came to be an important outlet for expressing personal feelings. Dekker attributed these changes to the growing individualism during that historical era in Holland as well as the changes in social conventions in regard to emotions and ideas about children.

One important point relevant to cohort effects is that the artifacts available to support memory may be very different from one generation to the next. The widespread use of videotapes and photographs to record personal experiences in the modern world stands in contrast to the experience of previous generations. These tools for recording memories are likely to have an impact on which events and which of their details are recalled over time.

Schudson (1995) underscored the point that societies also have dedicated memory forms that help both groups and individuals remember events. These forms include books, holidays, statues, and souvenirs (Schudson, 1995), and their nature and availability are likely to vary considerably across generations. With respect to historic events that individuals have either watched unfold or in some way taken part in, such markers may shape what and how personal experiences are eventually remembered (Jodelet, Pennebaker, & Paez, 1997). A widely discussed recent example is found in videotapes of the aircraft bombing of the World Trade Center that occurred in New York on September 11, 2001. It is possible that continually viewing these tapes on television in the days and months after the event may have altered some individuals' original memories of their personal experiences that day. Watching the videos could have the effect of reactivating and thus preserving individual event memories, or alternatively of confusing or distorting them through the introduction of post-event information not available at the time of the original event (e.g., Loftus & Hoffman, 1989). The point relevant to the present discussion is that in a cohort without this particular form of memory artifact, individual event memories would manifest differently.

A separate but related point is that the degree to which individuals remember shared, historic events in connection with their personal autobiographical recollections may differ across cohorts. Wang and Conway (2004) conducted a study that was not focused on cohort effects but is relevant in principle. In this questionnaire study, 40- to 60-year-old American and Chinese adults were asked to remember and briefly describe 20 specific, one-moment-in-time memory events that took place in their lives. The results indicated that Chinese participants provided an average of 3.4 memories that had a reference to historical events, while Americans on average did not even provide one

($M = 0.26$). Such a difference could as easily surface across cohorts as across cultures. In the case of China, it may be that the general milieu encourages citizens to attend to political events more than in the case of the United States. It may also be that the sweeping changes that have occurred in Chinese society during the lifetimes of adults presently in middle age provided captivating, personally relevant information with a high likelihood of becoming integrated into individuals' autobiographical memories. Across cohorts, both the degree of general political awareness and the nature, timing, and personal relevance of historic events that take place may affect the degree to which the events eventually become part of long-term personal event memory. In turn, such memories help define each generation's identity (Holmes & Conway, 1999).

Culturally Shaped Elements of the Social Environment

Cultural Differences

As we have noted, research indicates that variations in the proximal environments of childhood can influence the expression and retention of autobiographical memories. Some of the most marked normative variations in children's proximal environments are found across cultures, and thus investigators have turned their attention to how these differences influence memory for personally experienced events.

One major dimension along which theorists have placed various cultures is in terms of the degree to which they encourage individuals to think and act in independent versus interdependent ways (e.g., Markus & Kitayama, 1991; Fiske, Kitayama, Markus, & Nisbett, 1998). Some cultures, including those of the United States and some European countries, espouse the paramount value of autonomy, self-expression, and distinctive personal characteristics. Alternatively, other cultures, including many found in South America, East Asia, and Africa, place a premium value on interpersonal relationships and emphasize common goals and shared identities among people (Markus & Kitayama, 1991; Wang & Leichtman, 2000). To be sure, this characterization of cultural differences does not capture the views of all individuals or subcultural groups and it does not extend to all aspects of social functioning (Fiske, 2002; Oyserman et al., 2002). Nonetheless, it helps make sense of cross-cultural patterns that emerge across a variety of domains. Theoretically, cultural differences in independence/interdependence are closely connected with each of the memory-related aspects of the proximal environment we discussed earlier: variations in mother–child talk about the past, beliefs conveyed to children about the importance of past events, and variations in the extent of focus on the self. A growing body of literature including both adults and young children attests to the interconnections among these elements and their role in producing cultural differences in personal-event memories.

Some of the most direct evidence of cultural differences in the normative level of interdependence is the fact that scores on the Twenty Statements Test vary from country to country (Kuhn & McPartland, 1954; Triandis, 1989). A number of studies have documented that in cultures traditionally considered to have a relatively independent orientation, TST scores tend to be skewed in the direction of more private self-descriptions (Bochner, 1994; Trafimow, Triandis, & Goto, 1991). For example, Wang (2001b) gave the TST to Chinese and Euro-American college students and found that Americans had a much larger proportion of private self-descriptions than their Chinese counterparts, who had a larger proportion of collective self-descriptions. Other measures of self-description provide further support for cross-cultural differences in independence/interdependence. In a recent study, Wang, Cole, and Lord (2003) employed a method of intensive personal interviews to elicit self-descriptions in Euro-American and Malagasy young adults. Participants also filled out the Self-Construal Scale (SCS) following the interview (Singelis, 1994). Compared with Malagasy participants, Americans referred more frequently to their personal qualities and attributes and less to social roles and categories in their free self-narratives. Americans also showed greater strength of the independent self on the SCS.

Just as TST scores within a particular culture appear to be associated with the style and contents of autobiographical recollection (e.g., Wang, Leichtman, & White, 1998), across cultures this also seems to be the case. Wang (2001b) found that Chinese adults not only provided more collective self-descriptions than their American counterparts, but also evidenced differences in their autobiographical reports. When participants provided their earliest memory of childhood in a written questionnaire, Americans' memories were earlier, more autonomously oriented, and more likely to refer to specific, one-point-in-time events than those of Chinese participants. Analyses controlling for culture and gender indicated that individuals who described themselves in more self-focused and positive terms provided more specific and self-focused memories.

Using an interview method, Leichtman et al. (2003) also documented stylistic differences in the autobiographical memories provided by rural Indian adults and middle-class American adults. Native interviewers asked a series of questions about autobiographical memory, beginning with an open-ended question about whether participants remembered any event from childhood. Ninety-seven percent of American participants reported recalling a childhood memory, and 69% provided a specific one-point-in-time episode. In contrast, 57% of rural Indian participants reported having no recollection of childhood and only 14% provided a specific episode. To capture additional differences in the general nature of the memories, hypothesis-blind and culture-blind raters sorted culture-disguised versions of memories extracted from the transcripts into two equal piles. The piles were designated to contain "the richest, most vivid, detailed and accessible memories" and alternately "the least rich memories." The results indicated that 69% of American memories were sorted into the "richest" pile, while only 32% of the Indian memories were sorted into the "richest" pile. In this study, the two samples were chosen for maximum contrast in factors associated with culture and lifestyle. The results confirm that indeed, long-term access to specific autobiographical episodes may differ as a function of total cultural milieu.

There is currently empirical evidence that this pattern of differences between cultures in the timing, style, and content of adults' autobiographical recollections is associated with differences in the environments of childhood. In some of the earliest work in this vein, Mullen (1994) conducted a series of questionnaire studies on adults' earliest memories of childhood. The data indicated that both a mixed sample of Asian-American adults and a sample of Korean adults had earliest memories of childhood that were considerably later than those of Euro-Americans. Positing that these differences were related to social differences in children's environments in the two cultures, Mullen and Yi (1995) recorded natural conversations throughout a day in the homes of Korean and American mother–child dyads. The results indicated that during each hour they spent together, American mothers referred to three times as many past episodes as Korean mothers. There were also content differences in the conversations of the two cultural groups, with Americans focusing more on feelings, thoughts, and personal attributes and Koreans focusing more on social norms.

Subsequent studies contrasting parent–child conversation in Asian and North American cultures support the pattern that this work suggested (e.g., Choi, 1992; Miller et al., 1997; Wang, Leichtman, and Davies, 2000; Wang, 2001a). The body of evidence indicates that American parent–child conversation is distinguished by a relatively elaborative style in comparison with Asian parent–child conversation. For example, Wang, Leichtman, & Davies (2000) studied Euro-American and Chinese mothers at home with their 3-year-olds. Researchers asked the mothers to talk with their children in whatever way was natural about two past events and a story. When talking about both events and stories, many American mothers exhibited the classic elaborative style, asking many "wh" questions and elaborating on children's contributions. Chinese mothers instead typically exhibited a low-elaborative style, posing and repeating factual questions and rarely following up in the direction of the child's comments. In addition, consistent with the cultural emphasis on independence and autonomy, American mothers frequently prompted children to provide evaluative information about their thoughts, feelings, and predilections relevant to past events, with the child often cast as the central character of the story. (By way of illustration, recall the conversation between Patrick and his mother at the beginning of the chapter.) In contrast, Chinese mothers, who value to a great extent interpersonal harmony and behavioral conformity, tended to focus on rules and discipline when conversing with their children about the past and telling the story.

Leichtman et al. (2003) also documented striking differences in parent–child conversations in rural Indian and upper-middle-class American samples. Researchers videotaped 4-year-old children at home in the two countries and transcribed all conversations that occurred over the course of one hour. The results indicated that while American children heard an average of 3,090 total sentences and 20 sentences referring to distant-past events during the hour, Indian children heard an average of 718 sentences and 1 sentence referencing distant-past events. This difference between the number of sentences referring to distant past events was highly significant, even when analyses controlled for total number of sentences. In addition, the American children heard more evaluative language, more references to cognitive states, and more questions of all kinds (yes/no and "wh").

There is evidence that from an early age, children's narratives reflect the same kinds of cultural differences apparent in the conversations and memory reports of their parents. For example, Han, Leichtman, and Wang (1998) studied 4- and 6-year-old children from upper-middle-class, urban backgrounds in Korea, China, and the United States. Researchers asked children the same series of free-recall questions about recent events in their lives. The results indicated that American and Chinese children provided longer memory reports than Korean children, but on most other variables, the American sample stood apart from the Asian groups. American children evidenced a more detailed, elaborate style of talking about their memories than Asians, including more descriptives, more personal preferences, judgments, opinions, and more references to cognitive states in their reports. American children also gave many more memories that referred to specific one-point-in-time episodes as opposed to repeated or routine events.

Recent data from Wang (2004) also support the notion that cultural differences in memory and self-description are likely to be a function of differences in children's home environments, which include the parent–child conversations we have noted. This study indicated that cultural differences in both memory and self-concept emerge even before formal schooling has begun. Wang examined autobiographical memory and self-description among Euro-American and Chinese children in preschool through second grade ($N = 180$). Native female researchers interviewed children individually at school. During a "question-and-answer game," children recounted four autobiographical events and described themselves in response to open-ended questions. American children tended to provide lengthy, detailed, and emotionally elaborate memories and to focus on their own roles, preferences, and feelings when telling the story. In addition, they frequently described themselves in terms of personal attitudes, beliefs, and dispositional traits, and in a positive light. In comparison, Chinese children provided relatively skeletal accounts of past experiences that often centered on social interactions and daily routines, and they were more likely to describe themselves in terms of social roles, relationships, and context-specific behaviors in a neutral or modest tone. The cultural differences noted became larger and more stable with development. At the individual level, children who focused more on private aspects of the self gave lengthier memory accounts and placed more emphasis on personal roles and predilections.

Urban/Rural Differences

One important subcultural variable is the degree of urbanization. A number of studies have suggested that differences exist in the patterns of personal event memory in urban and rural contexts. Although there is likely to be wide variation within both urban and rural contexts from one region of the world to the next, extant data suggest that urban/rural differences may be consistent enough to have systematic effects on measures of autobiographical memory.

One example is Wang, Leichtman, and White's (1998) study of Chinese only and sibling children. In this study, in addition to only/sibling effects, the data showed significant urban/rural effects. Young adults who had grown up in urban environments reported earliest childhood memories dating from an average age of 43 months, significantly earlier than those of their rurally raised counterparts, whose earliest memories dated from an average age of 56 months. Participants from urban environments also provided lengthier accounts of their autobiographical memories. The sample in this study was taken from highly selective schools, making it unlikely that differences in global intelligence between groups were responsible for the effects. Instead, some Chinese theorists have suggested a pattern of socialization differences between urban and rural subcultures that might explain the results. In recent decades, urban Chinese families have apparently undergone larger changes in cultural values and childrearing practices than rural families, and urban parents are presently more likely to foster competition, independence, and self-actualization among their children (Ho, 1989; Wang & Hsueh, 2000).

Echoing this pattern of urban/rural differences in China, Leichtman et al. (2003) discovered urban/rural differences in the memory reports of urban and rural Indian adults. In this study, the two samples were matched in terms of socio-economic status, with both groups coming from lower-working-class backgrounds. The data indicated that compared with rural Indians, urban Indians were more likely to report having memories of childhood and were more likely to report both recent and childhood memories of specific, one-point-in-time events as opposed to general or routine occurrences. Urban Indian participants were also more likely to report talking about the past in their daily lives than were rural Indians. It may be that as individuals negotiate their identities in the more complex and socially mobile environments of city life, the unique attributes of the self – including a personal autobiographical history – come into relief.

Wang (2003) proposed that urban/rural differences in personal-event memory may result from different degrees of complexity of life experiences in the two settings. Change and novelty associated with city life produce the material out of which autobiographical memories can be developed and sustained, whereas repose and redundancy often associated with the countryside may render a life with few or no stories. It is possible then that, compared with the simple and stable life of rural areas, the relatively rich and complex lifestyle of the city could have contributed to the greater accessibility to early childhood events in the urban samples. This account may also in part be responsible for the cultural differences in autobiographical memory noted earlier. In Euro-American culture, changes and variations are often seen as equated with progress. This notion may create a variable, "exciting" lifestyle for its individuals and consequently many momentous and memorable events to dwell upon. In contrast, Asian cultures more often value stability, continuity, and a fully predictable life, which may lead to a life of repetition and relative "ordinariness" and thus, fewer memorable personal events.

Conclusions

In this chapter we have reflected on a broad array of influences on autobiographical memory. Developmental psychologists have looked first to the proximal environments of childhood to understand how factors outside the individual might bear on the intimate process of personal recollection. As we have noted, day-to-day social settings teach values and practices that affect what individuals eventually remember. What individuals believe about the importance of remembering past events, how they talk about events with significant others, and how they define themselves more generally helps determine the style and contents of autobiographical memory during and after childhood.

Even as beliefs, conversational styles, and self-views influence memory, these factors are themselves embedded in a larger socio-political framework. To gain a rich perspective on autobiographical memory requires that researchers tread into the traditional domains of anthropologists and sociologists, taking into account broader aspects of the societies in which people live. In particular, we have noted that the general political atmosphere of a society as well as specific government policies and historical transformations can affect what individuals remember. These overarching factors help to determine which specific aspects of experience individuals focus on, and also the manner in which memories are expressed.

As our examples have illustrated, some government policies can shape the functions of personal-event memory in the service of politics. Governments have occasionally encouraged distinct modes of autobiographical writing and, perhaps too, remembering. By modifying the family structure in fundamental ways, government policies can also shape individuals' daily settings and their patterns of interacting with significant others. These changes can in turn affect individuals' cognitions, including autobiographical memory and self-concept. Furthermore, a society's historical transformations in the realms of value orientation, ideology, and technology can produce new genres of autobiographical memory across generations.

Cross-cultural studies demonstrate the impact of both larger socio-political contexts and individuals' proximal environments on memory. The prevailing views of selfhood and the predominant social orientation of a society determine to a great extent how personal experiences are perceived, represented, and remembered. These cultural factors in the distal environment are mediated through organized daily activities between parents and children that have an impact on memory development from an early age. Urban/rural differences in autobiographical memory provide another illustration of such effects of the broader social context on personal remembering. There are bound to be other important contextual factors that we have yet to discover.

If there is one take-home lesson from the past decade of memory research, it is that personal event memory is never completely personal. This is to say that autobiographical memory is not a sole product of the individual mind or brain. Nor is it even a straightforward result of dyadic interactions with others. While the particular constellation of autobiographical memories that informs a person's behavior and sense of self may be unique, such memories are inseparable from the social and historical contexts in which they occur (Schudson, 1995; Leichtman, Wang, & Pillemer, 2003; Wang & Brockmeier, 2002). In this sense, the autobiographical memories of any one person are shaped by those of many other people, including many who have gone before.

The process of remembering always takes place at a particular social-political-historical moment and reflects the symbolic meaning system afforded by that moment. Autobiographical memory is thus part of the larger history co-authored by the many individuals of a given society.

References

Bochner, S. (1994). Cross-cultural differences in the self concept. *Journal of Cross-Cultural Psychology 25*, 2, 273–283.

Bronfenbrenner, U. (1979). *The Ecology of Human Development*. Cambridge, MA: Harvard University Press.

Brumberg, J. J. (1998). *The Body Project: An Intimate History of Adolescent Girls*. New York: Vintage Books.

Caldwell, L. (2002). *Bringing Learning to Life: The Reggio Emilia Approach to Early Childhood Education*. New York: Teachers College Press.

Ceci, S. J., & Leichtman, M. D. (1992). Memory, cognition and learning: Developmental and ecological considerations. In I. Rapin & S. Segalawitz (Eds.), *Handbook of Neuropsychology*. Holland: Elsevier.

Choi, S. H. (1992). Communicative socialization processes: Korea and Canada. In S. Iwasaki, Y. Kashima, & K. Leung (Eds.), *Innovations in Cross-Cultural Psychology* (pp. 103–122). Amsterdam: Swets & Zeitlinger.

Dekker, R. (2000). *Childhood, Memory and Autobiography in Holland: From the Golden Age to Romanticism*. New York: St. Martin's Press.

Dudycha, G. J., & Dudycha, M. M. (1941). Childhood memories: A review of the literature. *Psychological Review 38*, 668–682.

Fan, C. (1994). A comparative study of personality characteristics between only and nononly children in primary schools in Xian. *Psychological Science 17*, 2, 70–74 (in Chinese).

Fiske, A. P. (2002). Using individualism and collectivism to compare cultures – A critique of the validity and measurement of the constructs: Comment on Oyserman et al. (2002). *Psychological Bulletin 128*, 78–88.

Fiske, A. P., Kitayama, S., Markus, H. R., & Nisbett, R. E. (1998). The cultural matrix of social psychology. In D. T. Gilbert, S. T. Fiske, & G. Lindzey (Eds.), *The Handbook of Social Psychology* (Vol. 2) (4th ed.) (pp. 915–981). Boston: McGraw Hill.

Fivush, R., & Fromhoff, F. A. (1988). Style and structure in mother–child conversations about the past. *Discourse Processes 11*, 337–355.

Greenwald, A. G., & Pratkanis, A. R. (1984). The self. In R. S. Wyer & T. K. Srull (Eds.), *Handbook of Social Cognition* (Vol. 3) (pp. 129–178). Hillsdale, NJ: Lawrence Erlbaum.

Haden, C. (1998). Reminiscing with different children: Relating maternal stylistic consistency and sibling similarity in talk about the past. *Developmental Psychology 34*, 99–114.

Harley, K., & Reese, E. (1999). Origins of autobiographical memory. *Developmental Psychology 35*, 1338–1348.

Han, J. J., Leichtman, M. D., & Wang, Q. (1998). Autobiographical memory in Korean, Chinese and American children. *Developmental Psychology 34*, 701–703.

Hellbeck, J. (2001). Working, struggling, becoming: Stalin-era autobiographical texts. *The Russian Review 60*, 340–59.

Ho, D. Y. (1989). Continuity and variation in Chinese patterns of socialization. *Journal of Marriage and the Family 51*, 149–153.

Holmes, A., & Conway, M. A. (1999). Generation identity and the reminiscence bump: Memory for public and private events. *Journal of Adult Development 6*, 21–34.

Jiao, S., Ji, G., & Jing, Q. (1986). Comparative study of behavior qualities of only children and sibling children. *Child Development 57*, 2, 357–361.

Jodelet, D., Pennebaker, J., & Paez, D. (1997). *Political Events and Collective Memories*. London: Routledge.

Kassoff, L. B., & Wang, Q. (2002). Early autobiographical memories in Americans and French: Effects of culture on memory and self. Unpublished manuscript.

Kuhn, M. H., & McPartland, T. S. (1954). An empirical investigation of self-attitudes. *American Sociological Review 19*, 68–76.

Lee, L. C. (1992). Daycare in the People's Republic of China. In M. E. Lamb & K. Sternberg (Eds.) *Child Care in Context: Cross-cultural Perspectives* (pp. 355–392). Hillsdale, NJ: Lawrence Erlbaum.

Leichtman, M. D., Bhogle, S., Sankaranarayanan, A., & Hobeika, D. (2003). Autobiographical memory and children's narrative environments in Southern India and the Northern United States. Unpublished manuscript.

Leichtman, M. D., Holmes, E., & Pillemer, D. B. (2003). A clown came to the class: The impact of conversation and language status on children's event memories. Unpublished manuscript.

Leichtman, M. D., Pillemer, D. B., Wang, Q., Koreishi, A., & Han, J. J. (2000). When Baby Maisy came to school: Mothers' interview styles and preschoolers' event memories. *Cognitive Development 15*, 1, 99–114.

Leichtman, M. D., Wang, Q., & Pillemer, D. B. (2003). Cultural variations in interdependence and autobiographical memory: Lessons from Korea, China, India and the United States. In R. Fivush & C. A. Haden (Eds.), *Autobiographical Memory and the Construction of a Narrative Self: Developmental and Cultural Perspectives* (pp. 73–98). Mahwah, NJ: Lawrence Erlbaum.

Loftus, E. F., & Hoffman, H. (1989). Misinformation and memory: The creation of new memories. *Journal of Experimental Psychology: General 118*, 100–104.

Markus, H. R., & Kitayama, S. (1991). Culture and the self: Implications for cognition, emotion, and motivation. *Psychological Review 98*, 224–253.

McCabe, A., & Peterson, C. (1991). Getting the story: A longitudinal study of parental styles in eliciting narratives and developing narrative skill. In A. McCabe &

C. Peterson (Eds.), *Developing Narrative Structure* (pp. 217–257). Hillsdale, NJ: Lawrence Erlbaum.

Miller, P. J., Wiley, A. R., Fung, H., & Liang, C. H. (1997). Personal storytelling as a medium of socialization in Chinese and American families. *Child Development 68*, 557–568.

Mullen, M. K. (1994). Earliest recollections of childhood: A demographic analysis. *Cognition 52*, 55–79.

Mullen, M. K., & Yi, S. (1995). The cultural context of talk about the past: Implications for the development of autobiographical memory. *Cognitive Development 10*, 407–419.

Nelson, K. (1992). Emergence of autobiographical memory at age 4. *Human Development 35*, 172–177.

Oyserman, D., Coon, H. M., & Kemmelmeier, M. (2002). Rethinking individualism and collectivism: Evaluation of theoretical assumptions and meta-analysis. *Psychological Bulletin 128*, 3–72.

Pillemer, D. B. (1998). *Momentous Events, Vivid Memories*. Cambridge, MA: Harvard University Press.

Reese, E., Haden, C., & Fivush, R. (1993). Mother–child conversations about the past: Relationships of style and memory over time. *Cognitive Development 8*, 403–430.

Schudson, M. (1995). Dynamics of distortion in collective memory. In D. L. Schacter (Ed.), *Memory Distortion: How Minds, Brains and Societies Reconstruct the Past* (pp. 346–364). Cambridge, MA: Harvard University Press.

Sheingold, K., & Tenney, Y. J. (1982). Memory for a salient childhood event. In U. Neisser (Ed.), *Memory Observed* (pp. 201–212). San Francisco: Freeman.

Singelis, T. M. (1994). The measurement of independent and interdependent self-construals. *Personality and Social Psychology Bulletin 20*, 580–591.

Solomon, R. H. (1971). *Mao's Revolution and the Chinese Political Culture*. Berkeley, CA: University of California Press.

Super, C. M., & Harkness, S. (2002). Culture structures the environment for development. *Human Development 45*, 270–274.

Trafimow, D., Triandis, H. C., & Goto, S. G. (1991). Some tests of the distinction between private and collective self. *Journal of Personality and Social Psychology 60*, 649–655.

Triandis, H. C. (1989). The self and social behavior in differing cultural contexts. *Psychological Review 96*, 506–520.

Vogel, E. F. (1966), From friendship to comradeship: The change in personal relations in Communist China. In R. MacFarquhar (Ed.), *China under Mao: Politics Take Command*. Cambridge, MA: MIT.

Waldfogel, S. (1948). The frequency and affective character of childhood memories. *Psychological Monographs 62*, 1–39.

Wang, Q. (2001a). "Did you have fun?": American and Chinese mother–child conversations about shared emotional experiences. *Cognitive Development 16*, 693–715.

Wang, Q. (2001b). Cultural effects on adults' earliest childhood recollection and self-description: Implications for the relation between memory and the self. *Journal of Personality and Social Psychology 81*, 220–233.

Wang, Q. (2003). Infantile amnesia reconsidered: A cross-cultural analysis. *Memory 11*, 65–80.

Wang, Q. (2004). The emergence of cultural self-construct: Autobiographical memory and self-description in American and Chinese children. *Developmental Psychology 40(1)*, 3–15.

Wang, Q., & Brockmeier, J. (2002). Autobiographical remembering as cultural practice: Understanding the interplay between memory, self and culture. *Culture and Psychology 8*, 45–64.

Wang, Q., & Conway, M. (2004). The stories we keep: Autobiographical memory in American and Chinese middle-aged adults. *Journal of Personality, 72(5)*, 911–938.

Wang, Q., & Hsueh, Y. (2000). Parent-child interdependence in Chinese families: Change and continuity. In C. Violato, E. Oddone-Paolucci, & M. Genuis (Eds.), *The Changing Family and Child Development* (pp. 60–69). Aldershot, England: Ashgate Publishing Ltd.

Wang, Q., & Leichtman, M. D. (2000). Same beginnings, different stories: A comparison of American and Chinese children's narratives. *Child Development 71*, 1329–1346.

Wang, Q., Cole, J., & Lord, H. (2003). Self-narratives in Euro-American and Malagasy adults. Unpublished raw data.

Wang, Q., Leichtman, M. D., & Davies, K. I. (2000). Sharing memories and telling stories: American and Chinese mothers and Their 3-year-olds. *Memory 8*, 159–177.

Wang, Q., Leichtman, M. D., & White. S. H. (1998). Childhood memory and self-description: The impact of growing up an only child. *Cognition 69*, 73–103.

3   Toward a Better Story of Psychology

Sheldon White's Contributions to the History of Psychology, A Personal Perspective

William McKinley Runyan

Introduction

Entering Harvard as an undergraduate in 1946, Sheldon (Shep) White intended to study psychology. With strong prior interests in both literature and politics, scientific psychology seemed a reasonable extension of those interests, perhaps a way of being rigorously scientific about human behavior and experience. However, he was dropped into the middle of the fray of debate about what constitutes a properly scientific psychology (White, 2001).

It felt like being in a broken home, with White shuttling back and forth between two parents. On one side were the experimental psychologists in the basement of Memorial Hall, Edwin G. Boring, S. S. Stevens, and by 1948, B. F. Skinner. He took Psychology 1 with Boring, focusing on experimental studies of sensation, perception, and reaction time. "It was scientifically virtuous but dull as dishwater" (White, 2001, p. 2). On the other side was the newly formed Department of Social Relations, with personality and social psychologists, sociologists, and cultural anthropologists (Allport, Murray, Parsons, Kluckhohn), with the personality and social psychologists still located in Emerson Hall. He took Social Relations 1a with Allport, which had some colorful readings and lectures, but wondered "what did it all mean programmatically or scientifically?" (White, 2001, p. 2). Neither group seemed to have an adequate account of what it and the other group of psychologists were doing.

White attended graduate school at Iowa, a leading department of experimental psychology dominated by Hull–Spence theory. He experienced this as an improvement and had a "marvelous time" there. "One of the things I found most satisfying was that Iowa had a story – of who we psychologists are, how we got here, what we are trying to do" (p. 3). He was impressed that theoretical behaviorists like Kenneth Spence acknowledged that current experimental research may be limited and dull, but that science needed to start simply; yet over time, with theory building and "composition laws," one would be able to address more complex and interesting human behavior. "This wasn't a great story but it was a story" (p. 3).

Sheldon White's work in the history of psychology can be seen as breaking out of this world view, and moving toward a better story of psychology. Many of his generation shifted from behaviorism to cognitive psychology and cognitive neuroscience, but he also shifted from an internalist story of psychology to a story of psychology in its social and cultural contexts, and to a more pluralistic conception of what constitutes scientific psychology.

One traditional question is, How does one understand psychology as a natural science? White introduces and works with a number of additional questions: How does one understand psychology as an ethical enterprise? How does one understand psychology as a moral science? Is developmental psychology best understood as a natural science, a moral enterprise, or as a set of projects intertwined with social reconstruction? Is developmental psychology perhaps a science of personal and societal design?

These are unusual questions that look odd from a natural scientific perspective. Hadn't he learned that science is supposed to be a value-free inquiry into the mysteries of the natural world? Or, did he first learn that, then learn more about the social and historical embeddedness of psychology, and come to a different understanding of the value-saturated human science traditions?

In the spring semester of 1985–86, while writing and editing a book on the uses of psychology in historical interpetation (Runyan, 1988) and on sabbatical at Kohlberg's Center for Moral Development at Harvard, I visited the first session of Sheldon White's History of Psychology course to see how he was covering the field. There were readings from many familiar sources, but it soon became clear that something different was going on. This wasn't like any story about the history of psychology I'd heard before.

There was no textbook, but readings from primary sources in Helmholtz, Wundt, William James, John Dewey, J. M. Cattell, John Dewey, Morton Prince, Breuer and Freud, Wolfgang Kohler, B. F. Skinner, S. S. Stevens, Edward Tolman, George Miller, Karl Lashley, Gordon Allport, Robert Sears, Daniel Schacter, and other well-known figures. However, the pieces weren't falling into their familiar places. The balls weren't rolling into their accustomed slots. The conceptual framework was difficult to assimilate. However, it felt obviously right in many ways and seemed like it might be a better story of psychology.

Wundt was appearing not in his standard place as founder of experimental psychology, but.instead with his cultural-historical work as a contributor to early social psychology. The individual chapters of William James's *Principles of Psychology* were presented and analyzed. G. Stanley Hall and genetic-developmental psychology had an unusually prominent place. Francis Bacon was used to suggest that epistemology in philosophy often stems from a concern with social reform. Inquiry in developmental psychology was seen as often flowing from changes in social organizations, institutions, and programs for children and disadvantaged populations. There is not a rising tide of applause as the discipline gets more experimental. A different story of psychology was being developed here, one supported by more detailed knowledge of the intellectual and social organization of the discipline.

This was NOT a story of psychology becoming increasingly successful as a natural science, as it moved from Titchenerian introspection, to behaviorism and learning theories, to cognitive neuroscience. Rather, White kept talking about "cooperative empiricisms" employed by different groups of psychologists, often with different visions of the field. This included the early experimentalists, who appeared in a changed role, as not THE founders of psychology, but as one contending group among many. The story also includes the Child Study group at Clark University under G. Stanley Hall, clinical case analysis by Freud, neurologists, early social psychologists, learning theorists, cognitive psychologists, and a competing plurality of views about human nature that have affected social policy.

How to conceptualize psychology, and how to organize this pluralistic set of activities into a discipline? How did these "cooperative empiricisms" relate to the changing social organization of society? I was in trouble. How much did I know about 19th- and 20th-century social history, and how it was related to the rise and fall of different traditions in psychology? And what would I need to learn to be able to think critically about these kinds of arguments?

I thought I knew something about the philosophy of science, particularly about the rise and fall of logical positivism, with its loose connection to various behaviorisms (Smith, 1986), the later impact of Kuhn's cognitive and social-historical views, and the more radical sociological and Foucauldian approaches to scientific knowledge. However, that rug was also pulled out from under me, as White started analyzing philosophy of science not with Carnap, Hempel, or Nagel; not with Kuhn; not with Popper and falsificationism; not with James, Dewey, and pragmatism; not with rationalists versus empiricists or a Kantian synthesis; but with Francis Bacon. Francis Bacon (1561–1626)! Bacon was discussed in relation to his *Great Instauration* (1620), an effort to reformulate the sciences and their relation to society.

Bacon may be best known as an early philosopher of science, advocating induction, and as an early utopian, the author of *New Atlantis* (1627). What was he doing in a history of psychology course? Let me quote from notes on Bacon that White used in his History of Psychology course in the spring of 2000.

> Looking back at the past through a disciplinary telescope, the early psychologists saw a long lineage of ancestral philosophers of knowledge. But these "philosophers" – Thomas Hobbes, John Locke, David Hume, John Stuart Mill, Herbert Spencer – were not interested in epistemology for its own sake. They were men interested in political and religious reform, who addressed the problem of knowledge as foundational for a larger set of issues. What constitutes a sound notion? On what notion can good government be built? These writers were intellectuals, philosophes, members of the intelligentsia, "philosophers" in an older use of that word in English. They were leaders of Enlightenment efforts to create governments based on secular, rational, scientific social design.

In psychology, Bacon is sometimes mentioned as an early philosopher of science, but in White's view, "Bacon was a politician who led the active, chancy life of someone prominent in English public life. His advocacy of the inductive method was the first step in a larger project of a Great Instauration, a vision of a program of social reform that would inspire Descartes and Hobbes in the 17th century and come to fruition in the 19th century" (e.g., Comte, Mill, Spencer, Marx, and Engels).

Is this all true? I didn't then know enough to be able to judge, and I am still learning more about this field of issues. It is a large problem space, trying to relate theory and research in different traditions to social, institutional, and cultural history. At the time though, in the spring of 1986, I had the sense that this was a more detailed, better contextualized, and more complex story about the history of psychology than I was familiar with. It felt deeper, more socially relevant, and more intellectually adequate. In short, it seemed like a better story, one which conceptually left Boring's *History of Experimental Psychology* (1929/1950) in the dust. In later years, it provided a stimulating intellectual complement to Hilgard's *Psychology in America* (1987).

It was a story that I wanted to learn more about. On subsequent sabbaticals and years as a visiting scholar, I had a chance to again audit parts of his courses on the history of psychology and the history of developmental psychology, and talk with him about the problems raised. These were probably the most intellectually rewarding discussions I've had with anyone about psychology, continually raising new perspectives about what psychology is and how it fits into the world. It was a challenge to relate his perspective on psychology in its social contexts to my own primary interest in the study of lives. I used to feel that the most interesting conversations I'd ever had about psychology were with Henry Murray from 1970 to 1986, but over the last fifteen years, I've learned more from Shep White than anyone else, in person or in print, about the social and human meanings of psychology, and about the lives and careers of psychologists in different traditions. Getting together for a "quick sandwich" at the William James cafeteria often lasted three to four hours, or an afternoon chat would interfere with dinner plans. This chapter provides a welcome opportunity to think more carefully about the alternative views of the history of psychology that he was developing.

Debates about the need for a human science psychology to complement experimental natural science psychology have been kicking around for over a hundred years. Shep White's vision of developmental psychology as a human enterprise is, in my view, a major contribution to the human sciences and a way of understanding the details of work in different traditions in psychology related to wider social and cultural contexts.

He may have a better story of psychology, although not a perfect one. From my perspective, the social and cultural contexts of developmental psychology are illuminating, yet I also want to learn about the life histories of the people involved. The publications, with the exception of his work on G. Stanley Hall (White, 1992), often don't say a lot about this; but in conversation, White has empathic, critical, and insightful things to say about the lives and careers, about the "life plans and broken dreams" of many of those making a life in psychology.

With Emily Cahan, Shep White has traced the story of these human science traditions in psychology from Auguste Comte, John Stuart Mill, and Wilhelm Wundt, to Hugo Munsterberg and Gordon Allport (Cahan & White, 1992). Each called, in different ways, for a "human science psychology" or a "second psychology" to complement natural science laboratory-based experimental psychology. The tensions between these two visions came to life yet again in the split between experimental psychology and social relations at Harvard from 1946 to 1972, and though less visible, may not yet be resolved.

Cognitive neuroscience has an appealing story about itself in relation to psychology that has attracted many, and it seems likely to be more successful than earlier natural science visions such as Titchener's experimental psychology, or the behavioral and learning theory formulations that dominated from the 1930s through the 1950s. However, all three natural science programs, including cognitive neuroscience, have trouble dealing adequately with social-political contexts, cultural history, and the life histories of individuals. White has developed a vision of psychology in its social and cultural contexts that provides resources for reconstructing our understanding of the human science traditions in psychology. Rather than being dismissed as inadequately scientific, their methods and contributions need to be brought into clearer conceptual focus. It may turn out that social-cultural-historical approaches to psychology are indispensable complements to cognitive neuroscience and are even required resources for understanding the history of both "hard" and "soft" traditions in psychology in their social, cultural, and personal contexts.

This chapter discusses several of Shep White's contributions to the history of psychology, interwoven with a little about the contexts of his life and career. In particular, I'll draw on material from his publications "The Learning Theory Tradition and Child Psychology" (1970); "Psychology in All Sorts of Places" (1980) (a difficult-to-find chapter, which is perhaps my favorite); "Proposals for a Second Psychology" (Cahan & White, 1992) in the *American Psychologist*; and most recently, his Heinz Werner lectures at Clark University in May 2001 published as *Developmental Psychology as a Human Enterprise* (2001). These are supplemented by having audited his courses, the History of Psychology and the History of Developmental Psychology, and by having had talks and e-mail exchanges with him about these issues since the spring of 1986.

This is not a comprehensive review of all his contributions to the history of psychology; rather, as is inevitably the case, it is a personal perspective on how his work is perceived in light of my particular experience and interests. I have long been interested in the study of lives, and more recently in how the study of lives is related to the history of psychology (Runyan, 1982, 1988, 2003). I expect that others with backgrounds in developmental psychology, social policy, or the history and philosophy of science might well interpret his work differently.

Steps Toward a Better Story of Psychology

The Learning Theory Tradition and Child Psychology (1970)

As an associate editor of *Carmichael's Manual of Child Psychology* (Mussen, 1970), Shep White wrote the chapter on learning theory. This was not a raving endorsement of learning theory. The spell of Hull–Spence learning theory from graduate school at Iowa had been broken.

He granted that the stimulus-response tradition still remains an identifiable tradition, but "among child psychologists, as among psychologists in general, it is a waning tradition" (p. 657). Drawing on an analogy from Hebb

(1960), he said that in psychology, we are in the second American revolution. "The first American revolution overthrew introspection, the Psychology of Consciousness, and Titchenerian structuralism; it established stimulus-response analysis, the Psychology of Behavior, and the learning theories" (p. 657). Although often dated from Watson's 1913 paper, "Psychology as a Behaviorist Views It," the switch to behaviorism may have taken several decades to establish itself. The second ongoing revolution in 1970 was cognitive functionalism, with Piaget, Werner, Chomsky, ethology, and Russian psychologists (e.g., Luria) and an alignment with neurophysiology.

One surprising thing about the behavioral revolution was that although it had been central in theoretical work in academic psychology in the 1930s and 1940s, it did not become prominent in child psychology until the 1950s. Child psychologists may have been more influenced by a genetic point of view, as advocated earlier by G. Stanley Hall and later by Heinz Werner.

In a key paragraph near the end of the chapter, White says "We have all become a little tired of methodology, of scientific prospecti, of those seductive analogies between psychology and physics-seen-at-a-distance (White, 1970, p. 687)." As a result of this heresy, White says he was "excommunicated" from the learning theory community, and for a long time, Charles Spiker, his dissertation chair at Iowa, would not speak to him.

What led to the move away from behavioral learning theory? After White received his Ph.D. from Iowa in 1957, he started teaching at the University of Chicago in 1957, and said that people there, like Eckard Hess, just didn't find the Hull–Spence story credible. He published a number of experimental studies on learning and perception until the mid-1960s, but was troubled by the question: Is this a worthwhile way for a man to spend his life? By 1963–64, he was a fellow at the Center for Cognitive Psychology at Harvard. After moving to the Harvard Graduate School of Education in 1965, he started consulting on a number of social programs for children like Head Start, Follow Through, and Sesame Street. By 1973, he was lead author of a three-volume report, *Federal Programs for Young Children: Review and Recommendations*. White was ready for a different approach to psychology, both experimental and applied, and his relations with it. By the time of the 1978 Houston Symposium (White, 1980) discussed in the next section, he had a different way to conceive the stories that psychologists tell themselves about their discipline.

Psychology in All Sorts of Places (1980)

Psychologists are formed into an identifiable group through historical processes, including the creation of myths and factual historical accounts about their origin. White draws on the ideas of Mircea Eliade, historian of religion, about the function of tribal myths for initiating neophytes into the tribal traditions. In learning about the "Dream Time," or what happened at the beginning, the initiate also learns how to be "oriented" in this world, and what he or she must do to participate in it. White acknowledges that it is a huge leap, but suggests that the narrative histories of psychology, with stories about ancestors, also set forth a dream time, in which meaningful relations are created and orientation for the present is provided.

One significant difference is that narrative histories of psychology are debatable and corrigible. These histories can be tested against empirical evidence, and perhaps become "stories with footnotes" (White, 1980, p. 108). White says that when students are first exposed to a history of the discipline, such as Boring (1950) or Murphy and Kovach (1972), they often experience a "feeling of relaxation, of understanding of organization. '*Now* I see how the pieces fit together. . . .' '*Now* it all makes a little sense.'" (p. 110). Empirical historical research can lead to doubts about the received story and to construction of revised or new histories.

When things are going smoothly for the discipline, psychologists may not feel the need for a lot of specialized knowledge about its history, but can do their research, writing, and teaching and function effectively within the community with extant stories. One story goes as follows: "We view psychology as a kind of continuation of traditional philosophical inquiry, armchair philosophy become scientific" (p. 110). If we squint, and look in just the right direction, we can see a story that looks like that. "Our dream time being, roughly, at about the time of Sir Francis Bacon, the Novum Organum, and the rise of the spirit of science. A rising tide of scientific inquiry begat, on the one side, Hobbes and Locke, patriarch of the house of Skinner, and, on the other Descartes, patriarch of the house of Piaget" (White, 1980, p. 110).

Philosophical inquiry proceeds with an empiricist tradition (Berkeley, Hume, the Mills) and a rationalist tradition (Descartes, Spinoza, Leibniz). "In 1879 there begins, in Wundt's laboratory the scientific and experimental pursuit of psychology, philosophy pursued by other means. The laboratory of psychology grows, at first expressed in introspectionism, then in functionalism and behaviorism, finally emerging at present in information-processing and genetic epistemology" (p. 110). (If we continue the story to the present day, add cognitive neuroscience.) It seems that philosophical ideas about thinking are now being investigated with science and experimental methods, "and we realize the special value of our house, which is progress, scientific movement" (p. 111).

White suggests an alternative perspective from which to view the history of psychology. Psychologists often views the past as epistemological philosophy becoming epistemological psychology. However, White finds that "these epistemological movements are part of a larger picture, a broad effort to reconstruct knowledge in the interest of creating reformed government" (p. 111).

Francis Bacon was an advocate of induction, which we now see as limited. However, his work did not begin and end in ideas, but his project was to reconstruct methods of science, then reconstruct biological and social sciences, and finally, to reconstruct government.

"This program of comprehensive reconstruction caught the imagination of Thomas Hobbes and Rene Descartes." Two centuries later, "something like a fulfillment of Bacon's project of a Great Instauration – philosophical, scientific, and governmental truths all inter-rationalized to offer a social directive – emerges in the middle part of the nineteenth century" (p. 112). From the right, there is Herbert Spencer with the 10 volumes of his *Synthetic Philosophy*, arguing for laissez-faire economics, and called by his critics "Social Darwinism." From the left, there are Marx and Engels, developing the ideology of Communism. Both groups felt that Darwin's theory of evolution provided scientific support for their social-political views.

In relation to the history of psychology, around the beginning of the 20th century, there are visions of "scientific management," measuring people and their capacities, and their institutions, "factories, schools, governmental agencies, homes – bettered by rational analysis and calculated planning" (p. 112).

Human service agencies began to be professionalized, with government programs for the young, the old, the handicapped, the unemployed, and the poor, with a wave in the New Deal of the 1930s, and another wave with the War on Poverty in the 1960s. (One strand I would add to this is that the formation of personality psychology, beginning with Allport's *Personality: A Psychological Interpretation* (1937), can be traced back to Allport's dissertation in 1922 on "An Experimental Study of Traits with Special Reference to Social Diagnosis," which was done both in psychology and in social ethics, drawing partly on the ideas of Richard Clarke Cabot about differential diagnosis in medicine and the use of case histories. It also drew on Allport's exposure to "human science" traditions through the ideas of Stern and "personalism" that Allport learned more about in his postdoctoral year in Germany in 1922–23.)

The growth of psychology, particularly "applied psychology" and some of the "second psychologies" are "tied to, and formed by, contemporary concern to build a rational basis for education, social work, psychiatry, the courts" (p. 112). Applied psychology does not come after basic psychology, but they emerge together. The growth of psychology is part of a broader movement toward "rationalized social practice" (p. 112).

This says it more clearly than I understood when first hearing White's course. If psychology comes not just out of laboratory experimentation, but is also interwoven with the growth of social institutions and efforts to rationalize them, this is a different story than the one about epistemic issues in philosophy being tested in experimental psychology laboratories.

Proposals for a Second Psychology (Cahan and White, 1992)

Hugo Munsterberg (1863–1916) was invited to Harvard by William James in 1892 to run the Harvard Psychology Laboratory. Munsterberg had received his Ph.D. in psychology under Wundt, and then an M.D. He had criticized Wundt's work in a way that pleased James, he was intelligent and hard working, and it seemed he could be a valuable addition to the Harvard Psychology department. What is less known is that Munsterberg also had some exposure to the "human science" tradition in Germany, meeting with Rickert, one of the founders of human science in a discussion group that met at Max Weber's house.

Munsterberg's textbook *Psychology: General and Applied* (1915) argued that there were two branches of psychology, a natural science "causal" psychology, and a human science "purposive" psychology. In Munsterberg's view, the two psychologies "do not exclude each other, they supplement each other, they support each other, they demand each other" (Cahan & White, 1992, p. 224). Munsterberg, however, argued that psychology should be kept separate from history. In his autobiography, Gordon Allport (1967) reports listening to Munsterberg's lectures as an undergraduate and wondering if causal and purposive psychology could be reconciled or fused. For the rest of his career, Allport attempted to mediate relations between natural science and human science visions of psychology, in order to effectively study "individuality."

Cahan and White (1992) traced the story of these human science traditions in psychology from Auguste Comte, John Stuart Mill, and Wilhelm Wundt, to Hugo Munsterberg and Gordon Allport (Cahan & White, 1992). Each called, in different ways, for a "human science psychology" or a "second psychology" to complement natural science laboratory-based experimental psychology. The tensions between these two visions came to life again in the split between experimental psychology and Social Relations at Harvard from 1946 to 1972, and though less visible, are not yet resolved. Shep White's contributions to the social history of developmental psychology provide resources for rethinking the relations between natural science and human science visions of psychology and between cognitive neuroscience and social-cultural-historical psychology, which will be discussed later in this chapter.

Developmental Psychology As a Human Enterprise (2001)

In May 2001, Shep White gave the Heinz Werner lectures at Clark University, which resulted in the book *Developmental Psychology As a Human Enterprise* (2001). The lectures were given in two parts, the first "Child Study: Exploring New Contexts and Possibilities," and the second "Developmental Psychology as a Science of Personal and Societal Design."

The first lecture addresses the question, "What is the value of developmental psychology as a cooperative human enterprise?" He responds to three criticisms of developmental psychology, that it studies the obvious, that it is beset by pluralisms, and that its scientific status is questionable. The second lecture analyzes the programs of collaborative empiricism which emerged in developmental psychology. There was not just the single program of experimental research from Wundt's Leipzig laboratory, but a variety of research programs from the beginning, identified as early as Dewey (1887) or James (1890).

White argues that there were three relatively independent establishments of developmental psychology: G. Stanley Hall's Child Study movement at Clark University until World War I; the child development movement with child development centers and institutes, from roughly the 1920s to 1950; and the rise of theoretically based developmental psychology with Piaget, Werner, Vygotsky, and others beginning in the 1960s.

In the chapter discussed earlier, "The Learning Theory Tradition and Child Psychology" (1970), White indicated his disillusion with the Hull–Spence tradition that he'd learned as a graduate student at Iowa. By the 1960s, that tradition had begun to lose credibility with him and many other psychologists. This is often described as a paradigm shift within experimental psychology from behaviorism to the "Cognitive Revolution." White suggests it was something broader than that. It wasn't just a paradigm shift within experimental psychology, but a shift in conceptions of the relative place of experimentation and other methods within psychology.

Boring's *History of Experimental Psychology* (1929) had celebrated the opening of Wundt's Leipzig laboratory in 1879 as foundational in experimental psychology. This "birthdate" of psychology was reinforced in 1979 when the American Psychological Association celebrated the 100th anniversary of the event. However, it became clear by the 1960s that "clinical psychology, personality psychology, social psychology, and developmental psychology did not grow out of the brass-instruments laboratory at Leipzig" (pp. 4–5). Rather, the nonexperimental traditions had theories and research methods of their own, and needed histories of their own research traditions.

Working as a psychologist consulting on poverty programs for children, White began to "catch glimpses of a very different history of developmental psychology" (p. 5). In chapter 2 of vol. 1 of the three-volume report *Federal Programs for Young Children: Review and Recommendations* (1973), he reviewed a history of government programs for disadvantaged children and their major public purposes. "It was immediately evident to me that the history of public activities for children ran right into the history of developmental psychology, and it was at that point that I began to believe that the history of developmental psychology could only be fully understood by taking into account the "externalist" social and political forces impinging on the field" (p. 6).

"Part of the impetus for the establishment of developmental psychology came because American society formed a new system for the care, protection, and education of children in the later half of the 19th century" (p. 12). Some old roles, such as parent or teacher, were modified, while a number of new social roles were created, such as pediatrician, social worker, kindergarten teacher, or juvenile-court judge. New institutional structures were created for children, along with needs for new ways of conceptualizing children and human development. "While developmental psychology can reasonably be called a science, it cannot be what some have spoken about as a value-free science. Developmental psychology has served as a moral science, offering values and ideals to those concerned with the upbringing and education of American children" (p. 46).

He suggests that contemporary graduate training in developmental psychology should include more than training in how to do well-designed research. In addition, "students need an understanding of the larger purposes and meaning of their field" (p. 46). More work is needed on the social and political history of developmental psychology, and on the "diffusion of people, ideas, and methods back and forth between developmental psychology and the places and spaces of the "real world" (p. 46). (To me, it seems that Shep White's own work in analyzing the social institutional sources and uses of developmental psychology illustrates the power and value of a "second science" tradition in psychology.)

When Shep White entered Harvard in 1946, he found that the psychology department had broken in two, between experimental psychologists and the personality and social psychologists in Social Relations. In 1970, sociology withdrew from Social Relations, and in 1972, the cultural anthropologists returned to anthropology, and the experimental, social, personality, and developmental psychologists were combined in a Department of Psychology and Social Relations. In the spring of 1986, almost 40 years after his arrival as a freshman, as Chair of the Department of Psychology and Social Relations, his duty was to move, at a meeting of the Faculty of Arts and Sciences, that the name be changed back to a single unified "Department of Psychology." "It was a rare experience. How many children of a broken home are ever given the chance to repair the break?" (p. 47).

Cooperative Empiricisms in the Human Sciences: Nomothetic, Historical, and Experiential

The Harvard psychology department is now back in one unified department that is divided into four areas: Cognition, Brain, and Behavior; Developmental Psychology; Experimental Psychopathology and the Clinical Group; and Social Psychology. Experimental interests have evolved over the years from experimental psychophysics, to behaviorism, to cognitive psychology, and now to Cognition, Brain, and Behavior. There are a number of labs studying varying aspects of cognitive neuroscience, and the personality and clinical areas have been replaced by Experimental Psychopathology, with a Clinical Group added to it in recent years.

What, though, has happened with the "human science" traditions, designed to complement laboratory-based psychology? What happened with the social and cultural levels of analysis in the Social Relations Department? What happened with the study of individual lives? Are aspects of these human science traditions included in the four subject areas? Or is there a need to supplement them, and to complement cognitive neuroscience with greater attention to social-political contexts, cultural history, and life histories?

One of the problems with the "second psychologies" is that experimental psychology may be turning out more empirical research papers, while second psychologies are more often writing programmatic papers about "the need to broaden concepts of what science should be and do" (Cahan & White, 1992, p. 229). That may be in part because there is not yet an adequate conceptual framework, and/or an adequate institutional context, in which practitioners of second psychology can effectively pursue their research, publishing, and teaching. This may be one of the conditions which can motivate attention to philosophical issues, or to historical research and reinterpretation.

A phrase that Shep White frequently uses is that of "cooperative empiricisms," as practiced by experimental psychologists or by different generations of developmental psychologists. It may be that just such "cooperative empiricisms" are needed for the human science traditions. Dilthey (1887/1988) conceived his work on the human sciences as part of a larger "critique of historical reason." I would argue that processes involved in historical inquiry such as contextualizing, particularizing, and interpreting are central in case study interpretation, in analyzing cultural history, and in studying the social contexts of developmental psychology.

These historical-interpretive methods may be central to many of the second psychology or human science traditions discussed in Cahan and White (1992). Historical-interpretive methods may be as central to the human sciences as experimental methods are to natural science psychology.

One additional human science method can be conceived as "cooperative experientialism," or the processes through which a group of people make individual and collaborative efforts to better understand their own personal subjective experiences and that of others. This was pursued in the psychoanalytic and humanistic traditions, and efforts to better understand personal experience and meanings have been a significant part of the human sciences more broadly.

To summarize, there are at least three kinds of collaborative empiricisms: (1) nomothetic empiricism, which may be correlational or experimental; (2) historical empiricism, concerned with contextualizing, particularizing, and interpreting; and (3) personal, experiential empiricism, concerned with learning about the subjective experiences of self and others. While natural science visions draw on nomothetic empiricisms, testing general theories with quantitative and experimental methods; human science traditions concentrate more on interpreting particulars, drawing on historical-interpretive and personal-experiential empiricisms.

Lee Cronbach wrote about the "two disciplines of scientific psychology" (1957), experimental and correlational psychology; then, in "Beyond the Two Disciplines of Scientific Psychology" (1975), he referred to person X situation interactions, or the interaction of individual differences with situational-experimental conditions. Toward the end of his career, he talked about the value of historical accounts, and not only randomized experiments, in evaluation research (Cronbach, 1982). To extend Cronbach's language, there are not just "two disciplines of scientific psychology," but at least a "third discipline of scientific psychology," namely historical-interpretive psychology (Runyan, 2003, in press).

In psychology textbooks, there is often a hierarchical or "pecking order" discussion of research methods, starting with case studies used to formulate hypotheses, then correlational methods to explore quantitative relationships, and finally, experimental methods to more rigorously analyze causal relationships. This is true, but it is only part of the story. It is one way of thinking about the relationships between these three methods, organized around a search for general causal relationships. If one's purpose is to better understand an individual case, then relations between the methods change. Correlational and experimental studies become resources that can be employed to form interpretive hypotheses about the individual case, which then need to be rigorously examined with idiographic historical-interpretive methods (Runyan, 1982, 1997).

The relations between "natural science" methods and "historical science" methods are formulated in a useful way in Harvard's Core Curriculum. Historical science methods are concerned with explaining complex sequences of historically contingent events and processes. For example, in evolutionary biology, how to understand the evolution of particular species, or why dinosaurs became extinct 65 million years ago. In historical geology, how to understand the formation and history of the earth, or how to understand continental drift. In the spring of 1986, while auditing Shep White's course on the history of psychology, I was also auditing Stephen Jay Gould's course on "History of the Earth and of Life," with his making a case for "historical science" in both evolutionary biology and historical geology (cf. Gould, 1986, 1989, 2002).

In Harvard's Core Curriculum for undergraduate electives launched in 1978, there was debate about what science courses should be required. Undergraduates were required to take electives in both Science A and Science B. Science A courses "are intended to introduce students to areas of science dealing primarily with deductive and quantitative aspects and to increase the student's understanding of the physical world." For example, Science A-16 is "Modern Physics: Concepts and Development," and Science A-25 is "Chemistry of the 20th Century."

Science B courses are "intended to provide a general understanding of science as a way of looking at man and the world by introducing students to complex natural systems with a substantial historical or evolutionary component." For example, Science B-15 is "Evolutionary Biology" taught by E. O. Wilson, while Science B-16, "History of the Earth and of Life" was taught by Stephen Jay Gould, who had done much to argue for the importance of "historical science" as a way of scientific knowing. Historical science methods may be employed in biological, physical, or social sciences.

In auditing Gould's course and having occasional discussions with him, I was repeatedly struck with the relevance of these issues for the study of lives, and for the "human science" traditions in psychology. Historical science methods in psychology include processes such as contextualizing (relating psychology to external social, cultural, and historical contexts as well as to internal biological structures and processes), particularizing, forming and testing interpretive hypotheses, historicizing, and working toward more adequate narrative and interpretive accounts. Historical science methods may be as central to the "human science" or "second psychology" traditions as quantitative and experimental methods have been for the nomothetic "natural science" traditions in psychology.

Accounts of relations between life, work, and social-cultural contexts are examples of "historical science" inquiry of interest to psychologists trying to understand their discipline. Autobiographical accounts have been written not only by psychoanalysts but also by experimental psychologists. While working on his *History of Experimental Psychology* (1929), Edwin G. Boring set up the book series *A History of Psychology in Autobiography* (Murchison, 1930), inviting eminent psychologists to write intellectual autobiographies. The first volume was published in 1930, while Boring contributed a chapter of his own to vol. 4 in 1952, and a longer one in *Psychologist at Large* (1961). Skinner contributed a chapter to vol. 5 in 1967, and went on to publish a three-volume autobiography. The series has gone through eight volumes, broadening its focus when Gardner Lindzey became co-editor for vol. 5 in 1967, with the most recent, vol. 8, in 1989. Currently, Lindzey and I are organizing vol. 9 in the series.

The course of autobiographical and biographical inquiry sometimes leads to progress in understanding (Runyan, 1997). Consider, for example, the history of Freud interpretation, from Freud's own partially autobiographical writings, through the early critiques by Wittels in 1923, to Ernest Jones's three-volume biography (Jones, 1953, 1955, 1957), to Henri Ellenberger's massively informed *Discovery of the Unconscious* (1970), through Paul Roazen's research on the personal side of *Freud and His Followers* (1975), to critiques by Sulloway (1979) and many others, to Peter Gay's (1988) defense. This dialectic of advocacy and critique may have reached a more satisfactory synthesis in Louis Breger's *Freud: Darkness in the Midst of Vision* (2000). This is an account attempting to reveal both Freud's powerful intellectual insights, and how they're interwoven with dogmatism, error, and dictatorial treatment of his followers. The history of Freud biography illustrates both the potentials and limitations of the historical and interpretive processes utilized in the human sciences.

The success of human science inquiry in advancing our understanding of relations between work and life is also being demonstrated in the course of Darwin biography, from his own autobiography, to the letters edited by his son (1887), to the 12 published and annotated volumes of his correspondence recently completed, through the two volumes of Janet Brown's recent biography (1995, 2002). Another example of success in cumulative, progressively more adequate human science understanding of the relations between life and work is illustrated in the course of scholarship on William James, from his son's editing of William James's letters (1920), to Ralph Barton Perry's two-volume *The Thought and Character of William James* (1935), through Gay Wilson Allen's biography (1961), to *The Jameses: A Family Narrative* (1991) by R. W. B. Lewis, to recent biographies by Linda Simon (1998) and others. This biographical work is supplemented by the Harvard University Press's carefully annotated *The Works of William James* in 19 volumes, and the 11 (out of a projected 12) annotated volumes of the *Correspondence of William James* by the University Press of Virginia. This may be put down as mere "armchair" psychology, but may involve an amount of cumulative intellectual work which compares favorably with that in most quantitative analyses or laboratory experiments.

The objection may arise, "But how does this count as psychology? Isn't it part of humanistic scholarship?" YES! The human science side of psychology overlaps, and legitimately overlaps, with biography and history; just as the natural science side of psychology overlaps, and legitimately overlaps, with biology as in neuroscience, genetics, and evolutionary psychology.

If we start paring away the overlap of psychology with allied disciplines such as biology (on the natural science side), or biography and history (on the human science side), psychology will become a scrawny, emaciated reminder of what it might have been. In order not to become lopsided, psychology needs to be developed not only on its biological natural science side, but also on its historical human science side. The issue is repeatedly advocated by two centuries of those working on the human science or "second psychology" side of psychology (Cahan & White, 1992).

What is needed to move "toward a better story of psychology"? If Shep White is right, philosophical programs, back to Francis Bacon and on through the empiricists and rationalists, as well as scientific programs of "cooperative empiricism" in psychology were often related to programs for social-political reform. From my perspective, these intellectual and social-political programs can also be usefully understood in relation to the personal and life historical processes of the individuals involved. With Francis Bacon, as White argues, his concern with induction and philosophy of science were related to his interests in social-political reform. However, Bacon's intellectual ambitions and social-political aspirations may both need to be understood in relation to his personal history. His father died when Bacon was 18 in 1579, and as the fifth and youngest child of his father's second wife, Bacon died before he received an adequate inheritance, and thus Bacon was forced to try to make his fortune navigating the treacherous waters of court politics, when he would have preferred to spend his time on intellectual projects (Jardine & Stewart, 1998). Only after Bacon was impeached for bribery in 1621, did he have the last five years of his life to work with fewer interruptions on his major intellectual projects. "In later years, Bacon was careful to separate his life into a "before" period of intellectual intrigue, treacherous behavior of friends, and social climbing, and an "after" of austere scientific inquiry in a country retreat" (Jardine & Stewart, 1998, p. 19). Posterity was left with "two clearly incompatible versions of Francis Bacon. All subsequent biography has struggled to resolve them" (p. 19). In understanding the history of psychology, we too are left with questions about how to understand the varied relations between scientific inquiry, social-political interests, and the conduct of individual lives.

White convincingly argues that intellectual projects in philosophy and in psychology are often related to social, political concerns. I would add that both intellectual programs and social-political aspirations can often be illuminated by understanding their place in the life histories of particular individuals in their social, cultural, and historical contexts. Rather than seeing psychology through a solely intellectual lens as the empirical testing of philosophical speculations, perhaps psychology can be seen as part of a triangle of scientific-intellectual, social-political, and personal worlds co-constructing each other over the course of time.

Conclusion

Let's give the last word, or rather, the next to last word, to William James. One of his last published papers is "A Great French Philosopher at Harvard" in the *Nation*, on March 31, 1910. In reporting enthusiastically about the lectures of Emile Boutroux (1845–1921), James summarized some of his own late views about natural science versus human science approaches to psychology. "Carried away by the triumphs of chemistry, physics, and mathematics, these men imagined that the frame of things was eternally and literally mechanical, and that truth was reached by abstracting from it everything connected with personality . . . Boutroux took the diametrically opposite view. It is the element we wholly live in, it is what Plutarch's and Shakespeare's pages give us, it is the superabounding, growing, every-varying, and novelty-discovering. Its real shape is biography and history" (James, 1910/1978, pp. 169, 171).

James said lots of things, which can be used to support many different positions. The position I'll use him for here is to suggest the limitations of a natural science only view of the psychological world, and the need also for the varying, growing, and novelty-discovering disciplines of biography and history. These topics have been pursued for many years within the "human sciences" and various "second psychologies" (Cahan & White, 1992).

At Harvard, a concern for the study of lives and for psychology in relation to social and cultural contexts was one factor leading to a split between experimental psychology and a newly formed Social Relations Department in 1946, which was the situation faced by Shep White as an undergraduate from 1946 to 1951. As a graduate student at the University of Iowa, he was drawn to the experimental learning theory of Kenneth Spence and began work as an experimental child psychologist. By the time of his 1970 handbook chapter on "The learning theory tradition and child psychology," he had become disillusioned with that vision of scientific psychology and more interested in cognitive psychology. By the late 1960s he had become involved in consulting on social programs and policies for children (White et al., 1973). This work on social policy led him to see that the history of developmental psychology could be understood only in relation to "externalist" social, political, and organizational processes. Thus began a process of reconceptualizing the history of psychology, as well as reconceptualizing developmental psychology itself and its place in a world of designed institutions. One recent statement of this alternative vision is that developmental psychology "came into existence when people began to live in society composed of myriad designed institutions, when people needed to think about human motives and abilities and needs in order to create the institutions, and when individuals living in these new and slowly changing societies confronted historically new responsibilities for designing their own and their children's development" (White, 2003, p. 204).

When, as Chair of the Department of Psychology and Social Relations, White moved in 1986 that the name of the department be shortened to "Department of Psychology," this may have been associated with more harmonious relations between different groups of psychologists, now organized into the four areas of Cognition, Brain and Behavior; Developmental Psychology; Experimental Psychopathology and the Clinical Group; and Social Psychology.

What, though, has happened with the "second psychology," or "human science" traditions, and with the interdisciplinary perspectives of Social Relations? Cognitive neuroscience seems to have become increasingly influential as an integrative tradition, directing attention to underlying neurological structures and processes related to topics in each of the four areas of the department. What about social and cultural contexts of psychology? The relations of psychology with sociology and anthropology? Or the study of individual lives? Are parts of the earlier Social Relations projects worth retaining or developing?

With increasing attention given to biological levels of analysis, what do we do about the relations of psychology to social, cultural, life historical, and historical levels of analysis? Sheldon White's work linking developmental psychology to social policy and institutions and his research in the social history of developmental psychology are original and illuminating examples of interdisciplinary psychosocial inquiry. They provide much for us to build on in developing adequately pluralistic conceptions of scientific psychology, and in developing better stories of psychology, both retrospectively and prospectively.

References

Allen, G. W. (1967). *William James*. New York: Viking.
Allport, G. W. (1937). *Personality: A Psychological Interpretation*. New York: Holt.
Allport, G. W. (1967). Gordon W. Allport. In E. G. Boring & G. Lindzey (Eds). *A History of Psychology in Autobiography*, Vol. 5. New York: Appleton-Century-Crofts.
Bacon, F. (1620). *The Great Instauration*. Garden City, N.Y.: Doubleday, 1937.
Bacon, F. (1627). *New Atlantis; and, The Great Instauration*. J. Weinberger (Ed.). Arlington Heights, IN.: Davidson.
Boring, E. G. (1929/1950). *A History of Experimental Psychology*. New York: Century.
Boring, E. G. (1961). *Psychologist at Large*. New York: Basic Books.
Breger, L. (2000). *Freud: Darkness in the Midst of Vision*. New York: Wiley.
Brown, J. (1995). *Charles Darwin: Voyaging*. New York: Knopf.
Brown, J. (2002). *Charles Darwin: The Power of Place*. New York: Knopf.
Cahan, E. D., & White, S. H. (1992). Proposals for a second psychology. *American Psychologist 47*, 224–235.
Cronbach, L. J. (1957). The two disciplines of scientific psychology. *American Psychologist 12*, 671–684.
Cronbach, L. J. (1975). Beyond the two disciplines of scientific psychology. *American Psychologist 30*, 116–127.
Cronbach, L. J. (1982). *Designing Evaluations of Educational and Social Programs*. San Francisco: Jossey-Bass.
Darwin, F. (Ed.). (1887). *The Life and Letters of Charles Darwin*, 3 vols. London: Murray.
Dewey, J. (1887/1967). Psychology. In Jo Ann Boydston (Ed.), *John Dewey: Vol. 2. The Early Works, 1882–1898*. Carbondale and Edwardsville, IL: Southern Illinois Press.
Dilthey, W. (1887/1988). *Introduction to the Human Sciences*. Princeton, NJ: Princeton University Press.

Ellenberger, H. (1970). *The Discovery of the Unconscious*. New York: Basic Books.

Gay, P. (1988). *Freud: A Life for our Time*. New York: Norton.

Gould, S. J. (1986). Evolution and the triumph of homology, or why history matters. *American Scientist*, Jan–Feb.: 60–69.

Gould S. J. (1989). *Wonderful Life: The Burgess Shale and the Nature of History*. New York: Norton.

Gould S. J. (2002). *The Structure of Evolutionary Theory*. Cambridge, MA: Harvard University Press.

Hebb, D. (1960). The American revolution. *American Psychologist 15*, 735–745.

Hilgard, E. (1987). *Psychology in America: A Historical Survey*. San Diego: Harcourt Brace Jovanovich.

James, H. (Ed.). (1920). *The Letters of William James*. Boston: Atlantic Monthly Press.

James, W. (1890). *Principles of Psychology*, vols. 1 and 2. New York: Holt.

James, W. (1910/1978). A great French philosopher at Harvard. *The Works of William James*, Cambridge, MA: Harvard University Press.

James, W. (1920). *The Letters of William James* (edited by his son Henry James). Boston: Atlantic Monthly Press.

Jardine, L., & Stewart, A. (1998). *Hostage to Fortune: The Troubled Life of Francis Bacon*. London: Phoenix Giant.

Jones, E. (1953, 1955, 1957). *The Life and Work of Sigmund Freud*, 3 vols. New York: Basic.

Lewis, R. W. B. (1991). *The Jameses: A Family Narrative*. New York: Farrar, Straus, and Geroux.

Munsterberg, H. (1915). *Psychology: General and Applied*. New York: Appleton.

Murchison, C. (Ed.). (1930). *A History of Psychology in Autobiography, Vol. 1*. Worcester, MA.: Clark University Press.

Murphy, G., & Kovach, J. K. (1972). *Historical Introduction to Modern Psychology*, 3rd ed. New York: Harcourt Brace Jovanovich.

Mussen, P. H. (Ed.), (1970). *Carmichael's Manual of Child Psychology*, 3rd ed. New York: Wiley.

Perry, R. B. (1935). *The Thought and Character of William James*. Boston: Little, Brown.

Roazen, P. (1975). *Freud and His Followers*. New York: Knopf.

Runyan, W. M. (1982). *Life Histories and Psychobiography: Explorations in Theory and Method*. New York: Oxford University Press.

Runyan, W. M. (Ed.) (1988). *Psychology and Historical Interpretation*. New York: Oxford University Press.

Runyan, W. M. (1997). Studying lives: Psychobiography and the conceptual structure of personality psychology. In R. Hogan et al. (Eds.), *Handbook of Personality* (pp. 41–69). New York: Academic.

Runyan, W. M. (2003). From the study of lives and psychohistory to historicizing psychology: A conceptual journey. In J. Winer & J. W. Anderson (Eds.), *Annual of Psychoanalysis*, Vol. XXXI, *Psychoanalysis and History* (pp. 119–132). Hillsdale, NJ: The Analytic Press.

Runyan, W. M. (in press). Evolving conceptions of psychobiography and the study of lives: Encounters with psychoanalysis, personality psychology, and historical science. In W. T. Schultz (Ed.), *Handbook of Psychobiography*. New York: Oxford University Press.

Simon, L. (1998). *Genuine Reality: A Life of William James*. New York: Harcourt Brace.

Smith, L. D. (1986). *Behaviorism and Logical Positivism: A Revised Account of the Alliance*. Stanford: Stanford University Press.

Sulloway, F. J. (1979). *Freud, Biologist of the Mind: Beyond the Psychoanalytic Legend*. New York: Basic.

Watson, J. B. (1913). Psychology as a behaviorist views it. *Psychological Review, 20*, 158–177.

White, S. H. (1970). The learning theory tradition and child psychology. In P. Mussen (Ed.), *Carmichael's Manual of Child Psychology* (3rd ed.). New York: Wiley.

White, S. H. et al. (1973). *Federal Programs for Young Children: Review and Recommendations*, Vols. 1–3. Washington, DC: U.S. Government Printing Office.

White S. H. (1980). Psychology in all sorts of places. In R. Kasschau & F. S. Kessel (Eds.), *Psychology and Society: In Search of Symbiosis* (pp. 105–131). New York: Holt, Rinehart, & Winston.

White, S. H. (1992). G. Stanley Hall: From philosophy to developmental psychology. *Developmental Psychology 28*, 25–34.

White, S. H. (2001). *Developmental Psychology as a Human Enterprise*. 2001 Heinz Werner Lecture Series. Worcester, MA: Clark University Press.

White, S. H. (2003). Developmental psychology in a world of designed institutions. In W. Koops and & M. Zuckerman (Eds.), *Beyond the Century of the Child: Cultural History and Developmental Psychology* (pp. 204–223). Philadelphia: University of Pennsylvania Press.

White, S. H., & Phillips, D.A. (2001) Designing Head Start: Roles played by developmental psychologists. In D. L. Featherman & M. Vinovskis (Eds.), *Social Science and Policy Making: A Search for Relevance in the Twentieth Century* (pp. 83–118). Ann Arbor, MI: University of Michigan Press.

PART TWO

Designing Child and Family Policies

4   The Effects of Welfare Reform and Poverty Policies on Children and Families

Aletha C. Huston

Over the past 50 years, U.S. policies for low-income families with children have evolved and changed dramatically. Although poverty rates among families with children were higher in the 1950s than they have been since, policymakers gave relatively little attention to problems associated with child poverty until the War on Poverty began in the 1960s. Developmental psychologists participated in the war on poverty largely by creating, testing, and evaluating intervention programs for children, including Head Start, Follow Through, and many others. Economic interventions, subsumed in the label "welfare policy," that included cash assistance, medical care, and employment services for low-income families were, however, primarily the province of labor economists. Scholars and policy researchers designed, administered, and evaluated various policies, using sophisticated methods and theoretical models, from the 1960s onward, but there was little communication between economists and developmental psychologists.

In the late 1980s and the 1990s, these two research communities began to converge. Specialists in child development joined interdisciplinary teams to study the impacts of welfare and employment policies on children and families. Psychologists and sociologists spawned a series of empirical investigations, based in sophisticated theory, of the effects of poverty, family income, and income loss on the development of children and adolescents (e.g., Conger & Elder, 1994; Elder & Caspi, 1987; McLoyd, 1990, 1997, 1998). The result is a body of research, drawing on different methods and theoretical traditions, that not only informs policy, but also makes a contribution to developmental science.

In this paper, I describe recent work designed to understand the impacts of welfare and employment policies on children and families in relation to the theory and findings from naturalistic investigations. I begin with a little background on poverty, employment, and welfare trends and policies in the United

States, summarizing briefly the findings from correlational and longitudinal investigations of income effects on children. I then turn to experimental studies of policies designed to affect family income, employment, and welfare receipt. Finally, I offer some observations about the potential contributions of both naturalistic and experimental policy research to the theory and practice of developmental science, stressing both the advantages and pitfalls.

Historical Patterns of Poverty, Employment, Family Structure, and Welfare Changes in the Lives of U.S. Children

Poverty in families with children has been a persistent problem in the United States throughout our history. At the end of the 20th century, slightly fewer than one-sixth of children in the United States lived in a family with an income below the poverty threshold. The poverty rate for children declined to 15% in 1970, rose steadily until the early 1990s when it reached 22%, then declined to 16.3% in 2001 (see Haskins, chapter 6 in this volume). These rates are considerably higher than those in most other industrialized nations, largely because most other nations provide larger supplements for the incomes of poor families and also provide such services as health care and child care at considerably less cost than most U.S. parents face (Bergmann, 1996; Kamerman, 1996).

Single-mother and ethnic minority families have lower incomes and higher rates of poverty than do married-couple and white families. The median income for single-mother families is about one-third of the median for married couples and less than half the median for all families (U.S. Department of Health and Human Services, 2001). The number and percent of children living in single-parent families increased over the years from 1970 to 1999, so more children were affected by the high risk of poverty and low income associated with single-mother families. At the same time, income inequality increased, with families on the lower end of the income distribution experiencing a decline in real income while those at the higher end experienced considerable increases (U.S. Department of Health and Human Services, 2001).

Employment is the major source of income for most families, but employment alone does not raise all families out of poverty. Between 1985 and 1999, for example, there was a steady increase in parental employment in both single-mother and married-couple families. The percent of single-mother families in which the parent was employed went from 61% in 1985 to 79% in 2000; the percentage of children living in married-couple families in which both parents were employed increased from 57% in 1985 to 64% in 2000 (U.S. Department of Health and Human Services, 2001). Nonetheless, poverty rates among children continued to increase until 1993, declining after that. This decline began before the jump in the percentage of single mothers who were employed, which occurred after 1996, and coincided with large increases in earnings supplements through the Earned Income Tax Credit between 1993 and 1995, suggesting that a change in earnings alone was not enough to raise many families out of poverty, but earnings with public supplements did have that effect.

Developmental Study of Family Income Effects

These demographic patterns have led to a large body of research in developmental psychology investigating the relations of family income, parental employment, and income loss to children's development. The major purpose of this work was to understand the processes by which poverty and family income influence developmental patterns. McLoyd (1998) proposed a theoretical model in which the effects of economic poverty on children's psychological well-being are mediated by parental psychological distress, which in turn affects parenting practices. Both cross-sectional and longitudinal data support this model (see Huston, McLoyd, & Garcia-Coll, 1994; McLoyd, 1998; Mistry, Vandewater, Huston, & McLoyd, 2002). Conger and Elder (1994) have also demonstrated support for a model in which income loss affects children's adjustment through its effects on parental psychological distress and parenting practices. This work is guided by solid theory and a wealth of nonexperimental data, and all of it includes numerous controls for factors other than income that are associated with poverty (e.g., low education, minority ethnic group status).

Although no one denies the strong associations of poverty with a range of negative developmental outcomes, some economists have challenged the conclusion that income is the critical factor accounting for these effects. For example, Mayer (1997) conducted analyses of two large-scale longitudinal studies, using different methods to control for factors other than family income that might account for associations of family income with children's short-term and long-term achievement. She argues that conventional regression methods controlling for such correlates of poverty as race, low education, single-mother family structure, and physical disabilities are not satisfactory because one cannot covary all possible selection factors. It is always possible that people with different levels of income differ on unobserved characteristics that affect their children's development. For example, parents with higher incomes may have different levels of motivation, competence, or values than those with lower incomes. Mayer (1997) uses a variety of analytic strategies to account for such unobserved variables, and concludes that income per se has a relatively small effect on outcomes for children once you account for the effects of the many family, school, and neighborhood factors associated with poverty.[1]

These issues of selection, unobserved variables, and disaggregating the contribution of factors that are correlated in the real world are inherent in any nonexperimental research. In an ideal world, such studies would be complemented by experimental manipulations of income without changing other factors associated with poverty. No such "pure" experiments exist, but random-assignment experiments testing income and employment policies offer a different way of assessing the causal effects of family income and changes in income on children's development.

Income, Welfare, and Employment Policy Research

Income

Among the proposals generated during the War on Poverty of the 1960s was a federally guaranteed minimum income for families with children. The federal government funded a series of Income Maintenance experiments (sometimes called Negative Income Tax experiments) using random-assignment designs with large numbers of participants to test the impact of different levels of minimum incomes, with different tax rates as people's earnings increased. There were flaws in design and problems of differential attrition, but nonetheless, these experiments provide a way of evaluating the impact of supplementing family income without changing other family characteristics associated with poverty. The studies were designed primarily to assess economic impacts – work effort and family income. Although the programs did increase family income in some places, they also reduced work hours among some groups. As a result, policy analysts and policymakers concluded that a guaranteed income led people to reduce their work effort and would not be a wise policy to adopt in law (Ashenfelter, 1978; U.S. Department of Health, Education, and Welfare, 1983).

Developmental psychologists might draw different conclusions from these findings. Income guarantees raising families out of poverty and reductions of parental work hours could have benefits for children and for family life. In

---

[1] Some people might argue that "poverty" should not be disaggregated into single variables, but should instead be viewed as an accumulation of multiple sources of disadvantage. The economists' question, however, is how much change might be brought about by raising family income without intervening in other features of family's and children's lives. Hence, it makes sense to isolate income from other components of poverty.

two-parent families studied in the Income Maintenance experiments, for example, mothers reduced hours of employment much more than fathers did (Kershaw & Fair, 1976; Robins & West, 1980). Given that these families often had several children, it is possible that more maternal time at home provided some benefits for their families. In a very deprived rural sample, children's employment time was also reduced; again, this change may have been beneficial if it allowed young people to stay in school. Unfortunately, because the studies were not designed to assess effects on families and children, minimal data were collected on children's health, education, and behavior. There was some evidence of positive effects on educational progress for elementary school-age children, but not for adolescents. Nonetheless, children in experimental families were less likely than controls to drop out of high school (Mallar & Maynard, 1981; Salkind & Haskins, 1982). In a very deprived African American rural sample, family nutrition improved (Salkind & Haskins, 1982).

Earned Income Tax Credit

The major objection to a guaranteed minimum income was the possibility that it would reduce motivation to work. The Earned Income Tax Credit (EITC), a policy that provides an income supplement contingent on work through the income tax system, was adopted in 1975. The rationale had little to do with poverty or with the welfare of children. Instead, the new policy resulted from the fact that payroll taxes had increased considerably, putting an unfair burden on low-wage workers. In the 1990s, the EITC was expanded as it became a major policy instrument to "make work pay" and to ensure economic benefits for working poor families with children. The maximum benefit for a family with two children and a taxable income of about $12,000 increased from $1,511 in 1993 to $3,888 in 2000. Healthcare assistance, child care assistance for low-income families, and federal funding for after-school programs also expanded considerably during this period. For example, the total amount of federal funds for child care assistance to low-income families nearly doubled from 1991 to 2000 (Fuller, Kagan, Caspary, & Gauthier, 2002). These changes contributed to declines in poverty and increases in resources for working poor parents. It is difficult, however, to evaluate the effects of these changes on children because they were not tested experimentally, and naturally occurring variations cannot be evaluated because all workers are entitled to the EITC.

Employment and Welfare Experiments

Random–assignment experiments *have* been used to test a range of policies that are usually grouped under the rubric of welfare reform. The principal cash welfare program for poor families from 1935 to 1996 was Aid to Families with Dependent Children (AFDC); in 1996, it became Temporary Assistance to Needy Families (TANF). The vast majority of recipients are single mothers and their children. Beginning in the early 1980s and culminating in a major change in the law in 1996, the emphasis of the AFDC program shifted from providing support for stay-at-home parents to encouraging employment. After 1996, states could require welfare recipients to participate in employment-related activities, and assistance was time-limited. The number of families receiving cash assistance declined dramatically after 1996 as a result of the new policies (Greenberg et al., 2002).

These changes were preceded by a remarkable amount of high-quality research testing the effects of different policies designed to reduce welfare and increase employment among potential welfare recipients. Many of these investigations were initiated by states that requested and received waivers from the U.S. Department of Health and Human Services to test a variety of programs and policies intended to increase parents' employability and ability to be self-sufficient. The waivers were given on the condition that states do high quality evaluations of these policy variations, usually with random-assignment experiments. Not surprisingly, the major outcomes of interest were adult labor force participation, earnings, and welfare receipt (Gueron & Pauly, 1991; Friedlander & Burtless, 1995).

Although the initial studies, designed primarily by economists, included little attention to the consequences for children and family life, developmental psychologists soon began to play a role in this wave of research. Such policies as AFDC and TANF are, after all, designed to improve the welfare of children. Adults' eligibility for most benefits is contingent on their status as parents of minor children. Moreover, there was now a body of research that provided a theoretical and conceptual basis for understanding how parents' employment, income, and resources affect family patterns and children's development (e.g., McLoyd, Jayaratne, Ceballo, & Borquez, 1994; Zaslow, Moore, Morrison, & Coiro, 1995). In the late 1980s, the U.S. Health and Human Services Department launched the National Evaluation of Welfare to Work Study (NEWWS), including two embedded studies of children and family life, designed in part by developmental psychologists (Hamilton, Freedman, Gennetian, Michalopoulos, Walter et al., 2001; McGroder, Zaslow, Moore, & LeMenestrel, 2000). Several other demonstration experiments during the 1990s incorporated measures of children's development, parenting, and home environments (see Zaslow, Moore, Brooks, Morris, Tout et al., 2002). One of these was the New Hope demonstration project, in which I have been intensively involved.

New Hope

The New Hope project was a three-year random-assignment experiment initiated by a consortium of community groups in Milwaukee, Wisconsin. It was designed to test the effectiveness of a multifaceted employment-based anti-poverty program for families who are economically poor (see Bos, Huston, Granger, Duncan, Brock et al., 1999; Huston, Duncan, Granger, Bos, McLoyd et al., 2001). Unlike many welfare reform programs, its goal was to reduce family poverty as well as to induce employment. Hence, New Hope rested on different assumptions than those guiding welfare reform. Many other interventions and policies tested in other studies were designed primarily to reduce welfare use and increase employment without regard to changes in overall economic well-being.

The New Hope study used a random-assignment research design, assigning applicants to program or control groups by lottery. Adults in the program group were eligible for a package of benefits including job-search assistance and services of project representatives who provided information and advice about jobs, child care, and community resources. *When they worked 30 or more hours per week*, participants could receive wage supplements that were designed to raise total family income above the poverty threshold, subsidies for health insurance, and child care subsidies that exceeded those available through the welfare system. If they could not find a job that provided full-time work, they were eligible for community service jobs paying minimum wage; hours in those jobs qualified them for New Hope benefits. Although New Hope was not designed to demonstrate the effects of a time-limited program, individuals' eligibility for benefits lasted for three years because the program had limited funds.

Evaluations were conducted two and five years after random assignment. They included individual interviews with parents and children and mailed questionnaires to teachers of school-age children. The purpose was not only to test program impacts on children, but also to illuminate some of the pathways by which such impacts might occur. The conceptual model guiding the study appears in Figure 4.1. It draws heavily from models proposed by McLoyd (1990) from nonexperimental work and by Zaslow et al. (1995) to predict the effects of welfare policies on children. We expected that New Hope would have direct impacts on parental work hours, family income, and children's participation in paid child care as well as indirect effects on parents' psychological well-being, parenting practices, and the family environment. Hence, we measured parents' psychological well-being, parenting practices, child care and children's out-of-school activities as well as children's

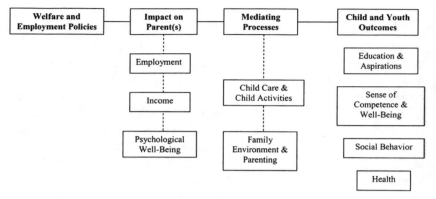

Figure 4.1. Conceptual model.

school performance and social behavior. An intensive ethnographic study, conducted with 46 families over the last three years of the study, provided valuable insights into the complexities underlying the overall patterns measured with quantitative methods (Weisner, Bernheimer, Espinosa, Gibson, Howard, Magnuson et al., 1999).

At both the two-year and five-year follow-ups, the New Hope program had significant and sizeable positive impacts on children's educational progress and aspirations and on their social behavior in school as reported by teachers. In most instances, children in New Hope families performed better than did children in control families. These impacts were much larger and more consistent for boys than for girls. Program group children scored substantially higher than control children on academic achievement measured by teacher reports, individual achievement tests, and parent reports. Program boys scored higher than controls on teacher-rated classroom conduct. Program group boys had higher educational expectations and occupational aspirations than did control group boys. These effects were still evident at the five-year follow-up, which was two years after parents' eligibility for benefits ended. The patterns are shown in Figure 4.2.

Program group boys had higher levels of positive social behavior and substantially lower levels of such problem behaviors as externalizing, internalizing, hyperactivity, and disciplinary problems, according to their teachers (see Figure 4.3). For girls, however, the effects on social behavior as reported by teachers were primarily negative. Contrary to prediction, teachers rated program girls lower on positive social behavior and higher than control girls on behavior problems, particularly at the five-year follow-up (Figure 4.3). Many of these effects were sufficiently large to have social as well as statistical

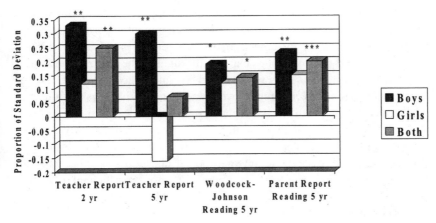

Figure 4.2. Impact of New Hope program on achievement.

significance, ranging from one-fifth to one-half of a standard deviation (see Bos et al., 1999; Huston et al., 2001, 2003; Mistry, Crosby, Huston, Casey, & Ripke, 2001 for details).

Demonstrating program effects is important, but, for purposes of advancing the science, it is important to understand why and how impacts occurred. To do this, we examined the child's social milieu. With the experimental design, we have used two approaches to drawing inferences about what mediates the

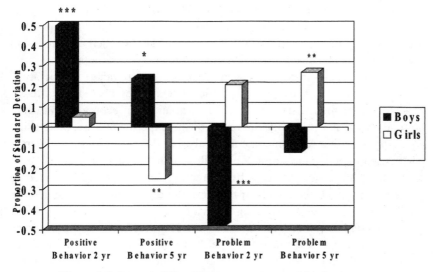

Figure 4.3. Impact of New Hope program on social behavior.

effect. First, we ask whether New Hope had an impact on the mediator (e.g., parenting). We can use the strong random-assignment experimental design to answer this question; differences between parenting practices of parents in the program and control groups can be attributed to the program and not to other factors. Second, we ask whether and how these mediators (e.g., parenting strategies) relate to children's development and well-being. This question must be addressed with nonexperimental analyses because the experiment did not directly manipulate parenting. Therefore, we examine within-group variations in parenting as predictors of variations in their children's development. Hence, we move from an experimental question – whether exposure to a particular policy affected a mediator – to a nonexperimental question – whether variations in the mediator, regardless of their origins, are related to variations in outcomes for children.

Two pathways were proposed in our original model. One of these was parents' psychological well-being and positive parenting. There were some small treatment effects on parents' well-being. New Hope parents reported less stress and more optimism about achieving their goals than did control parents, but there were no differences in depressive symptoms, self esteem, or perceptions of mastery (Bos et al., 1999). There were a few positive impacts on parental warmth and parent–child relations, but most of these were quite small and occurred only for subsamples (Huston et al., 2001). Hence, the policy tested in New Hope had small and inconsistent positive effects on our measures of parent–child interactions.

The nonexperimental analyses supported McLoyd's earlier work, suggesting that in families with less economic hardship, parents had better psychological well-being, were more warm and responsive to their children, and used more effective discipline. Their children displayed more positive social behavior in school – that is, they were more sensitive to others, cooperative, compliant to adults, and able to be independent. They also showed fewer behavior problems (Mistry et al., 2002). Variations in economic hardship, however, were not primarily the result of the experimental treatment; that is, the program increased income modestly, but did little to reduce parents' perceptions of economic stress. We concluded, therefore, that, although economic hardship is indeed related to parenting, and parenting is related to children's behavior, the effects of the New Hope program on children were not due to its impacts on parenting behavior.

The second possible pathway for New Hope effects on children was through children's experiences outside the family. For preschool and early school-age children, child care was examined, and for older children, out-of-school time and activities was potentially important. New Hope had strong effects on both child care and participation in structured activities at both the two-year and five-year follow-ups. Children in New Hope families were more apt to be in center-based as opposed to home-based child care in the preschool and early school years, and they were more likely to participate in before- and after-school care. Older children and adolescents spent more time in such structured out-of-school activities as lessons, religious classes, recreation centers, and clubs (Huston et al., 2001, 2003).

Although we lack information about the quality of the child care, there is now evidence that children who attend center-based child care have better cognitive and language skills and better school readiness than do children attending home-based care (NICHD Early Child Care Research Network, 2000, 2002). Other data indicate that the average quality of home-based care for low-income children is especially low (Coley, Chase-Lansdale, & Li Grining, 2001), so it is reasonable to infer that program impacts on the type of child care children experienced may have been partially responsible for their improved school performance. Similarly, there is extensive nonexperimental evidence that children who participate in structured out-of-school activities have better school performance and fewer behavior problems than do other children, particularly when they live in low-income families and neighborhoods (Mahoney, Larson, & Eccles, 2004; Pettit, Bates, Dodge, & Meece, 1999).

The New Hope results were widely disseminated in policy circles, and many accepted the conclusion that a program providing "generous" work supports can have positive consequences for children's development. But New Hope was one study with limitations. The sample members were volunteers who were perhaps less disadvantaged on average than were many parents in the welfare system. It took place in one geographic location in a midwestern state with a strong tradition of public supports for families. It was not clear why the results were more positive for boys than for girls. Moreover, it was impossible to determine which of the policy components were most important in producing the results.

The Next Generation

By the end of the 1990s, several random-assignment experiments testing employment, welfare, and income policies had generated information about impacts on children. The Next Generation project, led by Manpower Demonstration Research Corporation (MDRC) with collaborators in several universities, was established to do secondary analyses synthesizing the findings from these studies (Morris, Huston, Duncan, Crosby, & Bos, 2001; Morris & Duncan, 2002; Gennetian, Duncan, Knox, Vargas, Clark-Kauffman, & London, 2002). Child Trends did parallel and collaborative syntheses (Zaslow et al., 2002).

In one report, the effects of 11 programs on school achievement, social behavior, and health of elementary-school-aged children were examined. Four of these programs, one of which was New Hope, supplemented the earnings of working parents with public funds. As a result, family income increased as did parental employment (Bloom & Michalopoulos, 2001). All four programs led to higher school achievement, especially for children of long-term welfare recipients – a group of children who are particularly at risk. The improvements in achievement corresponded to an increase of five percentage points in a test score at the 25th percentile, raising it to the 30th percentile. Some of the programs also reduced problem behaviors such as hitting and bullying other children. For instance, one program reduced the proportion of children with high levels of problem behavior by almost eight percentage points. Finally, one program improved children's health (Morris et al., 2001).

The other seven programs mandated that parents participate in education or employment activities, but did not offer earnings supplements. These programs produced increased employment, but family income did not improve (Bloom & Michalopoulos, 2001). Parents simply exchanged welfare for work. These programs had few effects on children, and the effects found were as likely to be positive as negative. There was no evidence of serious harm to children, but there was also no evidence that increases in employment alone would, as some had hoped, promote children's well-being by enhancing parents' self-esteem, making family life more structured, and giving children more positive role models.

These studies provide consistent evidence that programs that supplement single parents' earnings from employment succeed in two ways – increasing employment and income for adults and improving children's well-being. Those that increase only employment do not improve income and have little consistent impact on children's well-being (Morris et al., 2001).

These conclusions apply to children in middle childhood, some of whom were as young as 3 years old when their mothers entered a program. There is little information about the consequences for infants and toddlers, but, at the other end of the age continuum, the impacts of some of these programs for adolescents were slightly negative. Across programs with or without earnings supplements, adolescents in program group families had slightly lower school achievement, were more likely to drop out of school, or were more likely to engage in minor deviant behavior (e.g., smoking and drinking) than were those in control group families (Gennetian, Duncan et al., 2002; Zaslow et al., 2002).

The second stage in the Next Generation analyses was to investigate the processes by which different types of policies affect children's development. Once again, we investigated two pathways: parenting and child care. There was little or no evidence of program impacts on survey measures of parenting in the Next Generation studies, but there were clear effects on use of child care. Therefore, we have done an extensive series of analyses to understand in more depth the ways in which policies affect decisions about child care.

Child care information was available in nine random-assignment evaluations testing 21 different welfare and employment programs with about 20,000 adult sample members. These programs generally increased parents' employment and use of paid child care – both formal and home-based – but not their use of Head Start (Chang, Huston, Crosby, & Gennetian, 2002). This finding suggested a possible conflict between parents' working hours and needs for child care on the one hand, and the structure and availability of Head Start on the other.

There were differences in the types of child care assistance offered across programs. In all locations, both control and program-group recipients of cash assistance were entitled to child care subsidies from a combination of state and federal sources while they received welfare and for a period after leaving welfare; limited amounts of assistance were also available for low-income parents outside the welfare system. These subsidy systems did not (and still do not), however, address many barriers to access, affordability, and reliability of child care that low-income parents face. For example, subsidies often do not cover the whole cost of care, and parents must pay the difference. Low reimbursement rates and payment delays make some providers reluctant to accept children whose care is subsidized. Parents sometimes have to pay providers out of pocket and then wait one to two months for reimbursement. Subsidies reach only a fraction of eligible children, and there are numerous bureaucratic hurdles to qualifying for child care assistance and for retaining eligibility (Adams, Snyder, & Sandfort, 2002).

Seven of the programs (including New Hope) offered "enhanced child-care assistance," which addressed at least some of these barriers. They offered some combination of the following: programmatic promotion of formal care, direct reimbursement of child-care providers, child care at the program site, child-care resource and referral agents in the welfare office, seamless transitions between welfare and other child-care funding streams when people left assistance, and subsidies to cover the market cost of formal care arrangements, which tend to cost more than home-based arrangements. In the other 14 programs, no additional child-care services beyond those available to control families were offered, so both program and control families had the same child-care assistance package.

Enhanced child-care assistance made a difference. Relative to programs that did not provide expanded child-care assistance, those that did so increased child-care subsidy use, lowered parents' out-of-pocket costs, and reduced the proportion of parents who reported having child-care problems that interfered with their employment (Gennetian, Crosby, Huston, & Lowe, 2002). Programs that implemented expanded child-care policies increased use of formal center-based care, confirming our finding from New Hope (Crosby, Gennetian, & Huston, 2001).

In summary, our efforts to understand the processes by which policies affect children's outcomes have come part-way. We now know that policies providing earnings supplements that increase overall family income lead to improved child achievement, but we do not know all of the paths by which those effects occur. We have evidence that improving child-care assistance leads parents to choose center-based formal child care more often than they do without that assistance. Enhanced child-care assistance increases parents' access to subsidies and reduces their costs, leaving them with more disposable income to use for other family needs, so it offers an important resource. Analyses are currently underway to determine whether formal center-based care experiences contributed to children's improved school performance.

Contributions to Developmental Science

Developmental psychologists often ask whether policy research has an effect on adoption of public policies, but less often ask what it contributes to the science of development. Lerner (1998) argues persuasively that policy research offers one way to study basic developmental processes. Policy conditions are ecological influences to be studied just as we investigate and theorize about the impacts of neighborhoods, families, and schools. The potential contribution of policy research to science depends, however, on whether it is guided by strong theory and whether it provides some insights into the processes by which distal economic and social conditions influence the development of children. Welfare and employment policies are not designed to affect children's behavior directly, but to influence their parents' employment and income, so developmental research needs a conceptual model spelling out the indirect paths of influence. The model that emerges in most of this research is similar in many respects to the one shown earlier in the chapter. Parents' economic behavior affects family resources, parent psychological well-being, parenting practices, and children's experiences in child care or out-of-school activities, which in turn affect children's cognitive and social development. Having such a model leads investigators to measure the relevant constructs so that the proposed links can be tested empirically.

When studies are well designed with tests of possible mediators, unexpected findings can be explored with process analyses. For example, negative effects of income and employment programs on adolescents were not predicted. The investigators tested several hypotheses about why these results occurred, including lack of adult supervision and exposure to older coworkers in the adolescents' own jobs. The strongest support occurred for the hypothesis that adolescent children were assuming responsibility for younger siblings when their mothers worked, and, in some cases, that responsibility interfered with their academic work and social opportunities. Among adolescents with younger siblings those in program group families not only performed less well in school, but were more likely than those in control families to drop out or be excluded from school. Adolescents without younger siblings were not affected negatively by their parents' participation in the programs (Gennetian, Duncan et al., 2002).

One of the major advantages of policy experiments is the opportunity to test income and employment effects with experimental designs, using large numbers of cases. Random–assignment studies have strengths and weaknesses that are, in many respects, complementary to the strengths and weaknesses of nonexperimental methods for investigating the effects of parent employment and family income. Most obviously, the experimental method allows firm conclusions about causal direction – something about the program caused the outcomes. Unobserved differences among individuals are unlikely to cause a difference between randomly assigned groups, at least when the number of cases is large.

On the other hand, policy experiments are generally designed to test a package of policies, but not to unravel the components of the policy that are most effective or to understand the processes by which effects do or do not come about. On occasion, different policy elements are contrasted. For example, in the NEWWS studies, some participants were placed in education-focused experiences before seeking work, and others were placed in programs designed to get them into the labor force immediately (McGroder et al., 2000). On the whole, however, it can be difficult to disentangle the contributions of different elements in the mix in a particular program. One can say with certainty that the program did or did not have an effect, but it is not possible to determine which components were important or why. Nonexperimental analyses permit more fine-grained identification of the unique contributions of different factors, and they lend themselves to testing complex theoretical models about the relations among such factors. The best of all possible worlds, then, is one in which both types of methods are used to converge on the same questions (and, of course, when they yield consistent answers). Multiple experiments with large sample sizes provide replication across sites and populations. For example, when a synthesis of 11 experiments shows consistently that programs that increase *both* family income and parent employment have positive effects on school-aged children's achievement and social behavior, that is more persuasive than any one study would be. Similarly, the consistency of slightly negative effects on adolescents in the same families raises intriguing developmental issues that require further exploration (Morris et al., 2001; Gennetian et al., 2002).

Research on economic conditions of families and children's development has brought a new mix of interdisciplinary collaboration into developmental science. Our New Hope team (like the teams for most other similar research) consists of economists, survey researchers, evaluation researchers, policy analysts, and anthropologists, as well as developmental psychologists. We have gradually learned to talk each others' languages and to appreciate the ways in which our methodological and conceptual approaches complement one another. This mix of disciplines casts our understanding of children's development in a different mold than one derived solely from psychology. For example, the theories of children's development informing this work emphasize not only intrapersonal and interpersonal socialization processes, but also human capital and material resources.

This work benefits from multiple methods, combining the rich description of ethnography with the generalizability and statistical power of systematic measures on large numbers of cases. We, and numerous other research teams, have gradually learned to go beyond using ethnography as a source of nice stories to an interactive process by which hypotheses are derived from ethnographic work, and interpretation of quantitative findings is aided by in-depth interviews and observations. For example, we had not predicted that New Hope would have more positive effects on boys than on girls. One reason for this difference was suggested in the ethnographic interviews. Parents often stated that gangs and other neighborhood pressures were more threatening to their elementary-school boys than to girls. As a response, mothers in the experimental group channeled more of the program's resources (e.g., child-care subsidies for extended-day programs) to their boys. One mother said, "Not all places have gangs, but [my neighborhood] is infested with gangs and drugs and violence. My son, I worry about him. He may be veering in the wrong direction . . . it's different for girls. For boys, it's dangerous. [Gangs are] full of older men who want these young ones to do their dirty work. And they'll buy them things and give them money" (Gibson & Duncan, 2004). Further quantitative analyses of both New Hope and national-sample survey data supported the interpretation that parents living in dangerous neighborhoods do indeed devote differential time and other resources to their boys relative to their girls (Romich & Weisner, 2000).

In some studies, videotaped observations of parent–child interaction have been conducted for a small sample, providing another kind of in-depth information that complements quantitative findings on a sample of thousands. For example, Zaslow and Eldred (1998) were able to evaluate the validity and meaning of survey measures of parenting, which were used on a large sample, by comparing them to observed behavior for the smaller videotaped sample. These multiple methods not only produce policy-relevant information, but also produce better science than do single methods.

Conclusion

In summary, during the last 20 years, developmental science has been enriched by a wealth of sophisticated theory and empirical investigation of the processes by which poverty and family income affect developing children's lives. Policy experiments, designed to test a range of employment and welfare policies, offer methodological and conceptual strengths that complement those of nonexperimental, naturalistic investigations. Both types of study support the notion that variations in family economic resources can have ramifications for children's school performance and behavior, at least at the low end of the income continuum. Both types of study also provide information about the processes by which parent employment and income influence children. Although nonexperimental investigations show consistently that economic hardship is related to parents' psychological well-being, warmth, and effective discipline, there is little evidence that policies that increase family resources have an effect on parenting warmth or parent–child relations. These policies do affect parents' choices about care for their children outside the family – specifically child care and out-of-school activities. Increased resources and programmatic support enable parents to use relatively expensive center-based child care and to increase children's participation in structured activities. Both parenting and experiences outside the family, therefore, appear to be likely paths by which income and employment are linked to children's behavior. Policy experiments that are interdisciplinary and use multiple methods have the potential to make important contributions to developmental science.

Acknowledgments

The Child and Family New Hope Study was initiated under the auspices of the MacArthur Foundation Research Network on Successful Pathways through Middle Childhood and was also funded by the W.T. Grant Foundation and the National Institute of Child Health and Human Development. The Next Generation Project is led by Manpower Demonstration Research Corporation and funded by the W.T. Grant Foundation, the Packard Foundation, and the MacArthur Foundation.

References

Adams, G., Snyder, K., & Sandfort, J. (2002). Getting and retaining child care assistance: How policy and practice influence parents' experiences. (Assessing the New Federalism Occasional Paper No. 55, March). Washington, DC: Urban Institute.

Ashenfelter, O. (1978). The labor supply response of wage earners. In J. Palmer & J. Pechman (Eds.), *Welfare in Rural Areas: The North Carolina-Iowa Income Maintenance Experiment*. Washington, DC: Brookings Institution.

Bergmann, B. (1996). *Saving Our Children from Poverty: What the United States Can Learn from France*. New York: Russell Sage.

Bloom, D., & Michalopoulos, C. (2001). *How Welfare and Work Policies Affect Employment and Income: A Synthesis of Research*. New York: Manpower Demonstration Research Corporation.

Bos, J. M., Huston, A. C., Granger, R. C., Duncan, G. J., Brock, T., & McLoyd, V. C. (1999). *New Hope for People with Low Incomes: Two-Year Results of a Program to Reduce Poverty and Reform Welfare*. New York: Manpower Demonstration Research Corporation.

Chang, Y. E., Huston, A. C., Crosby, D. A., & Gennetian. L. A. (2002). *The Effects of Welfare and Employment Programs on Children's Participation in Head Start*. (The Next Generation Project Working Paper). New York: Manpower Demonstration Research Corporation.

Coley, R. L., Chase-Lansdale, P. L., & Li Grining, C. P. (2001). *Low-Income Families and Child Care: Quality, Options and Choices*. Minneapolis, MN: Biennial Meeting of the Society for Research in Child Development.

Conger, R. D., & Elder, G. H., Jr. (1994). *Families in Troubled Times: Adapting to Change in Rural America*. New York: Aldine de Gruyter.

Conger, R. D., Ge, X., Elder, G. H., Jr., Lorenz, F. O., Simons, R. L., & Xiaojia, G. (1994). Economic stress, coercive family process, and developmental problems of adolescents. *Child Development 65*, 541–561.

Crosby, D. A., Gennetian, L. A., & Huston, A. C. (2001, September). *Does Child Care Assistance Matter? The Effects of Welfare and Employment Programs on Child Care for Preschool and Young School Aged Children*. (Next Generation Working Paper No. 3). New York: Manpower Demonstration Research Corporation.

Elder, G. H., Jr., & Caspi, A. (1988). Economic stress in lives: Developmental perspectives. *Journal of Social Issues 44*, 4, 25–45.

Elder, G. H., Jr., Van Nguyen, T., & Caspi, A. (1985). Linking family hardship to children's lives. *Child Development 56*, 361–375.

Friedlander, D., & Burtless, G. (1995). *Five Years After: The Long-Term Effects of Welfare-to-Work Programs*. New York: Russell Sage.

Fuller, B., Kagan, S., Caspary, G. L., & Gauthier, C. A. (2002). Welfare reform and child care options for low-income families. *Future of Children 12*, 1, 97–119.

Gennetian. L. A., Crosby, D. A., Huston, A. C., & Lowe, T. (2002). *How Child Care Assistance in Welfare and Employment Programs Can Support the Employment of Low-Income Families*. (The Next Generation Project Working Paper). New York: Manpower Demonstration Research Corporation.

Gennetian, L. A., Duncan, G. J., Knox, V. W., Vargas, W. G., Clark-Kauffman, E., & London, A. S. (2002). *How Welfare and Work Policies for Parents Affect Adolescents:*

A Synthesis of Research. (The Next Generation Project Working Paper). New York: Manpower Demonstration Research Corporation.

Gibson, C., & Duncan, G. J. (2004). Qualitative/quantitative synergies in a random-assignment program evaluation. In T. Weisner (Ed.), Discovering successful pathways in children's development. *Mixed Methods in the Study of Childhood and Family Life*. Chicago: University of Chicago Press.

Greenberg, M., et al. (2002). The 1996 welfare law: Key elements and reauthorization issues affecting children. *Future of Children 12*, 1, 27–57.

Gueron, J. M. (1987). Welfare to work programs: Lessons on recent state initiatives. *Policy Studies Review 6*, 733–743.

Gueron, J. M., & Pauly, E. (1991). *From Welfare to Work*. New York: Russell Sage Foundation.

Hamilton, G., Freedman, S., Gennetian, L. A., Michalopoulos, C., Walter, J., et al. (2001). *National Evaluation of Welfare-to-Work Strategies: How Effective Are Different Welfare-to-Work Approaches? Five-Year Adult and Child Impacts for Eleven Programs*. Washington, DC: U.S. Department of Health and Human Services and U.S. Department of Education.

Huston, A. C., Duncan, G. J., Granger, R. C., Bos, J. M., McLoyd, V. C., Mistry, R. S. et al. (2001). Work-based anti-poverty programs for parents can enhance the school performance and social behavior of children. *Child Development 72*, 318–336.

Huston, A. C., McLoyd, V. C., & Garcia-Coll, C. T. (1994). Children and poverty: Issues in contemporary research. *Child Development 65*, 275–282.

Huston, A. C., Miller, C., Richburg-Hayes, L., Duncan, G. J., Eldred, C. A., Weisner, T. S. et al. (2003). *New Hope for Families and Children: Five-Year Results of a Program to Reduce Poverty and Reform Welfare*. New York: Manpower Demonstration Research Corporation.

Kamerman, S. (1996). Child and family policies: An international overview. In E. F. Zigler, S. L. Kagan, & N. W. Hall (Eds.), *Children, Families, and Government* (2nd ed.) (pp. 31–48). New York: Cambridge University Press.

Kershaw, D., & Fair, J. (1976). *The New Jersey Income Maintenance Experiment*. Vol. 1. New York: Academic Press.

Lerner, R. M. (1998). Theories of human development: Contemporary perspectives. In W. Damon & R. M. Lerner (Eds.), *Handbook of Child Psychology: Vol. 1. Theoretical Models of Human Development* (5th ed.) (pp. 1–24). New York: John Wiley.

Mahoney, J. L., Larson, R. W., & Eccles, J. S. (Eds.) (2004). *Organized Activities as Contexts of Development: Extracurricular Activities, After-School and Community Programs*. Mahwah, NJ: Lawrence Erlbaum.

Mallar, C. D., & Maynard, R. A. (1981). The effects of income maintenance on school performance and educational attainment. In A. Kahn & I. Sirageldin (Eds.), *Equity, Human Capital, and Development* (pp. 121–141). Greenwich, CT: JAI Press, Inc.

Mayer, S. E. (1997). *What Money Can't Buy: Family Income and Children's Life Chances*. Cambridge, MA: Harvard University Press.

McGroder, S. M., Zaslow, M. J., Moore, K. A., & LeMenestrel, S. M. (2000, June). *National Evaluation of Welfare-to-Work Strategies. Impacts on Young Children and Their Families Two Years after Enrollment: Findings from the Child Outcome Study*. Washington, DC: U.S. Department of Health and Human Services, Office of the Assistant Secretary for Planning and Evaluation.

McLoyd, V. C. (1990). The impact of economic hardship on Black families and children: Psychological distress, parenting, and socioemotional development. *Child Development 61*, 311–346.

McLoyd, V. C. (1997). Children in poverty: Development, public policy, and practice. In I. Sigel & K. A. Renninger (Eds.), *Child Psychology in Practice* (5th ed.) (pp. 135–210). New York: John Wiley.

McLoyd, V. C. (1998). Socioeconomic disadvantage and child development. *American Psychologist 53*, 185–204.

McLoyd, V. C., Jayaratne, T. E., Ceballo, R., & Borquez, J. (1994). Unemployment and work interruption among African American single mothers: Effects on parenting and adolescent socioemotional functioning. *Child Development 65*, 562–589.

Mistry, R. S., Crosby, D., Huston, A. C., Casey, D. M., & Ripke, M. (2001). Lessons from New Hope: The impact of a work-based anti-poverty program for parents on children's well-being. In G. J. Duncan & P. L. Chase-Lansdale (Eds.), *For Better and for Worse: Welfare Reform and the Well-Being of Children and Families* (pp. 179–200). New York: Russell Sage.

Mistry, R. S., Vandewater, E. A., Huston, A. C., & McLoyd, V. (2002). Economic well-being and children's social adjustment: The role of family process in an ethnically diverse low-income sample. *Child Development 73*, 667–681.

Morris, P. A., & Duncan, G. J. (2002). Which welfare reforms are best for children? In Sawhill et al. (Eds.), *Welfare Reform and Beyond* (pp. 71–78). Washington, DC: Brookings Institution.

Morris, P. A., Huston, A. C., Duncan, G. J., Crosby, D., & Bos, J. M. (2001). *How Welfare and Work Policies Affect Children: A Synthesis of Research.* New York: Manpower Demonstration Research Corporation.

NICHD Early Child Care Research Network. (2000). The relation of child care to cognitive and language development. *Child Development 71*, 960–980.

NICHD Early Child Care Research Network. (2002). Early child care and children's development prior to school entry: Results from the NICHD Study of Early Child Care. *American Educational Research Journal 39*, 133–164.

Pettit, G. S., Bates, J. E., Dodge, K. A., & Meece, D. W. (1999). The impact of after-school peer contact on early adolescent externalizing problems is moderated by parental monitoring, perceived neighborhood safety, and prior adjustment. *Child Development 70*, 768–778.

Robins, P. K., & West, R. W. (1980). Program participation and labor-supply response. *Journal of Human Resources 15*, 499–523.

Romich, J. L., & Weisner, T. S. (2000). How families view and use the EITC: Advance payment versus lump sum delivery. *National Tax Journal LIII 4–2*, 1245–1265.

Salkind, N. J., & Haskins, R. (1982). Negative Income Tax: The impact on children from low-income families. *Journal of Family Issues 3*, 2, 165–180.

U.S. Department of Health and Human Services. (2001). *Trends in the Well-Being of Children and Youth, 2001.* Washington DC: Office of the Assistant Secretary for Planning and Evaluation, U. S. Department of Health and Human Services. www.aspe.hhs.gov/hsp/01trends.

U.S. Department of Health, Education, and Welfare. (1983). *Overview of the Seattle/Denver Income Maintenance Experiments: Final Report.* Washington, DC: Office of Income Security, U.S. Department of Health, Education, and Welfare.

Weisner, T. S., Bernheimer, L., Espinosa, V., Gibson, C., Howard, E., Magnuson, K. et al. (1999). *From the Living Rooms and Daily Routines of the Economically Poor: An Ethnographic Study of the New Hope Effects on Families and Children.* Albuquerque, NM: The Meeting of the Society for Research in Child Development.

Zaslow, M. J., & Eldred, C. A. (1998). *Parenting Behavior in a Sample of Young Mothers in Poverty: Results of the New Chance Observational Study.* New York: Manpower Demonstration Research Corporation.

Zaslow, M. J., Moore, K. A., Brooks, J. L., Morris, P. A., Tout, K., Redd, Z. A., & Emig, C. A. (2002). Experimental studies of welfare reform and children. *Future of Children* *12*, 1, 79–98.

Zaslow, M. J., Moore, K. A., Morrison, D. R., & Coiro, M. J. (1995). The Family Support Act and children: Potential pathways of influence. *Children and Youth Services Review* *17*, 231–249.

5   The Disconnect between Research and Policy on Child Care

Deborah Phillips and Kathleen McCartney

Research and policy on child care have developed along parallel tracks. Their influence on each other has been modest, despite the shared historical context in which each has evolved. This stands in stark contrast to Head Start (Zigler & Valentine, 1979; Zigler & Muenchow, 1992), a product of the 1960s and the War on Poverty, in which policymakers engaged researchers in a variety of roles, from designers to evaluators. Today, these roles have converged into what White and Phillips characterize as "a virtual industry of Head Start research," an industry that continues to be closely aligned with the policy community surrounding the program (2001, p. 83). The origins of modern-day child-care policy and research can also be traced back to the mid-1960s, when maternal employment and child-care usage began their steep upward trajectories. Why have research and policy on child care remained separate endeavors? Why has the relation between them evolved so differently from that between research and policy on Head Start? Can we hope for greater convergence in the years ahead?

To explore these questions about the disconnect between research and policy on child care, we begin by acknowledging the differing ways in which scientists and politicians think about child care. We then offer brief histories of child-care policy and research, which illustrate the mismatch between the central concerns and incentives guiding these two "distinct cultures," described by Shonkoff (2000). Next, we apply the roles for developmentalists outlined by White and Phillips (2001) for Head Start to child care. In conclusion, we outline lessons learned from history to portray possibilities for a more constructive science-policy alliance as the nation decides upon the future of child care.

What Is Child Care?

Efforts to place conceptual boundaries around "child care" are fraught with problems. Unlike Head Start, which is unified, albeit loosely, by its federal legislative authority and performance standards, child care is a remarkably heterogeneous service – ranging from care by relatives to center-based programs – that serves multiple needs. Its fuzzy boundaries have been blurred further by the growing number of state pre-kindergarten programs that, despite their separate funding streams, are often viewed by parents as a critical part of community child care. Even within the early childhood field, there are on-going debates about the adequacy of the term "care" to capture the many purposes, including the early educational purposes, met by child-care services (see Caldwell, 1991). Funding for child care is provided predominantly by parents, but is also subsidized through a dizzying array of federal and state appropriations. There are no unifying performance standards. Indeed, a growing share of child care, including government-funded services, now operates outside the purview of the 50-state regulatory provisions for child care, which ensure only minimal protections for children (Phillips, Lande, & Goldberg, 1990; Phillips & Zigler, 1987).

An appreciation that policy and science reflect differing perspectives on these definitional dilemmas is central to this chapter. With respect to policy, the unit of discussion is child-care-in-context (Phillips, 1984, 1991). Policy debates about child care tend to become embroiled in broader issues of public policy (e.g., immigration, unemployment, tax equity, welfare reform) that divert attention away from concerns directly pertinent to children's well-being. At the turn of the century, for example, child care, in the form of "day nurseries," was a mechanism for assimilating immigrant children and their parents into mainstream societal practices by, for example, offering parenting and hygiene classes (Grubb & Lazerson, 1982; Rothman, 1973). During World War II, publicly funded child-care services enabled women with children to work in wartime factories whose usual labor force had been depleted by the draft (Steinfels, 1973). Today, the central policy goal served by federal and state support for child care is that of moving families who are dependent on public assistance (Aid to Families with Dependent Children [AFDC], now Temporary Assistance to Needy Families [TANF]) toward economic self-sufficiency and, thereby, reducing public expenditures on welfare. The adult focus of these policy goals is distinct from the developmental goals of Head Start and its offshoot for infants and toddlers, Early Head Start, focused as they are on providing a comprehensive array of early education, health, screening, and social services to children living in poverty. Child-care policy, in contrast, reflects a view of child well-being as secondary to other national goals and defies the knowledge base affirming that all early environments – those that are explicitly educational and those that ignore this potential – influence development (Shonkoff & Phillips, 2000).

In contrast to policymakers, researchers view child care as a pervasive context in which development unfolds, second only to the immediate family (NICHD ECCRN, 2002a; Shonkoff & Phillips, 2000). Because most children experience some form of child care in the first year of life, it can be considered a normative experience. It is a social setting, where children establish bonds with caregivers and learn to work and play with peers, as well as an educational setting, where children learn school readiness skills. Sometimes experiences in child care constitute a source of protection or enrichment for young children; sometimes they are a source of risk (NICHD ECCRN, 1998; Phillips & Adams, 2001). From this perspective, child care, like Head Start, can be viewed as an early intervention that can either increase or diminish the odds of healthy development. Note that developmental researchers in essence provide answers to a single overarching question: How are children faring in child care? This question is, at best, of secondary concern in the world of policy, where child care is deployed as a service to promote programs for adults.

Child Care Policy

Numerous accounts of the history of child-care policy and advocacy describe the ebbs and flows of national, and hence policy, interest in child care (Cahan, 1989; Joffe, 1977; Hofferth, 1993; Gormley, 1995; Cohen, 2001; Kamerman & Kahn, 1987; Michel, 1999; Nelson, 1982; Whitebook, 2001; Phillips & Zigler, 1987). It is a reactive history in which the timing and fate of child-care policies are byproducts of other policy and demographic developments shaping the nation.

Federal Child Care As an Emergency Service

The first federal contribution to child-care services occurred in 1933 when President Franklin Roosevelt established emergency nursery schools under the Federal Emergency Relief Administration and the Works Progress Administration (WPA). These schools shared a dual purpose: to protect and educate preschoolers thrust into poverty by the Great Depression and to create jobs for unemployed teachers. By 1943, more than 300,000 children were attending these schools on a regular basis (Tank, 1980). This first excursion into federal involvement in child care established the policy framework that has survived largely intact to this day, namely that government involvement in child care is warranted during extraordinary times and for families beset with problems.

The WPA programs, however, went well beyond providing custodial care to these families. The early childhood professional and academic communities of the time were actively involved in the establishment and administration of these programs, which were high-quality, educationally oriented schools. In addition to staffing the programs with unemployed teachers, nurses, and social workers, state training institutions were established to ensure that these individuals understood *early* child development (Michel, 1999). A decade later when the economy improved, the WPA lost its funding, and the nursery schools were phased out.

But, extraordinary times returned with World War II. Women from all walks of life joined the workforce required by the war factories. Despite widespread discomfort with the implicit support for maternal employment involved in funding child care, President Roosevelt approved the use of public works monies from the Lanham Act for child care in 1942, thereby helping states pay for the nation's first "worksite" child-care centers (programs had to be established in war-disrupted areas). In many instances, these funds picked up where the WPA funds had left off. All child-care programs applying for Lanham Act funds had to be certified by the Federal Children's Bureau and Office of Education. During the four years of the Lanham Act, $52 million in federal money supported 3,102 centers in 47 states that eventually served 600,000 children (Cahan, 1989). Again, however, when normal times returned, federal funds were withdrawn; mothers were supposed to return home. By 1948, only California continued to fund the Lanham Act centers.

Child Care and Maternal Employment

Many mothers did not return home. Maternal employment among married women with children under 18 years rose from 8.7% in 1940 to 18.4% in 1950 and 27.6% in 1960 (U.S. Bureau of Labor Statistics, unpublished data). This trend proved to be significant for child care, but not because the nation saw fit to develop a universal child-care policy to accompany the steady, overall rise in working mothers. Rather, the general increase in maternal employment, combined with rising welfare costs, contributed to a shift in emphasis in the Aid to Families with Dependent Children (AFDC) program. Originally designed to protect children by enabling their impoverished mothers to care for them at home, policy began to shift toward increased incentives for these mothers to enter the labor force with their nonpoor peers and, ultimately, to reduce public expenditures on welfare. As in the past, policymakers recognized that encouraging work effort among mothers entailed providing child care for their children. In 1963, President Kennedy earmarked $800,000 for child care in the context of a welfare law (P.L. 87–543). In 1967, the Work Incentive Program (WIN) authorized the federal government to support the child-care costs of welfare recipients who were being trained for and placed in paid employment; however, an exemption for mothers with children under age six, enacted in 1971, kept WIN child-care payments very low.

These policies continued the theme of linking child care to maternal employment, but three important departures from the past warrant attention. First, the WIN and AFDC legislation yoked child care to welfare policy, as distinct from employment policy (WPA nurseries) and war policy (Lanham Act programs). Second, this yoking effectively placed child care on a par with other employment supports in the service of economic self-sufficiency, such as work uniforms and transportation, and situated child-care funding in the context of the broader goal to reduce public expenditures on welfare. Third, welfare-based child-care subsidies are directed to poor mothers who are generally viewed less sympathetically than prior target populations for federal child-care support (i.e., teachers who had suddenly found themselves unemployed and mothers working to support their country's war effort). Not coincidentally, the child-care provisions of these, and future, welfare reform laws emphasized the cost and supply of care. To provide more educationally oriented, higher-cost care would have defeated the overall cost-reduction goals of welfare reform, particularly in the absence of a ready supply of unemployed teachers, nurses, and social workers. Child care was now placed squarely in the service of promoting employment among welfare recipients.

Simultaneously, an alternative strategy for supporting families living in poverty emerged from the War on Poverty. Rather than focusing on the current generation of welfare parents, it sought to short-circuit intergenerational cycles of welfare dependence by providing comprehensive services to children living in poverty (Phillips, 1984, 1991). As described by White and Phillips (2001), Head Start appeared with "explosive speed" in 1965 in part to garner public support for the larger War on Poverty programs (e.g., VISTA, Job Corps, the Community Action Program), which were targeted for the truly disadvantaged (e.g., teens and adults living in poverty) (see also Greenberg, 1990a, 1990b; Zigler & Valentine, 1979; Zigler & Muenchow, 1992). Although rising welfare costs were not incidental to the creation of Head Start, of far greater influence were contemporary theories of development that identified the preschool years as a time when healthcare and nutrition, support for early learning, and encouragement of achievement motivation could propel children on a path toward school success and economic independence (White & Phillips, 2001). The Head Start strategy was focused primarily on child development goals, including the prevention of intergenerational poverty; as a result, program quality was of paramount importance.

By the end of the 1960s, these two strategies – child care as an adjunct to welfare focused on working mothers and Head Start as an investment in development focused on children – were firmly entrenched in federal policy. They exist alongside each other to this day as the centerpieces of our nation's efforts to intervene in the early environments of poor children.

The Comprehensive Child Development Act

In 1971, there was a chance for these two strategies to merge into a cohesive, universal child-care policy for the country. The opportunity was lost. The story of the Mondale–Brademas Comprehensive Child Development Act (CCDA) has been told many times, most recently in a highly readable book by Sally Cohen (2001). In November 2001, Vice President Mondale provided his own retrospective view of the Act as part of the Mondale Lectures on Public Service at the University of Minnesota (Mondale, 2001).

Motivated by the twin needs to address poverty and provide adequate care for children of employed mothers, Mondale sought to extend the Head Start model to the broader population of children with employed mothers across the economic spectrum. The statement of purpose accompanying the bill argues that "comprehensive child development programs are essential to the achievement of the full potential of America's children and should be available *as a matter of right* to all children regardless of economic, social, and family background" (S. 1512, p. 4). In 2001, Mondale referred to the bill as "the high point of national efforts to deliver justice to our children" (Mondale, 2001).

Despite having passed the House and Senate with wide margins, President Nixon vetoed the bill with what Mondale referred to as "a message that I will never forget"; it "was no ordinary veto," "had little to do with children," and could only be described as "savage" (Mondale, 2001). The message asserted that the Comprehensive Child Development Act of 1971 would "alter the family relationship, take away parents' authority over their children, and commit the vast moral authority of the national government to the side of communal approaches to child-rearing." This veto went well beyond divorcing child-care goals from child development goals. It explicitly pitted child care against the family in a zero-sum equation that, to this day, fuels public ambivalence about the relation between parental and "other" care (Sylvester,

2001). The reasons for Nixon's veto have been debated and likely reflect a convergence of factors. What is clear is that the Comprehensive Child Development Act incited deeply conservative interests that were becoming organized at the time of the legislation. A letter-writing campaign of unprecedented size and ferocity touting the rhetoric of conservative family values similar to that used in the veto message was mobilized in opposition to the Act. It was an exceedingly harsh confrontation that provided a harbinger of similar efforts mobilized around future child-care legislation as well as educational curricula, White House Conferences on Children, and other targets of conservative antipathy.

The demise of the CCDA marked a pivotal turning point in the lineage of federal involvement in child care that is of special importance for children and those who study them. The Act would not only have woven together adult- and child-focused poverty strategies and integrated child-care policies for poor and nonpoor families, but also would have required all funded programs to meet Federal Interagency Day Care Requirements (FIDCR). The FIDCR were designed to establish a floor of quality below which no federally funded program could fall. Since 1971, these three components (federal regulation, universality, and intergenerational services), all potentially beneficial for children and closely aligned with the child-care goals of interest to developmentalists, have remained outside the boundaries of federal policy discussions. Moreover, despite widespread perceptions that we are now spending unprecedented amounts on child care for low-income families, we would actually be spending more if federal funds had kept pace with the amounts deemed necessary in 1971 (Phillips, 2001). The $7 billion federal monies authorized for the CCDA in 1971 amount to $23.1 billion in 2001 dollars. Current federal direct expenditures on child care and Head Start are now approximately $19 billion.

In his closing comments at the 2001 Mondale Lecture, the Vice President noted that Congress failed to override the veto and speculated that the root cause of the CCDA legislation failure was a fear that some in government were bent to destroy the traditional family. Mondale states, "It was all the more difficult to combat these fears because we didn't yet have the scientific evidence to show the positive benefits of a stimulating educational environment."

Contemporary Child Care Policy

Since 1971, federal child-care policy, as reaffirmed in 1996 with the enactment of the Personal Responsibility and Work Opportunity Reconciliation Act (PRWORA or, more commonly, the 1996 welfare reform law, P.L. 104–193), has continued along its pre-CCDA path. Successive versions of welfare reform have consistently included funding for child care aimed at promoting self-sufficiency. They have also gradually removed exemptions from work requirements for women with young children. Whereas the WIN legislation exempted mothers with children under six years of age, the 1996 law removed all exemptions from participation in work-related activities based on the age of the children in the household. As of 2002, 19 states used this new flexibility to remove exemptions for parents whose youngest child is less than 1 year old (most require work when the infant reaches 3 months of age). An additional 23 states require mothers receiving benefits to work when their child is 1 year old (DHHS, 2002).

The question today is not whether but how the federal government defines its role in child care. Presently, this role remains firmly tied to goals that are adult-oriented, focused on poverty populations, designed primarily to remove an impediment to employment, and ultimately aimed at reducing federal expenditures on the poor by replacing public assistance with wages. Although no longer restricted to extraordinary times, federal child-care policy remains tied to families beset with problems. What is new, however, is that Mondale's wish for relevant research on child development and child care has been fulfilled. The existence of empirical data on the effects of child care holds the potential to create common ground and move at least some of the issues surrounding child-care policy (e.g., do children in settings that are in compliance with child-care regulations show better developmental outcomes than their peers not in such settings?) out of the no-man's land where political pushing and pulling can lead policy in almost any direction. We now turn to the history of this research.

History of Research on Child Care

Research Waves

Research on child care also began amidst the "scientific optimism" of the early 1960s that was associated with the War on Poverty (Caldwell, 1998). This optimism was based on Hunt's (1961) influential treatise on *Intelligence and Experience*, which emphasized the importance of early experience for later development. Hunt's arguments were used to justify numerous intervention programs, including child-care programs. Bettye Caldwell credits Charles P. Gershenson, Research Director of the U.S. Children's Bureau, for funding some of the earliest research on child care. Surely, credit must also be extended to Caldwell and other child advocates, who conducted pioneering studies.

Some of these early studies provided evidence that child care could help to prevent cognitive and language delays, especially for children from families with meager economic resources. Soon, however, studies began to report that child care could also pose risks, especially with respect to children's attachment relationships with their mothers. Caldwell argues that any early optimism was soon tempered by a "defensive posture" about child care from which researchers, practitioners, and parents have yet to escape.

Reviewers typically frame child-care research with respect to three waves (Belsky & Steinberg, 1978; McCartney & Galanopoulos, 1988; Lamb, 1998). The first wave consisted of comparisons of children in mother care with children in other care. These between-groups studies were simplistic for two main reasons: studies relied on convenience samples, often consisting of children attending university centers; and researchers did not consider family confounds of child-care experience, referred to as selection effects by developmentalists and endogeneity problems by economists and others. By today's methodological standards, the first wave studies are completely uninterpretable. Nevertheless, they helped to frame enduring debates about whether child care posed developmental risks or advantages for young children (McCartney & Phillips, 1985).

In the early 1980s, the second wave of studies began to appear, focusing on quality by using within-groups or correlational strategies. Statistical models began to include family variables to control for selection effects, beginning with the National Day Care Study (Ruopp, Travers, Glantz, & Coelen, 1977) and the Bermuda Day Care Study (McCartney, Scarr, Phillips, Grajek, & Schwarz, 1982). Debates about the best strategy for controlling for selection continue, residing in the fact that true versus spurious covariation between child-care variables and child outcomes cannot be differentiated. In other words, there is no universally accepted method for determining whether a child-care effect within a nonexperimental design represents a true effect of children's child-care environments or a selection effect associated with characteristics of the family.

Researchers assess quality with structural characteristics of child care (e.g., teacher–child ratios, group size, teaching training) or with process indicators of children's actual experiences in care (e.g., teacher–child interactions, characteristics of the curriculum). The two kinds of assessments are, of course, related (Howes, 1983). Structural characteristics are more policy-relevant, while process indicators reflect developmentalists' conceptions about environmental mechanisms such as caregiver sensitivity or language stimulation. Not surprisingly, albeit importantly, there is ample evidence from both structural and process assessments that higher child-care quality is associated with positive outcomes for children across cognitive, language, and social domains (for a review see Lamb, 1998).

Large, multisite, longitudinal studies are ushering in a third wave of research. The design of these studies is rooted in social ecology theory in which the child is viewed as nested within both child-care and family contexts. Their feasibility has been fostered by interdisciplinary collaboration, as well as by the growing expertise among developmental researchers with the methods and analytic strategies that characterize large-sample studies. One of the first examples of a third-wave study is the Cost, Quality, and Outcomes Study of 757 children attending one of 401 community child-care centers in four areas representing varying economic climates as well as state regulations for child care: Los Angeles County in California, the Hartford corridor in Connecticut, the Frontal range in Colorado, and the Piedmont region in North Carolina. Findings linked quality indicators with a variety of child outcomes, including language ability, pre-academic skills, and classroom behavior (Peisner-Feinberg & Burchinal, 1997). This study also provides some of the best evidence that child-care effects are moderated by variables like family economic resources. Bronfenbrenner (1979) predicted that the "main effects" on children's development would be interactions. By this he meant that influences like child care would not operate universally, but rather would be moderated as a function of child and family characteristics. For example, there is now substantial evidence in support of Peisner-Feinberg and Burchinal's finding that child-care quality effects are stronger for poor children (Barnett, 1998; McCartney, in press).

The most comprehensive study of child care to date is the ongoing National Institute of Child Health and Human Development Study of Early Child Care and Youth Development (NICHD SECCYD). The NICHD issued a request for applications under the direction of the Institute's Director, Dr. Duane Alexander, that resulted in 10 competitively selected grants, including one to each of the authors of this chapter, awarded in 1989. The original 10 principal investigators formed a research network that is conducting a collaborative study with a common protocol. Dr. Alexander's motivation to fund this project was derived in part from his participation in a one-day workshop on infant child care, sponsored by Zero to Three: The National Association for Clinical Infant Programs. The purpose of the workshop was to cool the heated controversy over whether infant child care was a risk factor, as suggested by Belsky (1986) and refuted by others on the grounds that available research evidence was limited, especially research on infants (Phillips et al., 1987). Thus, the NICHD study was not rooted in policy concerns but rather in developmental science.

The study is explicitly designed to answer the many questions about the relationship between child-care experiences and characteristics and children's developmental outcomes. The NICHD selected a research team, based on a competitive review of responses to a request for applications, located at universities across the United States, and at the NICHD. The strengths of the study include its prospective longitudinal design (1,364 families were recruited at birth in 1991), the geographic and socio-economic diversity of the sample (the sample is derived from 10 locations across the United States), the repeated assessment of children in their homes and child-care contexts, and the inclusion of observational and performance assessments in addition to survey data (see http://secc.rti.org for detailed information about the study).

To date, children in the study have been followed from birth through sixth grade. Children were observed in their child-care settings at five time points (6, 15, 24, 36, and 54 months). Settings included informal arrangements, such as relative care, as well as formal arrangements, including center-based care, public pre-kindergarten, and Head Start programs. Following developmental theory, the investigators developed a time-sampling measure of child-care quality that could be used across settings and that focused on caregiver sensitivity and stimulation of cognitive skills. Some of the field's most important findings about child-care quality are derived from this unprecedented study. The strongest findings are for cognitive and language outcomes, both of which were predicted by structural characteristic of child care (NICHD ECCRN, 1999, 2002b) as well as by process characteristics (NICHD ECCRN, 2000a, 2002c).

Findings about the importance of child-care quality are worrisome in light of typical care in the United States, which has been found repeatedly to fall below standards recommended by pediatric and early childhood professionals. For example, consider the low percentages of child-care centers from the NICHD study that met the caregiver–child ratio guidelines from the American Public Health Association and the American Academy of Pediatrics: 36% at 6 months, 20% at 15 months, 26% at 24 months, and 56% at 36 months (NICHD ECCRN, 1999). Given the extreme demands placed on caregivers by high child–teacher ratios, it is not surprising that, in the NICHD study, positive caregiving quality was observed to be characteristic of only 44% of settings across all types of care (NICHD ECCRN, 2000b).

The data from the NICHD study on whether child care poses a risk are mixed. With respect to mother–child attachment, there was no evidence that insecurity was associated with child-care experience, as indicated by the quality, amount, type, or stability of care (NICHD ECCRN, 1997a); there was, however, some indication that poor-quality child care coupled with poor-quality parenting might pose an increased risk of insecurity. With respect to behavior problems, there was evidence of risk associated with more hours in child care. This paper was so controversial within the field that the editor of *Child Development* published eight commentaries along side it. Some critics failed to replicate this finding with other samples (Love et al., 2003), while others pointed out the real possibility that unexplored third variables might be operating, such as temperament (Crockenberg, 2003) and parenting (Ahnert & Lamb, 2003). Newcombe (2003) questioned the ability to model relations between two variables with many others controlled by asking whether some controls control too much. This study generated much discussion, within the academy and beyond, because the stakes are high for parents, at least for some parents. We know from this study that any risk associated with hours did not operate universally, because only 15% of children in full-time care evidenced above-average behavior problems. Following Bronfenbrenner, the next task is to identify moderators of this effect. This is no easy task in nonexperimental work, because even large studies like the NICHD study tend to lack the statistical power necessary to detect interactions (McClelland & Judd, 1993).

Policy Research

In a sense, all research on child care is policy relevant. Nevertheless, most child-care studies are designed to answer scientific questions about associations between early experience and development rather than policy questions on targeted initiatives. Findings from scientific questions are only policy relevant in an indirect sense and typically only lead to general recommendations, for example, that higher quality child-care is better for children. In contrast, findings from policy questions are relevant in a direct sense and typically lead to specific recommendations, such as the thresholds of quality defined in state child-care regulations. Most of the policy-relevant developmental research on child care concerns so-called regulable aspects of care quality, specifically caregiver–child ratios, group size, and caregiver education and training.

The first, and perhaps best, example of research on child-care regulables is the National Day Care Study (NDCS), conducted by Abt Associates and funded by the Day Care Division of the Administration for Children, Youth and Families (Ruopp et al., 1977). This study is significant for two reasons. First, it is one of the few child-care studies that was designed specifically to address a policy debate, rooted in the 1968 Federal Interagency Day-Care Regulations. Second, this was one of the first large-scale, multisite studies of children. As such, it served as a model of how to do research on applied problems generally and on child care specifically. There is no doubt that other child-care researchers came to realize the importance of this approach to ensure the generalizability of their findings. For example, several multisite child-care studies conducted during the 1990s documented associations between the range of quality observed in licensed programs and the stringency of the state child-care regulations governing the programs (Phillips, Whitebook, & Howes, 1992; Phillips, Mekos et al., 2001). The hallmark of important studies like the National Child Care Staffing Study, the Cost Quality & Outcomes Study, and the NICHD Study of Early Child Care is their multisite approach.

The NDCS is really a collection of three studies. The first study was nonexperimental, focusing on naturally existing relations among regulated center characteristics in 64 centers from Atlanta, Detroit, and Seattle, cities chosen to reflect geographic, demographic, and regulatory diversity. The second two studies were each experimental. In study 2 ($n = 49$ centers), child–caregiver ratios were lowered in selected centers and untreated in other centers. In study 3 ($n = 29$ classrooms from 8 centers), children were randomly assigned to classes with varying levels of child–caregiver ratios and caregiver education.

The experimental studies produced "only scattered and largely nonsignificant effects" (Ruopp et al., 1977, p. 80). Most of the policy recommendations were derived from the nonexperimental study. The main finding was that group size and caregiver training/education were related to observed quality, as measured by social interaction, management, reflection, and aimless wandering, with group size being the strongest predictor. In contrast, child–caregiver ratio was only weakly associated with quality. Significantly, group size and caregiver training/education – unlike child–caregiver ratio – were unrelated to cost. Thus, the Abt research team was in the position to make regulatory recommendations regarding several key provisions of the FIDCR that would improve child-care quality with no additional funds required. The National Day Care Study stands alone in its findings on caregiver–child ratios. Virtually every other major study has revealed stronger associations between ratios and quality.

The National Child Care Staffing Study (NCCSS) (Whitebook, Howes, & Phillips, 1990; Phillips, Whitebook, & Howes, 1992) revisited the three NDCS sites in addition to Phoenix and Boston. This study was explicitly designed to address policy issues regarding (1) trends in the center-based child-care market since the 1977 NDCS; (2) the qualifications and stability of the nation's child-care workforce; (3) the contribution of child-care staff to the quality of care received by children; and (4) variation in the quality of care offered to children in centers governed by widely differing state child-care standards and managed under differing financial and legal auspices. In so doing, it set new ground by linking the adult work environment with research-based dimensions of care and by including measurement of regulatory and financial variables that constitute a central part of the policy ecology of child care.

Findings from the NCCSS documented the impact of the recommendations from the NDCS: during the interval between the two studies, child–staff ratios increased, while group sizes decreased. Follow-up studies of the Staffing Study sample in 1992 and 1997 (Whitebook, Howes, & Phillips, 1998) revealed staggeringly high turnover of both teaching staff and child-care programs over the decade of data collection, from 15% to 41%, further illustrating the value of adding longitudinal studies to the toolbox of child-care research. An unanticipated finding was that staff wages were the strongest predictor of child-care quality, stronger than even teacher education (see also Phillips et al., 2001). Although the NCCSS did a great deal to promote public education about the importance of adequately trained and compensated teachers, solutions to the child-care market failure have been slow in coming (Blau, 2001; Helburn & Bergmann, 2002).

The implementation of new ratio and education requirements in Florida offered Howes, Smith, and Galinsky (1995) the opportunity to conduct an important quasi-experiment. In 1992, regulations for child–caregiver ratios for infants changed from 6:1 to 4:1 for infants and from 8:1 to 6:1 for toddlers. In addition, for every 20 children, child-care facilities were required to have a caregiver with a Child Development Associate credential. The Florida Child Care Improvement Study used a pretest–posttest design to evaluate the effectiveness of these two requirements, with 880 children participating in each cohort. The findings were impressive. When ratios decreased, there was a significant increase in the overall quality of child care. Importantly, increases in quality were linked with better child outcomes. When compared with the pretest group, the posttest group of children engaged in more complex play with objects and with each other, were more securely attached to caregivers, had better language scores, and exhibited fewer behavior problems.

To date, the NICHD ECCRN network has published two papers that were designed to test policy questions about the importance of regulable aspects of child care. The first concerns an evaluation of a set of child-care center recommendations, jointly issued by the American Public Health Association and the American Academy of Pediatrics in 1992, for child–staff ratios, group size, and caregiver training. Greater caregiver training was associated with improved school readiness and language comprehension as well as with fewer behavior problems; better child–staff ratios were also associated with fewer behavior problems (NICHD ECCRN, 1999). The second paper tested a series of structural equation models and found a mediated path from both caregiver training and child–staff ratio through caregiver–child interactions to both cognitive and social competence (NICHD ECCRN, 2002b). Together, these two papers provide empirical support for policies that improve state regulations for caregiver training and child–staff ratios. They also demonstrate how policy research can be derived from developmental data sets. Perhaps these kinds of studies will usher in a fourth wave of research.

Although most of the research in this area concerns center-based care, most children attend informal care arrangements, especially during the first few years of life. Several studies have attempted to examine how children fare in family child care, provided either by a relative or an unrelated person. The findings from these studies tend to parallel those from studies of center-based care. For example, Galinsky, Howes, Kontos, and Shinn (1994) studied 225 children attending a family child-care program in either San Fernando/Los Angeles, California; Dallas/Fort Worth, Texas; or Charlotte, North Carolina. Quality was poor, especially for children from low-income families, characteristics of quality were intercorrelated, and quality mattered for child outcomes. Clarke-Stewart, Vandell, Burchinal, O'Brien, and McCartney (2002) studied a subsample of children from the NICHD ECCRN who attended family child care at 15, 24, and/or 36 months. Caregivers who were better educated and had received more recent training structured better learning environments and provided warmer and more sensitive caregiving. These researchers also tested new quality standards developed for the National Association of Family Child Care accreditation program (Modigliani & Bromer (1997). When settings were in compliance with these recommended age-weighted group size cut-offs, caregivers provided more positive caregiving. These findings make a case for regulating caregivers' education and training and for requiring that child-care homes not exceed recommended age-weighted group sizes.

Statistical Significance and Practical Importance

Until recently, significant findings were enough to demonstrate child-care effects to the policy community. Recently, however, debates about effect sizes have emerged in policy discussions of child care as well as other social programs (e.g., Layzer, Goodson, Bernstein, & Price, 2001). With respect to child care, Blau (1997), an economist, questioned whether regulable indicators of quality, for example, child–staff ratio, group size, and caregiver training, predict observed quality. Scarr (1999), a developmentalist, questioned whether any quality indicators predict child outcomes. In a review, she posited that "child care quality within the range of American child-care centers does not have important impacts on the development of children from ordinary homes" and that states should examine the impact of their regulations "on making child care affordable, available, and of sufficient quality to support good child development" (Scarr, 1999, p. 105).

Lamb (1998) critiqued the small-effects argument on conceptual grounds. He reminded developmentalists that "all aspects of behavioral development are multiply and redundantly determined, and, as a result, the absolute magnitude of each individual influence is likely to be quite small when all important factors are taken into account simultaneously" (p. 116). McCartney and Rosenthal (2000) critiqued the small-effects argument on practical grounds. They argued that even small effects with life and death consequences have practical consequences; for example, the effect size for the effect of aspirin in preventing heart attacks ($r = .03$) would be labeled small using an arbitrary numerical threshold, and yet the practical importance of this finding is great. Fabes et al. (2000) have suggested that small effects have practical importance if the effect is experienced by large groups of people, which is the case with respect to child care. McCartney and Rosenthal warn against embracing null findings, and, instead, suggest comparing effect sizes within and across studies. For example, in the NICHD study (NICHD ECCRN, 1999), child-care quality effects were about half the size of home quality effects. In this context, child-care effects hardly seem small.

Roles Played by Developmental Psychologists

This brief excursion through history highlights the conspicuous gap that characterizes prevailing political and scientific concerns about and goals for child care. Policymakers ask, "Are we providing enough child care so that parents on welfare can pursue employment undeterred?" Developmentalists ask, "Are we providing the kinds of child-care experiences that foster healthy growth and development?" Ironically, policymakers do care about children's experiences when Head Start is the focus of attention, as illustrated by the program's 25% funding set-aside for quality initiatives and on-going support for performance standards, literacy initiatives, and evaluation.

White (2002), in calling for a "politics of science," raised the intriguing question of whether science can ever shift the place of a program on the policy landscape. For our purposes, the question becomes one of moving child care closer to the developmental priorities that have guided the Head Start program. An examination of the roles developmentalists have played in Head Start suggests strategies to answer this question. Specifically, White and Phillips (2001) identified four roles: representation, demonstration, idealization, and evaluation. *Representation* involves building public awareness of an issue, problem, or underserved population; *demonstration* involves illustrating the potential outcomes of a program through model or demonstration projects; *idealization* involves portraying the broader possibilities of a program; and *evaluation* involves providing evidence on program effectiveness. Policymakers included social scientists in Head Start to foster its political success; and indeed Head Start is one of the most successful programs for children ever initiated, based on its longevity, funding levels, and bipartisan support. For this reason, an examination of these four roles as they pertain to child care offers a means to understand the disconnect between research and policy.

Representation

Representation refers to the use of research as a vehicle for building public awareness of an issue. A central role played by developmental psychologists during and since the 1960s has been to build public awareness and understanding of children's lives and needs. The ultimate purpose of these efforts to represent children through research is to mobilize public sentiment and public policy on their behalf. Although characterizations of poor children were instrumental to the development of Head Start (White and Phillips, 2001), which typically includes a child-care component, developmentalists have also attempted to influence child-care policy through broader representations of the development of all children. Researchers also have a long history of representing child-care programs and providers in studies aimed at describing the conditions and care that children experience when not in the care of their parents.

Representations of Children. Developmentalists who study child care have often found themselves in the position of representing the needs of children in the broader debates that subsume policies on child care. Perhaps the most long-standing example of this role is found in welfare reform debates. A central theme sounded by developmentalists has been the need to ensure that children are cared for in safe, developmentally beneficial settings, while their mothers participate in welfare-to-work programs. In 1967, for example, advocates for children were successful in attaching a requirement that child-care programs funded through the WIN program meet Federal Interagency Day Care Regulations (FIDCR). Child development scholars on the Federal Panel on Early Childhood, which was charged with drafting the regulations, represented the needs of children by arguing for small children–staff ratios (see Nelson, 1982 for an excellent history of the FIDCR). Representatives of the Department of Labor's Manpower Administration and the Bureau of the Budget vehemently and successfully objected to costly ratio provisions.

By the time of the major welfare reform overhaul of 1996, the issue of federal child-care regulations had long been moribund. The FIDCR were never fully implemented and, in 1981, were eliminated from all federal child-care legislation, effectively silencing the debate on this issue to the present day. However, other issues of central importance to children were up for discussion as a result of the anticipated large influx of new populations of children into child care, including infants. In addition to the topic of infant child care, active debates focused on whether child-care programs that are legally operating but generally not subject to state child-care regulations (e.g., care by relatives) should be eligible for public funds, whether mothers moving from public assistance to paid employment should be hired as child-care workers, and whether any monies would be set aside for quality improvement efforts.

Researchers were among the hundreds of individuals who testified as part of the 1996 welfare reform process, representing the needs of young children who were going to be placed in child care as a result of federally mandated maternal job training and work programs. The themes raised by developmental psychologists included the importance of quality child care, especially for children from impoverished families; the low supply of adequate infant child care; and the inequities that characterize the distribution of poor versus non-poor families into low versus higher quality child care (Burchinal, Roberts, Nabors, & Bryant, 1994; NICHD ECCRN, 1997b, 2002b; Phillips, Voran, Kisker, Whitebook, & Howes, 1994).

The Personal Responsibility and Work Opportunities Reconciliation Act of 1996 allows public funds to support child care in unregulated (but not illegal) programs, it mandates work (and thus child care) for parents of infants, and sets aside only 4% of the child-care funds for quality initiatives. It also, however, led to an increase in federal funding for child care by $4.5 billion over six years (Blank & Haskins, 2001). The open question raised by developmentalists today is *what* these increased dollars are purchasing and *whether* it is beneficial or detrimental for young children. Unfortunately, most of the large-scale evaluations of welfare reform effects on child outcomes (Morris, Huston, Duncan et al., 2001; Zaslow, Moore, Tout, Scarpa, & Vandivere, 2002) did not include adequate samples of infants and toddlers. The one study that allows us to get a glimpse of child care for this age group tells a mixed story (Coley, Chase-Lansdale, & Li-Grining 2001). Preschoolers in formal child-care centers (44% of the sample) typically received safe, stimulating, and nurturing care. Those in informal settings, particularly those that were not regulated (46% of the sample), often received unstimulating care from providers who were insensitive. The weekly costs of care across these two groups of arrangements, as reported by mothers, were surprisingly comparable.

Beyond the welfare context, developmental science has revealed more nuanced characterizations of early development that are also being fed into early childhood policy discussions, including those focused on child care. The National Academy of Science's report, *From Neurons to Neighborhoods* (Shonkoff & Phillips, 2000), summarized decades of research on early development into three central messages: while early development does not provide an indelible blueprint for adult outcomes, early damage can seriously limit future possibilities for growth; compensating for missed opportunities can be expensive and time-consuming; and initial pathways establish either a fragile or sturdy foundation upon which subsequent development is built. This report, in effect, identified what is at stake when children's early environments, including child care, fail to provide the nurturance, stimulation, and consistency that children need for healthy growth. The extent to which this portrait of early development will influence child-care policy is likely to hinge on the extent to which child care is portrayed less as a service for families and more as an intervention in young children's lives. Research that can accomplish this, as we discuss below, is just beginning to emerge.

Representations of Child Care. One of the earliest studies of child care was conducted by two early childhood experts from Teachers College (Reed & Raymond, 1929). The themes and concerns highlighted in this report are hauntingly similar to those sounded almost 50 years later in the 1972 National Council of Jewish Women's report, *Windows on Day Care* (Keyserling, 1972), and reiterated in numerous descriptive studies from the 1990s. Reed and Raymond, for example, studied day nurseries, nursery schools, and kindergartens located in six settlement houses in New York City (see Michel, 1999). They reported lack of professional qualifications among the staff, unacceptably large numbers of children per staff, poor hygiene and nutrition, and inadequate curricula. These studies, which read more like exposes than even-handed data gathering, clearly represented day care in a negative light. Although intended to alarm parents and compel policymakers to take corrective action, their predominant impact may have been to solidify public views of "institutional" child care as an undesirable service, acceptable only for families in desperate circumstances. They also cast child care as a custodial care service from which more legitimate initiatives, such as the WPA nurseries and the Lanham Act centers, needed to distance themselves.

The enduring impact of these early studies has been negligible as testified to by the current generation of such reports, which have confirmed the extensive variability in child-care staff and the quality of care they provide to children. What is different about these contemporary reports is that they have reached beyond center-based programs to include home-based arrangements and linked variation in quality to developmental outcomes, thus documenting the pervasive nature of the uneven quality of child care and its consequences for child development.

Developmental psychologists who study child care are not, however, a unified group and their differing perspectives have fueled substantial controversy and ambivalence about child care. One of the most lively illustrations of this derives from the so-called day-care wars, launched with Belsky's (1986) article for the journal of the National Center for Clinical Infant Programs. Because Belsky had co-authored a review of child-care research (Belsky & Steinberg, 1978), his concern was taken seriously by academics and by the public. He argued that infant day care posed a risk to mother–infant attachment and fostered aggressive behavior. A maelstrom of media attention included headlines that read, "Is Day Care Ruining Our Kids?" and "Brave New World: How Day Care Harms Children." Replies by other developmental psychologists (Phillips et al., 1987; Fein & Fox, 1988) and counter replies by Belsky (1987) provided a confusing array of representations of the developmental consequences of infant child care, alarmed many parents, and reinforced the views of many decisionmakers who did not want to lend their support to child-care legislation.

Although this controversy led directly to the initiation of the NICHD Study of Early Child Care in 1990 (NICHD ECCRN, 2002a), research on child care continues to be portrayed negatively in the media. Recent media coverage of evidence from the NICHD Study reporting both positive and negative consequences of child care (NICHD ECCRN, 2001a, 2001b) emphasized the negative and reignited the day-care wars with headlines such as, "New Study Critiquing Child Care Irks Parents" (*San Fransisco Chronicle*, April 20, 2001) and "Researchers in Child Care Study Clash Over Findings" (*Los Angeles Times*, April 26, 2001). In the process, developmental science and the scientists themselves were sometimes cast in unflattering terms.

Demonstration

Demonstration refers to psychologists' role in illustrating the potential outcomes of a program or policy through model projects. Psychologists and early childhood educators have played a variety of roles in the support of model child-care centers, from constituent to director. Sometimes, these centers are affiliated with universities and referred to as laboratory schools; in fact, one of us (McCartney) served as the director of the University of New Hampshire Child Study & Development Center. The purpose of laboratory schools is three-fold: (1) to serve as site for pre-service teacher training in early childhood education; (2) to serve as research sites; and (3) to serve as model schools (McBride, 1996). Osborn's (1991) history of these programs links their origin, in the early 1920s, with early research on child development; it is in this sense that these schools served as laboratories. For example, Gessell's work on maturation at Yale, Parten's work on play at the University of Minnesota, Wellman and Skeels work on intelligence at Iowa all were conducted in university lab schools (McBride, 1996). The most famous laboratory school is no doubt the one John Dewey founded at the University of Chicago.

In the mid-1960s, a number of model schools were founded as intervention programs for poor children, including preschool programs designed by Bereiter and Engelmann (1966) and Gray and Klaus (1965). Bettye Caldwell and Julius Richmond established one of the first of these university-based intervention preschools at Syracuse University in 1964. The Children's Center was portrayed as a "demonstration day-care center" for young children under 3 years from low-income homes with employed mothers (Caldwell & Richmond, 1965). The project was motivated by two pressures, one from employed mothers who needed good child care, especially for their infants, and the other by social scientists like Caldwell who hoped to test new ideas about the importance of early experience. The nation's ambivalence about child care is reflected in Caldwell's own analysis of the center: "We continued to seem uncertain about whether we must show the child-welfare field that children participating in our program were not harmed, or whether we could hope to demonstrate they showed significant developmental gains" (p. 33). Nevertheless, the Syracuse University school lab served as an influential model program, not only because it was the first to link child care with intervention for children from families with few economic resources, but also because of the research component that was so integral to the school (see Caldwell & Freyer, 1982). Other programs with this dual mission followed, notably the Abecedarian Project at the University of North Carolina with demonstrated child-care effects for cognitive and language development from early childhood through adolescence (Campbell & Ramey, 1994; Ramey & Ramey, 1990).

As is true across diverse arenas of child policy and practice, European countries have also served to demonstrate new possibilities for child care

(Kamerman, 1995). The legacy of the Montessori Children's Houses in Italy has been present in the United States for the past hundred years (Michel, 1999). Italy's influence continues with the Reggio Emilia Approach, developed in a northern town by Loris Malaguzzi and his followers (Edwards, Gandini, & Forman, 1998). Educators from all over the world have visited Reggio Schools to observe young children working collaboratively on projects that they have co-constructed with their teachers (see Gardner, 1993; Katz, 1993). The Reggio phenomenon illustrates the role that model schools still play in early care and education practice.

Idealization

The third role played by developmental psychologists who have contributed to Head Start involves articulating why a particular policy is the "right thing to do" (White & Phillips, 2001, p. 96) and what its broader possibilities might include. This blends what others have referred to as the knowledge-building and problem-exploring functions of research (see National Research Council, 1978). The goal is to direct fundamental understandings about development toward the accomplishment of social goals. For Head Start, this consisted of articulating the program's possibilities for improving child health and well-being, empowering poor parents, and serving as a catalyst for community action.

Given the more diffuse boundaries of child care, it is less obvious that psychologists have provided idealized views of what might be possible beyond urging policymakers to consider child care as a form of early intervention with all of the possibilities that have been envisioned for Head Start (Caldwell, 1991). There is, however, one striking parallel between the early history of Head Start and the contemporary context of child-care policy that warrants discussion. It links the high hopes for IQ modification that captivated public discussions of early intervention during the 1960s and the current fascination with early brain development.

As described by White and Phillips (2001) and others (Vinofskis, 1999; Zigler & Trickett, 1978; Zigler & Freedman, 1987), psychologists managed to graft existing theory about IQ modification (Bloom, 1964; Hunt, 1961) onto Head Start at a time when this fledgling program was seeking public acceptance. In a reminiscent fashion, the brief discussion of early brain development in the *Starting Points* report issued by the Carnegie Task Force on Meeting the Needs of Young Children in 1994 captured the public imagination and set in motion a train of events that aligned synaptic growth with early intervention (see Thompson & Nelson, 2001, for an excellent account of this story). Child-care advocates understandably seized the opportunity to justify their calls for quality improvement. Ultimately, the controversy that ensued about what many viewed as a misapplication of science for advocacy purposes (see, for example, Bruer, 1999; Kagan, 1998) led the U.S. Department of Health and Human Services to commission the Board on Children, Youth, and Families of the National Research Council and the Institute of Medicine (of which Sheldon White was the first chair) to conduct the study that become *Neurons to Neighborhoods* (Shonkoff & Phillips, 2000).

It is difficult to account fully for the prominence of these strands of research in policy discussions about early intervention and child care. One plausible scenario is that IQ modification in the mid-1960s and synaptic development in the mid-1990s provided scientifically grounded, uncontestable, hard-wired phenomena that everyone could agree society should promote. The outcomes are easily measured (for IQ) or visualized (for synapses), thus trumping other less tangible goals in the minds of policymakers who seek proof positive of program effects. In the case of early brain development in particular, the slides of "deprived" and "nondeprived" brains that were shown in Congressional hearing rooms and state capitols were extremely compelling to policymakers who are not well grounded in developmental science. Supporting early intervention programs almost put them on a par with neurosurgeons, sculpting brain development as it unfolds. As a result, interventions ranging from home visitation to pre-kindergarten programs to the gift of Mozart tapes to all new parents proliferated around the country.

It remains a stretch, however, to suggest that child-care policy – as distinct from other early childhood policies, such as Head Start and home visitation – benefited from this moment when neuroscience and early intervention met up, however dubiously. In fact, the virtual lack of child-care policies developed in response to the romance with neuroscience once again illustrates the extent to which child care is not viewed as child developmentalists view it, namely as an influential environment for early development.

Evaluation

The fourth role played by developmental psychologists, as described by White and Phillips (2001), involves them in the design, implementation, and interpretation of evaluation studies of Head Start. As with idealization, because child care is not an identifiable program, it has almost entirely eluded the evaluation enterprise. The NDCS still offers the only example of experimental research on child care as it is typically experienced in the United States. Evaluation research has historically been reserved for discrete, often model, programs with clear goals, such as the Perry Preschool Project, the Abecedarian Project, and the Infant Health and Development Program. A recent exception is an evaluation of Tulsa, Oklahoma's universal, school-based pre-kindergarten program, which has demonstrated the success with which systemic, population-wide interventions can foster school readiness (Gormley & Gayor, 2005; Gormley & Phillips, 2003).

This situation may be changing. Although child care remains outside the focus of ongoing evaluations of early childhood programs, some of these evaluations include assessments of child-care arrangements for children in the comparison and treatment. For example, the Congressionally mandated Head Start Impact Study, which will involve over 5,000 3- and 4-year-old children from a stratified, national sample of Head Start grantees, will include on-site observations of all forms of nonparental child care used by the children in the randomly assigned control group. Information about the types and hours of care used by the treatment children (those randomly assigned to Head Start) during hours when they are not in Head Start will also be gathered (see http://www.acf.dhhs.gov/programs/core/ongoing_research/ hs.impact_intro.html). It is significant that evaluation funds are being used to assess child care, though it is also important to understand that the child-care data are not experimental data.

A closer link between evaluation research and child care is exemplified by a new study of child-care subsidy strategies, conducted by the Manpower Demonstration and Research Corporation (MDRC). The study is focused on financial issues, specifically understanding how states' systems for subsidizing child care can be designed to accomplish the dual goals of improving children's well-being and supporting the employment of low-income parents. Four sites will be selected to participate in this multiyear random assignment study, which will assess such policy mechanisms as the levels of child-care subsidies or families' copayments and "tiered reimbursements" to child-care providers depending upon the quality of care they offer. To address the effects of these policies, data collection will include assessments of the child-care environments used by subsidized families.

Perhaps the longstanding gap between evaluations of intervention programs and correlational studies of child care is narrowing. This is an extremely promising development. It affords the opportunity to align variation in child-care quality with variation in the quality of early intervention programs, to consider this full spectrum of quality as it affects the development of treatment and comparison children, to address questions of whether and how typical child care used simultaneously with early intervention programs mediates their influence on developmental outcomes, and to evaluate the influence of giving low-income families access to higher quality child care through subsidy enhancements. Answers to these questions are needed to focus policymakers' attention on child care as an environment within which young children receive or fail to receive the interactions and experiences that foster their development.

Lessons Learned and Opportunities for the Future

Disparities between the driving issues addressed by research and policy are hardly restricted to child care. Science holds an uneasy place in an arena that White and Phillips characterize as "relying on bargaining, obfuscation, and compromise" (2001, p. 83). As others in our field have recently noted (McCartney & Rosenthal, 2000; Shonkoff, 2000), science has a minor part in the larger dramas that drive social policy. These dramas tend to be driven by social agendas and values through which scientific evidence is filtered and either used or ignored. This has certainly been true of child-care policy for which the fate of research has been profoundly shaped by its relevance to the larger agendas that subsume discussions of child care.

Even when research is woven into the fabric of policy decisions, it is often in a manner that highlights conflicting findings, fails to distinguish sound evidence from speculation, and obfuscates the practical significance of the findings. Research on child care has fallen prey to each of these hazards. Inconsistent portrayals of child care's developmental consequences within the scientific community have fueled controversy (as well as additional research) and confounded policymakers for whom the stakes associated with making bad decisions about allocating public resources are extremely high. Early speculation about the effects of infant day care framed policy debates about child care in the language of risk, which is only now being clarified by empirical evidence from the NICHD Study of Early Child Care and Youth Development. And, presentations of correlational data to support calls for greater investments in child-care quality have failed to address policymakers' practical questions about, for example, thresholds below which development is harmed or the economic payoffs that can be expected from quality improvement initiatives.

Applying the framework provided by White and Phillips (2001) to the relationship between child-care policy and research offers several insights into the policy–science gap and affords hope that the future holds opportunities for a more constructive alliance. The central lesson from history is the mismatch between the incentives guiding policy on child care and the concerns of scientists who seek to apply science to policy. In recent years, child-care policy has evolved in the context of welfare reform, which created incentives to enhance child-care supply, respond to parents' needs for flexibility, and reduce costs of care. Efforts to improve child-care quality – the facet of child care most strongly associated with its developmental effects – are inconsistent with efforts to increase supply and reduce costs. Even recent evidence raising concerns about the amount of children's exposure to child care is unlikely to alter the direction of public policy, given that the natural responses (e.g., more generous family leave policies, resumption of exemptions from welfare reform for mothers of young children) fly in the face of current policies.

To the extent that questions about child care and child development surface in the policy arena, they are now focused on the "magnitude of effects." Are the consequences of child care for children, documented in the research literature, large enough to warrant public investments in those dimensions of care (e.g., small ratios of children to adults, educated teachers, perhaps fewer hours) that matter for children? McCartney and Rosenthal (2000) make the case for an affirmative response. Yet, because child-care policy is decoupled from goals for children, the policy response has largely been negative. Clearly, continuing to conduct and communicate our research as we presently do is not a viable option if we accept White's (2002) proposal that we "recognize developmental psychology's agency . . . as a cooperative endeavor that has particular relevance to the problems and needs of contemporary society." So, what can we do? Each of the roles identified by White and Phillips (2001) suggests an answer.

The representation function of science is descriptive in nature and political in intent. The challenge is one of aligning the representations provided by research with prevailing political issues. In the case of child care, two issues are now prominent: welfare reform and early literacy. Welfare reform directs attention to the role of child care in either supporting or undermining its adult-focused goal of promoting employment. Representations of the child care that is purchased with federal welfare dollars are more likely to capture policymakers' interest than are broad representations of the vast variation in quality that characterizes child care more generally. Forthcoming reports from the federally funded National Study of Low-Income Child Care (Collins, Layzer, Kreader et al., 2000) will provide relevant evidence. These data may also be used to raise equity issues regarding access to quality care on behalf of welfare families as compared with other low-income families, as in past efforts to assess social class differences in access to quality care (NICHD ECCRN, 1997b; Phillips et al., 1994). Going one step further, analyses that link differing patterns of reliance on welfare-subsidized child care to the success with which families make the transition to and sustain employment would likely be of high interest to policymakers.

With regard to early literacy, efforts to focus representations of child care on dimensions that promote early literacy (e.g., language interactions, time spent reading) stand a greater chance of influencing policy discussions than do more generic portrayals of child-care quality. Along these lines, forthcoming data from the *Who Stays? Who Leaves? Longitudinal Study of the Child Care Workforce* conducted in Alameda County, California, reveal highly variable adult English literacy levels among both subsidized and nonsubsidized child-care providers, as well as no differences in literacy across Head Start, state-funded pre-kindergarten, and other center-based teachers (Phillips, Crowell, & Whitebook, 2003). This study is designed to provide a portrait of the early care and education workforce across both home- (60 licensed and 12 unlicensed home-based providers) and center-based (83 teachers and 42 directors) arrangements, serving low-income (subsidized and nonsubsidized) and middle-income children, as it changes over the course of three waves of data collection between August 2001 and March 2003. Importantly, adult literacy levels correlated with the quality of the language environments experienced by infants, toddlers, and preschoolers in both home- and center-based child care.

The question of demonstration and child care deserves some serious examination. There is a wide gap between child care in practice and both laboratory schools and early childhood demonstrations such as the Abecedarian Project and even Caldwell's Syracuse University Center. Exaggerated claims about what child care can accomplish based on these hot-house programs are unwarranted. In the long run, they can lull decisionmakers into complacency about modest investments and create a high stakes environment for accountability (Shonkoff, 2000). Perhaps for these reasons, demonstration and model programs remain aligned with the rhetoric of early intervention, not with child care. Even within this realm the leap from demonstration to scaled-up early interventions such as Head Start has been the topic of controversy (Zigler & Styfco, 1994).

This leaves developmentalists with the challenging task of identifying what a child-care demonstration ought to look like. Following the isolated example of the National Day Care Study, it could focus on systemically manipulating policy-relevant facets of child care and examining child outcomes. Beyond this, it could address the thorny issue of how best to meet the needs of children in the context of working families, an issue that the early intervention literature has largely set aside (see Phillips & Cabrera, 1996). In effect, this is the orientation of the new child-care subsidy demonstrations. Careful studies of small or large segments of the child care offered by other countries (see above) come quite close to demonstrating possibilities for child care in the United States. In practice, however, effective efforts to deploy the demonstration role of science, aligned as it has been with programs that are significantly better endowed than typical child-care programs, toward the goal of exploring possibilities for child care remain elusive. This illustrates, yet again, a disjuncture between persistent demands to "scale-up" child care to meet the needs of working parents and the necessarily tight focus of demonstration projects.

The idealization role played by developmentalists who have worked closely with Head Start is also problematic when grafted onto child-care policy. As with the demonstration function, it is difficult to envision capacities for a program with boundaries as diffuse as those for child care. The brief romance with neuroscience as a rationale for expecting more of child care had barely detectable repercussions. For reasons well articulated by Thompson and Nelson (2001), this is probably a blessing in disguise. As with leaps from hot-house interventions to national programs, leaps from child care to synaptic development are not only irresponsible, but also run the risk of setting loose a backlash that would likely further undermine public confidence in child-care programs.

A more productive approach to considering broader possibilities for child care focuses less on what investments in child care could accomplish and more on what Prewitt (1983) and Weiss (1980) have referred to as the subversion or enlightenment function of science. The enlightenment function addresses the value of science in bringing new concepts and issues to public and policy attention. It directs attention not to answering questions but to asking them. Some examples of this within the child-care field have involved expanding notions of quality care to encompass the adult work environment, specifically, wages (Whitebook, Howes, & Phillips 1990) and bringing concepts of equality and equity to bear on discussions of access to care (Phillips et al., 1994; ECCRN, 1997b). The intent, as with the idealization function, is to push policy discussions beyond their conventional boundaries to open up new possibilities for action. In the case of child care, the successful subversion of prevailing policy premises is likely to involve decoupling child care from welfare policy, bringing new questions and concepts to the quality debate, and bridging the illogical disjunction between early intervention (e.g., Head Start, Early Head Start, Early Reading First) and child-care policies.

Bringing the evaluation enterprise to studies of child care is a daunting and controversial task. On-going debates about how best to evaluate Head Start (see White & Phillips, 2001) offer important, but sobering lessons for the child-care field. Yet, it may be through this role that the greatest opportunities for bringing developmental goals more directly into discussions of child-care policy will emerge. Current evaluation studies are blurring the lines between research on early intervention and research on child care. In the process, child-care environments will necessarily be placed along a spectrum that includes the best of what government provides. This spectrum will then be linked to developmental outcomes that all agree are desirable (e.g., preliteracy, constructive social skills). Perhaps of greater importance are the possibilities that these data afford to conduct the kinds of cost-benefit analyses that will highlight, for budget-conscious policymakers, what varying levels of investment can produce. As we've been reminded by McCartney and Rosenthal, "when we allocate funds to programs that do not work, we waste precious resources. When we fail to allocate funds to programs that can and do work, we allow children to be at risk" (2000, p. 179).

We close this chapter on an optimistic note. Although research will always be an orphan child at the table where policy is made, in the end, both enterprises are involved in testing hypotheses about effective investments in the lives of children. Child care in today's policy discussions is primarily tied to investments focused on work as family policy. Child care in today's research discussions is viewed primarily as a context for development as well as a context for intervention for disadvantaged children. These are not inherently incompatible perspectives, despite that fact that they have evolved in parallel. We believe that representations of child care that are better aligned with prevailing policy concerns, efforts to portray the possibilities child care offers to children as well as families, and evaluations that demonstrate the lost opportunities of current investments in child care can each serve as strategies for shifting policy and research toward converging trajectories.

Acknowledgments

We are grateful to Bettye Caldwell for her valuable insights into the early history of research on child care and to Tom Cassells and Kristen L. Bub for their help with background research. We are also grateful to the other participants from this conference, whose comments and insights informed our work.

References

Ahnert, L., & Lamb, M. E. (2003). Shared care: Establishing a balance between home and child care settings. *Child Development 74*, 1044–1049.

Barnett W. S. (1998). Long-term effects on cognitive development and school success. In W. S. Barnett & S. S. Boocock (Eds.), *Early Care and Education for Children in Poverty: Promises, Programs, and Long-Term Results* (pp. 11–44). Albany: State University of New York.

Belsky, J. (1986). Infant day care: A cause for concern? *Bulletin of the National Center for Clinical Infant Programs 7*, 1, 1–7.

Belsky, J. (1987). Risks remain. *Bulletin of the National Center for Clinical Infant Programs 7*, 3, 22–24.

Belsky, J., & Steinberg, L. (1978). The effects of daycare: A critical review. *Child Development 49*, 929–949.

Bereiter, C., & Englemann, S. (1966). *Teaching Disadvantaged Children in the Preschool.* Englewood Cliffs, NJ: Prentice-Hall.

Blank, R. M., & Haskins, R. (Eds.). (2001). *The New World of Welfare.* Washington, DC: Brookings Institution Press.

Blau, D. M. (1997). The production of quality in child care centers. *Journal of Human Resources 32*, 354–386.

Blau, D. M. (2001). *The Child Care Problem: An Economic Analysis.* New York: Russell Sage Foundation.

Bloom, B. S. (1994). *Stability and Change in Human Characteristics.* New York: Wiley.

Bronfenbrenner, U. (1979). *The Ecology of Human Development.* Cambridge, MA: Harvard University Press.

Bruer, J. (1999). *The Myth of the First Three Years of Life.* New York: Free Press.

Bryant, D. M., Burchinal, M., Lau, L. B., & Sparling, J. J. (1994). Family and classroom correlates of Head Start children's developmental outcomes. *Early Childhood Research Quality 9*, 289–309.

Burchinal, M. R., Roberts, J. E., Nabors, L. Q., & Bryant, D. M. (1994). Quality of center child care and infant cognitive and language development. *Child Development 67*, 606–620.

Cahan, E. (1989). *Past Caring: A History of U.S. Preschool Care and Education for the Poor, 1820–1965.* New York: National Center for Children in Poverty.

Caldwell, B. M. (1991). Educare: New product, new future. *Journal of Developmental and Behavioral Pediatrics 12*, 3, 199–205.

Caldwell, B. M. (1998). *Child Care Research: Past, Present, and Future.* Unpublished manuscript, University of Arkansas.

Caldwell, B. M., & Freyer, M. (1982). Day care and early education. In B. Spodek (Ed.), *Handbook of Research in Early Childhood Education* (pp. 341–373). New York: Free Press.

Caldwell, B. M., & Richmond, J. B, (1965). Programmed day care for the very young child–A preliminary report. *Child Welfare 44*, 134–142.

Campbell, F. A., & Ramey, C. T. (1994). Effects of early intervention on intellectual and academic achievement: A follow-up study of children from low-incomes families. *Child Development 65*, 684–698.

134   *Deborah Phillips and Kathleen McCartney*

Carnegie Task Force on Meeting the Needs of Young Children. (1994). *Starting Points: Meeting the Needs of Our Youngest Children*. New York: Carnegie Corporation of New York.

Caughy, M. O., DiPietro, J. A., & Strobino, D. M. (1994). Day-care participation as a protective factor in the cognitive development of low-income children. *Child Development 65*, 457–471.

Clarke-Stewart, K., Vandell, D. L., Burchinal, M., O'Brien, M., & McCartney, K. (2002). Do regulatable features of child-care homes affect children's development? *Early Childhood Research Quarterly 17*, 52–86.

Cohen S. S. (2001). *Championing Child Care*. New York: Columbia University Press.

Coley, R. L., Chase-Lansdale, P. L., & Li-Grining, C. P. (2001). *Child Care in the Era of Welfare Reform: Quality, Choices, and Preferences*. (Policy Brief No. 01–4). Baltimore, MD: Johns Hopkins University, Welfare, Children, and Families: A Three-City Study.

Collins, A. M., Layzer, J. I., Kreader, J. L. et al. (2000). *National Study of Child Care for Low-Income Families: State and Community Substudy Interim Report*. Prepared for the U.S. Department of Health and Human Services, Administration for Children and Families. Cambridge, MA: Abt Associates.

Crockenberg, S. C. (2003). Rescuing the baby from the bathwater: How gender and temperament (may) influence how child care affects child development. *Child Development 74*, 1034–1038.

DHHS (2002). Fourth Annual TANF Report to Congress.

Edwards, C., Gandini, L., & Forman, G. (Eds.). (1998). *The Hundred Languages of Children: The Reggio Emilia Approach–Advanced Reflections*. Westport, CT: Ablex.

Fabes, R. A., Martin, C. L., Hanish, L. D., & Updegraff, K. A. (2000). Criteria for evaluating the significance of developmental research in the twenty-first century: Force and counterforce. *Child Development 71*, 212–221.

Fein, G., & Fox, N. (Eds.). (1988). Infant day care [Special Issue]. *Early Childhood Research Quarterly 3*, 3, 227–336.

Galinsky, E., Howes, C., Kontos, S., & Shinn, M. (1994). *The Study of Children in Family Child Care and Relative Care*. New York: Families and Work Institute.

Gardner, H. (1993). Complementary perspectives on Reggio Emilia. In C. Edwards, L. Gandini, & G. Forman (Eds.), *The Hundred Languages of Children* (pp. ix–xiii). Norwood, NJ: Ablex.

Gormley, W. T., & Gayer, T. (2005). Promoting school readiness in Oklahoma: An evaluation of Tulsa's pre-K program. *Journal of Human Resources*.

Gormley, W. T., & Phillips, D. (2003). *The Effects of Universal pre-K in Oklahoma: Research Highlights and Policy Implications*. CROCUS Working Paper # 2. Washington, DC: Georgetown University.

Gormley, W. T. (1995). *Everybody's Children: Child Care as a Public Problem*. Washington, DC: Brookings Institution.

Gray, S. W., & Klaus, R. A. (1965). An experimental preschool program for culturally deprived children. *Child Development 36*, 887–898.

Greenberg, P. (1969/1990a). *The Devil Has Slippery Shoes: A Biased Biography of the Child Development Group of Mississippi (CDGM): A Story of Maximum Feasible Poor Parent Participation*. Washington, DC: Youth Policy Institute. (Original work published 1969.)

Greenberg, P. (1990b). Head Start part of a multi-pronged anti-poverty effort for children and their families . . . Before the beginning: A participants' view. *Young Children 45*, 41–52.

Grubb, W. N., & Lazerson, M. (1982). *Broken Promises: How Americans Fail Their Children*. New York: Basic Books.

Harms, T., & Clifford, R. M. (1980). *The Early Childhood Environment Rating Scale*. New York: Teachers College Press.

Harvard University Project Zero and Reggio Children (2001). *Making Learning Visible*. Cambridge, MA: Project Zero.

Hayes, C. D. (Ed.). (1982). *Making Policies for Children: A Study of the Federal Process*. Washington, DC: National Academy Press.

Helburn, S. W., & Bergmann, B. R. (2002). *American's Childcare Problem*. New York: Palgrave.

Hofferth, S. L. (1993). The 101st Congress: An emerging agenda for children in poverty. In J. Chafel (Ed.), *Child Poverty and Public Policy* (pp. 203–243). Washington, DC: Urban Institute Press.

Howes, C. (1983). Caregiver's behavior in center and family day care. *Journal of Applied Developmental Psychology 4*, 99–107.

Howes, C., Smith, E., & Galinsky, E. (1995). *The Florida Child Care Quality Improvement Study*. New York: Families and Work Institute.

Hunt, J. McV. (1961). *Intelligence and Experience*. New York: Ronald Press.

Joffe, C. (1977). *Friendly Intruders: Child Care Professional and Family Life*. Berkeley, CA: University of California Press.

Kagan, J. (1998). *Three Seductive Ideas*. Cambridge, MA: Harvard University Press.

Kamerman, S. B. (1995). Child and family policy: An international overview. In E. Zigler, S. L. Kagan, & N. W. Hall (Eds.), *Children, Families, and Government* (pp. 31–50). New York: Cambridge University Press.

Kamerman, S. B., & Kahn, A. J. (1987). *Child Care: Facing the Hard Choices*. Dover, MA: Auburn House.

Katz, L. (1993). What can we learn from Reggio Emilia? In C. Edwards, L. Gandini, & G. Forman (Eds.), *The Hundred Languages of Children* (pp. 19–37). Norwood, NJ: Ablex.

Keyserling, M. D. (1972). *Windows on Day Care*. New York: National Council of Jewish Women.

Lamb, M. E. (1998). Nonparental child care: Context, quality, correlates, and consequences. In W. Damon (Ed.), *Handbook of Child Psychology: Vol. 4* (pp. 73–133). New York: Wiley.

Layzer, J. I., Goodson, B. D., Bernstein, L., & Price, C. (2001). *National Evaluation of Family Support Programs, Final Report Volume A: The Meta-Analysis*. Cambridge, MA: Abt Associates.

Love, J. M., Harrison, L., Sagi-Schwartz, A., van Ijzendoorn, M. H., Ross, C., Ungerer, J. A. et al. (2003). Child care quality matters: How conclusions may vary with context. *Child Development 74*, 1021–1033.

McBride, B. A. (1996). University-based child development laboratory programs: Emerging issues and challenges. *Early Childhood Education Journal 24*, 17–21.

McCartney, K. (in press). The family-child care mesosystem. In K. A. Clarke-Stewart & J. Dunn (Eds.), New York: Cambridge University Press.

McCartney, K., & Galanopoulos, A. (1988). Child care and attachment: A new frontier the second time around. *American Journal of Orthopsychiatry 58*, 16–24.

McCartney, K., & Rosenthal, R. (2000). Effect size, practical importance, and social policy for children. *Child Development 71*, 173–180.

McCartney, K., Scarr, S., Phillips, D., Grajek, S., & Schwarz, J. C. (1982). Environmental differences among day care centers and their effects on children's development. In E. F. Zigler & E. W. Gordon (Eds.), *Day Care: Scientific and Social Policy Issues* (pp. 135–156). Boston: Auburn House.

McClelland, G. H., & Judd, C. M. (1993). Statistical difficulties of detecting interactions and moderator effects. *Psychological Review 114*, 376–390.

Michel, S. (1999). *Children's Interests/Mother's Rights: The Shaping of America's Child Care Policy.* New Haven, CT: Yale University Press.

Modigliani, K., & Bromer, J. (1997). *The Providers' Self-Study Workbook: Quality Standards for NAFCC Accreditation.* Boston, MA: Wheelock Family Child Care Project.

Mondale, W. F. (2001, November). *Politics and the Well-Being of Children.* Presentation at the Mondale Lectures on Public Service. Minneapolis, MN: University of Minnesota.

Morris, P. A., Huston, A. C., Duncan, G. J., Crosby, D. A., & Bos, J. M. (2001, March). *How Welfare and Work Policies Affect Children: A Synthesis of Research.* NY: Manpower Demonstration Research Corp.

Nelson, J. R. (1982). The Federal Interagency Day Care Requirements. In C. D. Hayes (Ed.), *Making Policies for Children: A Study of the Federal Process* (pp. 151–199). Washington, DC: National Academy Press.

Newcombe, N. S. (2003). Some controls control too much. *Child Development 74*, 1050–1052.

NICHD Early Child Care Research Network. (1996). Characteristics of infant child care: Factors contributing to positive caregiving. *Early Childhood Research Quarterly 11*, 269–306.

NICHD Early Child Care Research Network. (1997a). The effects of infant child care on infant–mother attachment security: Results of the NICHD Study of Early Child Care. *Child Development 68*, 860–879.

NICHD Early Child Care Research Network. (1997b). Poverty and patterns of child care. In J. Brooks-Gunn & G. Duncan (Eds.). *Consequences of Growing Up Poor* (pp. 100–131). New York: Russell Sage Foundation.

NICHD Early Child Care Research Network. (1998). Early child care and self-control, compliance and problem behavior at twenty-four and thirty-six months. *Child Development 69*, 3, 1145–1170.

NICHD Early Child Care Research Network. (1999). Child outcomes when child care center classes meet recommended standards for quality. *American Journal of Public Health 89*, 1072–1077.

NICHD Early Child Care Research Network. (2000a). The relation of child care to cognitive and language development. *Child Development 71*, 960–980.

NICHD Early Child Care Research Network. (2000b). Characteristics and quality of child care for toddlers and preschoolers. *Applied Developmental Science 4*, 116–135.

NICHD Early Child Care Research Network. (2001a, April). Quality of child care and child outcomes. Paper presented at the biennial meeting of the Society for Research in Child Development, Minneapolis, Minnesota.

NICHD Early Child Care Research Network. (2001b, April). Further exploration of the detected effects of quantity of early child care on socioemotional adjustment. Paper presented at the biennial meeting of the Society for Research in Child Development, Minneapolis, Minnesota.

NICHD Early Child Care Research Network. (2002a). The NICHD Study of Early Child Care: Contexts of development and developmental outcomes over the first seven years of life. In J. Brooks-Gunn and L. J. Berlin (Eds.), *Young Children's Education, Health, and Development: Profile and Synthesis Project*. Washington, DC: U.S. Department of Education.

NICHD Early Child Care Research Network. (2002b). Child-care structure → process → outcome: Direct and indirect effects of child-care quality on young children's development. *Psychological Science 13*, 199–206.

NICHD Early Child Care Research Network. (2002c). Early child care and children's development prior to school entry: Results from the NICHD Study of Early Child Care. *American Educational Research Journal 39*, 133–164.

National Research Council (1978). *The Federal Investment in Knowledge of Social Problems. Vol. 1: Study Project Report*. Study Project on Social Research and Development, Assembly of Behavioral and Social Sciences. Washington, DC: National Academy of Sciences.

Osborn, D. K. (1991). *Early Childhood Education in Historical Perspective* (3rd ed.). Athens, GA: Education Associates.

Peisner-Feinberg, E. S., & Burchinal, M. R. (1997). Relations between preschool children's child-care experiences and concurrent development: The Cost, Quality, and Outcomes Study. *Merrill–Palmer Quarterly 43*, 451–477.

Phillips, D. (1984). Day care: Promoting collaboration between research and policy-making. *Journal of Applied Developmental Psychology 5*, 91–113.

Phillips, D. (1991). With a little help: Children in poverty and child care. In A. Huston (Ed.), *Children in Poverty: Child Development and Public Policy* (pp. 158–189). New York: Cambridge University Press.

Phillips, D. (2001, November). *Child Care: Then and Now*. Presentation at the Mondale Lectures on Public Service. Minneapolis, MN: University of Minnesota.

Phillips, D., & Adams, G. (2001). Child care for our youngest children. *The Future of Children 11*, 1, 53–62.

Phillips, D., & Cabrera, N. (1996). *Beyond the Blueprint: Directions for Research on Head Start Families*. Washington, DC: National Academy Press.

Phillips, D., & Whitebook, M. (2003, April) *Who Leaves? Who Stays? Stability and Quality of the Child Care Workforce through Time*. Paper presented at the meetings of the Society for Research in Child Development, Tampa, FL, April 24–27, 2003.

Phillips, D. & Zigler, E. (1987). The checkered history of federal child care regulation. In E. Rothkopf (Ed.), *Review of Research in Education* (Vol. 14, pp. 3–41). Washington, DC: American Educational Research Association.

Phillips, D., Crowell, N., & Whitebook, M. (2003, April). *Who Leaves? Who Stays? The Child Care Workforce over Time*. Paper presented at the Meeting of the Society for Research in Child Development, Tampa, FL, April 24–27, 2003.

Phillips, D., Lande, J., & Goldberg, M. (1990). The state of child care regulation: A comparative analysis. *Early Childhood Research Quarterly 5*, 151–179.

Phillips, D., McCartney, K., Scarr, S., & Howes, C. (1987). Selective review of infant day care research: A cause for concern. *Bulletin of the National Center for Clinical Infant Programs 7*, 3, 18–21.

Phillips, D., Mekos, M., Scarr, S., McCartney, & K. Abbott-Shim, M. (2001). Within and beyond the classroom door: Assessing quality in child care centers. *Early Childhood Research Quarterly 15*, 475–496.

Phillips, D., Voran, M., Kisker, E., Whitebook, M., & Howes, C. (1994). Child care for children in poverty: Opportunity or inequity? *Child Development 65*, 472–492.

Phillips, D., Whitebook, M., & Howes, C. (1992). The social policy context of child care: Effects on quality. *American Journal of Community Psychology 20*, 1, 25–51.

Prewitt, K. (1983). Subverting policy premises. In D. Callahan & B. Jennings (Ed.), *Ethics, the Social Sciences, and Policy Analysis* (pp. 293–304). New York: Plenum Press.

Public Agenda (2000). *Necessary Compromises: How Parents, Employers, and Children's Advocates View Child Care Today*. New York: Public Agenda.

Ramey, C. T., & Ramey, S. L. (1990). Intensive educational intervention for children of poverty. *Intelligence 14*, 1–9.

Reed, M. E., & Raymond, E. M. (1929). *Day Nurseries, Nursery Schools, and Kindergartens in Six Settlements in New York City*. National Federation of Settlements and Neighborhood Centers collection, supp. 1, box 109, folder 15., SWHA.

Rothman, S. M. (1973). Other people's children: The day-care experience in America. *The Public Interest 30*.

Ruopp, R., Travers, J., Glantz, F., & Coelen, G. (1977). *Children at the Center.* Cambridge, MA: Abt Associates.

Scarr, S. (1999, April). *What Can We Tell Working Parents?* Paper presented at the biennial meeting of the Society for Research in Child Development, Albuquerque, NM.

Shonkoff, J. P. (2000). Science, policy, and practice: Three cultures search of a shared mission. *Child Development 71*, 1, 181–187.

Shonkoff, J., & Phillips, D. (2000). *From Neurons to Neighborhoods: The Science of Early Childhood Development*. Washington, DC: National Academy Press.

Smith, S. (Discussant). (1999, April). *Selection Issues in Child Care: Estimating the Effects of Child Care on Child Outcomes*. Paper presented at the biennial meetings of the Society for Research in Child Development, Albuquerque, NM.

Steinfels, M. O. (1973). *Who's Minding the Children: The History and Politics of Day Care in America*. New York: Simon and Schuster.

Sylvester, K. (2001). Caring for our youngest: Public attitudes in the United States. *The Future of Children 11*, 1, 53–61.

Tank, R. M. (1980). *Young Children, Families, and Society in America Since the 1820s: The Evolution of Health, Education, and Child Care Programs for Preschool Children.* (Ann Arbor: University Microfilms International, 1980), 356–59.

Thompson, R. A., & Nelson, C. A. (2001). Developmental science and the media: Early brain development. *American Psychologist 56*, 1, 1–11.

Vinofskis, M. (1999). Do federal compensatory education programs really work? A brief historical analysis of Title I and Head Start. *American Journal of Education 107*, 187–209.

Washington Post, Kaiser Family Foundation, and Harvard University (2000, September). *Issues in the 2000 Election: Values.* Menlo Park, CA: Kaiser Family Foundation.

Weiss, C. H. (1980). *Social Science Research and Decision Making.* New York: Columbia University Press.

West, K. K., Hauser, R. M., & Scanlan, T. M. (1998), *Longitudinal Surveys of Children.* Washington, DC.: National Academy Press.

White, S. (2002, June). *Towards a Politics of Science for Developmental Psychology.* Presentation at the conference, "Developmental Psychology and the Social Changes of our Time," Wellesley, MA.

White, S. H., & Phillips, D. A. (2001). Designing Head Start: Roles played by developmental psychologists. In D. L. Featherman & M. A. Vinovskis (Eds.), *Social Science and Policy-Making* (pp. 83–118). Ann Arbor, MI: University of Michigan Press.

Whitebook, M. (2001). *Working for Worthy Wages: The Child Care Compensation Movement, 1970–2001.* Foundation for Child Development, Working Paper Series. New York: Foundation for Child Development.

Whitebook, M., Howes, C., & Phillips, D. (1990). *Who Cares? Child Care Teachers and the Quality of Care in America.* Final report of the National Child Care Staffing Study. Oakland, CA: Child Care Employee Project.

Whitebook, M., Howes, C., & Phillips, D. (1998). *Worthy Work Unliveable Wages The National Child Care Staffing Study, 1988–1997.* Washington DC: Center for the Child Care Work Force.

Zaslow, M. J., Moore, K. A., Tout, K., Scarpa, J., & Vandivere, S. (2002). How are children faring under welfare reform: Emerging patterns. In A. Weil & K. Finegold (Eds.), *Welfare Reform: The Next Act* (pp. 79–101). Washington, DC: The Urban Institute.

Zigler, E., & Freedman, J. (1987). Early experience, malleability, and Head Start. In J. Gallagher and R. Haskins (Eds.), *The Malleability of Children* (pp. 85–95). Baltimore: Brooks.

Zigler, E., & Muenchow, S. (1992). *Head Start: The Inside Story of America's Most Successful Educational Experiment.* New York: Basic Books.

Zigler, E., & Valentine J. (Eds.). (1979). *Project Head Start: A Legacy of the War on Poverty.* New York: Free Press.

Zigler, E., & Styfco, S. J. (1994). Is the Perry preschool better than Head Start? Yes and no. *Early Childhood Research Quarterly 9,* 269–287.

6 Child Development and Child-Care Policy

Modest Impacts

Ron Haskins

Whether developmental scientists have had an impact on the nation's day-care and preschool education policy is an important issue for several reasons. Social science research in general, and child development research in particular, is funded primarily by the federal government and foundations. Although I do not want to get entwined in the argument about the payoffs from basic versus applied research, there is little question that the federal government and foundations invest in child development research because they are seeking improved development of poor children, especially as measured by better academic performance in the schools. It follows that a major test of the validity of research-generated knowledge about development is whether knowledge can provide guidance for intervention programs designed to improve development, especially of poor children. An equally important issue is whether social scientists have learned to use their knowledge to influence policymakers as they formulate the nation's policy on day-care and preschool programs.

To examine the impact of child development research and researchers on the formulation of day-care and preschool policy, I adopt a straightforward approach. At the risk of some simplification, the historical record of the development of federal policy for day-care and preschool programs is divided into five episodes: the creation of Head Start in 1965; the battle over federal regulations as represented by the Federal Interagency Day Care Requirements (FIDCR); enactment of the Family Support Act of 1988; enactment of the pivotal child-care legislation of 1990; and the mega battle over the 1996 welfare reform legislation. After brief sketches of these seminal episodes in the formulation of federal day-care and preschool policy, I turn to a review of the major characteristics of federal child-care policy as it now stands. These characteristics are: dual track policy, federal regulations, parent choice, religious providers, and spending. My conclusion is that developmental scientists have

140

made reasonable contributions to the policy process but other forces have been even more important in policy development.

A preliminary issue deserves brief attention. It is useful to distinguish between day-care and preschool programs, especially if one is not too rigid about the distinction. Day-care and preschool programs form a continuum. On the one end are facilities that provide a clean, well-lighted place for care of young children while their parents work or attend school or training courses. On the other end of the continuum are programs that explicitly aim to stimulate children's development. In the public mind – and in the mind of most policymakers – the major goal of preschool education is to prepare children for the academic challenges of schooling. Traditionally, however, professional preschool educators and developmental researchers have also emphasized health care, nutrition, social behavior, and parent involvement. Terms such as "comprehensive care" and developing the "whole child" are sometimes used to capture the broad array of developmental goals of preschool programs. In observing the distinction between day-care and preschool education, it is not wise to draw any sharp lines. Indeed, as we will see, one of the major issues of day-care policy is whether facilities should be strictly regulated to ensure "quality" – and an important part of quality regulations is curriculum activities designed to stimulate children's development.

Crucial Episodes in the Development of Day-Care and Preschool Policy

Table 6.1 presents an overview of the major federal day-care and preschool education programs. In addition, there are at least 70 or 80 minor programs (U.S. General Accounting Office, 1994). Total federal spending on these programs exceeded $25.5 billion in 2003, a considerable sum of money by any standard. The programs listed in Table 6.1 are the outcome of nearly four decades of sharp partisan debate and action by Congress and various Presidential administrations. They are the current reality toward which past actions moved relentlessly, if somewhat inscrutably.

Head Start

One of the more interesting chapters in our story is that of Head Start. President Lyndon Johnson of Texas did more than almost any other American to advance the cause of civil rights. He guided the original civil rights bills through the Congress, first as Majority Leader of the Senate and then as President (Caro, 2002). However, Johnson also knew that simply establishing rights was not

Table 6.1. *Summary of State and Federal Spending on Preschool and Child-Care Programs*

Program	Spending (2003; millions)
Department of Education[a]	
Title I Grants	$284
Early Reading First	75
Special Education	
Infants and Families	437
Preschool Grants	390
Grants to States	512
Health and Human Services[b]	
Discretionary Child Care and Development Fund (CCDF)	2,100
Mandatory CCDF	2,717
Transfers from Temporary Assistance for Needy Families (TANF) Block grant to CCDF	2,000
TANF Direct Expenditures on Child Care	1,580
State CCDF Match and Maintenance of Effort Payments (MOE)	2,247
TANF MOE in Excess of CCDF MOE	750
Head Start	6,668
Social Services Block Grant (Title XX)	160
Department of Agriculture[c]	
Child and Adult Care Food Program	1,940
Tax Expenditures[b]	
Dependent Care Tax Credit	2,910
Employer Provided Child Care Exclusion	720
Employer Provided Child Care Credit	90
TOTAL	$25,580

[a] Education spending based on the proportion of children under age 5.
[b] HHS and tax expenditures are for children of all ages; 53% of CCDF children are under age 5.
[c] Only spending on children included in the estimate.
Source: Office of Management and Budget.

going to overcome the effects of centuries of slavery and Jim Crow. Thus, he also launched the War on Poverty with comprehensive legislation in 1964. The goal of much of this legislation was to place political power in the hands of local communities – especially minority communities – so they could organize and create programs to help themselves.

Johnson's closest advisor on his poverty programs was Sargent Shriver, an effective and relentless advocate for the poor. Shriver, whose wife Eunice Kennedy Shriver was also an activist on behalf of the poor and the disabled, was convinced that poor and minority children got off to a difficult start in life because their rearing environments did not help them achieve their developmental potential. Shriver had been head of the school board in Chicago and had already been thinking about early educational programs for poor children, both to help them academically and to employ teachers during the summer (Zigler & Muenchow, 1992). Shriver had visited Susan Gray's preschool program for poor children in Nashville and had been impressed with her evidence that poor children were profiting from the experience (Gray & Klaus, 1970). In December of 1964, Shriver asked Robert E. Cooke, a pediatrician at Johns Hopkins University, to quickly form a committee of experts and to lead them to make specific recommendations about a new preschool program that would stimulate the development of poor children. The task force met eight times in six weeks between January and February of 1965 before presenting the groundbreaking Head Start Program to Shriver (Zigler & Muenchow, 1992).

I doubt that there will ever again be an occasion on which developmental scientists and pediatricians have such direct input into the process of formulating a major new program for children. The Congressional enthusiasm over child development and preschool was just beginning to build. President Johnson was riding high, had already achieved several major Congressional victories, and had also pushed legislation through Congress authorizing his War on Poverty. It was as part of the War on Poverty that Johnson and Shriver decided to establish the Head Start preschool program as one element of their overall attack on poverty. And nobody was in position to stop them. Thus, the Cooke Committee was making recommendations that, when adopted by Shriver and Johnson, would immediately provide guidance for a major new program financed with federal dollars that did not require Congressional approval.

The program Shriver established was to become the best known and most popular of the War on Poverty programs as well as the most important single program in what, as we have seen (Table 6.1), was to become a crowded field of federal day-care and preschool programs. A major reason Head Start was able to achieve such exalted status was the solid foundation recommended by Cooke's committee and adopted by Shriver. Two features of their recommendations were vital to Head Start's staying power and continuing success. First, in what in retrospect is perhaps the most surprising and wise provision in the Committee's recommendation, Head Start was to offer "comprehensive" services. For the Cooke Committee, comprehensive services had a very specific meaning; namely, services that included healthcare, nutrition, preschool education, and parent involvement. This recommendation may seem commonplace today, but in 1965 what might be called "radical environmentalism" was sweeping the academic worlds of early education and child development. J. McVicker Hunt's *Intelligence and Experience* (1961) and Benjamin Bloom's *Stability and Change in Human Characteristics* (1964) had overcome several decades of predominance of the view that intelligence was genetically determined and therefore immutable. Intelligence was seen as malleable. Thus, the correct set of experiences during the preschool years could boost IQ and school performance. Both the President and Shriver often spoke as if intellectual development as measured by IQ was the major goal of Head Start.

However, when it became clear that the radical environmentalists were overly optimistic and that IQ and school achievement were difficult to boost, Head Start's defenders could respond by arguing that the major goals of the program included many activities crucial to a child's development other than mere IQ. Before the end of the 1960s, when Head Start was rocked by studies and reviews claiming that the IQ gains produced by the program faded quickly (Jensen, 1969; Westinghouse, 1969), the wisdom of the committee's emphasis on comprehensiveness became evident and Head Start was able to weather the storm.

A second vital provision of the committee's recommendation was that funds should bypass states and go to local sponsors so that poor communities could play a major role in the design and implementation of programs. Local control and the concept of "maximum feasible participation" in War on Poverty programs soon came to engender lots of opposition (Moynihan, 1970). But Head Start largely escaped the excesses that gave community action a bad, or at least a controversial, reputation. Two immense benefits accrued to the program because of this method of financing. First, even though the professionals on the Cooke committee wanted to start small and build up gradually so that program administrators and operators would have time to work out problems, Johnson and Shriver were operating on political logic that, given the money and energy available in 1965, called for mounting the largest possible program as quickly as possible. If the money had been channeled through state and local governments, it would have proven impossible to get much in place in less than a year. As amazing as it might seem, by the early summer of 1965 the Johnson administration had funded programs in more than 2,500 communities that enrolled 560,000 children (Zigler & Valentine, 1979, p. 70).

The second advantage conferred on Head Start by its quick buildup was that it created a constituency for the program all over the nation. There was at least one Head Start program in most Congressional districts. Thus, when trouble came – as it inevitably would – there were built-in supporters who could lobby Congress. Equally important, Head Start has now been through nearly four decades of annual appropriation battles. Constituent pressure on Congress has helped Head Start not merely survive annual appropriations, but grow at a very healthy rate in many years.

In sum, the Head Start initiative of 1965 set in motion a program that would grow to be the major federal activity for promoting the development of poor children before they enter school. The program has gained great favor among members of Congress and the American public and enjoys a widespread reputation for being a program that works. By 2003, the program cost about $6.7 billion and served more than 900,000 children. Its origins and history reflect the long-standing federal commitment to help the poor as well as the federal commitment to provide high-quality early education to poor children in order to, as President Johnson put it, bring poor children to the "starting line" of schooling equal with children of more affluent families.

There has always been plenty of controversy about Head Start. But it is one of the few War on Poverty programs that still survives. Indeed, it flourishes. Even so, the program does not have a good record of preparing poor children for schooling, something that many policymakers see as the major goal of federal preschool dollars (Haskins, 2003). In this regard, Head Start is still vulnerable today.

Child Development Act of 1971

Like Head Start, the Child Development Act of 1971 was ahead of its time. Most pieces of major legislation are years in the making and are often the result of a series of small steps that, taken together, constitute major change. As we have seen, Head Start, along with its embodiment of the big ideas of using preschool education to promote child development, influence parenting, and create opportunities for community organization and development, was created by administrative fiat with little or no legislative consideration. Rare event that.

Now came the 1971 child development legislation to greatly expand the very concepts embodied in Head Start. The legislation would make money available to local sponsors, including nongovernmental organizations and local governments representing 5,000 or more constituents, to design and conduct child development programs. Programs could be even more comprehensive than Head Start. Local sponsors, with heavy representation by parents and the poor, would submit a plan to the Department of Health, Education, and Welfare (HEW). Funds could be used for programs to diagnose physical or mental barriers to normal development, for prenatal services, for operation of programs for the disabled, for inservice training, and for all manner of preschool and after-school programs including summer, weekend, and overnight care. Families with incomes below $4,320 (around $16,000 in 2003) were eligible for free services, and families with incomes up to nearly $7,000 (about $26,000 in 2003) qualified for reduced-price services (Malone, 1971). Although it would have cost around $9 billion ($33.2 billion in 2003) to fully fund these eligibility levels (Steiner, 1976, pp. 111–112), the final bill authorized $2 billion ($7.4 billion in 2003) for the first year of operation.

It would be difficult to create a policy environment more conducive to the 1971 legislation than the one that actually existed. Marion Wright Edelman, who later founded the Children's Defense Fund, helped organize a diverse array of interest groups including children's organizations, women's groups, and organized labor to support the legislation. The chief lobbyist for the coalition was an experienced former HEW staffer who had strong relations with members of the House and Senate. Both Senator Mondale of Minnesota, who sponsored the bill in the Senate, and John Brademas of Indiana, who sponsored the bill in the House, were smart, relentless in planning and executing legislative strategy, and firmly committed to the children's cause. Moreover, on the basis of recommendations from his brash young adviser Daniel Patrick Moynihan, President Nixon had earlier issued a public statement about the importance of the early years that committed his administration to promoting child development. To this end, Nixon reorganized children's programs at HEW and created the Office of Child Development, apparently with the intention of both consolidating existing children's programs and creating new ones, all of which would be housed in one agency. To head the new office, Edward Zigler, a renowned developmental scientist who had played an important role in the creation of Head Start, was imported from Yale.

With this level of support and expertise, child development bills passed the House and Senate and flew through the House-Senate conference committee. Although there was considerable opposition from House Republicans, who wanted states – not local governments and nongovernmental organizations – to control the funds, the conference bill was easily approved by both Houses and sent to the President for a final signature.

Alas, President Nixon vetoed the bill with one of the most unexpected and, some would say, extreme veto messages in memory. Along with predictable criticisms of the bill such as opposition to allowing local governments to control the funds, the veto message included an exceptionally provocative passage stating that: "for the Federal Government to plunge headlong financially into supporting child development would commit the vast moral authority of the National Government to the side of communal approaches to child rearing over and against the family-centered approach" (Nixon, 1972).

The term "communal" raises the specter of communism, a card that Nixon had played on previous occasions to attack something or someone he did not like. But the more substantive issue is whether day care is "against" care by the mother in the child's home. The argument that out-of-home care was dangerous to attachment was prominent and persuasive to many during the 1950s and 1960s. Here was an issue that developmentalists knew something about. But it was possible to see this issue as one of politics versus science. Perhaps the strongest scientific case in the early 1970s was Bowlby's (1952) argument that separation anxiety could be detrimental to children's personality development. The particulars of Bowlby's work are much more sophisticated than this mere hint suggests, but there were plenty of social scientists and popular writers who claimed that children placed in day care while their mothers worked were at risk for emotional problems (Belsky, 1986; Phillips, McCartney, & Scarr, 1987). Meanwhile, the women's movement was gaining steam and for feminists the choice between staying home with babies or working was simple. Work was the route to liberation and babies could be well cared for by someone other than their mothers – no supporting evidence needed.

In the end, of course, women entered the labor force in droves and eventually more than 60% of women with preschool children went back to work (U.S. Census Bureau, 2001, p. 373), and most of them placed their children in group care of some sort. American families voted with their feet on the issue of "communal" child care regardless of the position implied by the "vast moral authority of the National Government." Moreover, the trend toward encouraging or even forcing welfare mothers to join the labor force got underway with President Kennedy's 1962 welfare reforms and, it should be noted, was strongly supported by the Nixon administration when its time came (Steiner, 1971). All of the federal welfare-to-work programs included explicit provisions for child care. The unstoppable demographic trend of mothers with ever younger children entering the labor force, coupled with the desire of both politicians and the public for welfare mothers to work, obliterated the arguments of a dwindling body of critics who believed the place for preschool children was in the home.

As a footnote to Nixon's "communal" care criticism, developmental scientists have not taken a consistent position on this issue. Most seem to have concluded, either by explicit statements or silence, that out-of-home care for very young children does not constitute a threat to their development. Yet, there is no question that child care increases rates of infectious illness (Haskins & Kotch, 1986). In addition, there is an ongoing debate among developmental scientists about whether separation from mothers on a routine basis during the first year of life damages the infant's personality development (Belsky, 1986; Phillips et al., 1987). Several very credible developmental scientists think there is evidence of problems (Brooks-Gunn et al., 2002; Waldfogel et al., 2002). No matter, a majority of mothers of young children are now in the labor force, their work is encouraged by numerous federal child-care policies, and major changes in their work status do not appear likely. Developmentalists have not spoken with one voice on this issue and therefore have not offered clear guidance to either parents or policymakers. Maybe they just could not stomach being in league with Richard Milhous Nixon.

Federal Interagency Day Care Requirements (FIDCR)

The long and intense struggle over FIDCR was another episode in which developmental researchers and advocates played a major role. The somewhat torturous story has been exceptionally well told by John Nelson (1982) and Gilbert Steiner (1976, 1981). Since FIDCR is more or less the opening chapter in the attempt to impose federal regulations on day care throughout the nation, and because developmentalists played an important role, the outline of the story is briefly repeated here.

Amendments enacted by Congress in 1967 to the Office of Economic Opportunity (OEO) legislation required OEO and the Department of Health, Education, and Welfare (HEW) to work together to coordinate their respective day-care and preschool programs. The interagency committee appointed the next year by HEW Secretary Wilbur Cohen reflected what is perhaps the major tension afflicting day-care and preschool education policy then and now; namely, the conflict between inexpensive care to simply provide a safe place for children while their mothers (or both parents) work or train versus relatively expensive care designed to promote child development. The amendments to the Aid to Families with Dependent Children (AFDC) program enacted under President Kennedy in 1962 placed a much greater emphasis on work than any previous reform legislation. Then as now, most members of Congress seemed to believe that if government encouraged or required work by welfare recipients, it followed that government was responsible for helping pay for child care. Indeed, as subsequent events demonstrated, many policymakers – and nearly all developmental scientists and child advocates – came to believe that merely helping welfare mothers pay for child care was not the only federal responsibility. Rather, much of the child-care debate was to focus on government responsibility for the supply and especially the quality of care. Taken together, this additional responsibility for supply and quality was a considerable expansion of federal authority and potentially, depending on implementation, of federal spending as well.

One of the major tasks of the interagency committee that wrote the initial version of the FIDCR regulations was to solve this conflict of cheap and stark versus expensive and enriched care. The conflict was more than academic. Developmental types from HEW, the Department of Education, and OEO wanted high-quality and "comprehensive" care that would promote child development. They represented, in short, the Head Start tradition. However, representatives from the Department of Labor wanted to promote work and regarded day care primarily as a work support. The extra cost of enriched care, to them, constituted an unnecessary expenditure that would make work programs too expensive. This argument is even more compelling today than it was in the 1960s. For a fixed amount of money, spending more on high-quality care means fewer families will receive subsidies; spending less for lower quality care means more families will receive subsidies. The mathematics of this tradeoff is unavoidable – and critical in the unfolding child-care debate.

On their face, the regulations drafted by the work group looked like the enrichment side had won a victory that might have set a precedent of the federal government accepting responsibility for day-care quality. The regulations required high staff–child ratios and mentioned all the hot-button issues that day-care regulators worry about including space per child, opportunities for parent involvement, safety and sanitation standards, and activities to develop the child's social, cognitive, and communication skills. And yet, on closer inspection (see Nelson, 1982, pp. 275–276), the regulations actually allowed lots of room for loose interpretation. For example, although the staff–child ratios were high, the regulations allowed clerical staff, housekeeping staff, and even volunteers to be counted in the ratios. In addition, the regulations specified that the ratios could not "normally" be violated. Similarly, space had to be "adequate," educational material "appropriate," and meals "adequate." Equally telling, enforcement was left to the federal agency that conducted the various child-care programs, thereby leaving plenty of room for interpretation by the Department of Labor and perhaps other agencies that wanted to emphasize work or training rather than day-care quality. Even senior officials at HEW let the word go out that the regulations would not be strictly enforced.

FIDCR and the general issue of federal day-care regulations was still very much up in the air. Richard Nixon was elected President in 1968 and, to everyone's surprise created the Office of Child Development and hired Ed Zigler to head the new agency. Zigler, well aware of the flaws in the FIDCR regulations produced during the Johnson administration, quickly received permission from HEW Secretary Robert Finch to revise them. By the spring of 1972, Zigler and his staff had completed the revision. The new version of FIDCR had lost its ambiguity, and the new version applied to both family day-care facilities and day-care centers. In addition, there were detailed provisions on age grouping, feeding, teacher wages, and teacher training and responsibilities. The new HEW Secretary Elliot Richardson gladly accepted Zigler's revised standards. Nixon's Office of Management and Budget (OMB) did not. In fact, OMB challenged the revised FIDCR on several levels.

OMB did not like the provisions on wages, raised serious concern about the cost of the high staff–child ratios, and rejected the idea that the federal government should have standards for family day care. Worse, OMB seemed to adopt a stance against the very concept of broad federal standards for child care. As explained by an obscure Assistant Director of OMB named Paul O'Neill (the same Paul O'Neill who later became CEO of Alcoa and Secretary of the Treasury under George W. Bush), the Zigler/Richardson draft FIDCR "cloud[ed]" the difference between the modest standards for day care needed for parents to work and the more far-reaching standards needed for "compensatory education" (Cohen, 2001). The memo went on to make the claim that compensatory education was a local and state – not a federal – responsibility. Given OMB's opposition, the Nixon administration put FIDCR to sleep.

To sleep, yes, but not yet to die. In 1975, after Nixon's downfall in the Watergate scandal, the Ford administration agreed to legislation creating Title XX of the Social Security Act. Title XX provided money to states to help poor and low-income families by providing them with social services. One of the eligible services was day care. The legislation limited day-care spending by states to care facilities that met the FIDCR guidelines. However, the FIDCR was still controversial. Advocates and child-care providers fought over whether the 1968 version or Zigler's 1972 version was better, OMB still opposed all but the most tepid federal standards, and HEW seemed to waver. But of greatest importance, Senator Russell Long, the powerful chairman of the Senate Finance Committee, opposed all federal standards. Long made certain that legislation was passed that delayed implementation of FIDCR until completion of an HEW study on the appropriateness of federal standards required by the 1975 Title XX legislation.

Although the study was completed in 1978, FIDCR had still not been implemented by 1979 when Joseph Califano became Secretary of HEW in the Carter administration. Under Califano and his successor Patricia Harris, HEW staff developed yet another version of FIDCR that met at least minimal standards. Although these standards failed to spark enthusiasm among child advocates and scholars, they nonetheless supported the new and weaker standards because these standards seemed to be the strongest ones possible at that moment given the continuing opposition from OMB and President Carter's indifference. In fact, if anything, Carter had serious questions about the wisdom of federal day-care standards (Cohen, 2001, pp. 66–67). HEW issued the revised FIDCR in the fall of 1981. Senator Long immediately responded by inserting a provision in budget legislation suspending implementation for one year. Although Senator Mondale and Senator Cranston tried to repeal the Long provision, they were not successful. Worse yet for those who had fought for over a decade for federal standards, the reconciliation legislation the following year eliminated FIDCR altogether.

Now, at last, FIDCR was dead. However, as subsequent events were to prove, the prospect of strong federal day-care regulations aimed at converting market day care into high-quality day care was far from dead.

Welfare Reform Legislation of 1988

Although day care remained a festering issue for many advocates and some Democratic members of Congress, the period between the demise of FIDCR and the welfare reform battle of 1987–1988 did not see major initiatives in either day-care or preschool education, although Head Start appropriations grew somewhat during this period. By 1987, several factors conspired to bring welfare reform – and along with it child care – to the public agenda. In the three decades between the onset of the War on Poverty in 1964 and passage of the sweeping reforms of 1996, welfare reform was either on the Congressional agenda or in the immediate foreground. Serious attempts to reform welfare had been made in the early 1970s under President Nixon (Moynihan, 1973) and again in the late 1970s under President Carter (Whitman & Lynn, 1981), but both efforts had failed. President Reagan came to office in 1981 making promises (or threats, depending on your politics) to reform welfare. He did make a few moderately important changes in the AFDC program in 1981, some of which were subsequently reversed, but the most far-reaching reforms under Reagan were achieved only after Congressional Democrats and the nation's governors (led by a little-known politician from Arkansas named Clinton) linked hands to initiate another major welfare debate in 1987–1988. This time, debate led to fairly substantial reforms that were enacted on solid bipartisan votes in both Houses.

The 1988 welfare reforms contained remarkable and far-reaching provisions on day care. That a major welfare reform law should contain such important provisions on day care simply demonstrates yet again the vital link between welfare and day care. Ironically, the emphasis on work requirements by conservatives ensured that a welfare reform debate necessarily meant a debate on day care. The argument that work requirements meant government responsibility for day care, combined with the impossibility of discussing welfare reform without discussing work, meant that welfare reform and day care were joined at the hip. The 1988 legislation made this relationship clear and indeed all but established it as a principle of federal policymaking on welfare reform for the foreseeable future.

Besides cementing the relationship between welfare reform and day care, another important provision established by the 1988 welfare reform law was that government would be required to pay for child care as mothers were making the transition from welfare to work. The final bill required government to help fund day care for a year after mothers left welfare. After 1988, every state set up a program to provide day care to mothers leaving welfare. Thus, when the next welfare reform debate rolled around in 1995–1996, it was simply assumed that government had to provide transitional day care to mothers leaving welfare.

In addition to establishing the two principles that government must, first, pay for day care if welfare mothers are required to work and, second, pay for care as mothers transition from welfare to work, a third important characteristic of federal policy adopted in 1988 provided funding for states to create and enforce their own regulations. After extensive negotiations, a somewhat complex compromise was reached. First, states could spend federal dollars only in facilities that met applicable state regulations. Second, states were required to develop "guidelines" for family day care, although the exact meaning of this requirement and its enforcement were left vague. Third, states had to ensure basic health and safety in day-care centers. Fourth, in exchange for this modest set of regulatory requirements, Republicans agreed to provide a small sum of money ($13 million per year) that would be given to states to improve their regulatory requirements, procedures, and oversight (Committee, 1989).

It is instructive to read the various versions of FIDCR regulations and compare them to these modest requirements placed in the 1988 welfare reform law. Between the demise of FIDCR in 1981 and these 1988 provisions, it seems fair to conclude that the scholars and advocates who wanted to improve the quality of day care through tough federal regulations were losing. But the landmark child-care legislation of 1990 presented another opportunity to increase spending on day care and to create modest federal regulations.

Child-Care Legislation of 1990

The child-care legislation enacted in 1990 on a bipartisan basis reinforced or established all of the defining elements of then current federal child-care policy. Sally Cohen (2001), the most important historian of federal child-care law, characterizes the 1990 law as "landmark" legislation. I see no reason to disagree with this characterization, except to clarify that the day-care provisions of the 1988 Family Support Act were important precursors to the 1990 legislation, especially on the issue of standards.

The major provisions of the 1990 law can be captured in five summary statements (Committee, 1996, pp. 648–651). First, the law established a new child-care grant program called the Child Care and Development Block Grant (CCDBG). This program gave states about $2.5 billion (subject to appropriation) over three years to provide day care to children under age 13 with a working parent. Funds were directed to low-income families by a provision that required states to spend the money on families under 75% (later changed to 85%) of state median income (the cutoff was about $54,000 in the average state in 2003). Because of the long-standing concern with day-care availability and quality, states were required to use 25% of block grant funds for activities to improve the availability and quality of care, to provide before- and after-school care, and to encourage early childhood development services. Of the 25% reserved for these purposes, at least 20% (or 5% of total funds) had to be used specifically for quality improvement. States had to spend the other 75% of their funds on day-care services (Committee, 1989, 1990; Spar, 1996).

Second, an additional grant program was established to provide day-care funds to states. This program was called the "At Risk" Child Care program because its funds were directed specifically at working families that were not on welfare but were considered by the state to be at risk for welfare if day care were not provided. Unlike the CCDBG, the At Risk program was an entitlement to states (meaning that the money did not have to go through the annual appropriation battle) funded at $300 million per year. The money was distributed among the states in proportion to each state's share of all children in the United States under age 13. An irreverent graduate student might ask, why were two grant programs established for more or less the same purpose? The answer: because both the Ways and Means Committee and the Education and Labor Committee in the House wanted their own program. So against all considerations of reasonable policymaking, the House insisted on two grant programs.

Third, the $13 million grant program for states to improve their standards, established by the 1988 reforms, was expanded to $50 million and a requirement that states spend at least half the funds on provider training was included in the new law.

Fourth, the law authorized day-care funds to be spent by states through grants, contracts, or "certificates" – a euphemism for vouchers. However, in an exceptionally controversial provision, states were required to make every qualifying parent aware that they had the option of using a voucher and then grant a voucher if the parent elected to use this form of financing. Thus, at least in theory, the final decision on where children would be placed in care was left to parents and not state officials or professionals.

Fifth, a somewhat messy provision on using government funds to pay for church-sponsored care was reached after many compromises. The issue of religious child care caused heated arguments throughout the two years of Congressional debate, as it had on many previous occasions and will again on many more in the future. The debates featured in-fighting among liberals, all of whom wanted to create a federal child-care program. The first version of the liberals' bill – the Act for Better Child Care (ABC) drafted by the Children's Defense Fund and a group of more than 70 advocacy organizations – required religious facilities to remove or cover religious symbols while children were participating in federally supported day care (Cohen, 2001). In addition, the ABC bill disallowed the provision of the 1964 Civil Rights Act that permitted religious facilities receiving federal dollars to discriminate in hiring in order to employ people who subscribe to their religious beliefs. As soon as these provisions became widely known, conservatives lashed out against them. Moreover, the provisions alienated important organizations in the liberal coalition, especially Catholic Charities, one of the most powerful and determined lobbies in the nation's capital. Even more damaging, the provisions probably could not command majorities in either the House or Senate. Thus, they had to be modified. When they were, several liberal groups – especially women's groups – left the ABC coalition. After lots of arguing and compromising, the final bill generally allowed religious providers to receive government support on the same basis as nonreligious providers. Moreover, under most circumstances sectarian providers can discriminate in hiring on the basis of religious belief. Further, care paid for by vouchers can include sectarian worship and instruction (Gish & Harper, 2002; Spar, 1996).

It would be difficult to overestimate the importance of this law. At the broadest level, because the 1990 legislation was combined with generous reauthorization of Head Start, the bipolar nature of federal policy for the preschool period was strengthened. The federal government would fund both a developmental program that provided high-quality and comprehensive services to poor children and a child-care program that served a broader group of families, was not necessarily comprehensive, and did not have high federal standards.

Equally important, the 1990 law seemed to confirm that not only was FIDCR dead, but the prospect of strong federal regulations took a giant step backward. Despite the mighty efforts of the Children's Defense Fund and other groups that lobby in the children's cause, as well as important Democrats in both the House and Senate, it was not possible to attract majority support for strong federal standards. Rather, states would continue to be responsible for regulations with only modest federal involvement. However, to stimulate action at the state level to create meaningful quality standards and to broaden the types of facilities to which they applied, the federal government increased from $13 million to $50 million the dedicated funds that could be used only to expand supply or strengthen standards and their implementation and enforcement. This set-aside to support quality child care was expanded in future legislation and may turn out to constitute the core of a long-term strategy to entice states to increase the quality of care by writing and enforcing their own standards. Although it might have been little consolation at the time, the funds for improving supply and quality are cleverly situated in the statute so that if any money is appropriated for the CCDBG, the set-aside for supply and quality is automatic. In this way, the authors of the provision were able to avoid the annual appropriations process to make sure their funds are actually available every year. In fact, the percentage set aside was increased somewhat in 1996 and is likely to be increased even more in future years.

Another feature of the 1990 legislation that is of long-term importance is the provision on vouchers. If states could contract with selected providers, it would be much easier to demand high-quality care, to monitor compliance with state regulations, and to ensure some continuity in child-care services over a period of years. On the other hand, experience showed that if parents could select care by use of a voucher, they would select a huge array of care, much of it provided in informal neighborhood settings that would be difficult or impossible – and in any case very expensive – to monitor (Divine-Hawkins, 1981; Gormley, 1995). In the Congressional debate of 1989–1990, few members of Congress came out explicitly against parent choice, but there is little question that Democrats and the Act for Better Child Care coalition preferred financing by contract while Republicans and conservative interest groups were firmly committed to vouchers. Because the Bush White House supported the Republican position and because the President's signature was required to cement the final compromise, Democrats agreed to the strong voucher requirement of the final bill. Today every state has an extensive voucher program.

Welfare Reform Legislation of 1996

The welfare reform legislation of 1996 is now generally agreed to be one of the most sweeping changes in federal social policy since the Social Security Act of 1935. The 1996 law replaced AFDC with the Temporary Assistance for Needy Families (TANF) block grant; all but eliminated welfare for noncitizens who entered the country after 1996; led to the termination of cash and health entitlements for drug addicts and alcoholics; created a controversial program on abstinence education; and made important changes in Supplemental Security Income, Child Support Enforcement, food stamps, child nutrition, and child care.

The child-care changes were substantial, but the new law retained most of the major features of the CCDBG created in 1990. It is only somewhat of an exaggeration to say that the thrust of the 1996 reforms was to end several child-care programs and put all the money from these programs, plus additional funds, in the CCDBG. This action substantially increased the amount of money available for day care and gave dramatic authority to the states to decide how to spend the money. According to the Congressional Budget Office (1996), the new law provided an additional $4.5 billion in budget authority for child care over the six years between 1997 and 2002 above the baseline of previous law.

As implementation unfolded, the 1996 law turned out to be a money machine for child care. In addition to the $4.5 billion in new entitlement money, the appropriations committees in the House and Senate provided the full $1 billion in discretionary money each year and even, beginning in 1998, took the rare action of appropriating funds above the $1 billion authorization level. By 2003, discretionary spending had grown to $2.1 billion. Moreover, taking advantage of a new provision in the 1996 law that allowed states to both spend TANF welfare funds directly on child care and, in addition, transfer up to 30% of TANF funds to the CCDBG, by 2000 states were spending more than $3.5 billion per year in TANF funds on child care. Thus, as shown in Table 6.1, spending on child care through the CCDBG had reached nearly $11.5 billion by 2003.

State flexibility in using child-care funds was increased by replacing the 20% set-aside for raising quality and increasing supply with a 4% set-aside. But because the 4% applied to all spending through the block grant, the unexpected increase in child-care spending since 1996 has meant that states must still spend a considerable sum of money on quality.

Finally, the 1996 bill eliminated all the child-care entitlements that existed in the programs associated with AFDC. Although advocates fought against this change, Republicans and governors were determined to give states a free hand in determining who should get child care and whether families should be required to make copayments. Republicans argued that the major goal of the reforms should be to increase the amount of money so that more families would receive subsidies. On this criterion, there is no doubt that many more families on and off welfare are now receiving services than at any time before 1996.

Keeping Score: Who Won on the Big Issues?

Based on this brief history, I turn now to an assessment of whether the major characteristics of federal day-care and preschool policy are consistent with the goals pursued by developmental scientists and child advocates. Current federal policy is characterized as consisting of five major issues, each of which was the object of political conflict as Congress and a series of presidents fought to establish day-care and preschool programs consistent with their own views. The five issues, the child advocacy and conservative position on each issue, and the outcome (current legislative status) of each issue are summarized in Table 6.2.

Dual Track Day-Care and Preschool Policy

Developmental scientists wanted all federally supported day care to be a positive force in children's development. Perhaps the most straightforward way

Table 6.2. *Child Advocacy and Conservative Positions and Outcome on Major Issues of Federal Child-Care Policy*

Issue	Child Advocacy Position	Conservative Position	Outcome
Dual Track	High-quality, federally regulated programs	Market	Mixed
Federal Regulations	Strong	Weak	Weak with set-asides
Parent Choice	Limited by state contracts	Full parent choice	Mixed, but parent choice guaranteed
Religious Providers	Regulated and restricted	Full participation and special accommodations	Full participation and special accommodations
Spending	High	Moderate	Substantial and growing

to ensure such a system would be to create a universal program of child care and development authorized, funded, and controlled by the federal government. A second method of creating universal developmental care would be to allow state and local governments to have major responsibility for day-care programs, but to impose strong federal quality standards on the care. In this section, I deal with the former; in the next, the latter.

The universal program strategy got off to a successful start with the creation of Head Start in 1965. The circumstances surrounding the birth of Head Start were exceptional in that a powerful president at the height of his powers was determined to establish the program and was able to do so by administrative fiat. In addition, the program was very large – with consequent broad political support from constituents – before it was required to undergo the rigors of the Congressional appropriations process. Moreover, no one thought of the program as universal; it was clearly a program for the poor. Although not evident at the time of its birth, Head Start could not expand beyond the poor without its advocates addressing a major problem; namely, the tradition of state and local control of education in the United States. A universal program seen as educational in its intent would have violated this tradition and would almost certainly have forced the public schools into strong action against the program – unless, of course, the program was part of the public schools. In any case, Head Start covers primarily poor children and even then, despite its healthy growth over nearly four decades, now serves only about 53% of poor 4 year olds. Head Start may eventually grow to cover all poor children, but it shows no signs of developing into a universal program.

Clearly, Head Start has advanced the goal of promoting child development, but child development is not the only goal of preschool programs. Beginning with the temporary day-care program established under the Lanham Act during World War II, federal support of day care has also served the goal of helping mothers (or both parents) work. When the war ended, federal support for day care disappeared until President Kennedy decided in 1962 to encourage mothers on welfare to work. His was a modest program, but it contained the seeds of an important policy idea; namely, that the federal government would accept major responsibility for day care if government encouraged or, as was eventually to happen, required welfare mothers to work. Thus, culminating in the Family Support Act of 1988 and the historic – if misnamed – Child Care and Development Block Grant (CCDBG) of 1990, the federal government created a second series of day-care programs that placed major control over policy in the hands of states. Here are the seeds of the major dichotomy in federal preschool policy: a high-quality program for the poor controlled from Washington with strict federal standards designed primarily to promote child development and a program of modest quality funded in major part by Washington but controlled by states designed primarily to promote work by low-income adults.

Two other factors should be mentioned briefly, both of which appear to move the federal mechanisms for supporting day care away from promoting a unified system that aims to stimulate child development. First, as shown in Table 6.1, there is substantial federal spending on day care through the tax code, primarily in the Dependent Care Tax Credit and the child-care exclusion programs. These programs, which enjoy strong political support, subsidize day care of every description and have absolutely no government-sponsored quality control mechanism of any type. Second, parental choice through use of vouchers is the major mechanism determining the type of day-care provider supported by federal dollars. In more than a decade, the voucher system has developed to the point that more than 80% of the care through the CCDBG is paid for by vouchers (Department, 2003). Again, parental choice and the resulting diversity of care arrangements make it difficult, if not impossible, to create a unified system of developmental care. Theoretically, it might be possible to encourage and educate parents to choose developmental care, but there is little evidence that discerning parental choice could move the day-care market toward providing uniform high-quality care (Blau, 2001; Gormley, 1995).

Clearly, the goal of creating a unified system of high-quality care has failed. After more than four decades of evolution, the federal government runs a dual system that consists of child development through Head Start and day care primarily through the CCDBG. In neutral terms, the current system could be described as "mixed" in that it is composed of both developmental care and care that is subject to modest regulation in most states – as well as lots of care that is completely outside government regulation. In large part because most market care is outside any effective regulatory and oversight system, much of that care is of indifferent quality. Such a useful, growing, yet diffuse system, which serves a master other than child development, does not meet the desires of developmental scientists or child advocates for a child-care system that promotes child development. Developmental scientists and child advocates have won only half of this battle.

Federal Regulations

Developmental scientists played a direct and important role in trying to subject all or most market day care in the United States to federal regulations. To this day, I would guess that a huge majority of developmentalists and child advocates would opt for strong federal regulations if they thought they could win the battle that would be required to establish some updated version of FIDCR. But Congress has consistently refused to impose federal regulations.

Republicans were always in the forefront of the fight against federal regulations. One of the major tenets of Republican philosophy is that government control of personal and family decisions is bad, and federal control is worse. Thus, all but a handful of Republicans are always willing to vote against federal standards. However, a surprising number of Democrats are also dubious about federal regulations. Many Democrats are aware that social programs are at best modestly successful, and, in large part because they represent cities, counties, and states – and often have served in legislative or executive bodies at these lower levels of government – they are wary of claims that the federal government knows best. Senator Russell Long, the leading Democrat on the Finance Committee in the Senate between 1966 and 1980, personally put the final hit on FIDCR. Another important Democrat, Congressman Wilbur Mills, Chairman of the Ways and Means Committee in the House between 1957 and 1975, had views on federal control of social programs that were similar to Long's and he too opposed FIDCR.

The history of attempts, headed almost exclusively by Democrats, to establish federal regulations provides little solace for those who want to use federal authority to directly increase the quality of day care. The long struggle over FIDCR, some of which occurred when Democrats controlled both Houses of Congress and the Presidency, ended with little more than a whimper. Now not even liberals know how to spell "FIDCR." Similarly, at a time when Democrats controlled both Houses of Congress, the partisan conflicts over day care in both the 1988 Family Support Act and the 1990 law that established the CCDBG did not result in anything like FIDCR-style federal regulations. If federal regulations cannot be established when Democrats control all or most of the levers of federal power, how can regulations be established when Republicans – the natural enemy of federal interference in family decisions – control either the Congress or the Presidency – as they appear poised to do for the foreseeable future.

As hard as it may be for developmentalists to accept, it seems likely that some things are more important than achieving child development through appeal to the strong arm of federal authority. Both Blau (2001) and especially Gormley (1995) have dealt with this issue in sophisticated detail, but even they, both of whom are more expert and more liberal than I, would grant the plausibility of the case against federal day-care regulations. At the most fundamental level, many Americans are naturally distrustful of central authority. Members of Congress usually demand a strong case before they will increase federal authority. This is especially true when the explicit purpose of federal authority is to interfere with parent choice. Economists have been conducting elegant analyses of market regulation for years, and there seems to be little disagreement that regulations limit choice. Moreover, in many cases regulations decrease supply and increase prices (Gormley, 1995). In the case at hand, the explicit intent of developmental scientists is to increase the quality of day care, primarily by controlling the number of children per adult, by stipulating minimum levels of training for caregivers, and by specifying curriculum activities. These requirements would not come free. Developmental scientists and child advocates have an answer to this problem – increase government subsidies, and if enough money is not available, just eliminate one aircraft carrier from the federal budget. Unfortunately, these arguments have been repeated ad nauseum in the nation's capitol with little effect beyond making their originator feel virtuous.

The mechanism for improving quality included in the 1990 grand compromise on day care shows more promise for improving quality. The essence of the compromise is to provide federal subsidies for states to create and enforce their own quality standards. This approach, though slow and of uncertain destination, avoids the bogie man of federal regulations and provides an obvious path for future policymaking through expanded federal and state funding. Through this set-aside mechanism, the issue of quality regulations is still alive, and it seems less likely than ever that direct federal regulation will play an important role in quality improvement.

Parent Choice

Republicans always made parent choice a central element in their approach to government subsidies for day care. The major question at issue is whether government or parents are going to decide the type of day-care facility in which children are placed. As we have seen, those who supported a more centralized system in which quality could be more easily achieved tended to support contracts and federal regulations, but if parents had the authority to select providers, contracts could not be used as the primary mechanism for funding day care. Hence, government officials would lose a great deal of control, especially because experience showed that parents would make day-care decisions on issues such as cost and convenience, and not necessarily on quality (Blau, 2001; Gormley, 1995).

The decisive moment for parent choice was the 1990 legislation that created the CCDBG. Although members of Congress – like developmental scientists and child advocates – never say they are against parent choice, on day-care issues Democrats have generally been much less enthusiastic about parent choice than Republicans. As in the case of federal regulations, the political philosophy of the two parties comes into play here. Republicans are naturally distrustful of government; Democrats believe government can serve as a primary vehicle for human improvement. On almost every social issue except abortion, Republicans want to maximize the choices of individuals and families and minimize the ability of government to make decisions for them. Democrats are not exactly the opposite because Democrats are not opposed to individual and family choices, but Democrats like government solutions a lot more than Republicans, even if sometimes supporting the government solution means reducing choices by families. When push comes to shove, and Democrats think the market and individual choices do not yield a satisfactory result, they are more willing than Republicans to impose the will of government. In the case of day care, Democrats think that high-quality programs are good for children and that when left to their own devices, many (perhaps most) parents do not choose high-quality care. Besides, if day care, like the public schools, is run by state and local government monopolies, it may be easier to ensure a given degree of quality.

Developmental scientists and child advocates are closer to Democrats than Republicans on the issue of parent choice. Like Democratic politicians, child advocates would not be caught saying that parent choice is not a good thing. Even so, given a choice between a program that would produce high-quality centers in which parents, especially low-income parents, could enroll their children as compared with a cash grant to parents, I think most developmentalists would choose the centers. The major justification is that in the long run, both the child and society will be better off if the preschool child attends high-quality care than if parents are given cash or allowed to make their own choices.

In any case, the seminal 1990 child-care legislation has put this issue to rest for the foreseeable future. The 1990 law, augmented by the child-care provisions in the 1996 welfare reform law, requires every state to offer parents a voucher that allows them to choose their own care. States have readily adopted voucher programs and now the overwhelming majority of day care supported through the CCDBG is paid for by vouchers. Parents select a wide variety of care, including lots of care from relatives and family day-care facilities. Moreover, in many states care by relatives, care in small family day-care settings, and care in churches is not subject to state regulation. It would seem to follow that future attempts to increase federal control over day care must either impose regulations on the entire market or work through mechanisms that influence parent choice. Based on the history of attempts to establish greater federal control of the day-care market, the former possibility seems beyond remote. The battle over quality, then, will take place at the state and local level, and a major part of the battle will consist of trying to influence the choices parents make in selecting child-care placements.

Religious Providers

The First Amendment of the Constitution provides that government cannot enact a law "respecting an establishment of religion." Nor can any law be passed "prohibiting the free exercise thereof." The application of this amendment to social services enjoys a long and colorful history. As a proud nonlawyer but a long-term observer and sometime participant, I would say that for the most part the history of this debate is a dazzling example of democracy in action. The problem is of utmost importance. When the Founding Fathers were writing the Constitution and its amendments, in a triumph of utilitarian over doctrinaire thinking, they concluded that the key to maximizing the benefits and minimizing the problems of religion was religious tolerance (Wilson, 2002). After centuries of slaughter, they interpreted the sweep of Western history to demonstrate that it was impossible to have state-supported religion without thereby creating deadly conflict within the borders of any nation. Equally repellant to them, any state that aggressively proselytized on behalf of its religion would be a great threat to peace among nations.

So they adopted a completely common-sense provision banning state "establishment of" or interference in the "exercise of" religion. But the real world is messy, and 200-plus years of jurisprudence have yet to settle exactly what these two phrases mean in practice. The fact that in America these conflicts are decided exclusively by informed debate and not bullets, and that our nation has never conducted a war in which religious doctrine was at issue, shows that the Founding Fathers have triumphed. Even so, the details are vital.

In the case of child care, there have been two primary details. First, the Civil Rights Act of 1964 allowed religious organizations receiving government funds to discriminate in hiring. Catholic day-care providers, for example, could hire Catholic teachers over equally or even more qualified Protestant or atheist teachers. This issue has received extensive discussion inside and outside Congress in almost every major child-care debate. One of the most extensive and spirited of these debates occurred on the floor of the House of Representatives during the partisan battles over the 1990 child-care bill. On this occasion, Congressman Don Edwards of California sponsored an amendment that would ban religious instruction and discrimination in hiring in any day-care facility receiving government funds (*Congressional Record*,

1990). After thorough and mostly pertinent debate, the House rejected the Edwards' amendment on a rather lopsided vote of 297 to 125. Discrimination in hiring is in.

The second major issue is the extent to which government funds can be used for religious instruction or proselytizing. Everyone agrees that use of government funds to directly promote any religion is unconstitutional because it would be "establishment" of religion. However, as always, the intermediate cases bring difficulty. If day care takes place in a church basement and there are pictures of Jesus and plaques with the Ten Commandments on the wall, isn't this a form of proselytizing? And what about reading stories based on the Torah or inspirational books about religion? If these conditions are interpreted as proselytizing and therefore Constitutionally banned, enormous change and confusion in day-care facilities would result. Around one-third of day care takes place in churches. So what to do with pictures of Jesus – or Vishnu for that matter? Cover them with cloth?

Although the original ABC bill proposed to do just that, a broader compromise was reached that did not require removing or covering religious symbols. Rather, members of Congress reasoned that if parents freely chose religious care, then government was not playing a role and could not be guilty of "establishing" religion. After all, the tax code provision subsidizing care selected by parents had been in the statutes since the 1950s and no one objected when parents selected religious care. Thus, all types of religious care could be supported under the voucher method of financing, but contracts could not be placed with religious providers because government would then be selecting a religious provider.

The major impact of this policy choice on the goals of developmental scientists is that it adds to diffusion and diversity in the day-care market. This policy had the effect of further strengthening parent choice, a primary source of market diversity which in turn makes strong regulation more difficult. Further, if at some future date a serious attempt is mounted to create a unified day-care program offered through the schools, parents wanting to retain their right to select a religious provider could constitute a formidable source of opposition to the universal policy.

Spending

An important issue in every policy decision is how much to spend on the policy. In the scholarly world, it is commonplace to look to economists for guidance on this question. The economists have an answer: make sure you spend your last dollar where it will do the most good. Good advice – with a modest problem or two. Whose good? How is the good measured and who gets to do the measuring? What are the total number of dollars available? Should you take dollars from other policies or programs to maximize a good achieved by a given program?

We should agree to bear in mind the economists' dictum to maximize good, while taking a more practical approach to deciding how much money to spend. Here is my recommendation. First, show that there is a real problem. Second, show that you have a solution that has a good chance of reducing the problem. Third, try to get as much money to solve the problem as the political system will bear.

In the case of day-care and preschool programs, social scientists are prone to produce big estimates of how much should be spent. Barbara Bergmann (Helburn & Bergmann, 2003), an emeritus professor at American University in Washington, DC, recommends $40 billion–$50 billion per year. David Blau (2001), a professor of economics at the University of North Carolina at Chapel Hill, has recently written a book arguing that around $95 billion per year is needed for a universal program of family allowances and day care. It is easy enough to see how such big numbers can be generated. A rough idea of the cost of universal preschool education can be computed by assuming that a quality program could be conducted for around $7,000 per child per year (Wolfe & Scrivner, 2003). The cost would be higher for infants and lower for older children, primarily because quality standards call for fewer teachers per child as children grow older. But if we accept an average cost of $7,000, and multiply by the number of children under age 5 (about 19 million), a universal program could cost as much as $133 billion. This figure is clearly too high because not all parents would put their children in a public program, many parents would wait until their children are age 1 or 2 or even older before putting them in group care, and so forth. It would also be possible to reduce costs by charging for care on a sliding-fee basis. Nonetheless, universal care starting in infancy, based roughly on the European model that so many American social scientists hold up as the ideal (Kamerman, 2000), would be very expensive.

Even so, I would not criticize scholars like Blau and Bergmann who recommend spending additional billions on a universal program. Indeed, for students of day-care and preschool education, it is edifying and challenging to read the spending estimates and accompanying policy justification they and other scholars produce. Estimates based on what a program would cost when fully implemented are a useful addition to the policy process. Besides, both reason and research could justify the conclusion that universal, high-quality day care might boost child development. It is at least as useful to consider, however, not what would be needed for a fully implemented program, but what the political system will bear and to go about getting it in a sophisticated way. On this criterion, child advocates and their allies among developmental scientists could improve their lobbying performance.

Advocates for new spending must assess a wide variety of factors to arrive at a reasoned judgment about a realistic target for increased spending in any given year or over a multiyear period. Since Congress creates a new budget every year, it is probably useful to build a funding strategy that includes annual goals. Whatever the goal, the first target should be the budgets produced by the White House and Congress each year. Briefly, the administration, based largely on detail work performed by the Office of Management and Budget, produces the President's budget by February of each year for the following fiscal year (which begins in October). Under the terms of the Budget Act, each House of Congress must also produce a budget and the budgets of the two Houses must be reconciled into a single budget that must then be passed by a majority vote in both Houses. The president plays no direct role in establishing the Congressional budget resolution, but – especially if either or both Houses are controlled by the same party as the White House – the president's budget often has considerable influence on the Congressional budget. Once approved, the Congressional budget is the blueprint for spending for the next fiscal year.

If child advocates manage to place a spending increase in either or preferably both the administration budget and the Congressional budget, the odds are high that the money will be forthcoming as Congress enacts authorization and appropriation bills during the course of the year. The opportunities to influence these budgets are legion but nearly all require connections with powerful members of administrative agencies, the White House, the Office of Management and Budget, the leadership in the House or Senate, or members of the Appropriations Committees in the House or Senate. Groups that lobby on a regular basis in Washington maintain relations with a select number of these well-placed individuals in order to ensure that their views and goals will, at a minimum, be heard. It is even rumored that lobbying groups have wined and dined and contributed to the political campaigns of such individuals.

Those favoring the children's cause often claim that they lack the resources to play this complicated and expensive game. Baloney. There are many influential organizations in Washington with exactly the types of contacts with executive and legislative branch agencies and the individuals just reviewed. These organizations include the Center on Budget and Policy Priorities, the Center for Law and Social Policy, Catholic Charities, the National Campaign for Better Jobs and Income, the Food Research and Action Committee, the Children's Defense Fund, and many others. And, of course, the exceptionally powerful organizations of state and local government – especially the National Governors Association, the American Public Human Services Association, and the National Council of State Legislatures – are always willing to accept more federal money for social programs and will lobby effectively to get it.

The history of federal support for preschool programs and day care illustrates that the Congressional and Executive branches are often willing to fork over large amounts of cash. Exhibit one is the Head Start budget. In constant dollars, Head Start funding has more than tripled from about $2.1 billion in 1965 to $6.7 billion in 2003. Similarly, spending on day care through the Child Care and Development Block Grant has exploded. Authorized at $750 million for 1991, by 2003 OMB estimates that combined federal and state spending will be well over $11 billion (Table 6.1).

On spending, it is a good bet that developmental scientists and advocates got more than they thought possible in 1996, although the growth of spending was due both to planned increases and to state decisions to use welfare money for child care. The second mechanism, the bigger of the two, depended on a traditional claim about welfare reform made by Republicans and largely dismissed by Democrats. Republicans had long argued that welfare spending, especially on entitlement programs, kept people on welfare, thereby confining them to dependency and wasting lots of public dollars that could be better spent for other purposes. The two undisputed and unprecedented effects of the 1996 reform law were to greatly reduce the cash welfare caseload and to greatly increase employment by former welfare mothers (Haskins, 2001). The exodus from the cash welfare rolls, combined with the fixed funding level of the TANF block grant, meant that by 1999 states collectively had about $8 billion or so each year in excess money that no longer needed to be spent on cash welfare. Hardly anyone, least of all child advocates, would argue that government funds are better spent on dependency-inducing welfare payments than on child care and other work supports that promote self-sufficiency.

Conclusion

Developmental scientists and child advocates give every indication of being disappointed about the current status of federal day-care and preschool education policy (Cohen, 2001). As Table 6.2 shows, they have won some and lost some. Even so, in 1965 there were virtually no federal investments in preschool education; today Head Start receives annual funding of $6.7 billion and serves over 900,000 children and families (in 2003). In 1965, there was virtually no federal spending on child care; today the CCDBG is funded at well over $11 billion and serves as many as 2 million children. In 1965, there were no federal programs that provided funding for disabled preschoolers; today there are three major programs that provide funding in excess of $1.3 billion. A minor problem with child advocates is that they tend to see the world through the eye of children's needs as advocates perceive those needs. However, Congress and the president make decisions about a huge range of policies, only one branch of which is programs for children and families. Many legislators, even many Democrats, could look back over the fruits of their labors since 1965 and conclude that they had won some important victories for children and families by creating several major programs and making substantial financial investments in day-care and preschool education.

It is true that the goal of a universal federal child development program of high quality serving all the nation's preschool children seems further away than ever. But the child-care system we now have certainly looks like a reasonable compromise among the conflicting preferences of liberal and conservative policymakers, researchers, advocates, federal and state administrators, parents, and the public. The public does not want to pay for a universal, high-quality, $100 billion per year program. Parents like to choose their own care, and lots of parents like care in church basements and in their neighborhoods. Many Americans are wary of government regulations, especially federal regulations.

In short, we have a typically American system of day-care and preschool education. A mix of quality, price, type of care, and government subsidies characterizes the child-care market. That is the way Americans like it; that is the way the system is likely to remain for the foreseeable future – within these broad parameters, improved quality, increased government subsidies, and better preparation for schooling are possible, especially if the current concern with the educational achievement of poor and minority children continues to grow (Haskins, 2003; Thernstrom & Thernstrom, 2003). There is a lot to like here.

References

Belsky, J. (1986). Infant day care: A cause for concern? *Zero to three 6*, 5, 1–9.

Blau, D. M. (2001). *The Child Care Problem: An Economic Analysis*. New York: Sage.

Bloom, B. S. (1964). *Stability and Change in Human Characteristics*. New York: Wiley.

Bowlby, J. (1952). *Maternal Care and Mental Health* (Monograph Series, No. 2; 2nd ed.). Geneva: World Health Organization.

Brooks-Gunn, J., Wen-Jui H., & Waldfogel, J. (2002). Maternal employment and child cognitive outcomes in the first three years of life: The NICHD study of early child care. *Child Development 73*, 4, 1052–1072.

Caro, R. A. (2002). *The Years of Lyndon Johnson: Master of the Senate.* New York: Knopf.

Cohen, S. S. (2001). *Championing Child Care.* New York: Columbia.

Committee on Ways and Means, U.S. House of Representatives. (1989). *General Explanation of the Family Support Act of 1988* (Public Law 100–485; WMCP: 101–103). Washington, DC: U.S. Government Printing Office.

Committee on Ways and Means, U.S. House of Representatives. (1990 and 1996). *Green Book: Background Material and Data on Programs within the Jurisdiction of the Committee on Ways and Means* (WMCP: 106–114). Washington, DC: U.S. Government Printing Office.

Congressional Budget Office. (1996, December). *Federal Budgetary Implications of the Personal Responsibility and Work Opportunity Reconciliation Act of 1996* (CBO Memorandum). Washington, DC: Government Printing Office.

Congressional Record. (1990). 101st Congress, 2nd Session. Vol. 136, pt. 36, H1312–H1322.

Department of Health and Human Services. (2003). *Child Care and Development Fund (CCDF) Report to Congress – Fiscal Year 2001.* Washington, DC: Child Care Bureau.

Divine-Hawkins, P. (1981). *Family Day Care in the United States* (DHHS Publication No. (OHDS) 80-30287). Washington, DC: U.S. Department of Health and Human Services.

Gish, M., & Harper, S. (2002, October 8). *Child Care Programs under the Child Care and Development Fund* (RL31605). Washington, DC: Congressional Research Service.

Gormley, W. T., Jr. (1995). *Everybody's Children: Child Care as a Public Problem.* Washington, DC: Brookings Institution.

Gray, S. W., & Klaus R. A. (1970). The Early Training Project: A seventh-year report. *Child Development 41*, 4, 909–924.

Haskins, R. (2001). Effects of welfare reform on family income. In R. Blank & R. Haskins (Eds.), *The New World of Welfare.* Washington, DC: Brookings Institution.

Haskins, R. (2003). Head Start gets makeover. *Education Next 4*, 1, 26–33.

Haskins, R., & Kotch, J. (1986). Day care and illness: Evidence, costs, and public policy. *Pediatrics* (Supplement) *77*, 6, part 2.

Helburn, S., & Bergmann, B. R. (2003). *America's Child Care Problem: The Way Out.* New York: Palgrave Macmillan.

Hunt, J. McVicker. (1961). *Stability and Change in Human Characteristics.* New York: Wiley.

Jensen, A. R. (1969). How much can we boost IQ and scholastic achievement? *Harvard Educational Review 39*, 1, 1–123.

Kamerman, S. B. (2000). Early childhood education and care: An overview of the development in the OECD countries. *International Journal of Educational Research 33*, 1, 7–30.

Malone, M. (1971, June 24). *Summary of Selected Proposals Related to Child Care* (71–162 ED). Washington, DC: Congressional Research Service.

Moynihan, D. P. (1970). *Maximum Feasible Misunderstanding.* New York: MacMillan.

Moynihan, D. P. (1973). *The Politics of a Guaranteed Income: The Nixon Administration and the Family Assistance Plan.* New York: Vintage.

Nelson, J. R. (1982). The politics of federal child care regulation. In E. F. Zigler & E. W. Gordon (Eds.), *Day Care: Scientific and Social Policy Issues* (pp. 267–306). Boston: Auburn House.

Nixon, R. M. (1972). Veto of the Economic Opportunity Amendments of 1971. *Public Papers of the Presidents of the United States: Richard Nixon, 1971.* Washington, DC: U.S. Government Printing Office.

Phillips, D., McCartney, K., & Scarr, S. (1987). Selective review of infant day care research: A cause for concern! *Zero to Three 8,* 1, 18–21.

Spar, K. (1996, October 7). *Child Care for Low-Income Families: Federal Programs and Welfare Reform* (96-780 EPW). Washington, DC: Congressional Research Service.

Steiner, G. Y. (1971). *The State of Welfare.* Washington, DC: Brookings Institution.

Steiner, G. Y. (1976). *The Children's Cause.* Washington, DC: Brookings Institution.

Steiner, G. Y. (1981). *The Futility of Family Policy.* Washington, DC: Brookings Institution.

Thernstrom, A., & Thernstrom, S. (2003). *No Excuses: Closing the Racial Gap in Learning.* New York: Simon & Schuster.

U.S. Census Bureau. (2001). *Statistical Abstract of the United States: 2001* (121st ed.). Washington, DC: U.S. Government Printing Office.

U.S. General Accounting Office. (1994). *Early Childhood Programs: Multiple Programs and Overlapping Target Groups* (GAO/HEHS-95-4FS). Washington, DC: U.S. Government Printing Office.

Waldfogel, J., Wen-Jui, H., & Brooks-Gunn, J. (2002). The effects of early maternal employment on child cognitive development. *Demography 39,* 2, 369–392.

Westinghouse Learning Corporation. (1969). *The Impact of Head Start: An Evaluation of the Effects of Head Start on Children's Cognitive and Affective Development.* Athens, OH: Ohio University.

Whitman, D., & Lynn, L. E. (1981). *President as Policymaker: Jimmy Carter and Welfare Reform.* Philadelphia: Temple.

Wilson, J. Q. (2002). The reform Islam needs. *City Journal 12,* 4, 27–35.

Wolfe, B., & Scrivner, S. (2003). Financing universal preschool for four-year-olds: The time has come. In I. Sawhill (Ed.), *One Percent for the Kids: New Policies, Brighter Futures for America's Children.* Washington, DC: Brookings Institution.

Zigler, E., & Muenchow, S. (1992). *Head Start: The Inside Story of America's Most Successful Educational Experiment.* New York: Basic Books.

Zigler, E., & Valentine, J. (Eds.). (1979). *Project Head Start: A Legacy of the War on Poverty.* New York: Free Press.

PART THREE

Designing Child Health Policies

7 Developmental Epidemiology

The Role of Developmental Psychology for Public Health in the 21st Century

Stephen L. Buka

Introduction

The leading causes of morbidity and mortality worldwide have been transformed dramatically over the past century. In the United States, since the early 1900s, there has been an unprecedented decline in the major infectious diseases of childhood, such as diptheria, scarlet fever, tuberculosis, and small pox. Simultaneously, there has been an increase in the prevalence of chronic diseases and disabilities, such as asthma, mental retardation, cerebral palsy, epilepsy, and childhood cancers. More recently there has been increasing concern for psychiatric, behavioral, and social disorders of childhood and a call for new methods to study and reduce these "new" psychosocial morbidities of childhood and adolescence (Buka & Lipsitt, 1994; Haggerty, Roughmann, & Pless, 1975).

This shifting profile of health concerns is not limited to either children or to the United States. Christopher Murray and Alan Lopez (1996) have conducted a comprehensive summary of the leading causes of mortality and disability, in 1990 and projected to 2020. To conduct this assessment, the Global Burden of Disease report calculated a single measure of the total "burden" that could be attributed to a particular disease or disorder, factoring in both the number of years lost (through premature death) and, for nonfatal diseases, the resulting losses in the quality of life. The resulting "Disability-Adjusted Life Year" (DALY) expresses years of life lost to premature death and years lived with a disability of specified severity and duration; one DALY represents one lost year of healthy life. Figure 7.1 summarizes the relative burden associated with 15 conditions, both in 1990 and projected for 2020. With increasing sanitary, public health, and medical advances worldwide, traditional causes of mortality and morbidity, such as respiratory infections, diarrhoeal diseases, and

174   *Stephen L. Buka*

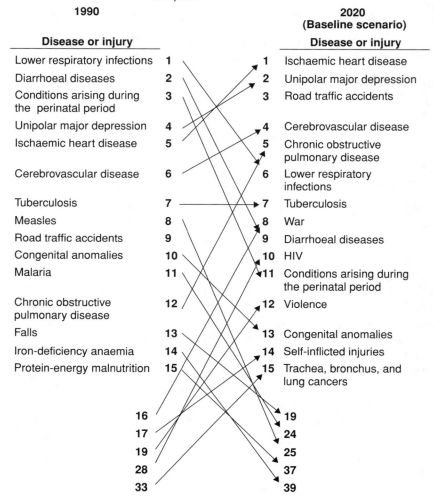

Figure 7.1. Change in the rank order of disease burden for 15 leading causes, world, 1990–2020. [Murray & Lopez, 1996 p. 375]

perinatal complications will have a dramatically reduced impact worldwide. And, conversely, conditions that have major behavioral, psychiatric, and psychological aspects, such as depression, motor vehicle accidents, losses due to war, violence, and self-inflicted injuries will lead global public health concerns in the coming generation.

Returning to the domestic situation for children, there are ample data in the United States to support this concern. For instance, evidence that the mental health of children and adolescents is an area warranting continued scientific and public health attention is well documented, most recently by the Office of the U.S. Surgeon General (USDHHS, 1999, 2001), the World Health Organization, and the National Institute of Mental Health (NIMH, 2001). Epidemiologic data suggest that roughly 20% of children ages 1–18 are in need of mental health services in the United States, half of which have mental illnesses severe enough to cause some level of impairment (Burns & Offord, 1972; Shaffer et al., 1996). Despite the high prevalence among children and adolescents, only about 5%–7% have received services for their disability (NIMH, 2001). This unmet need for services has raised concerns as children with emotional and behavior problems are at increased risk for dropping out of school, being in trouble with the law, and having an overall lower quality of life. Furthermore, mental disorders, particularly if left untreated, are likely to persist into adulthood. According to the 2001 Surgeon General's Conference on Children's Mental Health, about 74% of 21 year olds with mental disorders had prior mental health problems.

In addition to these social costs, there is a high fiscal burden associated with child and adolescent mental and behavioral disorders. A study in California found that 8.1% of hospital discharges for children ages 6–12 were for mental illness and that these children accounted for close to 90,000 days of hospitalization and $85 million in hospital charges in 1992 (Chabra, Chavez, & Harris, 1999). A national estimate of child mental health expenditures was recently produced by Sturm and colleagues (2001). In 1998, the total treatment expenditures for child and adolescent mental health were $11.75 billion including inpatient, outpatient, and medication costs. Unfortunately, the negative impact of poor child and adolescent mental health is felt worldwide and is likely to get worse. The World Health Organization predicts that by the year 2020, childhood neuropsychiatric disorders will become one of the leading causes of morbidity, mortality, and disability among children worldwide (USDHHS, 1999).

This summary of the global burden associated with child and adolescent mental disorder underscores the need for and utility of epidemiologic methods and data. As applied to behavioral morbidities of children, youth, and adults, epidemiologic investigations have been described as having three major purposes (Kellam & Ensminger, 1980). For public health planning purposes, epidemiology provides critical information regarding the prevalence of disorders, service utilization, treatment outcome, and costs. As epidemiology is the study of the distribution and determinants of disease in human populations, a second purpose of epidemiologic investigations is to advance understanding of the origins and course of behavioral morbidities. This includes understanding the significance of early circumstances, both biological and social, that contribute to the etiology and progression of disease, disorder, and dysfunction. Such data ideally lead to the third major application of epidemiology, the design and assessment of preventive and treatment interventions. As is apparent, the aims and approach of epidemiology have much in common with applied developmental psychology.

However, the limitations of traditional epidemiologic methods for studying complex social, behavioral, and psychiatric conditions are also apparent (Susser & Susser, 1996). There has been an overreliance on what has been termed "black box" epidemiology, with simple attempts to identify single risk factors. What is needed is to move beyond "risk factorology" to a more developmentally sensitive approach to epidemiologic investigations. As we have described previously (Buka & Lipsitt, 1994), we propose a new form of "developmental" epidemiology that draws on the theories, principles, and methods of (a) modern epidemiology, (b) developmental psychology, and (c) a variety of specific content domains including, psychiatry, education, and clinical psychology (Figure 7.2). The relative contribution of these applied areas will vary depending upon the condition under investigation, whether it be depression, drug use, violence, or teenage pregnancy. Consistent with others (e.g., Kuh & Ben-Shlomo, 1997), we call for a shift from an earlier emphasis on the "4 Ds" of traditional epidemiology: description of the distribution and determinants of diseases, to the "4 Cs" of developmental epidemiology: a focus on the causes and mechanisms underlying complex disorders, with recognition of the role of social contexts. We should specify from the outset that adopting a developmental orientation to the epidemiologic investigation of disorders of human populations does not imply a focus solely on infants and children. Rather, our view is that questions of the etiology and course of complex human disorders will best be answered by adopting a lifespan developmental orientation.

In this chapter, we describe and detail several features that help move epidemiologic investigations to become more developmental in nature. These principles of developmental epidemiology include (1) a lifecourse perspective (Ben-Shlomo & Kuh, 2002) that takes into consideration risk factors and processes that may exert an influence long before the manifestation of the outcome or disease state; (2) recognition of the role of multiple risks or component causes that combine to help explain the etiology of the outcome under study; and (3) attention to temporal sequences and a recognition that the order

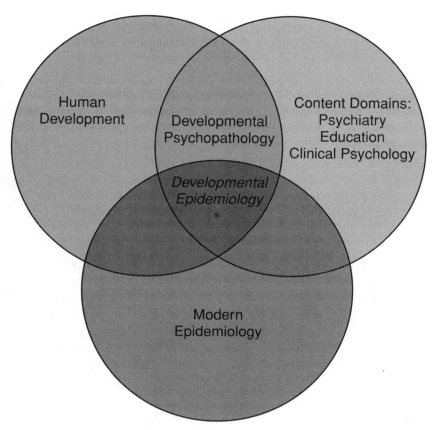

Figure 7.2. Developmental epidemiology: a multidisciplinary approach. (Buka & Lipsitt, 1994)

in which antecedent conditions are experienced or emerge may be critical in understanding etiology and prevention. While these first three principles all concern our conceptualization of risk conditions antecedent to the outcome of interest, the fourth principle focuses on conceptualization and characterization of the outcome condition, disorder, or disease. Developmentally informative epidemiologic investigations will also need to adopt a longitudinal approach to "disease classification," differentiating transient and time-limited forms of disorder from more stable and persistent versions. Examples of this approach, and details of these four principles of developmentally sensitive and informative investigations will be provided in the sections below.

Empirical examples of these principles will be drawn from a large-scale longitudinal study that we are conducting, drawing on the National Collaborative Perinatal Project (Niswander & Gordon, 1972).

The National Collaborative Perinatal Project: Developmental Epidemiology in the Field

History and Overview

The National Collaborative Perinatal Project (NCPP) was initiated 40 years ago to investigate prospectively the prenatal and familial antecedents of pediatric, neurological, and psychological disorders of childhood. Twelve university-affiliated medical centers participated in this national study, two in New England (Harvard Medical School and Brown University). The Project entailed a single study design involving the systematic collection of data through the prospective observation and examination of over 50,000 pregnancies through the first seven years of life. Obstetrical intake occurred between January 2, 1959, and December 31, 1965. Cases were selected on the basis of a sampling frame defined for each study center (Broman, 1987). Women in the study were representative of the patients receiving prenatal care in each participating center. At the conclusion of the study, a total of 55,908 births were recorded nationally, approximately 17,000 of which occurred in Boston/Providence. In the total population, follow-up rates for survivors were 88% at 1 year, 75% at 4 years, and 79% at 7 years. Major findings from the National Project have been summarized by Niswander and Gordon (1972), Broman, Nichols, & Kennedy (1975), Nichols and Chen (1981), and Broman, Bien, & Shaughnessy (1985).

Data from examinations and interviews were recorded by trained staff at each site beginning at the time of registration for prenatal care, using standardized protocols, forms, manuals, and codes. At the time of the first prenatal visit, a complete reproductive and gynecological history, a recent and past medical history, a socioeconomic interview, and a family history were recorded. A socioeconomic index (SEI) was assigned to each pregnancy, adapted from the Bureau of the Census and derived from the education and occupation of the head of household along with household income (Myrianthopoulos & French, 1968). Prenatal clinic visits were scheduled every month during the first seven months of pregnancy, every two weeks during the eighth month, and every week thereafter. An interval prenatal history covering the period since the last visit was recorded at *each* prenatal visit, along with results of pertinent laboratory tests and physical exams. Blood samples were collected for serology and for storage of frozen sera, and are available from the NIH repository for 98% of the pregnancies of the New England cohort (17,502 pregnancies and 48,695 separate samples, approximately three time points per pregnancy). After admission for delivery, trained observers recorded the events of labor and delivery, and the obstetrician in charge completed a summary of labor and delivery protocols. The neonate was observed in the delivery room and examined by a pediatrician at 24-hour intervals in the newborn nursery. A neurological examination was performed at two days. Nurses' observations and results of laboratory tests were recorded and a diagnostic summary of the nursery period was completed by a study physician.

After the neonatal stage, the child was scheduled for at least five subsequent assessments at ages 4 months, 8 months, 12 months, 4 years, and 7 years (assessments at 3 and 8 years were planned but discontinued). At each follow-up examination the mother was interviewed about the child's interval history, records of medical treatment obtained if appropriate, and physical measurements taken. Pediatric-neurological examinations occurred at 4 months, 12 months, and 7 years and psychological examinations at 8 months, 4 years, and 7 years. Interval histories were updated at 18 months, 2 years, 5 years, and 6 years. Family and social history information was obtained from the mother at intake and the seventh year. Diagnostic summaries were prepared by study physicians following the first and seventh year. Follow-up rates for the New England cohort surpassed the overall project rates; over 80% of the NE cohort completed the final full assessment at age 7.

Broman (1987) organized the thousands of study variables according to six epochs. A partial list is presented. For clarity of presentation, the original NCPP mothers (now ages 50–70) will be referred to as G1 (Generation 1), the offspring born in the NCPP from 1959 to 1966 (now ages 34–40) will be referred to as G2, and the children of the G2 offspring will be referred to as G3 (Hardy et al., 1997).

1. **Prenatal period.** Sociodemographic characteristics of the family, including G1 mother and father race, ethnicity, birthplace, age; mother's and father's parents' birthplaces; maternal and paternal educational attainment, occupation, and annual income; income of family during first three months of pregnancy; sources of income; number of persons supported and producing income; income changes during first three months of pregnancy; employment duration; number jobs past year; type of residence; duration at current residence; number of moves in the past five years; number of persons and rooms in household; detailed maternal medical and reproductive

history; paternal medical/psychiatric history (including first-degree relatives); repeat prenatal assessments including laboratory tests, self-reports of smoking, accidents, and illnesses; course and complications of pregnancy.

2. **Labor and Delivery.** Variables include length of labor, fetal heart rate, type of delivery, administration of anesthetics (type, duration, amount).

3. **Neonatal Period.** Birthweight, head circumference, gestational age, size for dates (small for gestational age), intrauterine growth retardation, Apgar scores, malformations, minor physical anomalies, genetic syndromes, breast/bottle feeding.

4. **Infancy.** Weight, height, head circumference (three times), test scores and behavior ratings from the research version of the Bayley Scales of Infant Development, fine and gross motor development, neurological soft and hard signs, two pediatric-neurological examinations, diagnostic summary of first year of life. Infant and maternal behavioral observations and ratings.

5. **Preschool Period.** Speech, language and hearing examination (partial sample only); physical measurements; age 4 psychological examination assessing intellectual functioning (Stanford–Binet Intelligence Scale), motor skills, concept formation ability (Graham–Ernhart Block Sort Test), and behavioral observations.

6. **Age 7.** *Reassessment* of demographic, socioeconomic, medical/psychiatric, family composition, residence, moves, and other family characteristics obtained at intake assessment (see 'Prenatal Period' above). *Child medical status*, based on a pediatric-neurological examination at age 7 and review of all medical records between 1 year and 7 years; neurological soft and hard signs. *Intellectual, academic, and perceptual motor functioning* assessed by the Wechsler Intelligence Scale for Children (WISC), the Wide Range Achievement Test (WRAT) the Goodenough–Harris Draw-a-Person Test, the Bender–Gestalt Test, the Auditory Vocal Association Test from the Illinois Test of Psycholinguistic Abilities, and the Tactile Finger Recognition Test. Behavioral observations and ratings.

Follow-up of the Providence Cohort of the NCPP

For the past 15 years we have been following members of both the Providence and Boston cohorts of the NCPP as adults (Buka et al., 1999; Buka,

Lipsitt, & Tsuang, 1988). The new name that we have given this long-term lifecourse investigation is the New England Family Study (NEFS). The Providence component of the NEFS includes 4,062 offspring, now ages 36–42. Of these, 1,780 of these have been selected for follow-up into adulthood. Selection for follow-up occurred in two separate phases; in each, a stratified random sample was drawn from the entire cohort to investigate the association between early life factors and adult psychiatric, behavioral, and social disorders. During phase one, initiated in 1984, 995 eligible subjects with and without pregnancy/delivery complications were selected for follow-up and 693 interviewed (Buka, Tsuang, & Lipsitt, 1993). In the second phase, initiated in 1996, 1,056 subjects with and without potential learning disabilities were selected and 720 were interviewed (Buka, Satz, Seidman, & Lipsitt, 1998). Interviews were typically conducted in person by well-trained lay interviewers; however, for approximately 15% of the sample respondents could not be met in person and were interviewed by telephone by the same pool of interviewers (Buka et al., 1993). Subjects were relocated using a variety of methods, including contact with family members and use of phone and address directories, internet services and the like. Following mailed introductions, researchers contacted the participants, described the adult protocol, and scheduled interviews at the subject home or study offices. Subjects were compensated at the rate of $10 per hour for their time. Adult follow-up interviews were conducted when the subjects were between the ages of 17 and 39; those individuals who were sampled during the first phase of the study were 17–27 years old, whereas those in the second phase were between 30 and 39 years old. Some subjects ($n = 146$) were interviewed twice (Gilman, Kawachi, Fitzmaurice, & Buka, 2003).

With this background, we proceed to demonstrate the first of four principles of developmental epidemiology.

Principles and Examples of Developmental Epidemiology

The Importance of Early Life Events for Adult Disorders

The past decade has witnessed renewed interest in questions of the long-term health effects of social and physical conditions that occur during gestation and childhood (Ben-Shlomo & Kuh, 2002; Kuh & Ben-Shlomo, 1997). Issues such as the impact of birth complications, critical and sensitive periods in development, and mechanisms explaining intergenerational transmission of

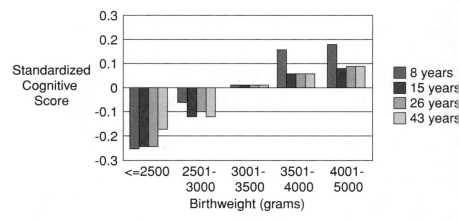

Figure 7.3. Mean differences in standardized cognitive scores by birthweight (compared to middle category), adjusted for sex, father's social class, mother's education, birth order, and mother's age. [Richards et al., *British Medical Journal*, 2001]

behavior and disease have long been a focus of inquiry in developmental psychology. These areas have traditionally received less attention in the field of epidemiology and for theories of disease causation and prevention. More recently, there has been particular interest in the long-term impacts of conditions occurring during the prenatal and perinatal periods and first few years of life. We provide several examples of the importance of this orientation for study of behavioral conditions, four from our work with the New England Family Study and the first from a similar long-term investigation in England.

Association between Birthweight and Intellectual Performance across the Lifecourse. While interest in the relationship of an infant's birth status to childhood functioning and intellectual performance has a long tradition, the longer-term outcomes associated with infant birthweight have only been documented more recently. One such effort was conducted by Richards, Hardy, Kuh, and Wadsworth (2001), who examined this relationship among 5,362 subjects followed from birth through age 43, as part of the 1946 United Kingdom birth cohort. As shown in Figure 7.3, at age 8 smaller babies (weighing less than 2,500 grams or approximately 5.5 pounds at birth) scored approximately 0.25 standard deviations lower on tests of general cognitive ability than normal weight babies (3,000–3,499 grams). Similarly, larger babies (above 4,000 grams) scored approximately 0.2 standard deviations higher.

The direct and graded relation between birthweight and cognitive performance persists well into adulthood. In a sample of 3,262 of these participants assessed at age 43, smaller babies still performed approximately 0.2 SD lower and larger babies about 0.1 SD higher than normal weight babies. The relationship of infant birthweight and general health status at birth on later cognitive performance persists throughout the lifecourse.

Perinatal Medication and Drug Abuse in Early Adulthood. Another set of conditions during the prenatal and perinatal periods that have impacts well into adult life involves medications and other substances prescribed to or taken by the pregnant woman. Previous studies in Sweden have suggested an association between drugs administered during labor and delivery and drug addiction (to both opiates and amphetamines) in adulthood (Jacobson, Nyberg, Eklund, Bygdeman, & Rydberg, 1988; Jacobson et al., 1990). We investigated this hypothesis using the New England Family Study (Nyberg, Buka, & Lipsitt, 2000). We identified 69 adults with well-documented histories of drug abuse or dependence to cocaine, hallucinogens, narcotics, and other hard drugs and compared them to 33 nonabusing siblings. There were significantly different levels of maternal medication during labor and delivery among the offspring who would go on to have a history of drug abuse, compared to their nonabusing siblings. Approximately one-quarter of the subjects who met diagnostic criteria for drug abuse had received high (three or more) doses of opiates or barbiturates during labor and delivery, compared to 6% of their unaffected siblings. While the mechanisms through which such long-term effects from infancy to adulthood operate remain obscure, the findings have analogs in the animal literature, suggesting that fetal exposure to opiates and other medications may alter neurodevelopment in a manner that influences psychological and physiological responses to these same and related substances in adulthood (Meyerson, 1985).

Maternal Smoking During Pregnancy and Risk of Tobacco Dependence among Adult Offspring. The long-term impacts of conditions occurring during the prenatal and perinatal period are also highlighted in our recent study of risks for tobacco dependence in adulthood. Cigarette smoking and nicotine dependence is clearly a huge public health concern of global significance (Murray & Lopez, 1996). Numerous theories, ranging from genetic to social marketing, exist to account for individual differences in levels of use and dependence. Most, however, focus on factors quite proximal to the youth at-risk for initiating smoking or the adult smoker who may or may not develop physiologic dependence to nicotine. In line with the general principle that we are presenting, developmentally informed studies of health behaviors and disorders that "emerge" later in life will increasingly benefit from considering risk conditions evident prior to the outcome. In particular, we have an interest in maternal smoking during pregnancy (MSP) as a potential determinant of later nicotine dependence among the adult offspring. A physiologic link between MSP and offspring smoking is plausible because nicotine, and other substances in cigarette smoke, cross the placental barrier and may have direct and long-term impacts on the neurological development of the fetus (Corrigall, 1991; Haass & Kubler, 1997; Koob & Le Moal, 1997). In particular, the nicotine that passes from mother to fetus stimulates nicotinic receptors, which are present from the early stages of fetal development (Ernst, Moolchan, & Robinson, 2001). This activity may cause permanent abnormalities in the brain's dopaminergic regulation (McFarland, Seidler, & Slotkin, 1991; Muneoka et al., 1997). These effects, which may even occur at lower nicotine doses and in the absence of notable fetal abnormalities (Navarro et al., 1989), may result in an increased liability to nicotine dependence compared to those who have not been exposed to tobacco smoke in utero (Griesler, Kandel, & Davies, 1998).

Accordingly, we used data on adult smoking and marijuana use in the New England Family Study to test two hypotheses (Buka, Shenassa, & Niaura, 2003). First, we predicted that individuals exposed to tobacco smoke in utero would be at particularly elevated risk of progressing from cigarette use to regular use and dependence. Second, such individuals would be at especially elevated risk for nicotine dependence in contrast to dependence to other substances, such as marijuana. We tested the hypotheses that (1) MSP was associated with a heightened risk of nicotine dependence, and risk of progressing from tobacco use to tobacco dependence, but not for early stages of smoking behavior; and (2) MSP predicted nicotine dependence but not marijuana dependence.

We used prospective data from the two samples of offspring in the New England Family Study, described above. Maternal smoking during pregnancy was assessed during each prenatal visit for 1,242 participants. Offspring smoking behavior and lifetime risk of nicotine dependence was obtained by structured interview using the Diagnostic Interview Schedule (Robins, Helzer, Croughan, & Ratcliff, 1981) at a mean age of 29 years. As predicted, offspring whose mothers reported smoking a pack or more of cigarettes during their pregnancy were significantly more likely to meet DSM criteria for lifetime tobacco dependence 29 years later than offspring of mothers who reported to have never smoked during pregnancy (odds ratio = 1.6, 95% confidence interval = 1.2, 2.1). The odds of progressing from ever smoking to nicotine dependence was almost twice as great for offspring whose mothers smoked during pregnancy (OR $= 1.9$, 95% CI $= 1.3, 2.9$). These significant differences remained after adjusting for participants' gender, age, and maternal socioeconomic status (SES) and age at pregnancy. The findings were specific for tobacco dependence; odds of marijuana dependence were not significantly elevated among the offspring of smokers. We concluded that offspring of mothers who smoked a pack or more of cigarettes during pregnancy are at elevated risk of developing nicotine, but not marijauana, dependence as adults. Also, interventions that can reduce maternal smoking during pregnancy may help prevent nicotine dependence in the subsequent generation.

Early Childhood SES and Lifetime Risk of Depression. The previous examples (birthweight, perinatal medication, and maternal smoking during pregnancy) have all involved early biological conditions and risk for adult disorders. We conclude this section with an example of the long-term sequelae of early social and environmental factors, focusing on the risk for later depression associated with childhood socioeconomic conditions (Gilman, Kawachi, Fitzmaurice, & Buka, 2002). Although previous epidemiologic investigations have demonstrated an increased risk of depression among individuals of lower socioeconomic status (SES) (Dohrenwend et al., 1992; Muntaner, Eaton, Diala, Kessler, & Sorlie, 1998; Murphy et al., 1991), many questions remain about the origins of these socioeconomic differentials (Dohrenwend, 1990; Piccinelli & Wilkinson, 2000). Mounting evidence of the long-term relation between early childhood conditions and the onset of depression raises the concern that SES differences in depression among adults originate during childhood (Johnson, Cohen, Dohrenwend, Link, & Brook, 1999; Kessler & Magee, 1993; Lundberg, 1993; Power, Hertzman, Matthews, & Manor, 1997; Sadowski, Ugarte, Kolvin, Kaplan, & Barnes, 1999).

Previous investigations of the long-term effects of childhood SES on depression have been limited by the use of retrospective reports of the childhood environment (Hallstrom, 1987; Jacobson, Fasman, & DiMascio, 1975; Kessler & Magee, 1993). Retrospective reports of childhood conditions are subject to measurement error that may be exacerbated by psychopathology (Calev, 1996; Crum, Bucholz, Helzer, & Anthony, 1992). We investigated prospectively the association between childhood SES and the first-time occurrence of a major depressive episode using the NEFS cohort.

Childhood SES, indexed by parental occupation, was assessed at the time of participants' birth and seventh year. A lifetime history and age at onset of major depressive episode were ascertained via structured interviews according to diagnostic criteria for 1,132 adult offspring. Survival analyses were used to model the likelihood of first depression onset as a function of childhood SES. The results indicated that participants from lower SES backgrounds had nearly a twofold increase in risk for major depression compared to those from the highest SES background independent of childhood demographic factors, family history of mental illness, and adult SES. Independent of the adult educational attainment of respondents, respondents from lower SES backgrounds had a risk of depression that was between 1.69 to 2.07 times higher than those from the highest SES background. We concluded that lower childhood SES is indeed prospectively linked to a higher risk of major depression in adults, and that social inequalities in adult depression, which might have resulted from lower socioeconomic attainment secondary to adult depression, originate early in life.

These findings, combined with those of other investigators (Fan & Eaton, 2001; Johnson et al., 1999; Ritsher, Warner, Johnson, & Dohrenwend, 2001; Sadowski et al., 1999), indicate that a developmental perspective is needed to understand the genesis of social inequalities in depression (Boyce et al., 1998; Buka & Lipsitt, 1994). One possibility is that during early childhood, disadvantaged social environments may have particularly adverse consequences for long-term mental health because of their effects on psychological development (McLoyd, 1998). Children in disadvantaged situations may acquire less control over their environment (Abramson, Seligman, & Teasdale, 1978) and may develop difficulties in forming intimate relationships (attachments) (Bowlby, 1977; Mickelson, Kessler, & Shaver, 1997); both of these factors may increase children's vulnerability to depression throughout the lifecourse. In addition, individuals from disadvantaged backgrounds may be more likely to experience stressful life events and be less capable of coping with such events when they occur (Brown & Harris, 1978). Other potential mediators of this association include material hardship, family disruption, strained social relationships, and poor physical health, each of which is related to depression (Berkman & Kawachi, 2000). While further research is needed to identify the pathways linking childhood conditions to SES differences in the incidence of major depression, the major point of this example is to again highlight that the search for the causes and potential prevention of depression, a major public health concern for adult populations, must consider developmental influences early in life.

Multiple Component Causes

The preceding section, titled the "Importance of Early Life Events for Adult Disorders," has been over-simplified to emphasize the view that a modern public health approach that focuses on psychiatric and behavioral conditions will need to consider conditions occurring well prior to the onset of the disorder. We have demonstrated how specific conditions or events in early life – birthweight, maternal smoking, and family socioeconomic circumstances – are associated with increased likelihood of a number of adverse outcomes many decades later. Two important caveats must be kept in mind, however. The first is, of course, that evidence of a mere association between earlier and later events may have little to no utility in the search for cause and prevention. Evidence of association does not provide evidence of causation, a fact well recognized by contemporary epidemiologists. Rather, there has been a movement toward a "modern" epidemiology that seeks to evaluate hypotheses about the causation of disorders and to relate these event occurrences to characteristics of people and their environment (Rothman, 1986). Although, we may never be able to rely on experiments, either natural or manmade, to test the hypothesis that maternal smoking during pregnancy increases nicotinic receptors and the risk for nicotine dependence among offspring, we nevertheless have available a set of logical and methodological procedures to help us approximate the results of such an experiment (Hill, 1965). So, as in most branches of behavioral and social science, the developmentally aligned form of epidemiology must struggle to distinguish causal and noncausal antecedents of conditions of study – to distinguish true risk "factors" from mere risk "indicators" (Miettinen, 1985). The "cause" of a disorder can be defined as any event, condition, or characteristic that plays an essential role in producing an occurrence of the disorder (Rothman & Greeland, 1998). Epidemiologic research seeks to determine which antecedent conditions are essential characteristics of the disorder occurrence (i.e., true risk factors) as opposed to mere risk indicators or confounding variables.

So, the first challenge in examining early origins of later disorder is to attempt to distinguish antecedents that may and may not have causal significance. The search for such single element causes may be naïve and largely unfruitful. Instead, both conceptual and practical wisdom suggests that there will be multiple developmental antecedents for most behavioral disorders, or, to paraphrase Garmezy, that "the interaction IS the main effect." Similarly, current epidemiologic reasoning argues against single models of causation and asserts that the cause of any effect likely consists of a constellation of components that act in concert (Rothman, 1976).

In the developmental origins of behavioral disorders, as in many facets of developmental science, conditions of interest are likely to arise from a constellation of converging risk conditions. There are many examples of conditions or "multiple risks" that contribute to disorder only when combined with other contributing factors. These conditions, nonetheless, do play a role in the causation of a disorder and have been termed "component" causes (Rothman, 1976). "Disorder" arises only when the entire critical constellation of component causes is present; this complete constellation has been described as a "sufficient cause" – the set of minimal conditions and events that produce disorder (Buka & Lipsitt, 1994; Rothman, 1976). Individual components may be regarded as necessary, but not sufficient, elements in the causal process. Any disorder may result from several different sufficient causes, which, in turn, represent the combination of multiple component causes. This general model has implications for conceptualizing the role of interactions (all component causes 'interact' in constituting a sufficient cause), and for understanding the strength of causality and the proportion of disorder attributable to a specific cause. Low childhood SES may be a strong and considerable causal element in the genesis of later depression, most likely not because it alone is a critical causal condition, but rather because low SES, when combined with many other subsequent events and conditions, may contribute to the development of depression through multiple pathways. Thus low childhood SES may be a component of multiple sufficient causes for depression and therefore, while not a sufficient cause in its own right, plays a large role in the total burden or prevalence of adult depression.

That individual conditions in early life may only contribute to later dysfunction and disorder in interaction with secondary factors is well recognized in developmental science. An early and key demonstration of this principle came from the work of Emmy Werner and her studies of the children of Kauai (Buka & Lipsitt, 1994). This landmark investigation followed 698 infants on the Hawaiian island of Kauai, from birth through age 30. A notable finding was the interaction between biological and environmental risk conditions. Approximately 10% of this sample were exposed to moderate to severe prenatal or perinatal stress (complications of pregnancy, labor, or delivery). Long-term sequelae of perinatal stress were mostly evidenced only for children at "double jeopardy" and who also experienced environmental stressors such as family instability and lower socioeconomic status: "Children who had suffered perinatal stress but lived in stable, middle-class families scored as well or better than children in poor, unstable households who had not experienced such a stress" (Buka & Lipsitt, 1994).

That early (and preventable) conditions of pregnancy and delivery may interact with subsequent environmental conditions to produce later disorder has been demonstrated in relation to adolescent violence and criminality as well. Using a Danish birth cohort, Adrian Raine and colleagues provide evidence of a biosocial interaction between birth complications and early maternal rejection in predicting adult violent crime (Raine, Brennan, & Mednick, 1994).

They reported on a cohort of 4,269 consecutive live births, with prospective data on birth complications, early maternal rejection (age 1 year), and measures of violent crime (age 18 years). Their results indicated that those who had experienced both birth complications *and* early child rejection were at elevated risk for violent offenses in adulthood, but that there was no increased risk for violent crimes associated with just one of these early conditions.

We have replicated this finding of an interaction between birth complications, adverse social circumstances during childhood, and adolescent offending with the NEFS study (Lipsitt, Buka, & Lipsitt, 1990). Among 1,552 Caucasian males in the Providence cohort, approximately 14% had been arrested for a property offense by age 18 and 7% for a violent offense against another person (such as robbery, assault, or rape). Children with birth complications and who grew up among families of lower socioeconomic resources were significantly more likely to be arrested for a violent offence (17%) than those who had only one or neither of these potential early risk conditions (6%). This outcome was specific to violent offending, neither birth complications nor lower SES, alone or in combination, increased the likelihood of property offenses by age 18. Here, as with the Raine finding, we see that an early biologic risk (birth complication) in combination with social disadvantage interact to increase the risk of violent, but not property offending by age 18. Given the high public health burden and cost associated with violence, such early and accumulating risks need to be considered in population-based prevention efforts (Buka & Earls, 1993).

Examining Temporal Sequences

Recognition that risks accumulate and influence the development and expression of later disorders leads to a third principle of developmental epidemiology: a need to investigate and specify the correct order of developmental sequences. In the above example, our explanation is that birth complications come first, contribute to a biologically vulnerable infant, who, when further exposed to a disadvantaged caretaking environment, may progress to develop violent behaviors. However, we may have the temporal sequence wrong. Instead, it is also possible that maternal disadvantage predated and contributed to the development of birth complications, and that only certain classes of birth complications (for instance, those secondary to maternal disadvantage) result in violence.

A highly visible example of getting the order wrong when multiple components are involved in the development of later disorders is evident in Herrnstein and Murray's work, *The Bell Curve* (Herrnstein & Murray, 1996).

In a popular description of this work (Herrnstein & Murray, 1994) they summarize their analyses as attempting to answer the question: "If you have to choose, is it better to be born smart or rich?" To address this, the authors use a nationally representative sample of 12,686 youth, ages 14–22, known as the National Longitudinal Survey of Labor Market Experience of Youth. This study included measures of general cognitive ability (e.g., intelligence), as assessed by the Armed Forces Qualification Test (AFQT) and a composite socioeconomic index (SES) based on parents' income, education, and occupation. Subjects were followed for 11 years and the authors conducted a series of regressions predicting adverse outcomes in adulthood, in relation to intelligence and SES scores at the beginning of the study. Based on these analyses, the authors attempt to determine whether intelligence (e.g., being "smart") or SES (being "rich") is a better predictor of adult disorder and dysfunction, and they conclude "the answer is unequivocally 'smart'" (Herrnstein & Murray, 1994).

How do they reach this answer? Unfortunately, while the authors seek to answer the question "is it better to be born smart or rich?" they conduct their analyses with measures of intelligence and SES obtained when the study sample were ages 14–22 – hardly at birth. What these analyses demonstrate, and they do indeed support this position, is that at approximately age 18 one's intelligence score is a stronger predictor than one's SES is predicting adverse outcomes in the next 11 years (setting aside other relevant criticisms of the study methods, such as greater error in the measurement of SES than intelligence).

However, the analyses do not test the question that the authors posed concerning the relative predictive influence of SES and intelligence *at birth*. We investigated this directly, again using the Providence cohort of the NEFS. For these analyses, we also restricted the analysis to Caucasian males ($n = 446$). Measures of cognitive ability were obtained when the subjects were aged 8 months (Bayley Scales of Infant Development), 4 years (Stanford–Binet), and 7 years (Wechsler Intelligence Scale for Children). A composite index of family SES was also calculated for these three ages, based on maternal and paternal educational level, occupation, and earnings (Myrianthopoulos & French, 1968). Using the same analysis method as Herrnstein and Murray we then conducted logistic regression models predicting adverse outcomes in early adulthood (when the subjects were, on average, age 23), such as failure to get a high school education. Our analyses yielded exactly the opposite conclusion as the *Bell Curve*. At 8 months, there was no association between childhood "intelligence" (as measured by the

Bayley Scales) and obtaining a high school degree, but there was a strong and graded association between family SES and obtaining a high school degree. *All* of the children among the top 5% of family SES completed high school, compared to only 53% of those of the lowest 5% of family SES. There was a clear and positive linear trend between family SES at birth and obtaining a high school degree. For those whose family SES was very high (top 5%), high (next 20%), moderate (middle 50%), low (next 20%), and very low (bottom 5%) the rate of obtaining a high school degree was 100%, 82%, 69%, 60%, and 53%, respectively. In sum, family SES, not intelligence at birth was the stronger predictor of high school completion (and other adverse outcomes, not shown).

By age 4, the relative influence of family SES and child cognitive ability had shifted somewhat. At age 4, both predicted later high school attainment, but the influence of family SES was greater than for child intelligence. Again, all of those of "very high" family SES completed high school, and similarly, all those who performed "very high" on the Stanford Binet completed high school. But as family SES moved from moderate, low, to very low, rates of high school completion fell from 69% to 59% to 33%. As child IQ moved from moderate, low, to very low, rates of high school completion fell from 76% to 64% to 52%. Again, family SES was the stronger predictor than childhood IQ of adult attainment.

By age 7, this pattern had reversed, slightly. Now, the association between childhood IQ and high school completion was a bit stronger than for family SES. For children whose IQ at age 7 was in the moderate, low, and very low ranges, the rates of high school completion were 72%, 47%, and 35%, respectively. For those whose family SES were in the moderate, low, and very low ranges, the rates of high school completion were 72%, 51% and 40%, respectively. By age 7, childhood IQ and family SES were statistically comparable predictors of later high school completion (and other key adult outcomes), with a nonsignificant indication that child IQ had a stronger relationship. And of course, as shown by the Herrnstein and Murray data, by age 18 this reversal has been completed, and cognitive performance, more than family SES is the stronger predictor of subsequent adult conditions, such as academic failure, criminality, and substance use and abuse.

Developmental Taxonomies

The preceding sections have all focused on the conceptualization and characterization of antecedent or "risk" factors in a developmental approach toward epidemiologic investigations: considering the role of early life factors; multi-component or interacting causal factors; and temporal sequences of risk conditions. An additional step in a developmental epidemiology approach concerns the characterization of the behavioral, emotional, and psychosocial outcomes of interest. Rather than relying solely on discrete states that are evaluated at a single time and place, a developmental approach uses an adaptational or organizational perspective to group behaviors, taking into consideration the expression of disorder or dysfunction over multiple contexts and times. The goal is to measure phases, sequences, or strands of behavior and functioning, rather than mere points; sequences of behavior along the lifecourse trajectory that are expressed over time and setting.

This view, and several of the preceding points, is depicted in Figure 7.4. At the bottom two panels of the figure, we illustrate how multiple component causes, either at a single, early timepoint or accumulating over time, may comprise a "sufficient" cause for later conditions or behavioral events of interest. In the top two panels we highlight the need to consider the stability of behavior, across time or setting. This permits the investigator to distinguish between risk factors for more time-limited or transient outcomes versus stable and persistent.

Two examples demonstrate this point. First, from the study of antisocial behavior and criminal offending, Moffitt (1993) proposed a developmental taxonomy that consisted of two hypothetically distinct groups of offenders (Piquero & Buka, 2002). The first group of offenders, adolescence-limited, is hypothesized to engage in crimes solely during the adolescent period. Moffitt expects the crime-type repertoire of these adolescence-limited offenders to include primarily property offenses such as theft and vandalism, as well as offenses involving behaviors that are sanctioned for adults, such as smoking and drinking. Importantly, these offenders are largely expected to refrain from involvement in violent acts. In contrast, Moffitt predicts a second, rarer group of offenders, termed "lifecourse persistent," that is hypothesized to engage in antisocial activities and criminal acts throughout the lifespan. Unlike their adolescence-limited counterparts, the lifecourse persistors are thought to continue their criminal involvement throughout most of their lives (i.e., they are unlikely to desist). Another important distinction between the two groups of offenders is the hypothesis that lifecourse persistors are expected to engage in the full range of criminal activities, especially those acts that take on a violent, person-oriented nature. In addition to differences in the persistence and forms of offending, Moffitt predicts that these groups will also differ in terms of antecedent risk conditions. The primary risk factors for the adolescence-limited group include physical

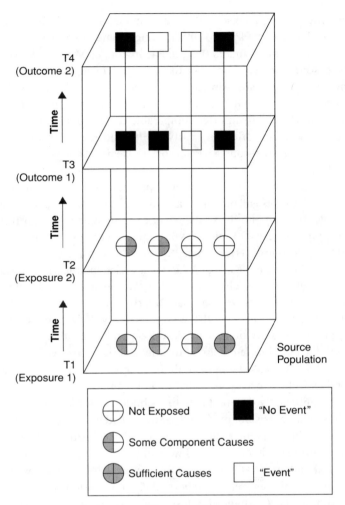

Figure 7.4. Schematic representation of prospective study with time-varying component causes and developmental classification of disorder. [Buka & Lipsitt, 1994]

maturation and association with delinquent peers; the primary determinants for lifecourse-persistent offenders are theorized to lie in the interaction between poor neuropsychological functioning and deficient home and socioeconomic environments.

Subsequent empirical research has tended to support some of the key hypotheses arising from Moffitt's typology (Bartusch, Lynam, Moffitt, & Silva,

1997; Moffitt, Caspi, Dickson, Silva, & Stanton, 1996; Moffitt, Lynam, & Silva, 1994; Tibbetts & Piquero, 1999), though some research has questioned the actual number of offenders (Nagin, Farrington, & Moffitt, 1995) and has uncovered some inconsistencies in the theory (Kratzer & Hodgins, 1999). Other models, such as Patterson and Yoerger's (1993) also distinguish between early- (and persistent) and late-onset offenders. Though differing in subtle ways, Moffitt and Patterson offer comparable explanations for the behavior of persons who begin offending early in life and persist in their problem behaviors over the lifecourse (Paternoster, Dean, Piquero, Mazerolle, & Brame, 1997).

The second example employs a developmental taxonomy to improve our understanding of risks and outcomes associated with learning disabilities. Using the New England Family Study, we have completed a 30-year follow-up study of approximately 400 children with signs of learning disabilities at age 7 and 400 healthy controls (Buka, Satz, Seidman, & Lipsitt, 1998). We reinterviewed 70% of this sample at age 35 and reassessed their learning disabilities with a thorough neuropsychological battery designed to identify a range of adult learning disorders. We were particularly interested in the antecedents and correlates of two classes of reading disability – those children whose reading problems were limited to childhood and those that persisted into adulthood. Of 115 children that met diagnostic criteria for reading disability at age 7, 52 (45%) persisted and could be diagnosed as reading disabled in adulthood as well. The subjects with "lifecourse-persistent" reading disabilities were significantly different than the "childhood-limited" or control subjects. Those with persistent reading disabilities had greater rates of academic difficulties during elementary and secondary school, histories of prenatal and attentional problems in childhood, lower lifetime earnings, and higher rates of antisocial and criminal behaviors (Buka et al., 1998). Those with persistent reading disabilities were also more likely to be of lower socioeconomic status and of lower IQ, suggesting less economic and cognitive resources to aid them in overcoming their childhood deficits. These findings suggest differences in the antecedents and consequences of persistent versus childhood-limited reading disabilities, important information for public policies and programs designed to prevent and ameliorate the severity of reading and other learning disabilities. Such fine-grained information results from the proposed developmental approach to the classification of disability, disorder, and dysfunction.

Such developmental approaches must also consider the relative stability of behaviors over time, and issues of heterotypic and homotypic continuity

(Rutter, 1989). The nature of human development is such that dispositions to behave in a particular way vary with age. The expression of hostility and aggression in a preschool-aged child differs dramatically from the appearance of aggression in a teenager or middle-aged adult. To study the continuities and discontinuities, as well as the transformations of behavioral expression across the lifespan requires observational and psychometric tools that honor the changing overt behavioral repertoire of the aging human. Although there are some domains of behavior, such as shyness (Kagan, 1989), that are consistently manifested over age, other domains of behavior, such as dishonesty, look quite different in the preschooler than in the adolescent. The challenge for developmental epidemiology is to employ such understanding of age-appropriate manifestations of underlying constructs to distinguish "lifecourse-persistent" subgroups that may involve different behavioral forms over time (heterotypic continuity). Erikson's (1982) allusion to the "tapestry" of development provides an apt metaphor for the changes in style of an attribute over the life stages while the trait substrate continues to persist and flow throughout the lifespan (Buka & Lipsitt, 1994).

Conclusion

The purposes of this chapter have been four-fold: (1) to demonstrate that the conditions that are and will increasingly afflict large populations worldwide are behavioral and social in nature; (2) that traditional methods of public health and epidemiologic inquiry will in most instances be inadequate to yield new insights into the causes and prevention of these conditions; (3) that there is much to be learned from the incorporation of theories and concepts from developmental psychology; and (4) to outline several principles to guide developmentally informed epidemiologic studies and analyses.

Fortunately, we are not alone in recognizing the critical need to infuse public health and public policy with methods and concepts from the developmental sciences. Others interested in methodology, disease and disorder causation, public health practice, and public policy have added to this growing literature (Costello & Angold, 1991; Keating & Hertzman, 1999). As Mustard & Lipsitt (1999, p. xi) write: "Given what we now know about the factors influencing the development of the brain, the biological pathways that affect learned behavior and health, and the long-term effects of a poor early childhood, how do we minimize poor environments for early child development? Clearly, the quality of early childhood affects the quality of the future population and prosperity of the society in which these children are raised . . . Lack of knowledge of infants' capabilities and of the environmental circumstances that best promote early growth and development is no longer a constraint to putting sound programs in place for enhancing children's development. Rather, in the words of the World Bank: 'Transforming this knowledge into action is the major limiting factor in implementing early child development programs and requires the combined support of governments, non-government organizations, the private sector and the media' (Young, 1997, p. 30)."

This call for a developmental epidemiology is not a mere academic exercise. If we are to use foresight in the application of science for the social good, the road ahead is clear. We must modify our methods of scientific inquiry to fit the behavioral and social conditions and concerns that are and will increasingly be apparent worldwide. This chapter has suggested several approaches for such an adaptation of traditional epidemiologic methods. We must adapt and expand effective programs that reduce the developmental impacts of early risk conditions and foster healthy development, and we must advocate for the implementation of such programs. This integration of science, service provision, and large-scale application through policy development has been a theme of this book and the work of Sheldon White. While policies based on developmental psychology have historically had the greatest impact on the classroom and preschool (White & Buka, 1987), the target of developmentally informed policies will need to expand in the coming generations. The work and legacy of White have provided models for the integration and application of developmental science for effective social policies and the social good; continuation and extension of these models are now the responsibility of the current and future generations of developmental scientists.

References

Abramson, L. Y., Seligman, M. E., & Teasdale, J. D. (1978). Learned helplessness in humans: Critique and reformulation. *Journal of Abnormal Psychology 87*, 1, 49–74.

Bartusch, D., Lynam, D., Moffitt, T. E., & Silva, P. (1997). Is age important? Testing a general versus a developmental theory of antisocial behavior. *Criminology 35*, 13–48.

Ben-Shlomo, Y., & Kuh, D. (2002). A life course approach to chronic disease epidemiology: Conceptual models, empirical challenges and interdisciplinary perspectives. *International Journal of Epidemiology 31*, 285–293.

Berkman, L. F., & Kawachi, I. (Eds.). (2000). *Social Epidemiology*. New York: Oxford University Press.

Bowlby, J. (1977). The making and breaking of affectional bonds. I. Aetiology and psychopathology in the light of attachment theory. An expanded version of the Fiftieth Maudsley Lecture, delivered before the Royal College of Psychiatrists, November 19, 1976. *British Journal of Psychiatry 130*, 201–210.

Boyce, W., Frank, E., Jensen, P., Kessler, R., Nelson, C., & Steinberg, L. (1998). Social context in developmental psychopathology: Recommendations for future research from the MacArthur Network on Psychopathology and Development. *Development and Psychopathology 10*, 143–164.

Broman, S. H. (1987). *Retardation in Young Children: A Developmental Study of Cognitive Deficit.* Hillsdale, NJ: Lawrence Erlbaum Associates.

Broman, S. H., Bien, E., & Shaughnessy, P. (1985). *Low Achieving Children: The First Seven Years.* Hillsdale, NJ: Lawrence Erlbaum Associates.

Broman, S. H., Nichols, P. L., & Kennedy, W. A. (1975). *Preschool IQ: Prenatal and Early Developmental Correlates.* Hillsdale, NJ: Lawrence Erlbaum Associates; distributed by the Halsted Press Division of Wiley.

Brown, G. W., & Harris, T. O. (1978). *Social Origins of Depression: A Study of Psychiatric Disorder in Women.* London: Tavistock.

Buka, S. L., & Earls, F. (1993). Early determinants of delinquency and violence. *Health Affairs 12*, 4, 46–64.

Buka, S. L., & Lipsitt, L. P. (1994). Toward a developmental epidemiology. In S. L. Friedman & H. C. Haywood (Eds.), *Developmental Follow-Up: Concepts, Domains, and Methods* (pp. 331–350). San Diego, CA: Academic Press, Inc.

Buka, S. L., Goldstein, J. M., Seidman, L. J., Zornberg, G. L., Donatelli, J. A., Denny, L. R., et al. (1999). Prenatal complications, genetic vulnerability, and schizophrenia: The New England longitudianl studies of schizophrenia. *Psychiatric Annals 29*, 3, 151–156.

Buka, S. L., Lipsitt, L., & Tsuang, M. (1988). Birth complications and psychological deviancy: A 25-year prospective inquiry. *Acta Paediatrica Japonica 30*, 537–546.

Buka, S. L., Satz, P., Seidman, L., & Lipsitt, L. (1998). Defining learning disabilities: The role of longitudinal studies. *Thalamus 16*, 2, 14–29.

Buka, S. L., Shenassa, E., & Niaura, R. (2003). Elevated risk of tobacco dependence among offspring of mothers who smoke during pregnancy: A 30-year prospective study. *American Journal of Psychiatry 160*, 11, 1978–1984.

Buka, S. L., Tsuang, M. T., & Lipsitt, L. P. (1993). Pregnancy/delivery complications and psychiatric diagnosis. A prospective study. *Archives of General Psychiatry 50*, 2, 151–156.

Burns, S. J., & Offord, D. R. (1972). Achievement correlates of depressive illness. *Journal of Nervous and Mental Disease 154*, 5, 344–351.

Calev, A. (1996). Affect and memory in depression: Evidence of better delayed recall of positive than negative affect words. *Psychopathology 29*, 2, 71–76.

Chabra, A., Chavez, G., & Harris, E. (1999). Mental illness in elementary-school-aged children. *Western Journal of Medicine 170*, 28–34.

Corrigall, W. (1991). Understanding brain mechanisms in nicotine reinforcement. *British Journal of Addiction 86*, 507–510.

Costello, A. J., & Angold, A. (1991). Developing a developmental epidemiology. In D. Cicchetti & S. Toth (Eds.), *Rochester Symposium on Developmental Psychopathology (Vol. 3)*. Hillsdale, NJ: Laurence Earlbaum Associates.

Crum, R. M., Bucholz, K. K., Helzer, J. E., & Anthony, J. C. (1992). The risk of alcohol abuse and dependence in adulthood: The association with educational level. *American Journal of Epidemiology 135*, 9, 989–999.

Dohrenwend, B. P. (1990). Socioeconomic status (SES) and psychiatric disorders. Are the issues still compelling? *Social Psychiatry and Psychiatric Epidemiology 25*, 1, 41–47.

Dohrenwend, B. P., Levav, I., Shrout, P. E., Schwartz, S., Naveh, G., Link, B. G., et al. (1992). Socioeconomic status and psychiatric disorders: The causation-selection issue. *Science 255*, 5047, 946–952.

Erikson, E. H. (1982). *The life cycle completed: A review*. New York: Norton.

Ernst, M., Moolchan, E., & Robinson, M. (2001). Behavioral and neural consequences of parental exposure to nicotine. *Journal of the American Academy of the Child and Adolescent Psychiatry 40*, 6, 630–641.

Fan, A. P., & Eaton, W. W. (2001). Longitudinal study assessing the joint effects of socio-economic status and birth risks on adult emotional and nervous conditions. *British Journal of Psychiatry 178* (Supplement 40), s78–s83.

Gilman, S. E., Kawachi, I., Fitzmaurice, G., & Buka, S. L. (2002). Socioeconomic status in childhood and the lifetime risk of major depression. *International Journal of Epidemiology 31*, 359–367.

Gilman, S. E., Kawachi, I., Fitzmaurice, G. M., & Buka, S. L. (2003). Socioeconomic status, family disruption, and residential stability in childhood: Relation to the onset, recurrence, and remission of major depression. *Psychological Medicine 33*, 8, 1341–1355.

Griesler, P., Kandel, D., & Davies, M. (1998). Maternal smoking in pregnancy, child behavior problems, and adolescent smoking. *Journal of Research on Adolescence 8*, 159–185.

Haass, M., & Kubler, W. (1997). Nicotine and sympathetic neurotransmission. *Cardiovascular Drug Therapy 10*, 657–665.

Haggerty, R. J., Roughmann, K. J., & Pless, I. B. (1975). *Child Health and the Community*. New York: Wiley.

Hallstrom, T. (1987). The relationships of childhood socio-demographic factors and early parental loss to major depression in adult life. *Acta Psychiatrica Scandinavica 75*, 2, 212–216.

Hardy, J. B., Shapiro, S., Mellits, E. D., Skinner, E. A., Astone, N. M., Ensminger, M., et al. (1997). Self-sufficiency at ages 27 to 33 years: Factors present between birth and 18 years that predict educational attainment among children born to inner-city families. *Pediatrics 99*, 1, 80–87.

Herrnstein, R. J., & Murray. (1994, October 10). The aristocracy of intelligence. *Wall Street Journal*, p. A12.

Herrnstein, R. J., & Murray, C. (1996). *The Bell Curve: Intelligence and Class Structure in American Life*. New York: Free Press.

Hill, A. B. (1965). The environment and disease: Association or causation. *Proceedings of the Royal Society of Medicine 58*, 295–300.

Jacobson, B., Nyberg, K., Eklund, G., Bygdeman, M., & Rydberg, U. (1988). Obstetric pain medication and eventual adult amphetamine addiction in offspring. *Acta Obstetricia et Gynecologica Scandinavica 67*, 677–682.

Jacobson, B., Nyberg, K., Gronbladh, L., Eklund, G., Bygdeman, M., & Rydberg, U. (1990). Opiate addiction in adult offspring through possible imprinting after obstetric treatment. *British Medical Journal 301*, 1067–1070.

Jacobson, S., Fasman, J., & DiMascio, A. (1975). Deprivation in the childhood of depressed women. *Journal of Nervous and Mental Disease 160*, 1, 5–14.

Johnson, J. G., Cohen, P., Dohrenwend, B. P., Link, B. G., & Brook, J. S. (1999). A longitudinal investigation of social causation and social selection processes involved in the association between socioeconomic status and psychiatric disorders. *Journal of Abnormal Psychology 108*, 3, 490–499.

Kagan, J. (1989). Temperamental contributions to social behavior. *American Psychologist 44*, 668–674.

Keating, D. P., & Hertzman, C. (1999). *Developmental Health and the Wealth of Nations: Social, Biological, and Educational Dynamics*. New York: Guilford Press.

Kellam, S. G., & Ensminger, M. E. (1980). Theory and method in child psychiatric epidemiology. In F. Earls (Ed.), *Studies of Children* (pp. 145–180). New York: Prodist.

Kessler, R. C., & Magee, W. J. (1993). Childhood adversities and adult depression: Basic patterns of association in a U.S. national survey. *Psychological Medicine 23*, 3, 679–690.

Koob, G., & Le Moal, M. (1997). Drug abuse: Hedonic homeostatic dysregulation. *Science 278*, 52–58.

Kratzer, L., & Hodgins, S. (1999). A typology of offenders: A test of Moffitt's theory among males and females from childhood to age 30. *Criminal Behaviour and Mental Health 9*, 57–73.

Kuh, D., & Ben-Shlomo, Y. (1997). *A Life Course Approach to Chronic Disease Epidemiology*. Oxford/New York: Oxford University Press.

Lipsitt, P. D., Buka, S. L., & Lipsitt, L. P. (1990). Early intelligence scores and subsequent delinquency: A prospective study. *American Journal of Family Therapy 18*, 197–208.

Lundberg, O. (1993). The impact of childhood living conditions on illness and mortality in adulthood. *Social Science and Medicine 36*, 8, 1047–1052.

McFarland, B., Seidler, F., & Slotkin, T. (1991). Inhibition of DNA synthesis in neonatal rat brain regions caused by acute nicotine administration. *Brain Research Developmental Brain Research 58*, 2, 223–229.

McLoyd, V. C. (1998). Socioeconomic disadvantage and child development. *American Psychologist 53*, 2, 185–204.

Meyerson, B. J. (1985). Influence of early beta-endorphin treatment on the behavior and reaction to beta-endorphin in the adult male rat. *Psychoneuroendocrinology 10*, 2, 135–147.

Mickelson, K. D., Kessler, R. C., & Shaver, P. R. (1997). Adult attachment in a nationally representative sample. *Journal of Personality and Social Psychology 73*, 5, 1092–1106.

Miettinen, O. S. (1985). *Theoretical Epidemiology: Principles of Occurrence Research in Medicine*. New York: Wiley.

Moffitt, T. E. (1993). Adolescence-limited and life-course-persistent antisocial behavior: A developmental taxonomy. *Psychological Review 100*, 4, 674–701.

Moffitt, T. E., Caspi, A., Dickson, N., Silva, P., & Stanton, W. (1996). Childhood-onset versus adolescent-onset antisocial conduct problems in males: Natural history from ages 3 to 18 years. *Development and Psychopathology 8*, 399–424.

Moffitt, T. E., Lynam, D., & Silva, P. (1994). Neuropsychologica tests predicting persistent male delinquency. *Criminology 32*, 277–300.

Muneoka, K., Ogawa, T., Kamei, K., Muraoka, S., Tomiyoshi, R., Mimura, Y., et al. (1997). Prenatal nicotine exposure affects the development of the central serotinergic system as well as dopaminergic system in rat offspring: Involvement of drug adminstrations. *Brain Research Developmental Brain Research 102*, 1, 117–126.

Muntaner, C., Eaton, W. W., Diala, C., Kessler, R. C., & Sorlie, P. D. (1998). Social class, assets, organizational control and the prevalence of common groups of psychiatric disorders. *Social Science and Medicine 47*, 12, 2043–2053.

Murphy, J. M., Olivier, D. C., Monson, R. R., Sobol, A. M., Federman, E. B., & Leighton, A. H. (1991). Depression and anxiety in relation to social status. A prospective epidemiologic study. *Archives of General Psychiatry 48*, 3, 223–229.

Murray, C., & Lopez, A. (1996). *The Global Burden of Disease: A Comprehensive Assessment of Mortality and Disability from Diseases, Injuries, and Risk Factors in 1990 and Projected to 2020 (Vol. 1)*. Cambridge, MA: Harvard University Press.

Mustard, J. F., & Lipsitt, L. P. (1999). Foreward. In D. P. Keating & C. Hertzman (Eds.), *Developmental Health and the Wealth of Nations* (pp. ix–xii). New York: Guilford Press.

Myrianthopoulos, N. C., & French, K. S. (1968). An application of the U.S. Bureau of the Census socioeconomic index to a large, diversified patient population. *Social Science and Medicine 2*, 3, 283–299.

Nagin, D., Farrington, D. P., & Moffitt, T. E. (1995). Lifecourse trajectories of different types of offenders. *Criminology 33*, 111–139.

Navarro, H., Seidler, F., Schwart, R., Baker, F., Dobbins, S., & Slotkin, T. (1989). Prenatal exposure to nicotine impairs nervous system development which does not affect viability or growth. *Brain Research Bulletin 23*, 187–192.

Nichols, P. L., & Chen, T.-C. (1981). *Minimal Brain Dysfunction: A Prospective Study*. Hillsdale, NJ: Lawrence Erlbaum Associates.

NIMH. (2001). *Blueprint for Change: Research on Child and Adolescent Mental Health*. Washington, DC: National Institute of Mental Health, National Advisory Mental Health Council Workgroup on Child and Adolescent Mental Health Intervention Development and Deployment.

Niswander, K. R., & Gordon, M. (1972). *The Women and Their Pregnancies: The Collaborative Perinatal Study of the National Institute of Neurological Diseases and Stroke*. Washington, DC: National Institute of Health.

Nyberg, K., Buka, S. L., & Lipsitt, L. (2000). Maternal medication as a potential risk factor for adult drug abuse in a North American cohort. *Epidemiology 11*, 715–716.

Paternoster, R., Dean, C., Piquero, A. R., Mazerolle, P., & Brame, R. (1997). Continuity and change in offending careers. *Journal of Quantitative Criminology 13*, 231–266.

Patterson, G. R., & Yoerger, K. (1993). A model for early onset of delinquent behavior. In S. Hodgins (Ed.), *Crime and Mental Disorder* (pp. 140–172). Newbury Park, CA: Sage.

Piccinelli, M., & Wilkinson, G. (2000). Gender differences in depression. *British Journal of Psychiatry 177*, 486–492.

Piquero, A. R., & Buka, S. L. (2002). Linking juvenile and adult patterns of criminal activity in the Providence cohort of the National Collaborative Perinatal Project. *Journal of Criminal Justice 30*, 259–272.

Power, C., Hertzman, C., Matthews, S., & Manor, O. (1997). Social differences in health: Life-cycle effects between ages 23 and 33 in the 1958 British birth cohort. *American Journal of Public Health 87*, 9, 1499–1503.

Raine, A., Brennan, P., & Mednick, S. A. (1994). Birth complications combined with early maternal rejection at age 1 year predispose to violent crime at age 18 years. *Archives of General Psychiatry 51*, 12, 984–988.

Richards, M., Hardy, R., Kuh, D., & Wadsworth, M. (2001). Birth weight and cognitive function in the British 1946 birth cohort: Longitudinal population based study. *British Medical Journal 322*, 7280, 199–203.

Ritsher, J. E. B., Warner, V., Johnson, J. G., & Dohrenwend, B. P. (2001). Intergenerational longitudinal study of social class and depression: A test of social causation and social selection models. *British Journal of Psychiatry 178, suppl. 40*, s84–s90.

Robins, L. N., Helzer, J. E., Croughan, J., & Ratcliff, K. S. (1981). National Institute of Mental Health Diagnostic Interview Schedule. Its history, characteristics, and validity. *Archives of General Psychiatry 38*, 4, 381–389.

Rothman, K. (1976). Causes. *American Journal of Epidemiology 104*, 587–592.

Rothman, K. (1986). *Modern Epidemiology*. Boston: Little, Brown.

Rothman, K., & Greeland, S. (1998). *Modern Epidemiology* (2nd ed.). Philadelphia: Lippincott-Raven.

Rutter, M. (1989). Pathways from childhood to adult life. *Journal of Child Psychology and Psychiatry and Allied Disciplines 30*, 23–51.

Sadowski, H., Ugarte, B., Kolvin, I., Kaplan, C., & Barnes, J. (1999). Early life family disadvantages and major depression in adulthood. *British Journal of Psychiatry 174*, 112–120.

Shaffer, D., Fisher, P., Dulcan, M. K., Davies, M., Piacentini, J., Schwab-Stone, M. E., et al. (1996). The NIMH diagnostic interview schedule for children, Version 2.3 (DISC-2.3): Description, acceptability, prevalence rates, and performance in the MECA study. Methods for the epidemiology of child and adolescent mental disorders study. *Journal of American Academy of Child and Adolescent Psychiatry 35*, 7, 865–877.

Sturm, R., Ringel, J., Bao, C., Stein, B., Kapur, K., Zhang, W., et al. (2001). National estimates of mental health utilization and expenditures for children in 1998. *Journal of Behavioral Health Services and Research 28*, 3, 319–333.

Susser, M., & Susser, E. (1996). Choosing a future for epidemiology: II. From black box to Chinese boxes and eco-epidemiology. [erratum appears in *American Journal of Public Health* (1996 August) 86, 8–1, 1093]. *American Journal of Public Health 86*, 5, 674–677.

Tibbetts, S. G., & Piquero, A. R. (1999). The influence of gender, low birth weight, and disadvantaged environment in predicting early onset of offending: A test of Moffitt's interactional hypothesis. *Criminology 37*, 843–877.

USDHHS. (1999). *Mental Health: A Report of the Surgeon General: Executive Summary*. Rockville, MD: U.S. Department of Health and Human Services.

USDHHS. (2000). *Report of the Surgeon General's Conference on Children's Mental Health: A National Action Agenda.* Rockville, MD: U.S. Department of Health and Human Services.

White, S. H., & Buka, S. L. (1987). Early education: Programs, traditions, and policies. In E. Z. Rothkopf (Ed.), *Review of Research in Education (Vol. 14).* Washington, DC: American Educational Research Association.

Young, M. E. (1997). Policy issues and implications of early child development. In M. E. Young (Ed.), *Early Child Development: Investing in Our Children's Future.* Amsterdam: Elsevier.

8 Ignoring Behavioral Science
Practices and Perils

Lewis P. Lipsitt

"I think there is a world market for maybe five computers."
Thomas Watson, Chairman, IBM, 1943

How amazing it is to behold the ways in which otherwise intelligent and creative people can be extraordinarily resistant to recognizing scientific advances at the threshold. Western Union, the greatest international communication system of the world, is said to have generated an internal memo in 1876, with this message: *"This telephone has too many shortcomings to be seriously considered as a means of communication. The device is inherently of no value to us."*

While many of these presumed verities are part of our scientific folklore, there is apparently no doubt that Lord Kelvin, an important contributor to the principle of the conservation of energy, and the president of the Royal Society in London, said in 1895, *"Heavier-than-air flying machines are impossible"* (Lindley, 2003).

Sometimes our vision of the future requires not a leap of faith but a scientific jump-start. Grass-roots visionaries are sometimes both imaginatively bolder and less delayed by establishmentarian constraints. Recent advances, for example, in childbirth practices involving less use of maternal anesthesia, the redesign of birthing areas in maternity hospitals, and the acceptance of nurse-practitioner midwives, have resulted largely from pressures brought by women resisting the old ways.

If the development and widespread use of the telephone, or of aircraft, or of computers had been delayed for a year or two, due to the short-sightedness of those in positions required to promote their development, perhaps little would have been lost in the total picture of things, especially in the long run. On the other hand, timing was everything during World War II; the U.S. government realized this, and thus launched the Manhattan Project, an intensive plan that

203

brought together the best science and the wisest physical scientists of the day to achieve nuclear fission.

The distinguished and secret coterie of scientists, including Enrico Fermi and Leo Szilard, intended to build the most destructive weapon in the world, and in this way to end the war. The issue of whether this was a social advance or an eventually disastrous undertaking for the peoples of the world will be debated endlessly, of course. In fact, when it became apparent to him and others just how dangerous this scientific advance could be for the world, Leo Szilard beseeched President Harry Truman to refrain from using the atom bomb to end the war in Japan. The psychological conflicts raised in others, e.g., by Heisenberg and Bohr, the prominent nuclear physicists famously involved in the earth-threatening nuclear dilemma, have been stunningly re-enacted in a play by M. Frayn (1998).

It might be argued that psychological science is no match, at least yet, for quantum physics, either in the clarity of its statements of lawfulness or in its precision of measurement. Nonetheless, it cannot be denied that humans today die as much from sloth of knowledge, and from behavioral misadventures even in the presence of adequate intelligence (Lipsitt & Mitnick, 1991; Salovey, Rothman, & Rodin, 1998), as from any other condition of humankind.

A solidarity of social and psychological scientific effort, similar to that of the Manhattan Project, designed to reduce death and morbidity, could hardly be expected to evoke such moral controversy as creating an atomic bomb. Yet, the world seems quite unprepared to mount such an effort, and one cannot help wondering why this state of affairs persists, despite the clear impact of behavioral mishaps, errors of judgment, and malicious adventurers on our nations, our families, our societies, and the world.

Beginning with the printing press, the most significant changes in human development have been technological. Our lives have been markedly shaped, indeed revolutionized, by the automobile, the light bulb, anesthesia, aircraft, the telephone, flush toilets, the transistor, penicillin, TV, velcro, stressed concrete, and skyscrapers. Most all of these advances have occurred in the last 100 years of human growth and development. The human body and our biological capacities, meanwhile, have not been significantly altered over the last thousands of years, notwithstanding that some "biologically timed" developmental processes such as the onset of menstruation have been speeded up, quite possibly if not very likely owing at least in part to the impingement of environmental influences on children and youth (Brooks-Gunn, 1987).

Our progenitors from dozens of generations ago had brains essentially the same as ours. One technological improvement after another now presses the human condition into a geometric growth function. The average lifespan increase of 20 years or more, in the most recent full century, has been due largely to advances in the biochemical sciences and technology, such as mass immunization, improved sanitation, electronically assisted diagnosis, and other public health measures.

At the same time, we are little improved in our ability to cope, or to self-regulate our behavior. It may be that technology has in some ways increased, rather than reduced, the stress in our lives, and diminished or constrained human capacity to cope. While our genetic dispositions or propensity for aggression are much the same now as twelve generations ago, the technology now exists to more easily destroy ourselves and others. Humans can do it now in a bigger way per act of devastation; witness the recent use of aircraft as missiles to crash into skyscrapers and kill thousands of people in just a few minutes.

At risk of effusively promoting the behavioral and developmental sciences to a degree beyond grandiosity, one must note nonetheless that the origins and development of behavior need to be much better understood if humans are to deal effectively with the dark side of human nature. Furthermore, if those new understandings are not deployed as *knowledge applications*, the annihilation of humankind through the behavior of misanthropes or out-of-control national leaders is not impossible.

Efforts to understand and thwart behaviors leading to mass destruction will surely follow advances in our understanding of, and the application of our knowledge about, more "local" problems of behavioral misadventure. There may be other ways of knowing, but there is no other *science* besides *behavior science* that can, through acquired knowledge, help promote reductions in homicide, suicide, and unintentional deaths due to behavioral errors of all sorts. One Manhattan Project will not be enough, obviously. The physicists had one major task to perform, one monumental goal. The behavioral and social sciences have a multiplicity of problems to solve. However, as in the case of the original, atomic-fission problem, scientific efforts must be directed toward specific, clearly stated goals. The great advances made recently in the understanding of "the genome," or the genetic structure of specific organisms, were regarded just a few years ago as unthinkably too complex to accomplish. When top scientists were put to work on the problem, however, the task progressed unthinkably fast!

Later in this chapter, crib death ("sudden infant death syndrome"), the biggest killer of infants in the first year of life, will be addressed as a domain of scientific investigation for which a mini-Manhattan Project might be expected to yield rapid and definitive progress, with marked diminution world-wide of such tragic and needless deaths of babies.

Prediction and control of human behavior is no less important as a domain of human understanding than the pursuits of scientists in the fields of physics, chemistry, biology, or astronomy. Yet our world culture has not yet got the message. The behavior sciences for many decades have been severely rejected, massively undertaught, poorly subsidized, and blatantly disparaged as weak and irrelevant in comparison with other scientific disciplines which have strong, clearly useful applications.

One caveat here is that in recent years, the condition of AIDS and its principal mode of transmittal, sexual behavior, have provided a springboard to acceptance of the importance of *behavior* both in individual life trajectories and in human destiny broadly conceived. Behavioral catastrophes such as the AIDS pandemic and the 9/11 World Trade Center and Pentagon disaster do alert the citizenry and government officials to the fact that human behavior is at the root of it, and thus a vigorous and well-supported behavior science must be appropriated and deployed to spar effectively with these adversities.

More young people in developed nations today die or become debilitated as a consequence of behavioral misadventures than from all diseases combined. Data supporting this assertion are available in the reports of the recent decade survey of the U.S. Centers for Disease Control and Prevention (2000), and the U.S. Department of Health and Human Services (2002). Deaths from inadvertence (accidents), homicide, suicide, the fall-out from excessive alcohol ingestion, tobacco habits, and the use of dangerous drugs, to all of which must be added bullying, terrorism, and warfare, are far in excess of all other causes, almost to middle-age. Even after age 35, the demographics of disease and disability reveal strong influences of behavioral and controllable environmental factors. Many older people incur a brain concussion and a broken hip from a fall while, for example, climbing on a ladder to change a light bulb. Such individuals are victims of a behavioral failure to anticipate that one's inner-ear function, balance, and motor function are not as keen as they once were.

Recent advances in behavioral and clinical science suggest that a better understanding of human mentality and behavior, and their origins, can significantly reduce addictive behavior, sociopathy, schizophrenia, aggressive behavioral disorders, learning disabilities, and birth defects. Many disorders of fetal development and those attributable to prematurity stem, in fact, from poverty, which is a "treatable" psychosocial disorder. Some nations, notably the Scandinavian countries, have been able to curb poverty through social and behavioral interventions with consequent reductions in early developmental disabilities (Keating & Hertzman, 1999).

Failure to heed clearly helpful scientific findings can place individuals and groups of people at great risk. If the steel in bridges, for example, is not specially treated, danger exists that the bridge will collapse. Similarly, the smallpox vaccine had to be developed and then administered to protect against future population afflictions. The need for this kind of preventive or preemptive defense is perhaps not as obvious in the behavioral and social sciences, but ignorance as well as mismanagement in the application of behavioral and environmental measures are at least as important here as in the application of the physical and medical sciences.

The behavior sciences are the least endowed with funding of all the sciences. Public opinion for many years seems to have held that the behavioral and social sciences are essentially frosting on the cake of a culture otherwise rich in resources for the support of scientific research. There is indeed a tendency, when behavioral inferences are drawn from data relating to adverse outcomes in human development, to emphasize the underlying neurophysiological or biochemical mechanisms associated with the process. This is an easy, but deceiving, path to follow, inasmuch as all behavior is mediated by the nervous system. Short of experience, however, the brain by itself is mindless. Without a personal and developmental history, and with no memorial content, the nervous system is empty, lacks operating structure, and is useless (McEwen & Schmeck, 1994).

Behavioral Misadventures Wanting Strong Science

Historical examples from the research domains of HIV/AIDS, already mentioned, and crib death or SIDS (to be dealt with in greater detail below), illustrate that ignoring the science of behavioral processes is widespread and is tragically detrimental to the well-being of humans everywhere. Observations of recent terrorist behavior, leading to a major public policy debacle, itself understandable only in behavioral terms, clearly are relevant. Following are some unfortunate human conditions that are behavioral in nature, each of them justifying a mini-Manhattan Project designed to better understand their origins and the conditions that perpetuate their presence in developed societies as sources of immense grief and despair.

Suicide and Other Behavioral Causes of Death

Most violent deaths are suicides. Worldwide, according to a recently released World Health Organization report (2002), people are much more likely to die by their own hand than as victims of armed conflict or murder. Globally, more than 1.6 million people died in the year 2000 in violent circumstances. Of those 1,600,000, 815,000 committed suicide, 520,000 were murdered, and 310,000 died in armed conflicts, including terrorist attacks. For every death from violent causes, hundreds more are injured and disabled. Violence is thus pervasive in the lives of millions of people annually, as each violent death has an impact on the lives of dozens of others.

That behavior is a root cause of much debility and social disintegration has not escaped the attention of some of the world's more sensitive leaders. When he addressed the human conditions that most cause dismay, disenchantment, and despair in people of all nations, Nelson Mandela urged that intensified efforts be made to address the widespread, but less visible, scourge of individual suffering, seen through the "pain of children who are abused by people who should protect them, women injured or humiliated by violent partners, elderly people maltreated by their caregivers, youths who are bullied by other youths and people of all ages who inflict violence on themselves" (WHO Report, 2002).

One person in the world commits suicide every 40 seconds, every minute there is a murder, and every 100 seconds someone dies as a result of armed conflict. All of these conditions are behavioral. Virtually none of it is caused by disease. A 2004 report of the U.S. Centers for Disease Control and Prevention reveals that about 68% of all deaths among persons aged 1–24 years are from only a few causes: motor-vehicle crashes (31%), other unintentional injuries (14%), homicide (13%), and suicide (10%) (*Morbidity and Mortality Weekly Report*, 9/13/2004).

In a recent treatment of the striking differences that occur in the health of nations world-wide, Keating & Hertzman (1999) displayed data showing convincingly that the rates of violence vary dramatically with national income. The rate of violent death is more than twice as high in low- and middle-income countries as in high-income countries, ranging from 32.1 per 100,000 persons to 14.4 per 100,000. The steepness of the socio-economic slopes across countries relates to many measures of well-being, including psychological durability or resilience and educational attainment.

In the United States, a suicide occurs every 17 seconds, for a total of approximately 30,000 suicides in each of the past several years (National Center for Health Statistics, 2002). There are in fact more suicides accomplished through the use of guns than homicides occurring by gunshot. That there is a strong environmental influence on the relative rates of homicidal and suicidal behavior is evidenced by the fact that in Africa and in South America, homicide rates are three times higher than suicide rates. In Southeast Asia and Europe, on the other hand, suicide rates are double the homicide rates.

Suicidal ideation and suicide attempts are rampant among the American young, according to authoritative data available from a recent inquiry (Centers for Disease Control and Prevention, 2002). Over a 12-month period, 28% (females 35%, males 22%) of the youths surveyed felt sufficiently sad or hopeless for greater than a two-week period that they stopped engaging in their customary life activities. The proportion of students "seriously considering attempting suicide" was 19%, 15% made a specific plan, and 9% had actually made an attempt (12% females, 6% males).

Sadness and hopelessness are psychological characteristics, widely agreed to be affected by the development of one's personal history, and by interpersonal relationships, especially including those with peers and parents. Much is still not known about those who have special perinatal and other early developmental vulnerabilities relating to addiction, suicide, and other major adversities (Jacobson, Nyberg, Gronbladh et al., 1990; Salk, Lipsitt, Sturner et al., 1985), and of the very early environmental conditions that may prime the individual to be sadly affected by personal events in the teenage and young adulthood years.

Abuse and Neglect of Children: A Behavioral Problem. From a U.S. Department of Health and Human Services Report for 2000, we learn that 17 children per 1,000,000 *died* in the United States from abuse or neglect. At each age, male children are rather more vulnerable than female, with the group under 1 year especially at risk.

Female parents are more than twice as likely to be the perpetrator of abuse than the male parent, but of course the child is typically under the care of the father much less. When the abuse is sexual in nature, the male parent is five times more likely to have been the perpetrator than the mother. Poverty and single motherhood are clearly important societal/cultural variables that are involved.

Teen Sexual Behavior. Almost half of all high school teenagers in the United States have had sexual intercourse at least once, according to data from the Youth Risk Behavior Survey (Child Trends, 2003), and fully 56% of these individuals reported that their first such experience occurred in the "comfort" of their (or their partner's) family home.

One of the most salient risk factors for children in our society, and for mothers as well, is unmarried teenage pregnancy. While one in three births to women of all ages in the United States occurs outside marriage, 80% of teen births in the year 2000 were nonmarital. This figure is somewhat lower than in the previous decade, overall, but for women aged 20–24 years the rate had risen. The teenage premarital birth *rate* (not numbers) for the hispanic and black populations is roughly double that for the same-aged white population, a race/ethnic phenomenon clearly confounded with socio-economic level. Of signal importance for our purposes here is that while childbirth in the United States usually takes place in a hospital, sexual intercourse and consequent pregnancies relate to human behavior and environmental conditions, not to disease. This is not to deny that adverse conditions of pregnancy following conception, such as inadequate medical monitoring of the mother and fetus, maternal malnutrition, and other factors, can lead to disease and injury. The entry point into many early developmental disorders, however, is pregnancy among teenagers whose lives are marked by poverty and the absense of a continuing partner.

Time and again, studies demonstrate that the socio-economic gradient prevails with respect to every outcome variable relating to health and welfare (see Keating & Hertzman, 1999). Children in the lowest socio-economic groups are most at risk for health problems, educational deficits, delinquency, early pregnancy, and poor adjustment. This is not to say that individuals in better-off economic circumstances never or seldom have such adverse developmental trajectories, but only to recognize that interventions designed to remove poverty as a condition of growing up will surely help to improve the health, educational, and welfare levels of the population.

Violent Behavior. Access to guns does not by itself necessarily mean that an individual with such access will use such weaponry. Under conditions of provocation, however, the accessibility of the weapon will surely increase the probability of its use. In 2001 (Centers for Disease Control and Prevention, June 28, 2002), 29% of male students and 6% of female students carried a weapon to school (a gun, knife, or club). Nationwide, almost 6% of high school students carried a gun on at least one day preceding a large national inquiry. Actual physical fighting had occurred during the year of the inquiry in 43% of the males and 24% of the females, and, during the year, fully 4% of the students had incurred sufficiently serious injuries from fighting as to require medical treatment.

Other Risk Behaviors

About 65% of all students have smoked cigarettes at some time, and about 30% are persistent, regular smokers. Almost 80% of the high school population has ingested alcoholic beverages but, more importantly perhaps, 30% of all the students surveyed had had five or more drinks (regarded as heavy or binge drinking) on at least one occasion in the previous 30 days of the survey

(34% male, 26% female). Such episodic heavy drinking was found to increase with age over the four high school years (Centers for Disease Control and Prevention, 2002).

While marijuana use as a lifespan risk has been debated, it is widely believed among health professionals and students of alcohol and drug addiction that prolonged use has response-slowing effects. Moreover, poly-drug users typically have experienced marijuana as an "entry drug." Among adolescents through senior high school age, 42% agreed to having used marijuana at some time in their lives (46% males, 38% females). About 25% of the males reported having used marijuana in the past 30 days. While it is quite possible that the 25% is a shifting population from month to month, one quarter of the high school students in any given month are apparently smoking marijuana. This is not to press the point that marijuana is necessarily an enormously *unsafe* drug, but to indicate that in this as in other relationships between the youth of the nation and their traditional authority figures, there are important disagreements as to what is acceptable and safe behavior. This may be seen also in unprotected sexual behavior, occurring currently when the importance of condom use is prominently announced wherever teenagers go. Some 34% of the high school population, from 9th to 12th grades, are sexually active, but of this group about 40% do not customarily use easily available condoms (Centers for Disease Control and Prevention, 2002).

Concerning other serious risk behaviors, it is noteworthy that almost 10% of the U.S. high school population has at least tried cocaine, in powder, crack, or free-base form, and 4% seem to have used it one or more times in the month preceding a national inquiry. One can go on, citing heroin, methamphetamine, and steroid use among the young. Substance abuse is part of our culture and, whatever may be said about addiction as a physiological process, there is no doubting that it begins, shall we say "purely and simply," as *behavior* and is sustained by a peer culture that supports deviancy and risk-taking. Whatever else one may believe about the complicity of the media, it has to be noted that some of our most popular television and other personal pastimes involve extreme sports, hurtful wrestling, gloveless boxing, and various forms of presumably nonlethal shooting games.

Behavioral Risks and Risk-Taking

"Priority health-risk behaviors, which contribute to the leading causes of mortality and morbidity among youth and adults, often are established during youth, extend into adulthood, are interrelated, and are preventable" (Centers for Disease Control and Prevention, 2002, p. 1).

In the United States, three-quarters of all deaths among persons aged 10–24 years result from only four causes: motor vehicle crashes, other unintentional injuries, homicide, and suicide. High school students are especially prone to engage in dangerous behaviors as evidenced by the following: In the 2001 survey, 14% had rarely or never worn a seat belt during the preceding 30 days, 31% had been a passenger in a vehicle in which the driver had been drinking alcohol, 17% had carried a weapon in the 30 days previous, 47% had consumed alcohol, and 24% had used marijuana. Almost 9% of the students had attempted suicide in the past 12 months, 46% of the students reported having ever had sexual intercourse, 42% of those sexually active had not used a condom during their most recent sexual contact, and 2.3% had at some time *injected* an illegal drug.

While addressing here the risk-behavior issues principally relating to young people and their vulnerabilities, it should be mentioned that in individuals *older than* 24 years of age in the United States, two-thirds of deaths occur from two causes, cardiovascular disease and cancer, and that the main risk behaviors for these two diseases are evident in adolescence: smoking behavior, failure to maintain adequate nutrition, and inattention to one's physical condition, including weight. *Behavior kills* at all ages, most especially the young, but older individuals carry with them the vestiges of their earlier behavior and adverse environmental conditions.

Crib Death: A Case of Neglect by Behavior Science

More babies die of "crib death" or the so-called sudden infant death syndrome (SIDS) than of all other causes combined (Burns & Lipsitt, 1991; Lipsitt, 1976, 1979, 2003). While exposure has occurred over the past decade of some cases of infanticide (itself a behavioral phenomenon), little attention has yet been given to the behavior and neuromotor development of the infant as a strong contributing factor to cases in which a post-mortem diagnosis of SIDS is made.

The rise and fall of nonbehavioral hypotheses, and the slow acceptance of behavioral factors in SIDS, is of historical interest, is a significant public health issue, and is relevant to the thesis of this chapter – that ignoring behavioral science in urgent life-and-death situations puts lives in peril and propels large numbers of families into grievous situations (Firstman & Talan, 1997).

Until the past few decades, when a baby died of no apparent or diagnosable cause with or without an autopsy, medical examiners frequently presumed the death was attributable to pneumonia or pneumonitis. Aggrieved parents usually accepted this medical explanation, and were frequently consoled to understand that their baby had died of a "disease" (Raring, 1975).

Circumstances conspired to increase the curiosity, eventually, of pediatricians, pathologists, and parents as to the "real cause" of the child's death (Naeye, 1980). Not infrequently, insinuations of investigators first arriving at the scene of the death stunned further the already shocked parents who were sometimes falsely accused of abusing their child. At the same time, pathologists and pediatricians were developing greater knowledge about the phenomenon of sudden and unexpected death of infants, and some found themselves empathizing increasingly with parents whose parenting skills were unwarrantedly approached with suspicion. This led to inquiries as to the evidence-supported mechanisms and processes underlying the death of an infant in the absence of foreboding signs that the child was ill, especially in the absence of postmortem clues as to the cause (Naeye, Messmer, Specht, & Merrit, 1976; Swift & Emery, 1973).

Fortified by a large investment of funds for research into the cause of crib death by the National Institutes of Health, and for services to the parents of SIDS victims, a grassroots movement was formed. Parents of SIDS victims joined with physicians who had personally experienced the death of an infant patient or were affected by parents whose lack of credible information as to the cause of their child's death compounded the severity of their loss (Firstman & Talan, 1997).

Despite the large investment of funds into the presumed medical causes of crib death, the phenomenon of SIDS has remained elusive. The definition of SIDS, as the death of an infant without apparent cause, has been institutionalized through legislation and medical consensus. However, the phenomenon remains a diagnostic mystery, with the coming and going of seemingly viable hypotheses that are not followed by indisputable verification. Although public attention to the phenomenon has lowered the frequency of false accusations of neglect or even murder, crib death remains today largely a diagnosis of ignorance – a residual diagnosis (Hunt, 2001). After expert attention has been paid to the death scene and the deceased baby has undergone a thorough autopsy, the medical examiner or pathologist certifies the death as "SIDS." The examiner asserts, in effect: "I don't know why this apparently healthy baby, without any apparent injury, without any identifiable disease, and with few prior indications of any difficulty, died."

The Phenomenon. The single most common cause of death in the first year of life, after the first few post-natal days, SIDS usually occurs at night while the infant and family are sleeping. Some of these infants are reported as having had a cold in the days preceding the death. Usually, however, the baby has been regarded as a normal child of good health just before the death.

Sometimes there are identifiable "predisposing conditions" which have been documented in epidemiological research. Maternal smoking, inadequate or late prenatal care, and poor socio-economic conditions have been documented in cohort studies of SIDS babies. In the United States, black infants are twice or three times more likely to die of SIDS and, from the little data available, Native American infants seem even more vulnerable. Race and ethnicity are probably confounded with poverty, but hispanic infants have thus far shown a lower incidence than blacks (National Center for Health Statistics, 2002). Although there is rather little data available on the drinking habits of parents of crib death babies, the existing data which would implicate excessive parental alcohol consumption (before or after birth) suggests that this may be a relevant antecedent, especially in interaction with other risk factors, but this needs much further research investigation (Friend, Goodwin, & Lipsitt, 2004).

The incidence of SIDS in most developed countries is presently around two deaths per 1,000 births. Of special interest is the fact that the reported rate of crib death has been halved in the last 10–12 years. This marked reduction, in other countries as well as the United States, has been attributed to the "back to sleep movement," which has involved instructions to parents, nurses, and day-care workers to place the infant for sleep on its back rather than in the prone position (Hunt, Lesko, Vezina, McCoy, Corwin et al., 2003).

The Timing. In about 85% of the cases, SIDS occurs between 2 months and 5 months of age. This "sensitive period" is of special fascination in connection with a biobehavioral hypothesis first proposed over a quarter-century ago (Lipsitt, 1979, 2003) and presented here as an example of behavior-science neglect.

Why is the child relatively free of vulnerability to crib death before 2 months of age and after 5 months? The answer quite likely resides in the nature of development and associated behavioral mechanisms in the first year of life.

Among the many hypotheses to emerge in the last three decades are some presumptions about the role of apnea, irregular breathing, hypothermia, cardiac anomalies, and hypothalamic dysfunction. Despite large investments in research on these phenomena, no specific medical or physiological hypothesis has yet been confirmed. Even hypotheses that would conjoin several ostensibly interacting conditions in a conflation of multiple risks as causes of crib death have not thus far received much evidentiary support (Hunt, 2001). It could well be that the search has taken the privileged investigators into well-traveled roads when new, perhaps riskier, divergent avenues might have been tried. Such a route would be through the science of behavior and behavioral development.

A directive was issued in 1994 from the National Institutes of Health and endorsed by pediatric societies (which actually began their campaign of instruction at least two years before) that babies should be placed on their backs, and not prone, when placed in position for sleeping (Hunt, 2001). Since then, the incidence of diagnosed SIDS cases has been reduced to half its previous level, a not inconsiderable advance. However, two extenuating conditions must be raised in evaluating whether the infant death rate has truly decreased: (1) the downward turn in rate of SIDS began to occur before the first back-to-sleep cautions were raised by the American Association for Pediatrics in 1992 (Lipsitt, 2003); and (2) the number of overall infant deaths has remained fairly constant, with more deaths being attributed to other causes than SIDS, for example, "cause of death undetermined," or "suffocation" (Task Force on Infant Sleep Position and SIDS, American Academy of Pediatrics, 2000).

A Viable Behavioral Hypothesis. Babies are born with a variety of reflexes, some infants manifesting these responses with greater intensity and lower thresholds for elicitation than others (Brazelton, 1973). Human infants born under adverse conditions, such as with the umbilicus around the neck, or to young mothers who smoke or do not seek obstetrical help early in their pregnancies (Scragg, Mitchell, Taylor et al., 1993; Protestos, Carpenter, McWeeny, & Emery, 1973) have been documented to be at special risk, although their babies do not appear to be clearly abnormal at or soon after birth. Actuarial statistics clearly point to special conditions that increase the probability of crib death occurring. In the United States, being black, of low socio-economic level, male, and premature are characteristics repeatedly found in epidemiological studies, although none of these conditions by itself can account for the deaths. Indeed, more than 90% of babies born with any of these characteristics survive.

Several investigators have proposed that some kind of compromise of respiration is involved in crib death (Swift & Emery, 1973; Anderson & Rosenblith, 1971; Lijowska, Reed, Mertins, Chiondi, & Thach, 1997; Lipsitt, 1976, 1979; Thach, Davies, & Koenig, 1988). Under such a hypothesis it may be presumed that any conditions which tend to lower the elicitability of reflexes at and shortly after birth may contribute to risk for crib death. However, the initial risk appears to be a contributor to greater risk between 2 months and 5 months of age than during the months preceding or following, due to developmental changes in the reflex repertoire and learned behaviors of the infant.

The *respiratory occlusion reflex*, evident in the first days of babies' lives, can be assessed easily, and appears on some scales of infant behavior (Brazelton, 1973; Anderson & Rosenblith, 1971). Newborns with weak defensive reflexes may be presumed to be in greater jeopardy at later ages, when important aspects of brain development depend upon the earlier appearance of reflexes of some minimal strength and ease of elicitation. The respiratory occlusion reflex, discussed by the British pediatrician Mavis Gunther (1961), copes with threats to respiration as a fixed-action pattern, well described by Gunther as involving various "fighting" maneuvers such as shaking the head side to side, pulling the head backward, raising the arms in a seeming attempt to remove the offending object, facial vasodilation, and mouth thrusting. This fixed action pattern is part of a behavior system necessary for survival in all mammals.

A viable theory about crib death, then, is that a behavioral insufficiency is implicated. More than 60 years ago, many years before the sudden infant death syndrome had been identified, the eminent psychobiologist and developmental researcher Myrtle McGraw (1942) presented findings indicating that subcortically mediated reflexes that babies manifest in the first weeks of life, as part of the behavioral repertoire of the human species, gradually wane in strength. In extensive longitudinal studies, she provided empirical demonstrations of the shifting character of these reflexes, particularly the swimming reflex, grasping, and the stepping reflex.

Between 2 months and 5 months of age, McGraw found, an important transition occurs, in which the reflexes which were initially "obligatory" become slower, more deliberative, and seemingly "voluntary." The initial reflex repertoire eventually yields to the more mature "deliberate" type of response. In its developmental progression from "reflexive" to "deliberate," McGraw documented a period of ambiguity, a transitory state that she labeled "disorganized behavior." She considered reflexes to be mediated principally by the brain stem, and the eventual "deliberate response" system to be a mark of maturing brain structures, specifically the growth of myelin sheathing and the proliferation of dendrites.

The intervening "disorganized and confused" behavior was said by McGraw to be a matter of two essentially conflicting psychobiological processes. When asked to describe the state of the baby during this intermediary period, she replied: "This occurs when the baby doesn't know whether he is supposed to be a reflexive creature or a learned organism" (McGraw, personal communication, May 25, 1979).

Especially interesting, and perhaps of major importance, is that McGraw's intermediate period of confusion is particularly evident, in her data, during the 2 month to 5 month age period in individual infants, and has a somewhat different time course in different infants. Such individual differences are evident in virtually all aspects of infants' growth and development, but the "peak of confusion" in most of the reflexes McGraw studied appeared to be around 130–150 days of age, which includes the age period during which most crib deaths occur.

There is scant basis for doubting that the developmental course of the respiratory occlusion reflex would be different from the other response systems that McGraw studied over time. Furthering support for a hypothesis implicating an aberration of the transitional respiratory occlusion response in vulnerable infants, Anderson and Rosenblith (1971) found that newborns who evidenced weak respiratory "defense" behaviors were more likely to succumb in the first year of life than babies who manifested vigorous defensive behaviors. Recently, the pediatric research laboratory of Thach (Lijowska et al., 1997) demonstrated a similar phenomenon, revealing individual differences among babies in their capacity for recovering the behaviors required to maintain survival levels of oxygen when threatened with oxygen deprivation during sleep.

A biobehavioral theory of crib death (Lipsitt, 1976, 1979) proposes, based on McGraw's developmental progression data, that if the reflex-to-learned-behavior transition is not made successfully between 2 months and 5 months of age, through acquisition of the life-saving learned respiratory defenses originating in the respiratory occlusion reflex, the baby will be unable to behave adequately when threatened with respiratory occlusion. Thus, initial neurobiological deficits associated with reflex insufficiency may compromise exposure to experiences that, in normal infants, lead to *learned, adaptive responses that can prevent death from suffocation.*

The new cautions that babies should be placed for sleep on their backs, and the new data suggesting that this care technique, itself a behavioral intervention, seems to have reduced the crib death rate in the United States by 50%, supports the contention made years before its implementation, that a behavioral process is of signal importance. Supportive data for a "respiratory occlusion" hypothesis importantly involving the *behavior* of the baby has existed for decades. Little support for behavioral research, however, has been evident, although there have been some exceptions (e.g., Thach, Davies, & Koenig, 1988). There has never been a call for proposals from the National Institutes that would *emphasize* the probable importance of babies' learned behavioral insufficiencies or aberrations. There has been a research lacuna in this area, judging from the existing literature on learning processes and other behavioral influences on SIDS.

Current State of SIDS Knowledge. A fair assessment of our state of knowledge concerning the origins of SIDS must include the defensible observation that the phenomenon is still a mystery. There has been no strong evidence emerging to provide a definitive cause. Nonetheless, the apparent success of the "back to sleep" caution, introduced in 1992, followed by a significant decline in diagnosed SIDS cases, augurs well for the hypothesis that respiratory occlusion constitutes a setting condition for the events leading to crib death. Moreover, the failure of some babies' capacities to lift their heads and retrieve their mouths and nostrils for breathing following such occlusion stands as a reasonable hypothesis concerning the final pathway to eventual suffocation.

Some infants learn to respond defensively to respiratory occlusion better than others. Although their reflexive behavior is sufficient in the first 2 months of life to maneuver into a safe position when their breathing is threatened, eventually the subcortical reflexive mediation of such responsivity gives way to neural development, with its attendant diminution of reflex defenses. If that transition does not take place seamlessly, as it does in most normal infants, the child of 2 months to 5 months of age will be in enhanced jeopardy of succumbing to SIDS.

While there seems a good basis to continue cautioning infant caretakers to place their infants in the supine position during sleep, there may be an even greater urgency to provide the baby with exercise during awake times, so that the infant will practice the psychomotor maneuvers important to keep his or her respiratory passages clear at all times. An argument may also be made, on the basis of extant information, that infants might be given deliberate practice in "objecting" to respiratory threats, and engaging in behaviors that are successful in removing the offending object. An example of significant enhancement of reflexive, subcortically controlled behavior facilitated by practice exists in the study of Zelazo, Zelazo, and Kolb (1972).

An enhanced program of research needs to be mounted on the reflexive behavior of the infant in the first months of life, especially with a view toward understanding better the transitional stage occurring during the critical or vulnerable period between 2 months and 5 months of age. To that end, it may be suggested that studies of conditioning or learning processes in the first 6 months of life must be accorded far greater priority than has been historically associated with research into crib death. Moreover, much more attention must be paid to the multiplicity of developmental events that control and presage human developmental trajectories (Buka & Lipsitt, 1994).

Last Words

We are at a critical place in scientific, technological, and social development, and must devote the same kind of passion and other resources to the behavioral sciences as we have invested in physical and chemical technologies. Major advances must now be made in social psychology, education, and child development, with the assistance and collaboration of the neurobiological and cognitive sciences. The technology of behavioral self-regulation, the study of empathy and altruism, the application of our best technical wits to the preservation of living humans, and the perpetuation of a livable world, must be a high priority on our global agenda.

All technological and scientific advances are in an important sense the products of behavior. Einstein behaved, and we got the theory of relativity; Salk behaved, and we got the polio vaccine; Heisenberg behaved, and we got the uncertainty principle; Thomas Watson behaved, and, despite his initial pronouncements about the uselessness of mass production of computers, most all of us now do at least some of our work on a computer.

Now people will have to behave again – to deploy the necessary energy, motivation, intelligence, cognitive perspicacity, funding, and willingness to take some risks. That's how we got the automobile, the airplane, the washing machine, and, perhaps following Niels Bohr's complementarity principle, the widespread global warfare for which we now seek behavioral steps to eradicate. This will take a Manhattan Project, or many of them, of a new and inspired sort. Major initiatives must address behavior, its origins, and its consequences. Behavior is the most important thing.

References

Anderson, R. B., & Rosenblith, J. F. (1971). Sudden unexpected death syndrome: Early indicators. *Biologia Neonatorum 18*, 395–406.

Brazelton, T. B. (1973). *Neonatal Behavior Assessment Scale*. Philadelphia: Lippincott.

Brooks Gunn, J. (1987). Pubertal pressures: Their relevance for developmental research. In V. B. Van Husselt & B. B. Whiting (Eds.), *Handbook of Adolescent Psychology* (pp. 111–130). New York: Pergamon.

Buka, S. L., & Lipsitt, L. P. (1994). Toward a developmental epidemiology. In S. L. Friedman and H. C. Haywood (Eds.), *Developmental Follow-up: Concepts, Domains, and Methods* (pp. 331–350). New York: Academic Press.

Burns, B., & Lipsitt, L. P. (1991). Behavioral factors in crib death: Toward an understanding of the sudden infant death syndrome. *Journal of Applied Developmental Psychology 12*, 159–184.

Centers for Disease Control and Prevention (2002). Youth Risk Behavior Surveillance, United States, 2001. *Morbidity and Mortality Weekly Report*, June 28, 2002, Vol. 51.

Child Trends (2003). *Research Brief*, August 2003 (No. 2003-16), Washington, DC: Child Trends.

Firstman, R., & Talan, J. (1997). *The Death of Innocents: A True Story of Murder, Medicine, and High-Stakes Science*. New York: Bantam Books.

Frayn, M. (1998). *Copenhagen*. Performed by Trinity Repertory Theatre, Providence, RI in 2003.

Friend, K., Goodwin, M. S., & Lipsitt, L. P. (2004). Alcohol use and sudden infant death syndrome. *Developmental Review 24*, 235–251.

Gunther, M. (1961). Infant behavior at the breast. In B. Foss (Ed.), *Determinists of Infant Behavior* (pp. 37–44). London: Methuen.

Hunt, C. E. (2001). Sudden infant death syndrome and other causes of infant mortality: Diagnosis, mechanisms, and risk for recurrence of siblings. *American Journal of Respiratory and Critical Care in Medicine 164*, 346–357.

Hunt, C. E., Lesko, S. M., Vezina, R. M., McCoy, M. J., Corwin, M. J., Mandell, F., Willinger, M., Hoffman, H. J., & Mitchell, A. A. (2003). Infant sleep position and associated health outcomes. *Archives of Pediatric and Adolescent Medicine 157*, 469–474.

Jacobson, B., Nyberg, K., Gronbladh, L., et al. (1990). Opiate addiction in adult offspring through possible imprinting after obstetric treatment. *British Medical Journal 301*, 1067–1070.

Keating, D., & Hertzman, C. (Eds.). (1999). *Developmental Health and the Wealth of Nations: Social, Biological, and Educational Dynamics*. New York: Guilford.

Lindley, D. (2003). *Degrees Kelvin: A Tale of Genius, Invention, and Tragedy*. New York: John Henry Press.

Lijowska, A. S., Reed, N. W., Mertins Chiondi, B. A., & Thach, B. T. (1997). Sequential arousal and airway-defensive behavior of infants in asphyxial sleep environments. *Journal of Applied Physiology 83*, 219–228.

Lipsitt, L. P. (1976). Developmental psychobiology comes of age. In L. P. Lipsitt (Ed.), *Developmental Psychobiology: The Significance of Infancy*. Mahwah, NJ: Lawrence Erlbaum.

Lipsitt, L. P. (1979). Critical conditions in infancy: A psychological inquiry. *American Psychologist 34*, 973–980.

Lipsitt, L. P. (2003). Crib death: A biobehavioral phenomenon? *Current Directions in Psychological Science 12*, 164–170.

Lipsitt, L. P., & Mitnick, L. L. (Eds.) (1991). *Self-Regulatory Behavior and Risk-Taking: Causes and Consequences*. Norwood, NJ: Ablex.

McEwen, B. S., & Schmeck, H. M., Jr. (1994). *The Hostage Brain*. New York: Rockefeller University Press.

McGraw, M. B. (1942). *The Neuromuscular Maturation of the Human Infant*. New York: Hafner.

Naeye, R. (1980). Sudden infant death. *Scientific American 242*, 52–62.

Naeye, R., Ladis, B., & Drage, J. S. (1976). SIDS: A prospective study. *American Journal of Diseases of Children 130*, 1207–1210.

Naeye, R., Messmer, J., III, Specht, T., & Merrit, F. (1976). Sudden infant death temperament syndrome before death. *Journal of Pediatrics 88*, 511–515.

National Center for Health Statistics (2002). Deaths Leading Causes for 2000. *National Vital Statistics Report 50*, 9–12.

Protestos, C., Carpenter, R., McWeeny, & Emery, J. (1973). Obstetric and perinatal histories of children who died unexpectedly (cot death). *Archives of Disease in Childhood 48*, 835–841.

Raring, R. H. (1975). *Crib Death: Scourge of Infants–Shame of Society*. Hixville, NY: Exposition Press.

Rosenblith, J. F. (1961). The modified Grahama behavior test for neonates: Test reliability, normative data, and hypotheses for future work. *Biologia Neonatorum 3*, 174–192.

Salk, L., Lipsitt, L. P., Sturner, W. Q., Reilly, M., & Levat, R. (1985). Relationships of maternal and perinatal conditions to eventual adolescent suicide. *Lancet* (March 16, 1985), 624–627.

Salovey, P., Rothman, A. J., & Rodin, J. (1998). Health behavior. In D. Gilbert, S. Fiske, & G. Lindzey (Eds.), *Handbook of Social Psychology*, 4th ed., Vol. 2. (pp. 633–683). New York: McGraw Hill.

Scragg, R. K. R., Mitchell, E. A., Taylor, B. J., Stewart, A. W., Ford, R. P. K., Thompson, J. M. D., Allen, E. M., & Becroft, D. M. (1993). Bed sharing, smoking, and alcohol in the sudden infant death syndrome. *British Medical Journal 307*, 1312–1318.

Swift, P. G. F., & Emery, J. L. (1973). Clinical observations on response to nasal occlusion in infancy. *Archives of Diseases in Childhood 48*, 947–951.

Task Force on Infant Sleep Position and Sudden Infant Death (2000): Report at year 2000. *Pediatrics: American Academy of Pediatrics 105*, 650–656.

Thach, B. T., Davies, A. M., & Koenig, J. S. (1988). Pathophysiology of upper airway obstruction in sleeping infants and its relevance for SIDS. In P. J. Schwartz., D. P. Southall, & M. Valdes-Dapena (Eds.), *The Sudden Infant Death Syndrome and Respiratory Mechanisms and Interventions* (pp. 314–328). New York: New York Academy of Sciences.

U.S. Centers for Disease Control and Prevention (2000). Atlanta, GA.

U.S. Department of Health and Human Services, Administration of Children, Youth, and Families (2002). *Child Maltreatment 2000*, Washington, DC: Government Printing Office.

Valdes-Dapena, M. (1978). *Sudden and Unexpected Death 1970 through 1975: An Evolution in Understanding*. (Pub. No. (HAS) 78-5255). Bethesda, MD: U.S. Department of Health, Education, and Welfare.

Watson, T. http://channels.netscape.com/ns/atplay/predictions.jsp

World Health Organization Reports (2000, 2002) published in Brussels, Belgium.

Zelazo, P. R., Zelazo, N. A., & Kolb, S. (1972) "Walking" in the newborn. *Science 177*, 1058–1059.

PART FOUR

Designing Effective Learning Environments for Children and Adolescents

9   A Cultural/Historical View of Schooling in Human Development

Barbara Rogoff, Maricela Correa-Chávez, and Marta Navichoc Cotuc

In this paper we examine changing arrangements of human development that have accompanied societal shifts to mass, compulsory "Western" schooling. We draw attention to the often taken-for-granted role of schooling in children's lives once extensive schooling has become the childhood norm in their communities. To do so, we examine two cases, involving very different histories and current conditions. We first examine the life patterns associated with the growth of mass schooling across the past centuries for European-heritage families in the United States, integrating the work of historians who have described the process. Then we examine the phenomenon across three generations of Mayan families in Guatemala, using our own interviews and observations.

In the United States one can generally assume that if a child is 6 years old, she is in the first grade, or if a child is in the first grade, she is about 6 years old. As Irwin et al. (1978) put it, "In Western industrialized countries, going to school has the same inevitability for children that death and taxes have for their parents" (p. 415).

Although psychologists often identify developmental transitions in terms of children's ages, age indexes *both* biological maturation and changing roles in cultural institutions.[1] As White (1975) has pointed out, age 5 to 7 years has for some centuries marked societal shifts in treatment of children, such as the standard onset of formal schooling in Europe and the United States. White and Siegel (1984) argued that a key feature of child development is the increasing involvement of children in wider societal institutions.

---

[1] Attention to the role of schooling and other societal institutions in children's lives does not require a mechanistic environmental causality view. We view biological maturation and engagement in cultural activities as mutually constituting each other (Rogoff, 2003).

225

Nonetheless, researchers commonly interpret children's age as simply a measure of maturation or general experience with the world (Wohlwill, 1970), overlooking the near-perfect association of age with experience in school in nations with compulsory schooling (Laboratory of Comparative Human Cognition, 1979). Indeed, European-American developmental transitions often center on children's participation in schooling, with children's development categorized in terms of progress in this institution: preschoolers, elementary age, high schoolers. Many studies have noted the relation of schooling to specific aspects of performance on cognitive tests (Rogoff, 1981; Sharp, Cole, & Lave, 1979). The common contemporary practice of equating children's development with age may be related to schooling's organization according to age and to the historical role played by developmental psychologists both in documenting changes according to age and in designing schooling.

Extensive experience with Western schooling appears to play a formative role in organizing childhood, for children and their parents worldwide. We are not arguing that it does so solo, but that its structure and practices play a role in shaping what developmental psychologists often think of as ordinary child development (Packer, 2001). The current ubiquity of Western schooling in the lives of children in most researchers' communities has made it difficult to discern alternative ways that children's lives have been structured in other times and places. This institution is taken for granted due to inevitability of many years of involvement, and treated almost as a 'natural' part of growing up. This 'naturalizing' of institutional experience makes sense:

> The members of an institution need not necessarily have been its originators; they may be second, third, fourth, etc. generation members, having "inherited" the institution from their forebears. And this is a most important point, for although there may be an intentional structure to institutional activities, practitioners of institutional forms need have no awareness at all of the reason for its structure – for them, it is just "the-way-things-are-done." The reasons for the institution having one form rather than another are buried in its *history*. (Shotter, 1978, p. 70)

Several key features of children's lives in societies with extensive schooling – segregation from adults into a children's world, association with peers in tightly limited age cohorts, comparisons of development according to age – arose in the recent history of compulsory, mass schooling.[2] Family

---

[2] Although formal instruction in societal institutions occurs in many societies other than those with formal Western schooling (Akinnaso, 1992), other forms of schooling generally do not oblige mass, universal instruction.

changes – such as decreases in family size, infant mortality, and children's contributions to sibling care and other family work – accompanied these shifts. Schooling's association with age-graded segregation from both adults and children of other ages restricts children's opportunities to learn from observing and becoming involved in the mature activities of their communities (Rogoff, 2003; Morelli, Rogoff, & Angelillo, 2003). The limited opportunities to observe and be involved in ongoing activities may increase the likelihood that children depend on others to organize their attention, motivation, and learning of the information and skills required in maturity, as in schools (Rogoff, Paradise, Mejía Arauz, Correa-Chávez, & Angelillo, 2003).

In a *Scientific American* article written more than a quarter of a century ago, Bronfenbrenner argued that unhealthy changes were arising because of the segregation of children from community and family life, due to the structure of societal institutions such as industry and schools:

> If a child is to become a responsible person, he not only must be exposed to adults engaged in demanding tasks but also must himself participate in such tasks. . . . Our children are not entrusted with any real responsibilities. Little that they do really matters. They are given duties rather than responsibilities; the ends and means have been determined by someone else and their job is to fulfill an assignment involving little judgment, decision making or risk. This practice is intended to protect children from burdens beyond their years, but there is reason to believe it has been carried too far in contemporary American society and has contributed to the alienation of young people and their alleged incapacity to deal constructively with personal and social problems. The evidence indicates that children acquire the capacity to cope with difficult situations when they have an opportunity to take on consequential responsibilities in relation to others and are held accountable for them. . . . The institution that has probably done the most to keep children insulated from challenging social tasks is the American school system. (1974; p. 60)

In the ensuing decades, U.S. children have become further segregated from mature community and family lives and spent greater time as the wards of bureaucracies. Children under 5 and youths over 16 spend more and more time in institutions that separate them from the ordinary, productive lives of adults.[3]

Developmental psychology is an active player in the story, as White has pointed out in his historical accounts of this field's role in designing

---

[3] As of 1987, more than a third of 3- to 4-year-olds and almost a fourth of 20- to 24-year-olds were in school (Angus, Mirel, & Vinovskis, 1988).

institutions of modern society (especially those addressing health, education, and welfare) and in establishing normative developmental markers and milestones associated with particular ages and schooling. During the 20th century, the new field of developmental psychology grew to play a role in designing methods and ideas for use by "'distal bureaucrats' who do not deal predominantly with flesh-and-blood children, families, or practitioners but with symbolic representations of large numbers of them" (White, 1999, p. 12).

Developmental research has made key contributions to the design of cultural institutions and practices that are now central to U.S. childhood: "Child science . . . legitimated the idea of age-graded elementary education, . . . classified students based on the construction of the concept of intelligence quotient, and . . . psychologists [were] enlisted as the appropriate arbiters of developmental truth in American society" (Hawes, 1997, p. 65).

Coming to a clearer understanding of the role of the ubiquitous institution of schooling in the lives of U.S. children and families, and its growing role worldwide, is important for illuminating the nature of child development. In addition, an understanding of the historical/cultural role of schooling is essential for considerations of researchers' and policymakers' future contributions to the design of institutions and practices for children in the United States and worldwide. In this paper, we first review the growth and roles of schooling for U.S. children and families across several centuries, and then we examine data regarding the growth and roles of schooling for Guatemalan Maya children and families over three generations.

Compulsory Mass Schooling in European-American Communities

It has only been for about a century that U.S. childhood has routinely and extensively involved school attendance. In colonial America, families were expected to teach children to read at home (Getis & Vinovskis, 1992). Before 1800, only 40%–60% of the U.S. male population attended school, usually for only a few years (LeVine & White, 1987). The school day and school year were also shorter than at present, and less central to the learning experiences of childhood.

With the onset of industrialization in the 1800s, schooling increased. In 1830, 35% of white children ages 5 to 19 attended school; in the 1870s, the figure had increased dramatically to 61% (Chudacoff, 1989). Enrollments in public school increased three-fold from 1840 to 1900 and most children completed several grades of elementary school; in 1910, three fourths of the population over age 25 had five or more years of schooling (Myers, 1996).

As industrialization spread, in the early 1900s, schooling was made compulsory and time spent in school increased (Chudacoff, 1989; Hernandez, 1994). Compulsory schooling was sponsored by movements that also restricted children's work – labor unions tried to protect jobs for adults, and child welfare workers attained laws protecting children from dangerous working conditions (Bremner, 1971; Chudacoff, 1989; Hernandez, 1994). From 1870 to 1940, school enrollment increased from 50% for children aged 5 to 19 years to 95% for children aged 7 to 13 years and to 79% for children aged 14 to 17 years.

Children who were enrolled also became more regular in their attendance (LeVine & White, 1987). The number of days spent in school each year doubled between 1870 and 1970, rising from 78 days to 162 days attended per enrolled student (Angus, Mirel, & Vinovskis, 1988).

In addition, higher schooling became required for economic advancement. In 1889–1890, enrollment in secondary schools in the United States included only 7% of 14- to 17-year-olds; in 1919–1920, 32% were in school, and by 1929–1930, 51% were enrolled (Chudacoff, 1989). By the middle of the 1900s, most U.S. children and youth spent a great deal of their day at school or, given the increases in schooling across generations, interacting with their rather extensively schooled parents and siblings (Hernandez, 1997).

Changes in the Role of Schooling in Children's Learning

Along with the change to enrolling all children, the purposes of schooling and its role in children's learning have changed since it began to be a mass, compulsory institution. For example, the definition of functional literacy has transformed greatly over this time (Myers, 1984, 1996; Resnick & Resnick, 1977; Wolf, 1988): In the United States of the 1700s and the early 1800s, the definition of literacy was being able to sign one's name or an X to legal documents. In 1800, only 58% of Army enlistees were able to sign their names; in the 1880s, 93% were able to do so (Myers, 1996).

> The purpose of schools was to teach students to sign their names, to make lists, to record information, to copy word lists, to read a few essential words, to read a few things aloud from memory, to have some awareness of how devotional books were organized, to know some religious passages "by heart," to know how to write a few numbers, to be able to arrange numbers in inventory columns, and, possibly, to be able to do a few, simple arithmetic calculations. (Myers, 1996, p. 49)

It was not school's job to teach children about the world; this was usually up to the family, and it often did not involve the use of books. As much as half of the U.S. population did not have books in their home in 1859 (Myers, 1996).

In the late 1800s, literacy became the ability to read and recite memorized passages, not necessarily with comprehension (Myers, 1996; Resnick & Resnick, 1977). This shift occurred as the United States sought order in recovering from a civil war and in incorporating influxes of immigrants,[4] and as industrialization spread.

With the decrease in children sharing in the family work on the farm – the most common setting of U.S. childhood until this point – the responsibilities of schools changed. Schools were given the job of teaching children obedience, industriousness, and punctuality (Graff, 2001). They taught primarily through a "drillmaster" model, leading children in unison in reciting their lessons and testing how many texts and facts from the text they could recite (Myers, 1996).

> The acts of reciting passages aloud, giving reports aloud, summarizing a version of literal meaning (metaphorical and historical), learning to write some, learning diction, and learning to copy dictation were intended to socialize children from homes where one parent was home all day; to teach English to nonnative speakers; to socialize immigrants and natives into U.S. traditions; to overcome the shortage of printed materials in schools; to police the student population by teaching them "discipline;" and, according to many observers, to sort the population, even where segregation laws had been dropped, into segregated groups based on gender, economic class, and race or ethnicity. (Myers, 1996, p. 75)

In the early 1900s, the definition of reading began to involve literal understanding of unfamiliar passages. At this time, Army testers sought recruits for World War I who could read instructions for operating equipment, and the efficiency goals of increasingly centralized industry required workers who could extract information from text (Myers, 1996; Resnick & Resnick, 1977).

---

[4] By 1909, 58% of students in the 37 largest U.S. cities were children of immigrants from 60 different ethnic backgrounds (e.g., 72% in New York, 67% in Chicago, 64% in Boston; Cremin, 1961). With increasing diversity and numbers, New York City undertook bureaucratization of the school system as early as the first half of the 1800s, seeking the efficiency of labor-saving machinery by breaking the curriculum into small steps and regimenting students as well as teachers in the beginnings of a uniform system (Kaestle, 1973).

Schooling became centralized, with many regulations for sequence of instruction and forms of assessment, and with many administrators to oversee the bureaucracy. Although teachers still relied heavily on questions to structure their engagement with students, the system of instruction no longer included reciting whole passages but rather focused on "bits-and-pieces interrogation of the student's mind" (Myers, 1996, p. 87).

> This shift from oral recitations of whole pieces to oral answers about smaller bits meant that most classrooms began to seem like quiz shows focusing on small bits of information, not the memory dumps of whole pieces typical in many traditional recitation classes. (Myers, 1996, p. 88)

Industrial models were used to transform the organization of schooling, employing "rational" models based on assembly line efficiency as in Ford's factories (Packer, 2001; Tyack & Tobin, 1994). The "scientific management" approach promoted by the new cadre of school administrators fit well with E. L. Thorndike's idea of organizing instruction and measurement around "elements." Thorndike's 1904 book (*An Introduction to the Theory of Mental and Social Measurement*) advocated that teachers should break tasks into sequenced parts, have students repeat each part in order and often, and reward students with grades or stars or other forms of feedback (Myers, 1996). The invention of the multiple choice test item followed a decade later.

Metrics were also developed to compare students – both IQ testing and standardized grades. Grading on a curve was introduced by Max Meyer in 1908 in the journal *Science* (proposing that the top 3% be ranked excellent, the next 22% labeled superior, the middle 50% judged medium, the next 22% inferior, and the bottom 3% failing). Standardized grading on a curve and IQ testing spread widely a few years later during the era of "scientific efficiency" in which education experts and administrators applied industrial models for factory production to schools.

> Since Americans were, in the first 30 years of the twentieth century, inundated by dozens of immigrant groups who were so radically different first from "Americans" and then from each other, the emphasis on differences now measurable by scientifically validated tests was translated from the realm of the senses to that of statistics. This made the differences seem firmer, sharper, and also more controllable. At a time when democracy seemed threatened by heterogeneity, counting, sifting, and ranking provided a form of order and containment. (Fass, 1980, p. 439)

However, by the end of the 20th century, "higher" levels of literacy were expected for all U.S. children, requiring them to make inferences and develop ideas through written material. This was the first time that critical literacy was set as a goal for all children, although some children of the elites had this goal long before (Myers, 1996; Resnick & Resnick, 1977; Wolf, 1988). Of course, some of the structures of schooling that developed in the old factory model, such as use of age and standardized tests to organize the treatment of children, have become "naturalized" in conceptions of childhood and of learning in highly schooled societies.

Use of Age As a Metric of Human Development

Age became a measure of development and a criterion for sorting people, with the rise of industrialization and efforts to systematize human services such as education and medical care in the last half of the 1800s in the United States and some other nations (Chudacoff, 1989). Specialized institutions were designed around age groups. Developmental psychology began at this time, along with pediatrics, old-age institutions, and age-graded schools.

Before this time, people in the United States often did not know their ages, and students advanced in their education as they learned (Chudacoff, 1989). Over the past century and a half, the cultural concept of age and associated practices relying on age-grading have come to play a central, though often unnoticed, role in ordering lives in the United States.

Age-Graded Bureaucracies. Bureaucratic institutions for children such as school often cluster one-year age groups for adults' convenience. Until large numbers of children were required to attend school, dividing children according to age was not involved even in schooling's ordering of the curriculum (Chudacoff, 1989; Serpell, 1993). Gradations based on students' progress through the curriculum began in the 1500s in European schools; the levels were not determined by time since birth (Ariès, 1962; Serpell, 1993).

Rough gradation based on age began in the early 1800s, with the usual very wide age range narrowing to about a six-year range within a given class (Ariès, 1962; Serpell, 1993). In North America of the late 1700s and early 1800s, there was not a standard age of entry or completion, and it was not unusual for 3- or 4-year-olds to be in the same classroom as teenagers (Angus, Mirel, & Vinovskis, 1988; Chudacoff, 1989).

> Since children differed widely with respect to when they had begun school, how many terms they had attended, how regular their attendance had been, how much time they could find at home to study, and so

forth, not to mention differences in talent and motivation, age was a poor predictor of which child would be studying at which level in each subject. Teenage boys who had grown up out of the reach of a school might find themselves learning the alphabet alongside children of four or five. (Angus, Mirel, & Vinovskis, 1988, p. 216)

In the mid-1800s, a system of "graded instruction" was developed that ordered the subjects to be taught into a sequence according to difficulty, and arranged them into the amount of work expected in one year for the average child (Angus, Mirel, & Vinovskis, 1988; Hamilton, 1989). However, the children were advanced through these grades on the basis of their attainments, not their age. Some efficiency accompanied the grouping of children according to their level of accomplishment, and teachers began to instruct the whole class, giving the same lesson to all, rather than having individuals or small groups recite.

In the late 1800s, segregation of U.S. schoolchildren by age became formalized, when the schools instituted standard starting ages as part of the legal requirements of compulsory schooling. Age-grading served bureaucratic needs, in the face of great increases in the numbers of schoolchildren (due in part to industrialization, urbanization, and immigration). Handling instruction bureaucratically also followed the preference of the late 1800s to organize a "rational" system of uniform classification, curricula, textbooks, and discipline, using age as a metric to categorize pupils within the efficiency model of the factory system (Chudacoff, 1989).

> Awareness of age and the age grading of activities and institutions were part of a larger process of segmentation within American society during the late nineteenth and early twentieth centuries.... New emphases on efficiency and productivity stressed numerical measurement as a means of imposing order and predictability on human life and the environment. Scientists, engineers, and corporate managers strove for precision and control through the application of specialization and expertise. These same endeavors were applied to human institutions and activities – schools, medical care, social organizations, and leisure. The impetus for rationality and measurement also included the establishment of orderly categories to facilitate precise understanding and analysis. Age became a prominent criterion in this process of classification. (Chudacoff, 1989, p. 5)

With the employment of a standard starting age, age-batches could be given the same instruction. In France and the United States, organizing instruction into stages for batch-instruction helped administrators supervise teachers (Anderson-Levitt, 1996; Tyack & Tobin, 1994). However, the bureaucratic employment of age to sort students yielded problems with children who did not fit the developing norms.

Timing and Measuring Development. A growing concern with timing of development stemmed in large part from administrators' concern in the early 1900s with the number of children who were "behind" the grades in school that were designated for them, challenging the bureaucratic efficiency of age-grading (Anderson-Levitt, 1996; Chudacoff, 1989). Psychologists such as E. L. Thorndike and Lightner Witmer began to collect and analyze age/grade data from a number of large U.S. cities, initiating the school-efficiency movement which soon made age/grade tables a routine part of school districts' annual reports (Angus, Mirel, & Vinovskis, 1988).

Calculations of the financial costs of students repeating grades were debated among school and business leaders, and psychologists played leading roles in seeking the causes of "retarded" progress through the grades and in devising systems for "child accounting" (Angus, Mirel, & Vinovskis, 1988).

> The newly emerging profession of psychology saw in the concept of age-grading a measurement tool that could lend scientific legitimacy to their work [and] the same can be said of the emergent field of scientific school administration. [They were] enthralled by statistics and numbers. (p. 223)

However, the standards they set for progress through the grades proved difficult to meet. For example, New York had sparked the concerns about "retardation" by reporting that 39% of students were over-age in 1904, but in 1922, New York's over-age rate was still 31% (Angus, Mirel, & Vinovskis, 1988). Business leaders often criticized the schools' inefficiency, as students took eight or nine years to finish the six elementary grades.

To address the concerns regarding the large proportion of students who were "over-age" for their grade, mental testing developed about this time. The invention of mental testing was based on work in developmental psychology, especially in France and the United States, building on the recent development of laboratory techniques in German psychophysics (e.g., in Wundt's laboratory) and of statistical methods in England (e.g., by Pearson and by Spearman; Fass, 1980). In France, Alfred Binet and colleagues developed tests of mental age as practical tools for schools of the early 1900s to sort out feeble-minded children who needed "special" education.

The intelligence quotient was soon invented to compare tested mental ages to children's chronological ages (by Terman, the Stanford psychologist, in 1916). Americans, particularly, became obsessed with defining and measuring mental age, creating an American industry that lasted for more than 50 years, and established age norms and developmental schedules (Chudacoff, 1989; Fass, 1980). "Psychologists suddenly found themselves in a lucrative business with skills very much in demand" (Fass, 1980, p. 446).

Contemporary levels of correspondence between age and school grade did not occur until the 1940s or 1950s, with automatic ("social") promotion based on age as a solution to the bureaucratic problem of age/grade discrepancies (Angus, Mirel, & Vinovskis, 1988). This was accompanied by the use of mental testing of various sorts, chronological age, and "ability" grouping to sort individuals for various educational and career opportunities, so that children could be advanced year-by-year according to their ages but sorted into tracks that determined their future instruction and chances.

Many changes in family structure and roles accompanied the shift to mass, compulsory education. Of course, many other features of life changed during industrialization, accompanying the spread of mass, compulsory schooling.

Family Changes Associated with Increases in U.S. Schooling

As children spent more of their days in age-graded schooling, they were less available to help in family economic endeavors. Their economic contributions to the family decreased due to compulsory schooling and child labor laws. With children's increased schooling and decreased economic contributions, children became costly rather than contributors to the family larder or pocketbook (LeVine & White, 1986, 1987).

Family sizes decreased in the period of increasing schooling, in part due to children's changing economic roles (Hernandez, 1994). From 1865 to 1930, smaller families (with only one to four children) grew from 18% to 70%. The median number of siblings in the families of adolescents plummeted from 7.3 to 2.6.[5]

Small family size and school attendance limit the experience children have in caring for younger children (Harkness & Super, 1992; Martini, 1994; Whiting & Edwards, 1988). For example, now that 5- to 10-year-old Kikuyu

---

[5] Infant mortality dropped over the same period. Around 1800, U.S. women averaged seven live births, of which a third or a half would not survive to five years of age (Ehrenreich & English, 1978). Around 1890, 20% of white children and 40% of black children died before age 15 (Hernandez, 1994). In the 1900s, child mortality in the United States dropped due to improvements in sanitation and nutrition; more recent advances in drugs and immunization have contributed to further drops. By 1973, only 2% of white children and 4% of black children died by age 15.

(Kenyan) children usually attend school, they are no longer available to serve as child nurses for their toddler-aged siblings, although they are the preferred age for this job. This means that Kikuyu mothers now need to rely on children under age 5 to help care for and entertain their toddlers (Edwards & Whiting, 1992).

The age-range of children's interactions with children at home, as well as at school, is thereby restricted. With older children in school, younger children spend less time in their company. In addition, the reductions in number of children tightened the spread of siblings' ages to a narrow range (Chudacoff, 1989). Now that many very young children attend institutional care settings, their days too are increasingly age-graded. Consistent with this segregation, middle-class North Americans emphasize children's peer relations over relations with brothers and sisters (Angelillo, Rogoff, & Morelli, manuscript; Ruffy, 1981; Wolfenstein, 1955).

Now, within nations with near-universal schooling extending throughout childhood, it is difficult to imagine childhood relationships and learning in any other way than that structured by this institution. Looking to other nations where schooling is not so ubiquitous provides important information on distinct ways that childhood can occur when schooling is not such a primary institution as well as information on the role of schooling itself in children's lives. Changes in recent generations in communities where schooling is just now taking hold provide opportunities to consider aspects of childhood that seem to relate to increases in schooling.

Western Schooling's International Spread

The impact of schooling on childhood has grown worldwide in the twentieth century, as Western schooling has spread around the world from its European and North American origins (LeVine & White, 1986). In many parts of the world, Western schooling was initially exported as a means of "civilizing" populations in the colonial eras. The first Western schools in many colonies were introduced as part of the missionizing process (Spring, 1996). Teaching of skills such as literacy was accompanied by insistence on the cultural practices and values of the missionaries, including obedience, punctuality, settled life and private property, and use of a colonial language, in addition to Christianity (Lomawaima, 1994; Spring, 1996).[6] In advice to the British

---

[6] At the same time, in some settings the colonial powers restricted access to literacy and the colonial language, as a way of dominating subjugated populations.

Parliament in 1847, a well-known educator claimed that the aim of colonial education was to instill Christianity, habits of self-control, and moral discipline, "as the most important agent of civilization for the colored population of the Colonies" (J. P. K. Shuttleworth, quoted by Willinsky, 1998, p. 100).

For example, an "army" of teachers arrived in the Philippines from the United States at the beginning of the 1900s, to instill new attitudes toward wealth and work. The desire for new things, it was thought, would motivate Filipinos to new standards. A domestic science teacher stated, "It is true we are teaching them to want things they have never had or cared to have before; but the incentive to have more will promote the ambition to work" (Cleaves, 1994, p. 7).

Compulsory mass schooling had spread to 80% of countries by 1985, and at least 90% of all children, worldwide, currently spend some time in school (Meyer et al., 1992). Generally, in countries that introduced elementary schooling following the European and American nations, enrollments grew by about 5% per decade from 1870 to 1940, and by about 12% per decade after World War II, accompanying international efforts for all children to attend school (Meyer et al., 1992).

Although secondary schooling has occurred for almost all youth in countries like the United States and Germany for many decades, it has jumped from approximately half of youth in 1980 to about three-fourths in 2000 in Argentina, Egypt, and China. In other nations, the increase has also been dramatic but has started from a much lower baseline, such as in India (moving from a third to a half of youth over this time) and Nigeria (moving from a fifth to a third; Arnett, 2002).

In the next section, we examine changes in schooling over the past 60 years in the Guatemalan Mayan community of San Pedro, as schooling has changed from enrolling only a few children for only a few years, to enrolling almost all children, with some going on to achieve Ph.D., M.D., and law degrees. Schooling had been introduced by Catholic priests from Spain in prior centuries, but it was not until the late twentieth century that this Western institution began to have widespread importance in the daily lives of many indigenous Mayans of San Pedro. We have had the privilege of studying some of the associated changes.

Growth of Schooling
in Three Guatemalan Mayan Generations

The role of schooling in the lives of children and families stands out among the rapid changes in recent generations in San Pedro. Our study of these processes spans three decades, from 1974 to the present, but focuses especially on data gathered in 1976 and in 1999.

In 1976, San Pedro was a town of about 5,000 inhabitants, whose lives were based primarily on traditional subsistence corn-and-beans agriculture, carried out by the men, with handwoven textiles and handmade tortillas made by the women. Travel out of town was on foot, in canoes across Lake Atitlán to neighboring towns, or in motor boats that came to the town dock three times per week. Most people from San Pedro married others from San Pedro, and lived in households in proximity to other kin, as had been the case for several centuries. By 1999, the town had grown to more than 10,000 inhabitants, not counting the many local people who have now emigrated to the capital city, other Guatemalan cities, and some to the US.

Almost all the inhabitants of San Pedro (known as "Pedranos" and "Pedranas" masculine and feminine forms) were and are Mayan Indians. They speak the Mayan language, Tz'utujil, which is unrelated to Spanish – the language employed in national government, commerce in cities, and in schools. During most of the 1900s, schooling was sponsored primarily by the Guatemalan government, expanding on the first San Pedro school, established as a mission school in 1799 (Aguirre, 1972).

To examine changes in involvement in Western schooling, we use data gathered across 23 years on 60 families from San Pedro. The 60 families all had a 9-year-old child in 1976, when Barbara Rogoff did her dissertation study (1977) with them with the assistance of Marta Navichoc Cotuc and several other San Pedro research assistants.

Rogoff has done research in San Pedro over the past 30 years, studying child-rearing practices and participating in the life of the community, living in the town for a total of about two years over the three decades. Navichoc Cotuc joined in the research 28 years ago, and is a native of San Pedro. Rogoff and Navichoc Cotuc repeatedly interviewed and videotaped families, observed children and their siblings and parents, and in the early years gave cognitive tests to the children. Maricela Correa-Chávez joined in the research four years ago, and has conducted interviews and observations over about four months of living in San Pedro. Navichoc Cotuc is a native speaker of the local Mayan language, Tz'utujil; Rogoff speaks and understands it conversationally; Correa-Chávez is studying it. All three speak Spanish, which is used widely as a second language in San Pedro.

Continuing informal contact with the 60 children and families across the decades from 1976 was followed up with formal interviews in 1999 by Rogoff and Navichoc Cotuc. The main interviews in 1976 and 1999 were conducted with adults in the families' homes, in whichever language they were most comfortable. Some interview information was also obtained from the 9-year-olds in 1976 in a rented room where the children came repeatedly for memory tests, which they regarded as a voluntary school. Our information thus involves interview data collected in 1976 and 1999, regarding

- people who by 1999 were the grandparent generation (*Generation 1* – parents of the 9-year-old children of 1976);
- people who in 1999 were in the parent generation (though some of this generation did not have children; *Generation 2* – they had been 9 years old in 1976); and
- people who in 1999 were the children of Generation 2 (*Generation 3*).

There was considerable mortality of San Pedro children born nine years before the study began in 1976 (35% of that birth cohort had died by age 9, mostly in the first year of life, according to municipal birth records). However, attrition of the sample since then has been minimal, allowing a follow-up that is unusually complete. One of the 60 children who made it to age 9 died of illness as a youth. The remaining 59 were about 33 years old in 1999, and 48 of them still lived in San Pedro. Information was available on all of them, including those who had emigrated.[7]

The 60 children who participated in Rogoff's dissertation study in 1976 were selected from the 9-year-olds of three of the five neighborhoods of San Pedro, and fairly well represented the general population of the town except for the stipulation that they were attending (or had been enrolled in) school.[8] In 1976, about a quarter of the town's 9-year-olds had not attended school. The 60 9-year-old children's level of schooling ranged across four grade levels – about half of them (48%) were in first grade, and most of the rest were either in Castellanización (introduction to Spanish, the language of schooling; 27%) or second grade (22%); two of them (3%) were in third grade. Their average age at school entry was 6.7 years (Rogoff & Lave, 1979); Guatemala's legal public school entry age was 7 years (Irwin et al., 1978).

The ages of the 9-year-olds (average = 9 years, 2 months; range 8 years, 7 months to 10 years, 0 months) were ascertained by municipal birth records in 1976. The parents' estimates of the children's ages often differed from the birth records by a year or two. The parents' estimates of their own ages were based on very rough guesses. Mothers often asked Rogoff to estimate their

---

[7] Sadly, another of the 60 has died subsequent to the data presented here, murdered by a robber in the capitol city.

[8] Only two families that were approached did not give permission for their children to participate in the study.

own ages, and their own estimates were often in 5- or 10-year increments. Some mothers responded to Rogoff's census question regarding their own age along these lines: "How old am I? Hmmm, well, I don't know. How old would you say, Barbara? Maybe 40? . . . Or maybe more like 50? . . . Put 50."

Schooling Does not Stand Alone

We are not suggesting that schooling is the force behind all the changes in children's lives across generations in San Pedro. Schooling is part of a constellation of changes (Rogoff & Angelillo, 2002), many of which depend on each other. However, we argue that schooling is a key part of the changes and an increasingly important part of children's experience in San Pedro, as in the United States and many other locales worldwide.

Some changes across the generations *can* be attributed directly to changes in schooling. For example, children who spend substantial portions of most days in age-graded schools cannot be involved in care of young siblings during that time. Hence, their child-care responsibilities are diminished; in 1976 needing the children to provide child care was a common reason for nonattendance (on some days, or in some years, or altogether). As another example of a causal link, certain levels of schooling are prerequisite for a number of the occupations that are increasingly commonly held (and aspired to) within San Pedro, such as teacher and accountant. Without schooling, these jobs are off limits.

A number of other changes in San Pedro may also be connected with schooling in a more general fashion, because schooling and other experiences contribute to fluency in Spanish, and this opens up other possibilities for occupations and travel, which in turn encourage greater Spanish fluency. In 1976, Generation 1 males generally spoke some Spanish (73% spoke it "more or less") and females generally spoke none (61%) or a little (25%). By 1999, Generation 2 males usually spoke Spanish well (85%) and females generally did too (68%). In Generation 2 in 1999, 12% of males and 6% of females also spoke some English. At the same time, all individuals in Generations 1, 2, and 3 spoke the Mayan language Tz'utujil – a central marker of Mayan identity.

A number of other forms of communication with the "outside world" have increased dramatically over these years. In 1976, although 87% of the Generation 1 households had electricity supplying at least one light bulb, only 6% had a television. Most households had only a Bible (68%), and the remaining 32% had no books. By 1999, all Generation 1 households had electricity, 78% had a television, 5% had a VCR, and one had a photocopy machine. In 1999, only 23% of Generation 1 households had no books and 38% had only a Bible, while 30% had other books and 8% had shelves of books; 38% of Generation 1 households had a typewriter in 1999 (none had a computer).[9]

In what follows, we examine increases across the three generations in the extent of schooling, accompanied by narrowed age-grading and changes in educational and occupational aspirations, actual occupations, and children's contribution to family work. In addition, increased schooling is accompanied by dramatic decreases in number of children born, yielding limitations in number of siblings. We relate these findings to other research that suggests that with increases in schooling, mothers also appear to be more likely to interact with their children in ways that resemble the formats of schooling and less often to engage in the sort of collaborative group endeavors that seem to characterize traditional indigenous family and community organization (Chavajay & Rogoff, 2002; Rogoff, Mistry, Göncü, & Mosier, 1993).

Increases in Involvement in Schooling

From Generation 1 to Generation 2, a dramatic shift occurred from almost no schooling for most children, to considerable numbers of youth achieving higher degrees. In both generations, the extent of schooling was less for girls than for boys (see Table 9.1).

The prevalence of schooling is quite related to the level of schooling that has been available locally for the different generations. In 1936, third grade was the highest grade available locally, and school comprised only a few children (mostly boys) of varying ages, who generally attended for only a year (Chavajay & Rogoff, 2002). By 1953, the top grade extended to sixth grade (Demarest & Paul, 1981). Still for years, many did not attend school, a third-grade education was common, and graduation from sixth grade was a

---

[9] When adult Generation 2 households lived apart from Generation 1 households, the patterns were similar to those described here, although Generation 2's households were a little more austere than their parents' households. One third of married Generation 2 individuals lived in households combined with their parents' households. Unmarried Generation 2 individuals lived in their parents' household if they lived in San Pedro. (Of 8 unmarried individuals, 4 lived in San Pedro.) Of the 34 Generation 2 married households that were separate from Generation 1 households, 27 lived with the other spouse's parents or in a separate household in San Pedro, and 7 lived in another town or city.

considerable accomplishment. In 1972, grades 7–9 became available and in 1995, a teacher-training school encompassing grades 10–12 opened.

In the Yucatán, in communities with primarily Mayan background, the most powerful predictor of how many grades an individual would attend was the number of grades available in the individual's town (during roughly the same era as our Generation 1; Sharp, Cole, & Lave, 1979). Few individuals attained more schooling than that available in their town. The number of grades available in town served as a ceiling, and people reported aspirations set at about 70% of the highest amount of schooling available in their towns. (Maternal schooling was also a strong predictor of individuals' schooling in the path analysis reported by Sharp and colleagues.)

Few of San Pedro's Generation 1 received more schooling than was available locally. Many had no schooling at all (67% of the females and 33% of the males), and the majority had two or fewer grades of schooling (including those with no schooling: 87% of the females and 63% of the males). Almost none had completed more than six grades, with the exception of two who completed career studies equivalent to 12 grades.

By Generation 2, much more schooling was available in San Pedro. However, some children enrolled in 7th through 9th grades in distant cities, even though these grades had become available in San Pedro; their families believed they would thereby get a better education. In addition, a number of Pedranos and Pedranas pursued more schooling than the highest grade level available in town. Families could better afford the added expenses of studying out of town than in the previous generation (about half of the students attending 7th through 9th grades in 1976 studied in distant cities; Rogoff & Lave, 1979).

In Generation 2, the extent of schooling was much higher than in Generation 1, as can be seen in Table 9.1. All children had some schooling – a selection criterion for being in the study. [10] About half of Generation 2 completed one to six grades (61% of the females and 44% of the males), another 7%–10% completed seven to nine grades, and 30% of the females and 48% of the males completed the 12 grades required for entry into careers such as teacher and accountant (and one of the males had a higher degree). The level of schooling achieved by Generation 2 children was not

---

[10] This selection criterion may have meant that their parents – Generation 1 – had more schooling than average for the town; the 25% of children who were not in school in 1976 may have had parents who had attended less school than the Generation 1 parents. However, data from a random sample of 239 households carried out in 1974 show similar levels of parental schooling as the present data.

Table 9.1. *Extent of Schooling in Generations 1 and 2*

	Generation 1		Generation 2	
Highest Schooling	60 Females	60 Males	30 Females	29 Males
0	40 (67%)	20 (33%)	0	0
1–2	12 (20%)	18 (30%)	5 (17%)	5 (17%)
3–4	6 (10%)	17 (28%)	8 (27%)	3 (10%)
5–6	1 (2%)	4 (7%)	5 (17%)	5 (17%)
Básico (7–9)	0	0	3 (10%)	2 (7%)
Career (12+)	1 (2%)	1 (2%)	9 (30%)	14 (48%)

significantly correlated with their mothers' or their fathers' limited level of schooling.[11]

Greater Level of Schooling than Neighboring Mayan Towns

San Pedro's rate of schooling is considerably greater than in the neighboring Tz'utujil Mayan towns. In 1962, 40% of children were enrolled in San Pedro's school, a proportion much higher than in the larger Tz'utujil town of Santiago Atitlán, only a few miles away (Paul, 1968). Moreover, in Santiago Atitlán, the rate of schooling did not increase between 1964 and 1990. Across these decades in the neighboring town, a steadily high rate of attrition prevailed: Compared with the number of children in first grade, there were 38%–47% fewer children in second grade and 78%–89% fewer in sixth grade (Carlsen, 1997). By comparison, in the San Pedro Generation 2 data, for schooling during the same era, just 17% of the children attended only one to two grades, and over half of the children completed six grades or more.

In two other Tz'utujil towns a short walk from San Pedro along the lakeshore – San Juan and San Pablo – schooling was also less prevalent than in San Pedro. Although children are required by Guatemalan law to attend school from age 7 to 14, only 67% in San Juan and 18% in San Pablo were enrolled in 1978, and those usually attended primary school irregularly and seldom remained in school after age 10 or 11 (Loucky, 1988). When they were needed at home, their work took priority over schooling, which

---

[11] Moreover, for the most part, as young adults, both Generation 1 and Generation 2 individuals seemed to have married without much consideration of schooling level; their spouses' level of schooling was not correlated with their own. The exception was that Generation 2 women who had six or more grades of schooling almost all married men with similar extent of schooling.

was not expected to be of much use. By age 7, children were becoming dependable for many significant subsistence tasks, and apparently were more heavily involved in them in the two neighboring towns than in San Pedro, where schooling had taken a greater hold.

The variability in uptake of Western schooling in these Tz'utujil Mayan towns underlines the importance of not assuming uniformity across even closely related communities. San Pedro is known among Indian towns in this region for its interest in schooling.

San Pedro's emphasis on schooling can be seen in its teachers and other professionals. In 1936 the one teacher in town was non-Mayan (Chavajay & Rogoff, 2002), and still in 1976 most teachers in San Pedro were non-Indians from elsewhere in Guatemala. However, by the late 1990s most San Pedro teachers were Pedranos or Pedranas. In 1997, 114 of the 130 teachers employed in San Pedro were natives of San Pedro (12 were from other Mayan communities and 4 were not Mayan; Chavajay & Rogoff, 2002). In fact, San Pedro has been supplying a high proportion of teachers for the state as a whole (including staffing schools in Santiago Atitlán, San Juan, and San Pablo). A 1994 estimate indicated that San Pedro likely contributed more teachers working in the whole state of Sololá than all 18 of the state's other municipalities combined (Paul, 1994). In addition, in the late 1990s, about 100 students from San Pedro were attending universities (Chavajay & Rogoff, 2002) and about a dozen Pedranos and Pedranas had received or were studying for medical, law, or Ph.D. degrees.

Narrowed Age-Grading Accompanying Increased Schooling

In 1999, we asked about the schooling of the child of the Generation 2 individuals who was the closest in age to 9 years and the same gender if possible (Generation 3). Of the 59 surviving Generation 2 individuals, 27 had a child aged 6 to 14 years (average age was 8.8 years).

Generation 3 children were all in school, and their current grades closely matched those expected by their ages in an age-graded system. Most of the children (16 of 27) were in the expected grade, and almost all the rest were in the grade above (3) or below (5) the grade associated with their age – variation which would often be the case in strictly age-graded schools due to differing birthdates throughout the year. Only 3 of the 27 Generation 3 children were in a grade that was more than one grade different than the expected grade for their age (all 3 were two grades below). This is a narrower age range per grade than when Generation 3's parents were 9 years old.

The wide spread of ages within grades in the generation corresponding to Generation 2 was clearly apparent in a nearly random sample of 126 San

Pedro children aged 6 to 13, censused in 1974 by Rogoff. Only a few of the 6-year-olds and half of the 7-year-olds had entered school. At ages 8 and 9, 77% of the children had enrolled in school (ranging from Castellanización to second grade), and at ages 10 to 13, 88% of the children had some schooling, although 12% of the 10- to 13-year-olds had already quit school. There was a 6-year range within each of the first three grade levels (with children of ages 6–11 years in the preliminary "Castellanización" class, to learn Spanish to enter first grade, also 6 to 11 years in first grade, and 8 to 13 years in second grade). From third to sixth grades, the youngest ages crept up (11, 10, 11, and 13 years), but we cannot determine the oldest age because the top age examined was 13. However, the 10–11-year-olds who were still in school ranged from Castellanización to fifth grade and the 12–13-year-olds who were still in school ranged from second to sixth grades.[12]

It appears that in the time between the childhoods of Generation 2 and 3 (the 1970s and 1990s), schooling in San Pedro had become fairly tightly age-graded. Before that, children started at different ages and attended less continuously (across days and across years). Many of the Generation 2 children also struggled more to learn Spanish (because Spanish was used less in homes and in the community overall). Because speaking Spanish was a prerequisite for entry to first grade, which was taught solely in Spanish, more variation in this skill probably contributed to the wide spread of ages in each grade.

Aspirations for Schooling Rise Too

Children's aspirations regarding how far they would go in school rose dramatically across Generations 2 and 3 (see Table 9.2). Those who were 9 years old in 1976 (Generation 2) were asked how far they expected to go in school ("What grade do you think you'll go to?"). In 1999, the same question was asked of the Generation 3 children.

---

[12] In San Marcos, a few miles away, children (and teachers) attended school sporadically in 1980; on average children missed about half of the school time, due in large part to needs for their help at home and little confidence that school served a useful purpose. About half of the children enrolled in Castellanización and primary school were repeating the grade that they were in – for the second, third, fourth, or fifth time (Richards, 1987). In Castellanización (introduction to Spanish), only 2 of the 32 children who were not repeating this grade ended up passing into first grade, and of the 30 children who were already repeating this grade, only half ended up passing it.

Table 9.2. *Highest Grade Children Expect to Complete,*
in Generations 2 and 3

	Generation 2		Generation 3	
	30 Females	30 Males	13 Females	14 Males
Don't know	0	3 (10%)	2 (15%)	0
0–2	8 (27%)	5 (17%)	0	0
3–4	7 (23%)	11 (37%)	0	0
5–6	14 (47%)	9 (30%)	1 (8%)	4 (29%)
Básico (7–9)	1 (3%)	2 (7%)	3 (23%)	3 (21%)
Career (12+)	0	0	7 (54%)	7 (50%)

Almost all (95%) Generation 2 children had aspired to six or fewer grades when they were 9 years old (although many of them in fact went on to complete many more grades). In contrast, fully half of Generation 3 children aspired to complete at least 12 years of schooling. The change in aspirations could be based on the increased availability of schooling locally, the dramatically greater levels of schooling of their own parents, the improved economic circumstances across decades for many families, and other cohort differences supporting increased levels of schooling. It could also be that the Generation 3 children are predicting their schooling more accurately, based on more information about what is available (due to more schooling being available in town and more information about schooling available via television and other media by 1999).

The Generation 2 children's schooling aspirations correlated positively with their mothers' level of schooling ($r = .30$, $p = .01$). This effect seems to have come from the Generation 2 girls ($r = .44$, $p = .008$); the correlation for boys did not approach significance ($r = .06$). (There was no correlation with fathers' level of schooling.) Surprisingly, Generation 3 children's schooling aspirations were not correlated with their mothers' or fathers' levels of schooling. Perhaps Generation 2 girls were more likely to be encouraged in their schooling if their mothers had any schooling, and by Generation 3, the potentials of schooling in people's lives were more visible (in town and on television), providing more wide-based encouragement to go on in school.

Aspirations for Adult Occupation Transform with the Generations

The children in Generations 2 and 3 were asked (in 1976 and 1999) what work they expected to do when they grew up ("What work do you think you might do when you grow up?"). The children's aspirations in Generation 2

Table 9.3. *Children's Anticipated Occupations, in Generations 2 and 3*

	Generation 2		Generation 3	
Anticipated Occupation (as child)	30 Females	30 Males	13 Females	14 Males
Weave, embroider*	13 (43%)		2 (15%)	
Make tortillas, cook	12 (40%)		2 (15%)	
Wash, sweep up	5 (17%)			
Farming, cultivation		23 (77%)		3 (22%)
Gather firewood		5 (17%)		1 (7%)
Become mayor		1 (3%)		
Teacher			2 (15%)	2 (14%)
Accountant, secretary			3 (23%)	1 (7%)
Student (higher education)		1 (3%)	3 (23%)	
Doctor, lawyer				2 (14%)
Pastor				2 (14%)
Carpenter				2 (14%)
Musician				1 (7%)
Don't know			1 (8%)	

* Girls who expected to weave or embroider often also mentioned making tortillas and cooking.

(1976) resembled the kind of work that they were already doing to help in their family and the kind of work their same-sex parent did (see Table 9.3). Girls anticipated weaving, embroidering, making tortillas, and washing clothes and dishes. Boys anticipated farming and gathering firewood. Most of these children could anticipate that as adults they would continue to participate in extended household production and work on family land. The only Generation 2 children who fell outside this pattern were a boy who expected to go on to higher education and a boy who anticipated becoming mayor.

By Generation 3 (1999), few children had aspirations resembling those of Generation 2 as children. (Only 30% of the girls and 27% of the boys had aspirations like their Generation 2 parents had as children.) Most of the others aspired to go on in their studies and work in specialized careers such as teacher, accountant, pastor, and doctor.[13]

[13] Of the 5 Generation 3 children whose same-sex parent had a career requiring extensive schooling, all wanted such careers themselves. In addition, 1 girl whose mother had a little store wanted to become an accountant, 4 girls wanted to weave or work at home like their mothers, and 3 boys wanted to become a musician, a carpenter, or to work the fields like their fathers. The other children's occupational aspirations did not seem related to those of their same-sex parent (and relations with the other-sex parent's occupation seemed minimal).

Table 9.4. *Adult Occupations of Generations 1 and 2*

Adult Occupation	Generation 1		Generation 2	
	29 Females	30 Males	30 Females	29 Males
Weave, embroider*	19 (63%)		15 (50%)	
Make tortillas, cook	6 (20%)		5 (17%)	
Midwife	1 (3%)			
Farming, cultivation		27 (90%)		6 (21%)
Market/store sales	3 (10%)	3 (10%)	3 (10%)	3 (10%)
Teacher			3 (10%)	5 (17%)
Accountant, manager, sec'ty			3 (10%)	2 (7%)
Student (higher education)			1 (3%)	
Doctor				1 (3%)
Pastor				1 (3%)
Carpenter, tailor, shoemaker				4 (14%)
Factory worker				3 (10%)
Truck driver				2 (7%)
Security guard				1 (3%)
Musician				1 (3%)

* Women who identified their work as weaving or embroidering often also mentioned making tortillas and cooking.

Adult Occupations Move from Agricultural and Home Production to Include Teaching and Other New Positions

To compare the actual adult occupations of Generation 1 and 2, we examined occupations of the same-sex parent of each of the Generation 2 individuals (see Table 9.4). Many of the Generation 2 females followed the same occupations as their mothers, with the addition of paid careers for about a fourth of them. The Generation 2 males, however, shifted markedly from their fathers' occupations – only a third of them followed the occupations of their fathers, and the other two thirds followed new careers.

Many of the new occupations have high schooling prerequisites, requiring completion of 12 grades to qualify for them. All of the Generation 2 individuals who are in the professions of teacher, accountant, manager, secretary, doctor, pastor, or still studying have completed twelve or more grades. This comprises 7 (23%) of the females and 9 (31%) of the males (and none of their parent generation). The other Generation 2 individuals who have completed 12 or more grades are in the following occupations: 2 females work at home cooking; 2 males work in sales, 2 in factories, and 1 in carpentry. The other levels of schooling seem to be spread randomly among the other kinds of work (both traditional and new) that do not require completion of 12 grades, for the rest of the Generation 2 females and males.

Some of the pressure to adopt wage-earning occupations may come from the decreasing landholdings available to each generation across the 20th century. Guatemala has the most extreme discrepancy between landholdings of the wealthy and the poor in Latin America: In about 1980, 1% of the population controlled 66% of the land, whereas 96% of the population controlled only 16% of agricultural land (Early, 1982, as cited by Loucky, 1988). This imbalance is exacerbated by the rapid increase in population, such that already-small plots of land are subdivided into plots too small to sustain a family. In 1979, 77% of rural Guatemalan households had insufficient holdings for subsistence (Early, 1982, as cited by Loucky, 1988). The population of San Pedro has grown from about 2,000 in 1941 to over 12,000 in 2002, despite a great deal of outmigration to cities, where there are often not sufficient jobs to support them.

Extensive schooling does not guarantee a good job. A number of Pedranos and Pedranas employed as teachers as of 1994 had jobs in private schools with poor remuneration, in hopes of moving into a well-paying government teaching position, and about 25% of those who were trained as teachers were not employed as teachers (Paul, 1994). About a third of these had other positions in office jobs in the capital or were doing well as agriculturalists; however, the others worked in trades in San Pedro or in available jobs in the capital. Some of these may be represented among the Generation 2 individuals who have more than 12 years of schooling but are working in homemaking, sales, factory work, and carpentry, which do not require such high levels of schooling.

Possible Generational Changes in Schooling's Relation with Occupations

Going to school may provide different occupational benefits for Generations 1, 2, and 3, associated with the dramatic differences in prevailing levels of schooling as well as available occupations. For Generation 1, who completed just a few grades, learning Spanish – useful in commerce – may have been a primary effect of school attendance. Primary schooling may have provided skills used in transitioning from agriculture and home-based production to merchant and traveling roles. In prior generations, the value of schooling for agricultural careers was questioned by San Pedro parents. For Generation 2, credentialing needed for salaried professions may commonly be the effect of completing 12 grades of schooling. With secondary schooling, Pedranos and Pedranas may join the bureaucratic workforce.

Consistent with these speculations, a path analysis indicated that for Generation 1, Spanish fluency was more closely related than schooling to adult income and family wealth (Rogoff & Lave, 1979). (Generation 1's Spanish fluency was itself predicted by extent of schooling and contact with Spanish speakers in the course of work and everyday life.) However, Generation 1 men's involvement in nonagricultural careers (such as teaching, tailoring, and ministry) was predicted by their level of schooling, perhaps due to credentialing barriers in many such occupations or perhaps due to a need for higher levels of literacy in some of them. Generation 1's Spanish fluency was also more related than was their schooling to the extent of schooling of their Generation 2 offspring, but family wealth, fathers having nonagricultural careers, and mothers' contact with non-Pedranos were even more directly related to Generation 2's schooling. By the time the available level of schooling included secondary school (as was the case for Generation 2), the credentialing effect may have been much stronger in relating extent of schooling to other aspects of San Pedro lives.

The reasons that Generation 2 and 3 children gave for attending school were also consistent with the idea of changing benefits of schooling. Many Generation 2 children (47% of them) said that learning Spanish was their reason for going to school, whereas only 15% of Generation 3 children gave this reason. Between 1976 and 1999, the general usage of Spanish has increased greatly, so it may be more taken for granted, and also easier to learn because of the greater prevalence of Spanish on television, in local tourism, and in everyday local use (in addition to the increase in schooling and the advent of bilingual Mayan–Spanish early schooling). Generation 3 children's reasons for attending school included being students in order to get a good job, cited by 37% of them and none of the Generation 2 children. (The remaining children in both generations reported that they went to school to learn to read and/or write, or did not have a reason.)

Children's Work Contributions Decline

The increases in children's schooling across the generations have been accompanied by decreases in their contributions to family work. With increasing days and years spent in school and with decreasing numbers of siblings, fewer boys were involved in caring for siblings, but most girls still had some childcare responsibilities. (See Table 9.5.) However, the amount of time spent in child care is probably much less for both girls and boys (based on casual observation of frequency of seeing a child tending a baby, and commentary of San Pedro parents; Magarian, 1999).

Table 9.5. *Number of Children Doing Each Type of Work (as Reported by Parents)*

Type of Work	Generation 2		Generation 3	
	30 Girls	30 Boys	13 Girls	14 Boys
Tending a baby	18 (60%)	16 (53%)	8 (62%)	1 (7%)
Weaving	26 (87%)		0	
Washing clothes	21 (70%)		8 (57%)	
Making tortillas	12 (40%)		4 (29%)	
Selling (store or street)	5 (17%)	1 (3%)	0	0
Cleaning houses for pay		1 (3%)		
Farming/cultivation	1 (3%)	17 (57%)	1 (7%)	5 (36%)
Fishing		6 (20%)		3 (21%)
Picking coffee	0	0	2 (14%)	9 (64%)

Children also participate less in other family work. For example, no girls of Generation 3 are involved in weaving, whereas 87% of their mothers (at age 9) had been weaving or beginning to weave – a primary job of San Pedro women of prior generations. (Half of the Generation 2 girls who were involved in weaving were at the level of play-weaving, in which girls set up little looms using found materials and practice weaving.) There also seems to be a slight decrease in children's washing, making tortillas, and selling (peddling or helping in a family shop).

Somewhat fewer boys of Generation 3 than Generation 2 are involved in tending family corn, bean, onion, and fruit crops – formerly the main male occupation. However, in 1999, the children – especially boys – picked coffee beans on family trees or for pay (for Pedranos with larger landholdings), accompanying the increase of this cash crop since their parents were children.

There are also differences in the number of types of work each child does (using the types listed in Table 9.5; see Table 9.6). In Generation 3, a higher proportion of the children are reported not to be doing work at all, which was less common in Generation 2, χ-square $= 8.02$, $p < .009$. (In both generations, boys are more often the ones doing no work.)

The average number of different types of work done by the children has decreased from Generation 2 to Generation 3, t (85) $= 3.00$, $p = .003$. The change is mostly among the girls: Generation 2 girls averaged 3 types of work, whereas Generation 3 girls averaged only 1.7 types of work. The boys' number of types of work changed little, averaging 1.5 and 1.3 types of work in Generations 2 and 3.

These changes are consistent with LeVine and White's (1987) contrast of children's roles in agrarian communities versus in middle-class communities

Table 9.6. *Number of Types of Work by Children in Generations 2 and 3*

No. of Types of Work	Generation 2		Generation 3	
	30 Girls	30 Boys	13 Girls	14 Boys
0	0	3 (10%)	2 (15%)	5 (36%)
1	1 (3%)	12 (40%)	3 (23%)	3 (21%)
2	9 (30%)	12 (40%)	6 (46%)	3 (21%)
3	9 (30%)	3 (10%)	1 (8%)	3 (21%)
4	10 (33%)		1 (8%)	
5	1 (3%)			
Average	3.0	1.5	1.7	1.3

in industrialized nations, where parents provide economic and social support to children without expecting tangible returns. Middle-class occupations result in many children needing to make their future careers in work that their parents do not know how to do, in contrast with agrarian traditions. Thus, childhood becomes a time of preparation for uncertain employment in adulthood, instead of ongoing involvement in family and community productive activities (Rogoff et al., 2003).[14]

In prior generations, children in San Pedro contributed importantly to the resources of their family; such contributions were also noted in work done in 1978 in the nearby Tz'utujil towns of San Juan and San Pablo (Loucky, 1988). "Maya children represent positive net economic value by adolescence. This contributes to continuing upward pressure on fertility and school abstention" (p. xi).

Fertility and Infant Mortality Decline, and with Them, Number of Siblings

Generation 1 parents had a relatively large number of children, several of whom usually died in early childhood. We compare Generation 1 and 2 childbearing at the age of 33, in order to hold constant the number of years available to bear children. We also limit the comparison to the Generation 1 parent that is of the same gender as the individuals included in Generation 2 ("same-sex Generation 1").

By the time the same-sex Generation 1 individuals were an estimated 33 years old, in about 1968, they had had an average of 6 children (see Table 9.7). Of course, many continued to have children after age 33; females

---

[14] The number of chores that the Generation 2 children did was not significantly correlated with the limited amount of schooling of their mothers or their fathers.

Table 9.7. *Fertility and Child Mortality of Same-Sex Generation 1 and 2 Parents*

	Same-Sex Generation 1		Generation 2	
	30 Females	29 Males	30 Females	29 Males
Average # children born				
by age 33	6.6	5.5	2.4	2.0
Range	3–15	3–9	0–7	0–6
# with no children at 33	0	0	4 (13%)	5 (17%)
# with 1–2 children	0	0	15 (50%)	16 (55%)
# with 3 or more	30 (100%)	29 (100%)	11 (37%)	8 (28%)
Ave. # babies died by 3 years				
across childbearing	1.9	1.7	0.3	0.1
Range	0–13	0–7	0–3	0–2
# w/ no babies that died	4	8	23	26
Ave.# died age 3–18*	0.2	0.7	0*	0.04

* *Note:* Generation 2 had less opportunity for older children to die, as Generation 2 was only 33 at the time of data collection.

averaged 8.4 live births (range 3 to 18) across their childbearing years. Across their childbearing years, they reported that about 2 of their children died.[15,16] Generation 1 males, marrying a couple of years older, had had a smaller average number of children born by age 33, but they caught up (Generation 2 males' fathers' total number of children born was 9.1; range 3 to 16).

When Generation 2 was 33 years old, in 1999, they had an average of 2 children per family and only an average of 0.2 had died. It is striking that about two thirds of Generation 2 had 0 to 2 children by age 33, whereas none of their same-sex parents (in Generation 1) had this few children at age 33.[17] It

[15] It seems that the mothers reported fewer mortalities than those documented in the municipal death records; probably they did not report the deaths of some babies who died in the first days or weeks of life. This may make sense given high birth and mortality rates, in retrospective reporting across several decades.

[16] These fertility figures are similar to those of neighboring Santiago Atitlán, where the average mother had eight live births in the mid-1960s (according to Early's data, reported by Carlsen, 1997). The rate of infant and child mortality, although high, is perhaps less than in prior decades. In Santiago Atitlán in 1950, more than 50% of children died between ages 0 and 4; by the mid-1980s, half of the women of Santiago Atitlán reported losing no children (Carlsen, 1997). In nearby towns of San Juan and San Pablo, about a fifth of children were reported to have died, according to 1978 information that resembles figures in San Pedro (Loucky, 1988).

[17] Of course, the parents are not a random sample of people of their generation; they were selected on the basis of having a 9-year-old in 1976, so all had

is also striking that during their childbearing years, almost all of Generation 1 had at least one child die, and usually 2, whereas at age 33, almost all of Generation 2 had lost no children.

Generation 1 women as a whole (all 60 of them, mothers of both Generation 2 females and males) had slightly fewer children born the more years they completed in school ($r = -.20$, $p = .06$). However, the relation between the Generation 1 men's extent of schooling and their number of children did not approach significance ($r = -.12$). Generation 2 individuals, at age 33, had significantly fewer children born the further they went in school, $r = -.31$, $p = .009$. [The correlation was about the same for Generation 2 females ($r = -.27$) and for Generation 2 males ($r = -.31$).]

The generational changes in fertility and mortality mean that the family experiences of Generation 3 are far different than those of Generation 2. Only about a third of Generation 3 children have more than 1 sibling, whereas all of the Generation 2 children had several siblings. Half of the Generation 3 children have one or no siblings, and Generation 3 children do not exist at all for 9 of the Generation 2 individuals who are childless.

So across the generations, we see large increases in schooling, in age-grading, and in aspirations for schooling and school-based occupations (as well as greater involvement in school-based occupations); this is accompanied by children's lesser involvement in sibling care and other contributions to their households, and fewer siblings to engage with. San Pedro children have become more unique in their families and more segregated from household and community activities as they spend increasing time in schools, in preparation for work that differs from that of their parents and grandparents. The changes seem to be transforming childhood from being a contributing segment of family and community worlds to being segregated and preparing to contribute to bureaucratic organizations that pay salaries (if they are fortunate to be both successful in school and in competing for the limited posts available).[18]

---

at least one surviving child by the design of the study. Nonetheless, the differences between generations in the same families are notable.

[18] Schooling in many systems is designed to fail some proportion of students, many of whom approach their subsequent lives as failures, unlike in generations where schooling was not an option (see Serpell, 1993). The unavailability of jobs for which students have prepared also means that a number of successful students become unsuccessful in the job market. The consequences of failed aspirations (for the individual, family, and community) are worthy of study, especially as the school/work system that children enter in "developing" and post-industrial societies is often designed for a

More School-Like Adult–Child Interactions

With greater experience of school and fewer children, more of whom were likely to survive, other studies have shown that San Pedro mothers were more likely to interact with their children in ways that were similar to those of middle-class European-American mothers. With their toddlers, they gave language lessons, acted as peers in conversation and play, and used mock excitement and praise to motivate involvement in their own agenda (Rogoff et al., 1993). With older children, highly schooled San Pedro mothers took a more managerial role and divided a task among themselves and three children, rather than approaching it as a collaborative group (Chavajay & Rogoff, 2002). In families with little or no involvement in schooling, there was greater use of interactional patterns that appear consistent with traditional indigenous social organization – keen observation, supportive assistance, and fluid coordination in groups engaged in shared endeavors (Chavajay & Rogoff, 2002; Rogoff et al., 1993). (Maternal experience in school has also been found to relate to mother–child interaction in a number of other communities around the world; Laosa, 1980; Mejía Arauz et al., in preparation; von der Lippe, 1999.)

In related findings from Cuernavaca, México, mothers who had 6 to 9 years of schooling were more likely to desire and give birth to a smaller number of children, as well as to discuss family planning with their husband, compared with mothers who had 1 to 5 years of schooling (LeVine, LeVine, Richman, Tapia Uribe, Correa, & Miller, 1991; Miller, 1997). The more-schooled mothers were more likely to respond to their infants' vocalizations and looks with vocalizations, perhaps modeling after school experiences. LeVine et al. (1991) summed up their view of the role of schooling as follows:

> As schooling becomes institutionalized, mothers who have acquired this model in the classroom increasingly prepare their children for school, engaging them in pedagogical interaction at younger and younger ages. This means verbal responsiveness to the child during infancy, which has the effect of producing a verbally active toddler who frequently initiates demands for maternal attention during the post-infancy years. Such children are on the average less compliant and more "difficult" and "exhausting" to raise, reinforcing the mother's assumption that child care is a labor-intensive task – requiring more of her time and energy
>
> considerable proportion to fail – a striking contrast with lives a few generations back where almost everyone had work and made valued contributions in the community.

than it did for her own mother (prior to female schooling in an agrarian community) and inducing her to bear fewer children. (p. 486)

A Moment in Time?

The observations of changes accompanying schooling in San Pedro complement the historical analysis of the role of widespread schooling in the lives of U.S. children. With extensive involvement in Western schooling, children's lives seem increasingly to involve segregation from adults and association with close-in-age peers and siblings, accompanying smaller family size, decreased infant mortality, and reduced contributions by children to sibling care and other family work. When schooled children grow up, they seem to adopt some of the ways of schooling in dealing with their own children – such as attempting to manage children's attention and learning, employing more managerial roles, and less side-by-side pitching in together on a common productive endeavor.

At the turn of the twenty-first century, in middle-class communities in the United States, and increasingly in other communities around the world such as in the Mayan town of San Pedro, schooling seems to have become sufficiently obligatory and widespread that it is becoming "naturalized" in people's thinking about childhood. People often assume that the conditions of childhood surrounding schooling are simply the way children and families "are." Our aim is to call attention to them as a rather unique historical/cultural phenomenon that has wide and deep consequences for children's everyday lives as well as those of their families of origin and their subsequent families when they grow up.

LeVine and White (1987) have pointed out that the similarities across societies in the conditions of childhood accompanying compulsory and extensive schooling – such as small family size, low infant mortality, and limited economic contributions from children – stem from very different histories. The histories vary among different European and American nations, as they do among different neighboring Tz'utujil Mayan towns. In particular societies, these developments relate to industrialization, urbanization, and local childrearing philosophies in different manners and distinct sequences across the last few centuries. Despite the differing origins and routes, compulsory schooling has become a ubiquitous aspect of childhood, along with its accompanying features such as small family size, reduced infant mortality, reduced child contributions to family and community, and increased age segregation.

The historical changes leading to the present do not end in this moment. New generations will face changed circumstances and will develop new approaches that resemble current forms of childrearing in some ways and depart from them in others, reflecting distinct cultural histories as well as local and global change.

Despite its current ubiquity, compulsory, extensive mass schooling itself is a short experiment. Even during its century of existence in the United States, a number of transformations in its purposes and formats can be seen (along with some sturdy continuities, such as age-grading and standardized "measures" of students).

Although developmental researchers often treat schooling as a "natural" part of child development, as Diana Slaughter-Defoe has pointed out (in a planning meeting on child development and learning at NSF; July 1998), there is reason to question whether schooling will continue to play the same role throughout the coming century.[19] She posed the question, if schools are likely to cease to exist in 75 years, how should developmental researchers and policymakers currently be conceptualizing and contributing to the design of arrangements for children's learning and development? We regard this thought experiment as extremely valuable for broadening the perspective on how future practices and institutions can be designed to support children's development for the circumstances of the future.

Investigating the arrangements for children's learning in settings where Western schooling has not been prevalent for generations provides key information for considering resources for aiding children's learning. Such research not only helps us understand the role of Western schooling in children's lives in societies where this institution is central to children's lives, but also draws attention to the ways that children learn in communities where schooling is not pervasive. In many such settings, children learn by keen observation in the process of being involved in their communities' activities with people of a wide age range, motivated by the importance of the activities and the value of their contributions (Rogoff et al., 2003).

In commenting on the reduction in children's opportunities to engage in shared endeavors with adults, working side-by-side to accomplish a joint task together, Heath pointed out the importance of such situations for child and

---

[19] Her speculation was based in part on increasing use of home schooling, private schooling, and opportunities for other forms of learning (such as distance learning and use of the internet as an learning resource).

youth development:

> Currently, aside from agricultural households, relatively few [U.S.] families spend time in cross-age tasks that require planning, practice, and productive work across a period of several weeks or months. Yet these are the very situations in which children are most likely to engage in work on tasks beneficial to them and others and to receive extensive authentic practice [in] planning ahead, linking current actions to future outcomes, and self-assessing and self-correcting their own behaviors and attitudes. (1998, p. 217)

Such involvement is an important feature of a number of voluntary community youth organizations such as drama, arts, sports, and service clubs. In such settings, young people often learn and demonstrate important planning, hypothetical thinking, language, and leadership skills (supported by adult mentors and coaches) that they frequently do not show in schools (Heath, 1998).

Of course, schooling does not necessarily need to segregate children from the adult world or from making contributions to their communities (Bronfenbrenner, 1974). Efforts to improve the formats of schooling can be informed by greater understanding of the roles of schooling and of changing community structures in children's lives. Indeed, some innovative schools employ processes of intent participation that have long characterized children's contributions to their family and community lives in communities in which schooling has not been a central activity of childhood (Rogoff, Goodman Turkanis, & Bartlett, 2001; Rogoff et al., 2003).

As Shep White (1999) has eloquently pointed out, it is part of the role of developmental psychology to contribute to the design of societies' institutions for children. To do so most effectively requires some understanding of the powerful roles and the diverse trajectories of institutions such as schooling and family and work organization in children's lives across time and place.

Authors' Note

This chapter has benefited from decades of guidance by Shep White and Ben Paul. Their intellectual engagement, integrity, and commitment to children and families have provided theoretical vision as well as practical and moral support to this work. We also deeply appreciate the interest and collaboration of the 60 San Pedro children and their families, who welcomed our involvement in their lives and provided us with hospitality and information whenever we showed up. We also acknowledge helpful comments and other forms of assistance from Pablo Chavajay, Elena Gonzalez, Beatrice Whiting, Michael Cole, Sylvia Scribner, Bob LeVine, and Jerome Kagan. The work relied on financial support from a National Science Foundation Fellowship for Graduate Study, a NIMH Traineeship in Cross-Cultural Research in Human Development, a research grant from Harvard University Department of Psychology and Social Relations, a NICHHD grant (#HD10094 to Jerry Kagan), and Barbara Rogoff's endowed chair (the UCSC Foundation Professorship in Psychology), along with a Ford Foundation Fellowship and a NIMH Traineeship in Developmental Research (T32-MH20025) to Maricela Correa-Chávez.

References

Aguirre, Gerardo G. (1972). *La cruz de Nimajuyú*. Guatemala City.

Akinnaso, F. N. (1992). Schooling, language, and knowledge in literate and nonliterate societies. *Comparative Studies in Society and History 34*, 68– 109.

Anderson-Levitt, K. M. (1996). Behind schedule: Batch-produced children in French and U.S. classrooms. In B. A. Levinson, D. E. Foley, & D. C. Holland (Eds.), *The Cultural Production of the Educated Person: Critical Ethnographies of Schooling and Local Practice* (pp. 57–78). Albany, NY: SUNY Press.

Angelillo, C., Rogoff, B., & Morelli, G. (manuscript). Age and kinship of young children's child partners in four communities.

Angus, D. L., Mirel, J. E., & Vinovskis, M. A. (1988). Historical development of age stratification in schooling. *Teachers College Record 90*, 211–236.

Ariès, P. (1962). *Centuries of Childhood: A Social History of Family Life*. NY: Random House.

Arnett, J. J. (2002). The psychology of globalization. *American Psychologist 57*, 774– 783.

Bremner, R. H. (Ed.) (1970; 1971). *Children and Youth in America. A Documentary History. Vols. I–II, 1600–1932*. Cambridge, MA: Harvard University Press.

Bronfenbrenner, U. (1974). The origins of alienation. *Scientific American 231*, 53–57, 60–61.

Carlsen, R. S. (1997). Under the gun in Santiago Atitlán. In *The War for the Heart and Soul of a Highland Maya Town* (pp. 123–149). Austin TX: University of Texas Press.

Chavajay, P., & Rogoff, B. (2002). Schooling and traditional collaborative social organization of problem solving by Mayan mothers and children. *Developmental Psychology 38*, 55–66.

Chudacoff, H. P. (1989). *How Old Are You? Age Consciousness in American Culture*. Princeton, NJ: Princeton University Press.

Cleaves, C. (1994, November). *Domesticated Democrats: Domestic Science Training in American Colonial Education in the Philippines*, 1900–1910. Paper presented at the meetings of the American Anthropological Association, Atlanta.

Cremin, A. L. (1961). *The Transformation of the School: Progressivism in American Education, 1876–1957.* New York: Knopf.

Demarest, W. J., & Paul, B. D. (1981). Mayan migrants in Guatemala City. *Anthropology UCLA 11,* 43–73.

Edwards, C. P., & Whiting, B. B. (1992). "Mother, older sibling and me": The overlapping roles of caregivers and companions in the social world of two- to three-year-olds in Ngeca, Kenya. In K. MacDonald (Ed.), *Parent-Child Play: Descriptions and Implications.* Albany, NY: SUNY Press.

Ehrenreich, B., & English, D. (1978). *For Her Own Good: 150 Years of the Expert's Advice to Women.* Garden City, NY: Anchor Press/Doubleday.

Fass, P. S. (1980). The IQ: A cultural and historical framework. *American Journal of Education 88,* 431–458.

Getis, V. L., & Vinovskis, M. A. (1992). History of child care in the United States before 1950. In M. E. Lamb, K. J. Sternberg, C.-P. Hwang, & A. G. Broberg (Eds.), *Child Care in Context* (pp. 185–206). Hillsdale, NJ: Lawrence Erlbaum.

Graff, H. J. (2001). The nineteenth-century origins of our times. In E. Cushman, E. R. Kintgen, B. M. Kroll, & M. Rose (Eds.), *Literacy: A Critical Sourcebook* (pp. 211–233, 705–713). Boston MA: Bedford/St.Martin's.

Hamilton, D. (1989). *Towards a Theory of Schooling.* London: Falmer Press.

Harkness, S., & Super, C. M. (1992). Shared child care in East Africa: Sociocultural origins and developmental consequences. In M. E. Lamb, K. J. Sternberg, C.-P. Hwang, & A. G. Broberg (Eds.), *Child Care in Context* (pp. 441–459). Hillsdale, NJ: Lawrence Erlbaum.

Hawes, J. M. (1997). *Children Between the Wars: American Childhood, 1920–1940.* NY: Twayne.

Heath, S. B. (1998). Working through language. In S. M. Hoyle & C. Temple Adger (Eds.), *Kids Talk: Strategic Language Use in Later Childhood* (pp. 217–240). Oxford: Oxford University Press.

Hernandez, D. J. (1994, Spring). Children's changing access to resources: A historical perspective. *Society for Research in Child Development Social Policy Report 8,* 1, 1–23.

Hernandez, D. J. (1997). Child development and the social demography of childhood. *Child Development 68,* 149–169.

Irwin, M., Engle, P. L., Yarbrough, C., Klein, R. E., & Townsend, J. (1978). The relationship of prior ability and family characteristics to school attendance and school achievement in rural Guatemala. *Child Development 49,* 415–427.

Kaestle, C. F. (1973). *The Evolution of an Urban School System: New York City, 1750–1850.* Cambridge, MA: Harvard University Press.

Laboratory of Comparative Human Cognition. (1979). Cross-cultural psychology's challenges to our ideas of children and development. *American Psychologist 34,* 827–833.

Laosa, L. M. (1980). Maternal teaching strategies in Chicano and Anglo-American families: The influence of culture and education on maternal behavior. *Child Development 51,* 759–765.

LeVine, R. A., LeVine, S. E., Richman, A., Tapia Uribe, F. M., Correa, C. S., & Miller, P. M. (1991). Women's schooling and child care in the demographic transition: A Mexican case study. *Population and Development Review 17,* 459–496.

LeVine, R. A., & White, M. I. (1986). *Human Conditions: The Cultural Basis of Educational Development*. New York: Routledge & Kegan Paul.

LeVine, R. A., & White, M. I. (1987). The social transformation of childhood. In J. B. Lancaster et al. (Eds.), *Parenting across the Life Span: Biosocial Dimensions*. NY: Aldine de Gruyter.

Lomawaima, K. T. (1994). *They Called It Prairie Light: The Story of Chilocco Indian School*. Lincoln, NE: University of Nebraska Press.

Loucky, J. (1988). *Children's Work and Family Survival in Highland Guatemala*. Ph.D. dissertation, University of California at Los Angeles. University Microfilms International, #8803983.

Magarian, L. (1999, December). *Portraits of Change: Women's Lives over 58 Years in a Mayan Town: San Pedro la Laguna, Guatemala*. Unpublished thesis, Stanford University.

Martini, M. (1994). Peer interactions in Polynesia: A view from the Marquesas. In J. L. Roopnarine, J. E. Johnson, & F. H. Hooper (Eds.), *Children's Play in Diverse Cultures*. Albany: SUNY Press.

Meyer, J., Ramirez, J., & Soysal, Y. (1992). World expansion of mass education, 1870–1980. *Sociology of Education 65*, 128–149.

Meyer, M. (1908). The grading of students. *Science 28*, 243–250.

Miller, P. M. (1997, April). *The Effect of Schooling on Maternal Behavior in Low-Income Mexican Mothers*. Paper presented at the meeting of the Society for Research in Child Development, Washington, DC.

Morelli, G., Rogoff, B., & Angelillo, C. (2003). Cultural variation in children's access to work or involvement in specialized child-focused activities. *International Journal of Behavioral Development 27*, 264–274.

Myers, M. (1984). Shifting standards of literacy–The teacher's Catch-22. *English Journal 73*, 26–32.

Myers, M. (1996). *Changing Our Minds: Negotiating English and Literacy*. Urbana, IL: National Council of Teachers of English.

Packer, M. J. (2001). Cultural and critical perspectives on human development. In M. J. Packer, & M. B. Tappan (Eds.), *Changing Classes: Shifting the Trajectory of Development in School* (pp. 113–146). Albany, NY: State University of New York Press.

Paul, B. D. (1968). San Pedro la Laguna. In F. Rojas Lima (Ed.), *Los pueblos del Lago de Atitlán* (pp. 93–158). Guatemala: Seminario de Integración Social Guatemalteca (no. 23).

Paul, B. D. (1994, November). *Grade-School Teachers and other Professionals in San Pedro la Laguna*. Unpublished manuscript, Stanford University.

Resnick, D. P., & Resnick, L. B. (1977). The nature of literacy: An historical exploration. *Harvard Educational Review 47*, 370–385.

Richards, J. (1987). *Language, Education, and Cultural Identity in a Maya Community of Guatemala*. Ph.D. dissertation, University of Wisconsin, Madison. (University Microfilms International #8801496).

Rogoff, B. (1977). *A Portrait of Memory in Cultural Context*. Ph.D. dissertation, Harvard University.

Rogoff, B. (1981). Schooling and the development of cognitive skills. In H. C. Triandis & A. Heron (Eds.), *Handbook of Cross-Cultural Psychology* (Vol. 4). Rockleigh, NJ: Allyn & Bacon.

Rogoff, B. (2003). *The Cultural Nature of Human Development.* New York: Oxford University Press.

Rogoff, B., & Angelillo, C. (2002). Investigating the coordinated functioning of multifaceted cultural practices in human development. *Human Development 45,* 211–225.

Rogoff, B., & Lave, J. (1979, July). General or specific effects of schooling on family occupations and economics and education of offspring. Unpublished manuscript.

Rogoff, B., Goodman Turkanis, C., & Bartlett, L. (2001). *Learning Together: Children and Adults in a School Community.* New York: Oxford University Press.

Rogoff, B., Mistry, J., Göncü, A., & Mosier, C. (1993). Guided participation in cultural activity by toddlers and caregivers. *Monographs of the Society for Research in Child Development 58,* 7, Serial No. 236.

Rogoff, B., Paradise, R., Mejía Arauz, R., Correa-Chávez, M., & Angelillo, C. (2003). Firsthand learning through intent participation. *Annual Review of Psychology 54,* 175–203.

Ruffy, M. (1981). Influence of social factors in the development of the young child's moral judgments. *European Journal of Social Psychology 11* 61–75.

Serpell, R. (1993). *The Significance of Schooling: Life-Journeys in an African Society.* Cambridge, UK: Cambridge University Press.

Sharp, D. W., Cole, M., & Lave, C. (1979). Education and cognitive development: The evidence from experimental research. *Monographs of the Society for Research in Child Development 44* (Serial No. 178), 1–2.

Shotter, J. (1978). The cultural context of communication studies: Theoretical and methodological issues. In A. Lock (Ed.), *Action, Gesture, and Symbol: The Emergence of Language* (pp. 43–78). London: Academic Press.

Spring, J. H. (1996). *The Cultural Transformation of a Native American Family and Its Tribe, 1763–1995.* Mahwah, NJ: Lawrence Erlbaum.

Thorndike, E. L. (1904). *An Introduction to the Theory of Mental and Social Measurement.* New York: Teachers College.

Tyack, D., & Tobin, W. (1994). The "grammar" of schooling: Why has it been so hard to change? *American Educational Research Journal 31,* 453–479.

von der Lippe, A. L. (1999). The impact of maternal schooling and occupation on child-rearing attitudes and behaviors in low income neighborhoods in Cairo, Egypt. *International Journal of Behavioral Development 23,* 703–729.

White, S. H. (1999, April). *Developmental Psychology in a World of Designed Institutions.* Paper presented at the meetings of the Society for Research in Child Development.

White, S. H., & Siegel, A. W. (1984). Cognitive development in time and space. In B. Rogoff & J. Lave (Eds.), *Everyday Cognition: Its Development in Social Context* (pp. 238–277). Cambridge, MA: Harvard University Press.

Whiting, B. B., & Edwards, C. P. (1988). *Children of Different Worlds: The Formation of Social Behavior.* Cambridge, MA: Harvard University Press.

Willinsky, J. (1998). *Learning to Divide the World: Education at Empire's End.* Minneapolis: University of Minnesota Press.

Wohlwill, J. F. (1970). The age variable in psychological research. *Psychological Review 77,* 49–64.

Wolf, D. P. (1988). Becoming literate: One reader reading. *Academic Connections* (College Board), 1–4.

Wolfenstein, M. (1955). French parents take their children to the park. In M. Mead & M. Wolfenstein (Eds.), *Childhood in Contemporary Cultures*. Chicago: University of Chicago Press.

10   The Rise of the American Nursery School

Laboratory for a Science of Child Development

Barbara Beatty

American nursery schools served both as laboratories for the derivation of a science of child development and as consumers of this new science. Nursery schools grew out of the larger preschool movement of eighteenth- and nineteenth-century infant schools and kindergartens and from new conceptions of childhood. Treatises on how to educate young children, medical advice and child rearing manuals, Darwin's theory of evolution, and other early work in biology and comparative psychology laid the groundwork for the study of child development. G. Stanley Hall's child study movement of the 1890s was the main precursor. Edward L. Thorndike's educational psychology added new quantitative methodology. All of this came together in the environment of the nursery school, where psychologists, teachers, and parents sought new scientific information about children, and young children were readily available for research (Beatty, 1995; Koops & Zuckerman, 2003; Sears, 1975; Smuts and Boardman, 1986; White, 2003).[1]

Driven by societal needs and concern for children's well-being, the nursery-school movement and child development research were based on the belief that scientific knowledge about young children, child rearing, and preschool education could ameliorate larger social problems. The flood of immigrants and increasing industrialization, urbanization, and poverty heightened existing worries about child welfare. The growth of cadres of experts in the sciences, social sciences, and children's professions created a new infrastructure. The roaring economy and more organized private charities and government agencies provided financial and political support. The success of the public

[1] I am grateful for the comments of Sheldon H. White, Emily Cahan, and David Pillemer, whose insights added greatly to my understanding of the linkage of the history of preschool education and developmental psychology. An earlier version of this chapter was given as a paper at meeting of the Society for Research in Child Development in 1995.

kindergarten movement in the early twentieth century turned preschool educators' attention to younger children. The result was a burst of research in the 1920s and early 1930s on young children, most of it done in nursery schools (Beatty, 1995; Bremner, 1971; Muncy, 1991; Schlossman, 1981; Ross, 1990). The American nursery-school movement stemmed from the British nursery-school movement, which was explicitly linked to psychology. Deeply concerned about the health of poor and working class children and a great believer in the beneficial effects of ventilation and hygiene, British socialist Margaret McMillan started a nursery school in 1913 for children from 1 year to 6 years of age in the London slum of Deptford. In keeping with McMillan's medical model of preschool education, the teachers were called nursery nurses. McMillan was influenced by the sensory psychology of Edouard Seguin and others, and thought that young children's minds and memories could be expanded through a sensorial pedagogy somewhat like that of her contemporary Maria Montessori. Grace Owen, the sister-in-law of psychologist James McKeen Cattell, was also prominent in the British nursery-school movement and in its translation to the United States. Future American nursery-school leaders studied with McMillan and brought nursery-school ideas back to this country (Beatty, 1995; Lascarides & Hinitz, 2000; McMillan, 1921; Steedman, 1990).

American child welfare activists were also involved in the movement's beginnings. Wealthy, progressive Iowa City matron Cora Bussey Hillis, who had lost children due to illness, began efforts in 1906 that would lead to the Iowa Child Welfare Research Station at the State University of Iowa, in Iowa City. Arnold Gesell, who was also the country's first public school psychologist, opened a clinic in 1911 at Yale University, to treat young children with school adjustment problems. Greenwich Village radical Caroline Pratt who had started a playgroup for young children in 1913, collaborated with Harriet Johnson and Lucy Sprague Mitchell to found the Bureau of Educational Experiments in 1916 and its nursery school (Antler, 1987; Beatty, 1995).

Associated with colleges, universities, or training institutes, many early nursery schools were begun with the goal of producing scientific research, and served the children of well-to-do, well-educated parents who wanted their children to be educated in progressive, scientifically designed environments. Other nursery schools were begun as part of settlement houses, the urban communal organizations where social reformers lived and worked. These, such as the nursery school at Jane Addams's famous Hull House in Chicago, served the children of poor and immigrant parents, many of whom were less receptive to scientific notions about child rearing. Leaders of the kindergarten movement, especially Patty Smith Hill, who started a nursery-school course at

Teachers College, were also very active in promoting nursery schools (Beatty, 1995; Lascarides & Hinitz, 2000).

Private philanthropy was the most immediate impetus behind the rapid growth of nursery-school-based research. In 1923, Beardsley Ruml, a University of Chicago trained psychologist, and Lawrence K. Frank, a University of Chicago trained economist with connections to the nursery-school community, began distributing large sums of Laura Spelman Rockefeller Memorial funds to projects designed to advance child welfare through scientific research. By 1925, Ruml and Frank had awarded more than a million dollars to such research, and gave out another $10 or $11 million before they left the fund in 1930 (Cahan, 1991; Grant, 1994, p. 14; Schlossman, 1981, p. 297; Sears, 1975, p. 20). Much of this money went to child development institutes at Teachers College, Yale, and at the Universities of Minnesota, Iowa, California, and Toronto, and to other institutions and researchers, as well. Headed by psychologists, all of the institutes were associated with nursery schools (Sears, 1975; Senn, 1975; Smuts & Boardman, 1986).

Two major bibliographic efforts documented the growing amount of child development and nursery-school research. In 1929, the National Society for the Study of Education (NSSE) published its *Twenty-Eighth Yearbook, Preschool and Parental Education* (Whipple, 1929). In 1935, the National Association for Nursery Education (NANE) published a comprehensive bibliography, *Nursery School Education* (Bradbury, Skeels, & Swieda, 1935). Both included hundreds of articles from *Child Development*, the *American Journal of Psychology*, *Pedagogical Seminary*, the *Journal of Genetic Psychology*, the *Journal of Educational Psychology*, the *American Journal of Orthopsychiatry*, the *Journal of Experimental Psychology*, and other psychology journals and texts. The NSSE yearbook covered early research through studies published in 1928; the NANE bibliography covered work published mostly between 1928 and 1934 (Bradbury, Skeels, & Swieda, 1935; Whipple, 1929). Since there was relatively little overlap between the two, and some editors worked on both compilations, these may have been intended as continuation volumes.

As these many studies attest, participants in the nursery-school movement saw the enterprise as a large psychological experiment. Viewed from this perspective, the movement's goals can be framed as research questions. Although there were many interrelated topics and subcategories, examination of nursery-school sources suggests six main lines of inquiry. (1) Could nursery schools improve young children's health, physical growth, and motor development? (2) Could nursery schools enhance young children's mental development and language? (3) Could nursery schools enhance young children's social and emotional development? (4) Could nursery schools alleviate the problems of emotionally, behaviorally, and otherwise troubled children? (5) Could parent education and parent involvement in nursery schools positively influence children's development? (6) Could nursery schools help women combine career interests and motherhood without adversely affecting their children?

There were other questions that did not initially make it onto the main agenda or were removed temporarily. A seventh question about sensory development appears but was stifled when Maria Montessori's ideas were rejected as unscientific by American psychologists and educators, though sensorial activities were part of the nursery-school curriculum, and a focus of some child development research (Beatty, 1995, p. 118). Language development was emerging as a separate line of inquiry. There was also great interest in play, artistic development and creativity, and nursery-school materials. The question of whether nursery schools could alleviate the effects of poverty was introduced, as well. Consequently, the themes of measurement, of developing accurate metrics and norms for gauging development, and of recordkeeping cut across all of these questions (White, 1999).

The NSSE and NANE bibliographies are revealing pieces of data. Like posed, black and white Depression-era photographs of psychologists and nursery-school educators peering over clipboards recording observations of young children, they document the emergence of child psychology before it had crystallized as a profession. Their categories reveal the nascent structure of the field and the interconnectedness of psychology research with the practical concerns of nursery educators and parents. The items included show the kinds of research that psychologists studying young children in the 1920s and 1930s thought were important. Examined together, the two bibliographies demonstrate the close linkage of the rise of the American nursery and development of developmental psychology.

Origins and Organization of the NSSE and NANE Bibliographies

The NSSE and NANE bibliographies were joint efforts by psychologists and nursery educators who collaborated on many other child-related projects. The founding of the federal Children's Bureau in 1912 and the National Research Council's (NRC) Committee on Child Development in 1925 brought scientists and social scientists together to address the need for more scientific information about young children (Cahan, 1991). Meanwhile, the nursery-school movement was becoming more professionally organized. In 1925, Patty Smith Hill called together a group of nursery-school educators, parent educators, and psychologists, who met annually, and, in 1929, became the National Association for Nursery Education (Beatty, 2001; Lascarides & Hinitz, 2000; NAEYC, 1976). Other conferences and publications added to the momentum.

The fact that the NSSE, which had originated in the 1890s as an organization for the promotion of the science of education, chose to devote one of its yearbooks to preschool and parent education reflected the coming of age of these fields. Made-up mostly of psychologists, the membership of the *Twenty-Eighth Yearbook*'s advisory committee represented the many interlocking themes it addressed. The chair, Lois Hayden Meek (later Stolz), who headed the American Association of University Women's child study campaign, was soon to take over the Teachers College Institute of Child Welfare from Helen Thompson Woolley, who was also on the committee. Woolley had directed research efforts at the Merrill–Palmer Institute in Detroit, which was headed by Edna Noble White, who, along with Patty Smith Hill, was the other preschool educator in the group. Arnold Gesell was on the committee, along with Douglas Thom, a leader in the mental hygiene and child guidance movements. The volume was dedicated to the recently deceased Bird Baldwin, the first director of the Iowa Child Welfare Station, the seventh member of the committee (Beatty, 1995; Grant, 1994; Whipple, 1929, p. iv).

One publication led to another. Many of this same group participated in the 1930 White House Conference on Child Health and Protection. The White House Conference's Committee on the Infant and Preschool Child, headed by University of Minnesota Institute for Child Welfare director John E. Anderson, also produced a large volume of reports (White House Conference on Child Health and Protection, 1931). That same year, 1930, Dorothy E. Bradbury, who had worked on the NSSE bibliography, and Esther Leech Skeels, both from the Iowa Child Welfare Research Station, began a second survey of nursery-school-based research. In 1931, NANE appointed a bibliography committee, headed by Anderson, Meek, George Stoddard (who took over at the Iowa Station after Baldwin died), and Mary Dabney Davis of the U.S. Bureau of Education, who was president of NANE the year the NANE bibliography came out. An influential group, Anderson, Meek, and Stoddard also worked with Davis on the National Advisory Committee for the Federal Emergency Nursery Schools, which underwrote the bibliography's publication (Davis, 1935; Bradbury, Skeels, & Swieda, 1935, p. vi; Grant, 1998; Michel, 1999).

The first volume, the NSSE yearbook, reflected some lack of certainty about the future of the nursery-school movement and of child development research. The nursery school and parent education movement was "too recent to predict its outcome with assurance," wrote NSSE editor Guy Montrose

Whipple (Whipple, 1929, p. ix). Meek and the other NSSE committee members were equally measured about the status of child development research. They hoped that "the deficiencies and limitations" of Hall's child-study movement, which they credited with paving the way, and "the cumulative improvement of investigatory methods" would "rest the present-day movement on a broader and somewhat firmer scientific foundation." Writing in the late 1920s, they were not fully confident about their new science of child development. "It remains to be seen" (Whipple, 1929, p. 453).

There was also some lack of clarity about the ages of the children under discussion. Meek explained preschool signified the "age period from two to six years," because the term "preschool" had initially been used by "child hygienists and public health workers" to refer to "the gap in child health provisions between the infant welfare station and the public school" (Meek in Whipple, 1929, p. 3). Meek and the yearbook committee, however, preferred the more "flexible," "inclusive" continuity of the "whole period of infancy and early childhood, from birth up to elementary-school entrance at the age of six or seven" (Meek in Whipple, 1929, pp. 3–4).

The NSSE yearbook committee struggled with the definition of child development research, as well. Here again they pushed for breadth. The expansiveness and lack of clarity of the term *development* was useful, they said, as "'development' in its broadest sense is a unifying concept which supersedes the old duality of mind and body." Child development was "a subdivision of human biology," they wrote, in which age was "the defining characteristic," a "correlation of all the psycho-biological sciences upon the focal problem of the development of the individual" (Whipple, 1929, p. 454).

The organization of the two volumes was similar. Both included chapters with descriptive information or lists of studies on nursery-school philosophy, history, organization, procedures, and training, and surveys of different types of nursery schools in the United States and other countries. Both contained separate chapters on "Research," with abstracts of experimental studies. But the NANE bibliography put habit formation, play, and art within the research chapter, while the NSSE yearbook placed these in a separate chapter "Methods of Educating Preschool Children" that mixed experimental studies with descriptive accounts. This differing categorization reveals much about differences in what was considered scientific research, a tension that would grow as some psychologists began distancing themselves from the more practical work of the nursery school (Bradbury, Skeels, & Swieda, 1935; Whipple, 1929).

The research chapters contained references from about the same number of publications, 238 in the NSSE yearbook and 236 in the NANE bibliography, though the NSSE volume listed studies within these publications as individual items under separate headings. Bradbury colleagues noted that they had only included research that had "a definite bearing on nursery school procedures or the effect of nursery school practice upon the child," not "all the researches using nursery school children" (Bradbury, Skeels, & Swieda, 1935, p. 88). If they had, it would have been a very large number. The nursery-school movement grew rapidly in the six years between the publication of the two volumes, as did child development research. A survey in the NSSE yearbook listed 84 nursery schools in existence in 1928; by 1930 a U.S. Office of Education survey found 262 (Davis and Hansen, 1933, p. 1; Whipple, 1929, pp. 239–241). The *Abstracts of Child Development* for 1928 alone, published by the NRC's Committee on Child Development, listed 1,232 titles (Whipple, 1929, p. 455).

The NSSE yearbook authors also examined the amount of different types of child development research being done within the field as a whole. In 1927, the NRC's Committee on Child Development had conducted a survey of child development researchers and their research. Based on their analysis of this *Directory of Research in Child Development*, which listed 425 researchers, the NSSE yearbook committee included estimates of approximately how many researchers were working on what topics (Whipple, 1935, pp. 456–457). In her introduction to the NANE bibliography, Mary Dabney Davis captured this scientific tone of the nursery-school movement. The large number of new studies, she said, was evidence of "the scientific sponsorship which has been given the development of nursery-school education and shows the care with which the activities of the program" were "continually being analyzed and developed" (Davis, 1935, p. v).

Health, Physical Growth, and Motor Development

The first of the six over-arching research questions, on the effects of nursery schools on young children's health, physical growth, and motor development, was the primary emphasis of the British nursery-school movement. Fresh air circulated freely throughout the classrooms, children played outside for long hours, and their bodies were inspected and bathed daily. This focus on health carried over to American nursery schools, where throats were checked each morning, children were sent home if there were signs of disease, eating a nutritional diet was emphasized, and hand washing and other sanitary routines took up much of the day (Beatty, 1995).

There was a great deal of child development research on health. Based on the NRC directory, the NSSE yearbook authors estimated that 26% of child development researchers were working on health and disease-related topics, and 18% on nutrition and diet (Whipple, 1929, p. 457). The yearbook's research chapter listed 39 studies on nutrition, including animal research on the effects of cod liver oil, irradiated milk, and cocoa and chocolate consumption in rats (Whipple, 1929, pp. 628–643). The yearbook authors noted that though some of these studies were "highly technical," they were also "practical." Just as child development was "rooted in the medical and biological sciences," nursery education was "influenced by the physical and hygienic requirements of the child," and not a "mere readaptation of the scholastic concepts of educational psychology to less mature age-levels" (Whipple, 1929, pp. 461–462).

The NANE bibliography was more practical, with prescriptive recommendations for nursery-school health programs and how to educate parents about physical hygiene. There were entries on "midday meals" and on how children's clothing could promote better health, such as a report on a play suit "designed for nursery school children to wear in cold and damp weather" (Bradbury, Skeels, & Swieda, 1935, pp. 67–69, 70). The research chapter contained studies on nutrition and infection, with one that found that "nursery school children consistently contracted fewer diseases" than children who did not attend, a topic of continuing debate today (Bradbury, Skeels, & Swieda, 1935, p. 98).

Much research in American nursery schools focused on charting patterns of children's physical growth and motor development. The NSSE authors estimated that 24% of researchers were working on physical growth and listed 55 studies on motor development and 62 on physical growth, on topics like reflexes and anthropometric statistics, including many citations from Arnold Gesell's classic work on physical and motor development (Whipple, 1929, p. 457). The yearbook also contained studies on the use of tracing paper for improving young children's writing and on tempos in walking, running, and skipping (Whipple, 1929, pp. 479, 484). The NANE research chapter listed four studies on motor development, on topics like eye–hand preferences and when children had sufficient motor control to be able to dress themselves, an issue of obvious interest to nursery-school teachers and parents. But there was also a study on "bi-lateral transfer in motor learning" from one side of the body to the other (Bradbury, Skeels, & Swieda, 1935, p. 99).

Mental Development and Language

Whether and how nursery schools could enhance mental development and language was a second main question. Much nursery-school research focused on developing intelligence scales for young children and on ascertaining the effects of nursery-school attendance on children's IQs. The Preschool Laboratories of the Iowa Child Welfare Research Station were especially known for such work, and for research which challenged prevailing notions of fixed intelligence. The first director, Bird Baldwin, was much involved in designing tests, and George Stoddard, who took over when Baldwin died, developed the famous Iowa tests and did much research on the nature of intelligence (Cravens, 1993).

The NSSE yearbook reflected psychologists' intense interest in issues related to mental development and intelligence testing. The yearbook committee refused to take sides in the ongoing debate over abstract thought versus behavioral learning, but said that in research with young children the behavioristic approach necessarily came more to the fore. They estimated that 20% of psychologists in the NRC's child development directory were working on "mental development and behavior other than intelligence measurement and mental hygiene," while 9% were working on "intelligence and its measurement" (Whipple, 1929, p. 457). They reviewed the history of this work: Darwin, Preyer, Hall, James Mark Baldwin, Binet and Simon, Terman, and others. The section on recent research was equally eclectic: Bird Baldwin and Lorle Stecher's 1924 *Psychology of the Preschool Child*; Nancy Bayley's performance tests, which though not yet standardized were deemed worthy of "further experimentation;" Lois Meek's 1925 "A study of learning and retention in young children;" John Watson's 1925 "What the nursery has to say about instincts;" and the 1923 revision of Robert Yerkes's scale for measuring mental ability (Whipple, 1929, pp. 575, 576, 584, 587).

Interestingly, the NSSE yearbook also highlighted Piaget's 1926 *The Language and Thought of the Child*, which was summarized favorably under both intellectual and language development. The Jean-Jacques Rousseau Institute in Geneva where Piaget was working had received $15,000 in Laura Spelman Rockefeller money in 1925 and its nursery school, the Maison des Petits, was mentioned earlier in the volume (Hseuh, 2004, p. 30). The yearbook authors praised Piaget's "clinical method," and recommended Piaget's "two volumes on *The Development of Child Logic*," for "the fresh light which they cast on the mental processes, and incidentally on the personality of the young child" (Whipple, 1929, p. 459). The mention of personality may have been a reference to a positive review in 1927 of Piaget's work in *The Psychoanalytic Review* (Cahan, 2003). That same year, nursery-school educator Lucy Sprague Mitchell of the Bureau of Educational Experiments had favorably reviewed *The Language and Thought of the Child* in the journal *Progressive Education* (Cahan, 2003). Coming at the peak of this period of early interest in

Piaget's work, the positive references in the widely circulated NSSE volume demonstrated that some psychologists and nursery educators in the late 1920s were well aware of the value of Piaget's methods.

As interestingly, Piaget's work did not appear in the sections on mental or language development in the NANE bibliography, even though Lois Meek was on the committee for both publications. This may have been due to the influence of another NANE bibliography committee member John Anderson, who was deeply critical of observational biography and survey methods (Cahan, 2003).

The NANE bibliography included Beth Wellman's groundbreaking 1932 analysis of 600 2- to 5-year-olds, which "indicated that attendance in preschool, at least in the Iowa Child Welfare Research Station, was characterized by an increase in intelligence quotient" (Bradbury, Skeels, & Swieda, 1935, p. 93). Wellman's research provoked a storm of criticism from hereditarians associated with Terman who believed that IQ was fixed, and attempted to debunk Wellman's work (Cravens, 1993).

The NANE bibliography listed other studies on the effects of nursery-school attendance on intelligence. Florence Goodenough's analysis of intelligence scores of 28 children before and after they attended the University of Minnesota Child Welfare Institute nursery school found almost "a zero correlation" between "gain in IQ and length of attendance" (Bradbury, Skeels, & Swieda, 1935, p. 93). In another study, Goodenough found that in 388 2- to 5-year-olds given the Binet test "there was a steady decrease in the average intelligence of the children according to social class" as measured by their fathers' occupations (Bradbury, Skeels, & Swieda, 1935, p. 124). The NANE bibliography did not include Helen Thompson Woolley's work at the Merrill–Palmer Institute, however, where she found that the intelligence quotients of the nursery-school children increased rapidly compared with those on the waiting list (Beatty, 1995, p. 153). As with Piaget's research, this may have been excluded because it relied heavily on case studies of individual children. Although the determinism of Lewis Terman and his Stanford associates initially drowned out these nursery-school-based studies, the nursery-school environment was an incubator for the idea that intelligence was malleable and environmentally influenced.

Unlike the NSSE yearbook, the NANE bibliography divided mental development studies into five categories: sensory, imagination, learning and problem solving, comprehension, and language. The five studies of sensory development focused on form and color perception, taste, and visual and auditory stimuli. Imagination was represented by one study, in which material was presented to children on a tachistoscope (Bradbury, Skeels, & Swieda,

1935, pp. 99–100). The 26 studies on learning and problem solving included one that found that "changes in bodily position affect a child's memory for the position of objects." Another compared 28 nursery-school children "in five different situations arranged in duplication of Kohler's insight experiments with apes" (Bradbury, Skeels, & Swieda, 1935, pp. 101, 103).

Language was also the topic of considerable research. Of the 143 studies listed in the NSSE volume under language, most are on children's vocabulary, such as one by the Child Study Committee of the International Kindergarten Union, which attempted to ascertain the vocabulary of kindergarten children before they entered first grade (Whipple, 1929, p. 503). The yearbook included many studies on infant language, and subsections on sound production, stages of language development, the relation of language and thought, parts of speech, sentences, and special vocabularies, such as for color, number, time, and distance (Whipple, 1929, pp. 546–566). Piaget's *The Language and Thought of the Child* was again included, with an explanation of his distinction between a child's "implicit and explicit understanding," and the statement that children "do not understand each other until the age of 7 years" (Whipple, 1929, p. 527). There was also a detailed explanation of Piaget's categories and subcategories of egocentric and socialized speech (Whipple, 1935, pp. 565–566).

The NANE bibliography contained 17 items on language. A study on responses to animal stories was listed, on which compiler Dorothy Bradbury was the second investigator. Another, on grammatical errors in "305 records of the spontaneous conversation of 220 children aged eighteen months to six years, covering a total of 22,994 sentences or 99,289 running words," demonstrated the detail in which research on language development was conducted in nursery schools (Bradbury, Skeels, & Swieda, 1935, p. 107).

Social and Emotional Development

Showing how nursery schools could promote social and emotional development was a third research question. The treatment modality studied was usually play. Focusing on children's play, of course, predated the nursery school; nineteenth-century infant schools and kindergartens had stressed play. Kindergarten founder Friedrich Froebel had developed a set of intricate, rigidly sequenced play materials and activities to enhance children's symbolic development, and games and songs to promote socialization and cooperation. American kindergarten educators modified Froebel's formal, adult-directed curriculum of "gifts" and "occupations" to include spontaneous "free play" (Beatty, 1995, 2000; Brosterman, 1997).

The educational philosophy of the nursery-school movement extended this more child-centered approach and made free play with blocks and other materials the centerpiece of the nursery-school day. The first American nursery school, begun by Caroline Pratt in 1913, focused on the very American goal of children's liberation through play. Espousing a philosophy of socio-emotional health and individual creative expression, Pratt also sought to liberate children from what she saw as the oppression of societal strictures and the private family (Antler, 1987; Beatty, 1995). Harriet Johnson, who directed the Bureau of Educational Experiments' nursery school, which opened in 1919 next door to Pratt's school, developed wooden unit blocks and other play materials to maximize children's play experiences. Her illustrated 1922 pamphlet, *A Nursery School Experiment*, included long, verbatim scripts of children's dramatic play. A sample copy of a child's individual daily record contained detailed, time-sampled notations of child–adult and child–child "Social Contacts" (Johnson, 1922, p. 124).

The NSSE yearbook included a summary of the contentious history of research on emotions, and stated that the study of children's social development was growing (Whipple, 1929, p. 601). The authors' analysis of the NRC survey, however, did not show any researchers working on social development (Whipple, 1929, p. 457). The Yearbook included studies on "laughter in preschool children" and on the "growth of social perceptions," and an entire section on play, but in a separate chapter on child activities, not in the research chapter (Whipple, 1929, p. 603). Written primarily by Harriet Johnson, it listed studies ranging from older work similar to G. Stanley Hall's, comparing the play of "civilized children" to "adult savages," to an Iowa Station study on developing play apparatus to promote motor control in preschool children (Whipple, 1929, pp. 703, 704).

The NANE bibliography also had a special chapter on play and play equipment, with 23 items, including Harriet Johnson's classic 1933 *The Art of Block Building*. Most dealt with blocks, apparently not inappropriately, as observational research on free play in a preschool laboratory "showed a decided preference on the part of 4-year-old children for blocks, which were the first choice again and again" (Bradbury, Skeels, & Swieda, p. 75).

Unlike the NSSE yearbook, the research chapter of the NANE bibliography did have a heading on play, along with headings on emotional development and social development, with 38 items, confirming that interest in this topic was increasing. Under emotional development, a 1932 study by Gladys F. Ding and Arthur T. Jersild of 59 Chinese nursery and kindergarten children found that "laughing and smiling occurred most frequently in connection with motor activity" (Bradbury, Skeels, & Swieda, 1935, p. 113). Other studies examined anger, fears, mood levels, and other indices of emotion. Under social development there were studies of quarrels, competition, cooperation, popularity, and reactions to strangers.

Gender differences were also emerging as a topic of child development research. A 1930 study by Robert C. Challman on friendship, a much studied subject, found that "children from twenty-seven to forty-five months of age appeared to discriminate decidedly on the basis of sex" (Bradbury, Skeels, & Swieda, 1935, p. 115). Studies by K. M. Banham Bridges in 1927 and 1929 found that 3-year-old boys "showed more singleness of purpose, and spent longer time at their favorite occupations," while four-year-old boys "were more often distracted and talked more frequently than girls" (Bradbury, Skeels, & Swieda, 1935, p. 119).

Emotional and Behavioral Problems

A fourth question focused on preventing and alleviating the problems of emotionally and behaviorally troubled or otherwise "abnormal" children. Some nursery schools, such as the Guidance Nursery School started in 1926 by Arnold Gesell at the Yale Psycho-Guidance Clinic, and the habit clinic nursery schools started in Boston in the 1920s by Douglas Thom, served populations of "problem" children. Linked to clinical psychology and the mental hygiene and child guidance campaigns, and to Watson's popularization of Pavlovian behaviorism, these nursery schools sought to normalize child behavior, especially that of children from poor and immigrant families, whose parents were also thought to be problematic (Grant, 1998; Horn, 1988; Jones, 1999). Clinic nursery schools like Gesell's in New Haven and Thom's in Boston treated children referred involuntarily by social workers, but also children from well-to-do families brought in voluntarily by worried parents. Many other nursery schools enrolled a few children with problems and had consulting psychologists and child-guidance workers on their staffs to deal with problems as they arose (Beatty, 1995; Grant, 1998).

Like G. Stanley Hall, under whom he had done his doctoral work at Clark, Gesell was much interested in deviance. Hall had taken a great interest in the kindergarten movement; Gesell was much involved with nursery schools. Hall had identified adolescence as a key time in development; Gesell declared the primacy of the preschool period "for the simple but sufficient reason that it comes first" (Gesell, 1923, p. 2).

Like many others in the early nursery-school movement, Gesell and Thom were proponents of habit training, a method espoused by Watson for substituting the problematic actions of young children and their mothers with supposedly more adaptive, well-adjusted ones. Habit training, which enjoyed a vogue in the 1920s, was used to treat an amazingly wide range of conditions, from eating and feeding difficulties to personality disorders, convulsions, psychoses, and mental retardation (Thom, 1924). Not surprisingly, this "taming" of "troublesome" children, who could create enormous difficulties for teachers and mothers, resulted in the production of a large amount of child development research (Jones, 1999; Grant, 1998).

The NSSE yearbook had an entire chapter devoted to habit training and the establishing of regular nursery-school routines, with 65 studies on eating, sleep, bladder training, and other habits. The yearbook authors' estimated that 21% of child development researchers in the NRC directory were working on "behavior and habit problems, personality traits and personality adjustment, emotional balance and general mental hygiene" (Whipple, 1929, p. 457). Work by both Watson and Gesell appeared frequently in these listings.

The NANE bibliography also listed numerous studies by Gesell, 16 in all, more than by any other psychologist in the volume – but not one reference to Watson, suggesting how quickly his work fell out of favor. The NANE bibliography listed 72 items related to emotional and behavioral problems. Like the NSSE yearbook, there was a chapter on "Nursery School Procedures," with studies on habit formation, mostly on naps and bathroom routines, and on mental hygiene, including one on the relationship between psychiatric social workers and nursery schools (Bradbury, Skeels, & Swieda, 1935, pp. 71, 72). There were 10 items on "Personality Problems," including studies on adoption and on early indicators of juvenile delinquency, a topic of great social concern (Bradbury, Skeels, & Swieda, 1935, p. 73). The research chapter had another 27 studies on habit formation, also largely on sleeping and eating habits. For instance, "longer night sleep for the older children" was found to be correlated with "a shorter nap" (Bradbury, Skeels, & Swieda, 1935, p. 111). Of obvious interest to nursery-school teachers and parents, study of children's sleeping and eating habits would eventually become subfields of their own.

Parent Education and Parent Involvement

A fifth research question concerned ways parent education and parent involvement could improve child-rearing practices and enhance children's development. Promoting parent education was one of Lawrence Frank's main goals in directing Laura Spelman Rockefeller Memorial funds to child development research and nursery schools. It was the central emphasis of the Rockefeller-sponsored program started in 1922 by Edna Noble White at the

Merrill–Palmer Institute in Detroit. White, who had studied at Deptford with McMillan and chaired the National Council on Parent Education, thought families needed individual counseling as well as group meetings to improve their parenting skills (Smuts, 1980).

Because it was center for preparental and parental education nationwide, many scientific and popular publications were published under Merrill–Palmer's auspices. Elizabeth Cleveland's widely distributed 1925 child-rearing manual, *Training the Toddler*, written while she was at Merrill–Palmer, emphasized a "scientific approach" that directed mothers to establish and follow invariant routines, with what Cleveland called "unrelenting regularity" (Cleveland, 1925, 36; Watson, 1928). Helen Thompson Woolley's research at Merrill–Palmer showed that parent education, combined with nursery-school attendance, could help prevent developmental retardation, personality disorders, juvenile delinquency, and other problems (Beatty, 1995, pp. 153–155).

Promoting parent involvement, a less prescriptive form of parent education, was a central theme of Abigail Eliot's work at the Ruggles Street Nursery School in the Roxbury section of Boston. Eliot, who had also studied with McMillan, favored a more collaborative approach than White. Stressing the importance of "establishing mutual confidence between school and home," Eliot encouraged the staff of the nursery school, which she took over in 1922, to get to know parents well and meet with them informally (Eliot, 1926, p. 187). She invited mothers to come visit the nursery school and held integrated meetings for the school's black and white parents, who came from mostly lower-income backgrounds. In 1926, Eliot began the Nursery Training Center of Boston, which eventually became the Eliot–Pearson Department of Child Study at Tufts University (Beatty, 1995).

With the support of the Laura Spelman Rockefeller Memorial, which funded Eliot, parent education evolved into a robust line of psychological research on parent–child relations. The NSSE yearbook included a history of the parent education movement, an extensive survey of parent education programs, and a section on "Experiments in Preparental Training" with teenagers, which often used nursery schools "as laboratories" (Whipple, 1929, p. 355). Studying parent education was listed as a motivation for researchers in the section on emotional and social development, which included a study in progress on "Parent–child relationship as a factor in nursery school adjustment," with a test of reactions to strangers (Whipple, 1929, pp. 600, 612–613).

The NANE bibliography listed 19 items under "Parent Education," including studies of parent education programs in many cities and states, and in "nursery schools of negro colleges" (Bradbury, Skeels, & Swieda, 1935,

p. 81). It also listed the NSSE yearbook, along with publications by the National Congress of Parents and Teachers, the forerunner of the P.T.A. Parent education, too, would become a huge, and hugely profitable, field.

Combining Marriage, Career Interests, and Motherhood

The question of whether nursery schools could help women combine marriage, career interests, and motherhood without adversely affecting their children's development was a sixth line of research. Given the traditional view that it was harmful for young children to be cared for outside of the home, it was imperative that nursery educators and psychologists prove that being away from home for a limited period of time while attending nursery school was good for young children. All research on how nursery schools enhanced young children's physical, mental, social, and emotional development thus obliquely addressed this general issue.

Nursery-school educators and researchers were divided about how much time young children should spend out of the home. Most early nursery schools had sessions that were longer than three hours, often the length of a school day (Beatty, 1995, p. 159). Although not many middle-class mothers were in the job market before World War II, many were involved in volunteering and other career-type activities and personal interests. Many mothers from lower-class backgrounds did work outside of the home, and some put their children in day nurseries, which were criticized as unhealthy environments for young children. Most nursery educators sought to distance the nursery school from day nurseries, but the Depression-era federal Emergency Nursery Schools, most of which operated for the length of full school day, pushed child-care issues to the fore (Beatty, 2001; Cahan, 1989; Michel, 1999; Rose, 1999).

The career dilemmas of the growing number of women psychologists also highlighted the issue of child care. Since it dealt with young children, a traditionally female concern, nursery-school and child development research circumvented conventions that discouraged even married women from middle- and upper-class backgrounds from working for pay or having full-time careers. In 1924, Laura Spelman Rockefeller Memorial fellowships and scholarships for child study and parent education research began being awarded, mostly to women (Cahan, 1991, p. 240). The NSSE yearbook research chapter, which was based on earlier publications, contained mostly studies by relatively well-known male psychologists, with a sprinkling of well-known women. By contrast, by 1935, most of the studies listed in the NANE bibliography were by women. In the NANE research chapter, 180 out of

233 studies, or 77%, clearly had female authors, most listed as first authors, and there may have been more as some were cited with initials only. Nursery schools thus provided both a locus and focus of research for female psychologists.

The obstacles psychologist Ethel Puffer Howes met in her career led directly to nursery-school research on how women could coordinate their professional and personal interests with their child rearing. Howes, who had completed doctoral work in Harvard's new Psychology Department in 1898 where she taught as an assistant but was not listed in the catalog, was not awarded her degree until 1902, by Radcliffe, because Harvard would not confer a doctorate upon a woman (Cahan, 1991; Scarborough and Furumoto, 1987). These difficulties, which worsened after she married, led Howes, with support from the Laura Spelman Rockefeller Memorial, to start the Institute for the Coordination of Women's Interests, at Smith College in 1926. The Institute included a home-food-supply experiment, a home-assistants service, and a cooperative nursery school, which was open for a full school day. Like other cooperatives, the Northhampton Cooperative Nursery School served as a form of child care, but also required mothers to be involved in various aspects of the program, including spending time assisting in the classroom (Hewes, 1998). The mothers involved whom Howes surveyed all said that they found it and Howes' other projects enormously helpful in maintaining or regaining their professional and personal interests (Beatty, 1995, p. 164). Although the Institute for the Coordination of Women's Interests was short-lived, Howes' studies were precursors of modern research on the effects of maternal employment, child care, and other family support variables on children's development.

NSSE yearbook chair Lois Meek, who had worked for the American Association of University Women, was also very concerned about child care. The yearbook, which included sections on the history of the day nursery movement and on different types of day nurseries, emphasized that criticisms of day nurseries were not supported by research. Low quality of care was the problem, not day nurseries per se. There was "conclusive evidence," yearbook authors stated, that these criticisms were "not valid when applied to the inherent nature of the day nursery, but only valid when applied to the quality of its service" (Whipple, 1929, p. 94). But day nurseries and nursery schools were intrinsically different. A day nursery was for relief purposes, to help needy families, and could never be "a true nursery school." A nursery school was an educational institution, with "a definite educational goal," focused on the developmental needs of the child (Whipple, 1929, p. 104). The Yearbook then outlined health and education standards for day nurseries and listed research on model day nurseries in Philadelphia (Michel, 1999; Rose, 1999; Whipple, 1929, p. 106).

Like the NSSE yearbook, the NANE bibliography emphasized the distinction between day nurseries and nursery schools. But by the 1930s, this clarification was becoming less necessary as nursery schools were increasingly promoted as half-day programs, a change that would have long-lasting consequences for mothers and children. Iowa Station director George Stoddard was an especially strong advocate of half-day rather than full-day programs (Beatty, 1995, pp. 159–160). The NANE bibliography listed studies on cooperative nursery schools, including Howes' work, and on other types of nursery schools and day nurseries that enrolled children of working mothers, including nursery schools in France, Russia, and other countries that were beginning to provide more forms of child care (Michel, 1999). There was even a national feasibility study of costs, by Stoddard, a staunch proponent of universalizing nursery education (Bradbury, Skeels, & Swieda, 1935, p. 62).

Conclusion

Nursery schools and child development research in the 1920s and 1930s were symbiotic, pluralistic, eclectic movements. Many nursery schools were sites of practical work and research on most, if not all of these questions about young children's physical, motor, mental, social, and emotional development, and on troubled children and parent education. Defining women's roles as mothers and how much time children should spend outside of the home was a pervasive, underlying theme. Children's, parents', and teachers' immediate needs shaped this research, as did larger societal concerns. As Sheldon White argues, developmental psychology came into existence in a "world of designed institutions," like nursery schools, and had intertwined internal and external, theoretical and practical agendas (White, 2003, p. 206).

Drawing from many sources, nursery-school educators and psychologists derived ideas from their ongoing interactions with each other and with children and mothers. Traces of Watson and Thorndike were mixed with hints of Freud and Piaget, and other emerging psychological strains. G. Stanley Hall's genetic psychology and Gesell's maturationism pervaded most of these efforts; interest in intelligence testing abounded. It was all very fluid, syncretic, and pragmatic, with awareness of differing schools of thought and methodologies but a desire to blend and meld them. This was the "primordial ooze" from which developmental psychology arose (White, 1999).

Despite this interactivity, relationships among the participants were not equal. This was a complex hierarchy, with many rungs. University-trained psychologists had the upper hand. Nursery-school directors and parent educators, then teachers, then parents, and children followed. In addition to intrinsic and intellectual satisfactions and other personal benefits, each group had things to gain from this uneasy alliance.

Psychologists got financial support and subjects for their research, and a larger terrain for the study of child development within academia. Nursery-school directors were attracted to the intellectual and professional prestige associated with science, and by the credibility and usefulness of scientific expertise in their work with parents and children. Nursery-school teachers were attracted by the attention of academics to what went on inside their classrooms, by the promise of better understanding of the children they taught, and by the hope that this knowledge would translate into more effective classroom techniques. Parents who shared these values hoped to gain useful advice about child rearing, and how to deal with difficult children.

What the children got out of all this, of course, is much harder to ascertain. They clearly got more attention from more adults, which was probably both annoying and satisfying. They got asked lots of questions and were constantly tested and observed. They got to attend preschool programs in specially designed environments, with attractive new play equipment, and activities that were intended to be socially, emotionally, artistically, and mentally stimulating. But some nursery-school-based research promulgated practices that were restricting, and could have had harmful as well as helpful consequences for children and parents. Habit training, for instance, was very rigid, and the obsessive focus on establishing and maintaining regular daily routines, and added attention paid to the smallest details of child and family life could have been a source of anxiety for mothers (Grant, 1999).

Between 1929 and 1935, the years when the NSSE yearbook and NANE bibliography were published, descriptions of nursery schools and child development research became more positive. As Beth Wellman from the Iowa Station wrote in 1929 the "problem of the preschool laboratory" was "the determination of laws and principles of development that will aid in a better understanding of children in general" (Bradbury, Skeels, & Swieda, 1935, p. 21). By 1935, one senses that many would have agreed with NANE president Mary Dabney Davis that the nursery-school and child development movements had gained real "momentum," and that solutions to this problem were well underway (Davis, 1935, p. v).

This affirmative answer to questions about the effects of nursery schools on young children may have been as much a foregone conclusion as an empirical finding. Nursery educators and psychologists doing nursery-school-related research were committed to the cause of helping young children. Many of these investigations were designed to produce information that could be put to immediate use. When the finding that naptime was inversely correlated with nighttime sleep was published in *Child Development* in 1932, some nursery schools may have begun shortening the 4-year-olds' naps. However, not all nursery-school directors read *Child Development*, and nursery schools' and parents' views on sleep did not always coincide (Bradbury, Skeels, & Swieda, 1935, p. 111). It is hard to know whether and how some of this was actually used.

Many American parents and the public at large appear to have been less convinced. Despite the growth in the number of nursery schools, overall attendance remained relatively low. By 1932 there may have been 500 nursery schools nationwide, enrolling between 10,000 and 15,000 children out of a total preschool population of about 16 million (Tank, 1980, p. 294). Preschool education did not really catch on until working mothers entered the labor market in large numbers after the war (Michel, 1999; Rose, 1999; Takanishi, 1977; Tank, 1980). African Americans and other parents from minority and lower-income backgrounds were the most resistant. Some refused to put their children into nursery schools, even when offered publicly supported programs, and actively dismissed or ignored "modern," scientific advice (Beatty, 1995; Grant, 1998; Michel, 1999; Rose, 1999). With some exceptions, this was a movement by and for elites, which was not fully accepted by the "others" whom it sometimes attempted to study and serve.

From the perspective of gaining knowledge about child development, at least that of middle- and upper-income children, the nursery-school movement was a huge success. As the NSSE yearbook, NANE bibliography, and other publications document, phalanxes of psychologists and nursery educators collected masses of data and published multitudes of studies, and in the process, came away with more questions and topics for research.

After the 1920s, as Laura Spelman Rockefeller Memorial funding dried up, some developmental psychologists retreated into academia, away from the messy, intractable problems of children, schools, and families. But pressing human questions and needs continued to tug at the profession. In the 1960s, when the War on Poverty refocused interest on preschool education and provided funding for programs and research, developmental psychologists were in the forefront of the campaign. Under closer, more sophisticated scrutiny, the whiff of advocacy that had hung over earlier nursery-school-based research raised larger doubts. Project Head Start and its offspring helped support new studies on how to maximize child health and development and brought large numbers of new psychologists back into explicitly useful research. Some had never left, understanding that developmental psychology was inextricably linked to questions about social policy and the design of social programs for children and families.

References

Antler, J. (1987). *Lucy Sprague Mitchell: The Making of a Modern Woman.* New Haven, CT: Yale University Press.

Baldwin, B., & Stecher, L. I. (1925). *The Psychology of the Preschool Child.* New York/London: D. Appleton & Company.

Beatty, B. (1995). *Preschool Education in America: The Culture of Young Children from the Colonial Era to the Present.* New Haven, CT: Yale University Press.

Beatty, B. (2000). The Letter Killeth: Americanization and multicultural education in kindergartens in the United States, 1856–1920. In Roberta Wollons (Ed.), *Kindergartens and Cultures: The Global Diffusion of an Idea.* New Haven, CT: Yale University Press.

Beatty, B. (2001). The politics of preschool advocacy: Lessons from three pioneering organizations. In Carol J. De Vita & Rachel Mosher-Williams (Eds.), *Who Speaks for America's Children? The Role of Child Advocates in Public Policy.* Washington, DC: The Urban Institute.

Bradbury, D. E., Skeels, E. L., & Swieda, W., Eds. (1935). *Nursery School Education: A Classified and Annotated Bibliography Including References Published up to December, 1934.* Washington, D.C.: National Association for Nursery Education.

Bremner, R. H., (Ed.). (1971). *Children and Youth in America: A Documentary History.* Cambridge, MA: Harvard University Press.

Brosterman, N. (1997). *Inventing Kindergarten.* New York: Harry N. Abrams.

Brown, J. (1992). *The Definition of a Profession: The Authority of Metaphor in the History of Intelligence Testing, 1890–1930.* Princeton, NJ: Princeton University Press.

Cahan, E. (1989). *Past Caring: A History of U.S. Preschool Care and Education for the Poor, 1820–1965.* New York: National Center for Children in Poverty.

Cahan, E. (1991). Science, practice, and gender roles in early American child psychology. In F. Kessel, M. Bornstein, and A. Sameroff (Eds.), *Contemporary Constructions of the Child: Essays in Honor of William Kessen* (pp. 225–249). Hillsdale, NJ: Lawrence Erlbaum.

Cahan, E. (2003). *American Educators and Psychologists Encounter Piaget's Early Works.* Paper, Annual Meeting of the Society for Research in Child Development.

Cleveland, E., (1925). *Training the Toddler.* Philadelphia: Lippincott.

Cravens, H. (1993). *Before Head Start: The Iowa Station and America's Children.* Chapel Hill, NC: University of North Carolina Press.

Danziger, K. (1990). *Constructing the Subject: Historical Origins of Psychological Research.* Cambridge, UK: Cambridge University Press.

Davis, M. D., & Hansen, R. (1933). *Nursery Schools, Their Development and Current Practices in the United States.* Washington, DC: U.S. Department of the Interior, Office of Education Bulletin, No. 9, GPO.

Davis, M. D. (1935). Introduction. In Bradbury, D. E., Skeels, E. L, & Swieda, W. (Eds.) *Nursery School Education: A Classified and Annotated Bibliography Including References Published up to December, 1934.* Washington, DC: National Association for Nursery Education.

Eliot, A. E., (1926). Educating the parent through the nursery school. *Childhood Education 3*, 183–189.

Gesell, A. (1923). *The Pre-School Child.* New York: Houghton Mifflin.

Grant, J. (1994). Lois Meek Stolz. In M. Schwartz (Ed.), *Women Educators in the United States, 1820–1933* (pp. 372–379). Westport, CT: Greenwood.

Grant, J. (1998). *Raising Baby by the Book: The Education of American Mothers.* New Haven, CT: Yale University Press.

Hewes, D. (1998). *"It's the Camaraderie": A History of Parent Cooperative Preschools.* Davis, CA: Center for Cooperatives, University of California.

Horn, M. (1989). *Before It's Too Late: The Child Guidance Movement in the United States, 1922–1945.* Philadelphia: Temple University Press.

Hseuh, Y. (2004). "He sees the development of children's concepts upon a background of sociology": Jean Piaget's honorary degree at Harvard University in 1936. *History of Psychology 7*, 20–44.

Johnson, H. (1922). *A Nursery School Experiment.* New York: Bureau of Educational Experiments.

Johnson, H. (1928). *Children in the Nursery School.* New York: Bureau of Educational Experiments.

Johnson, H. (1933). *The Art of Block Building.* New York: The John Day Company.

Jones, K. W. (1999). *Taming the Troublesome Child: American Families, Child Guidance, and the Limits of Psychiatric Authority.* Cambridge, MA: Harvard University Press.

Koops, W., & Zuckerman, M. (2003). *Beyond the Century of the Child: Cultural History and Developmental Psychology.* Philadelphia: University of Pennsylvania Press.

Lascarides, C., & Hinitz, B. (2000). *History of Early Childhood Education.* New York: Falmer Press.

Meek, L. H. (1925). A study of learning and retention in young children. *Teachers College Contributions to Education,* No. 161. New York: Columbia University Press.

McMillan, M. (1921). *The Nursery School.* New York: Dutton.

Michel, S. (1999). *Children's Interests/Mothers' Rights: The Shaping of America's Child Care Policy.* New Haven, CT: Yale University Press.

Mitchell, L. S. (1922). Introduction to H. Johnson, *A Nursery School Experiment.* New York: Bureau of Educational Experiments.

Muncy, R. (1991). *Creating a Female Dominion in American Reform, 1890–1935.* New York: Oxford University Press.

National Society for the Study of Education (1929). *Twenty-Eighth Yearbook, Preschool and Parental Education.* Bloomington, IL: Public School Publishing Company.

NAEYC Organization History and Archives Committee (1976). NAEYC's first half century. *Young Children,* September, 467.

O'Donnell, J. M. (1985). *The Origins of Behaviorism: American Psychology, 1870–1920.* New York: New York University Press.

Piaget, J. (1926). *The Language and Thought of the Child.* (Trans. by M. Warden). New York: Harcourt Brace & Company.

Pratt, C. (1924). *Experimental Practice in the City and Country School*. New York: E. P. Dutton.

Rose, E. (1999). *A Mother's Job: The History of Day Care, 1890–1960*. New York: Oxford University Press.

Ross, D. (1990). *The Origins of American Social Science*. New York: Cambridge University Press.

Scarborough, E., & Furumoto, L. (1987). *Untold Lives: The First Generation of American Women Psychologists*. New York: Columbia University Press.

Schlossman, S. L. (1981). Philanthropy and the gospel of child development. *History of Education Quarterly 21*, 275–299.

Sears, R. (1975). *Your Ancients Revisited: A History of Child Development*. Chicago: University of Chicago Press.

Senn, M. (1975). Insights on the child development movement in the United States. *Monographs of the Society for Research in Child Development 40*, 304 (Serial no. 161).

Smuts, A. (1980). Edna Noble White. In B. Sicherman & C. H. Green (Eds.), *Notable American Women: The Modern Period* (pp. 728–729). Cambridge, MA: Harvard University Press.

Smuts, A., & Boardman, J. W. , Eds. (1986). *History and Research in Child Development. Monographs of the Society for Research in Child Development*. Chicago: University of Chicago Press.

Steedman, C. (1990). *Childhood, Culture, and Class in Britain: Margaret McMillan, 1860–1931*. New Brunswick, NJ: Rutgers University Press.

Takanishi, R. (1977). Federal involvement in early childhood education (1933–1937). In L. Katz (Ed.), *Current Issues in Early Childhood Education*, Vol. I (pp. 139–162). Norwood, NJ: Ablex.

Tank, R. M. (1980). *Young Children, Families, and Society in America since the 1820s: The Evolution of Health, Education, and Child Care Programs for Preschool Children*. Ph.D. dissertation, University of Michigan.

Thom, D. (1927). *Everyday Problems of the Everyday Child*. New York: D. Appleton.

Watson, J. B. (1925). *Pedagogical Seminary* 32: 293–326.

Watson, J. (1928). What the nursery has to say about instincts. *Psychological Care of Infant and Child*. New York: W. W. Norton.

Whipple, G. M., Ed. (1929). *Twenty-Eighth Yearbook of the National Society for the Study of Education, Preschool and Parental Education*. Bloomington, IL: Public School Publishing Company.

Whipple, G. M. (1929), "Editor's Preface, " in National Society for the Study of Education, *Twenty-Eighth Yearbook, Preschool and Parental Education*. Bloomington, IL: Public School Publishing Company.

White House Conference on Child Health and Protection, Committee on the Education and Training of the Infant and Preschool Child. (1931). *Nursery Education*. New York: Century.

White, S. H. (1991). Three visions of a psychology of education. In L. T. Landesman (Ed.), *Culture, Schooling, and Psychological Development*. Norwood, NJ: Ablex.

White, S. H. (1983). The relationship of developmental psychology to social policy. In E. Zigler, S. L. Kagan, & N. Hall (Eds.), *Children, Families, and Government: Preparing for the 21st Century*. New York: Cambridge University Press.

White, S. H. (1995). *Child Development, 1930–1934: Organizing a Research Program.* Paper presented at symposium, "The Children's Cause: Some Early Organizations," Society for Research in Child Development, Indianapolis, IN.

White, S. H. (1999). Personal conversation with author.

White, S. H. (2003). Developmental psychology in a world of designed institutions. In W. Koops and M. Zuckerman (Eds.), *Beyond the Century of the Child: Cultural History and Developmental Psychology* (pp. 204–224). Philadelphia: University of Pennsylvania Press.

11   Actualizing Potentials

Learning through Psychology's Recurrent Crises

Michael Cole and Jaan Valsiner

It was presumably the philosopher George Santayana who commented that those who do not know the past are doomed to repeat it. Yet study of the history of psychology has rarely, if ever, been used as a tool by social scientists to help them avoid the pitfalls of the past. Instead, social scientists use the study of the history of the discipline as a tool to plan and organize their work. Sheldon (Shep) White represents a distinctly different model of how to view the history and practice of psychology. In the 1970s, Shep began writing articles on the history of psychology that were pointedly designed to be used by the current practitioners of the discipline to help them to reflect upon their own practices (White, 1976, 1978; Cahan & White, 1992).

The Nature of Knowledge in Science: From Crises to Potentials

Contrary to the fast-paced reporting of science to the lay public – by journalists and scientists – scientific knowledge grows slowly and is subject to various periods of stagnation and even regression. Both evolution and involution in scientific thinking are linked with social events (Danziger, 1990). Usually such periods are filled with the tension created between the avalanche of new ideas (in new contexts) and the rigidities of the previous habits of thought. This tension may emerge along a multitude of parameters – between theory and (social) practice; ways of knowing and religious dogmas (remembering Galileo's troubles about moving celestial objects at his time and arguments about stem cell research in our own); generality and fragmentation within a discipline; and the "stress of interdisciplinarity" – a discipline resisting the incoming streams of ideas from other disciplines. All of these situations can be described as "crises."

It seems that psychology is a discipline where the creation of crises is a regular pastime. In his essay *The Historical Sense of the Psychology's Crisis*

(1926/1982), Vygotsky criticized the fractionation of psychology into many, seemingly incommensurate, enterprises, each of which is ruled by a central phenomenon, its initial discovery, and its associated conceptual apparatus. These initial ideas are extended to adjacent phenomena and somewhat generalized – salivary reflexes to leg flexion in Pavlov's case or well-formed figures to problem solving in the case of Gestalt Psychology, for example. Then the phenomenon is generalized far beyond its initial field of application to become an all-encompassing world view, applicable to all of psychology and perhaps all of science. A second way of creating a world view is to start from ideological positioning – that of "slogan marxist" or "slogan free market" claims.

Vygotsky's voice was part of a wider dialogue about the nature (and the future) of psychology in the 1920s. In parallel with Vygotsky, Karl Bühler, in his Viennese environment, developed a similar critique of the psychology of the 1920s. His treatment of the state of psychology – in his book *Die Krise der Psychologie* (Bühler, 1927/1978) – concentrated on similar themes: a rigid focus on study of behavior was ignoring the essential meaningfulness of human psychological phenomena. Applied psychology of the time was equally problematic – psychological ideas were taken and over-generalized to contemporary social issues. The result was the dominance of rigid ideas – seemingly useful in practice, high in social appeal (e.g., consider the notion of intelligence), yet unproductive for making sense of human psychological realities.

The problem – conceptual crisis in psychology, as its role in a society proliferates – is crucial in our day as much as it was in the 1920s. How do scientific ideas lose their usefulness? They become generalized and mapped onto the ideological discourses of the given society at the given time. For example, the dialectical philosophy of Hegel was part of the German *Naturphilosophie* trend in the 19th century and produced valuable thought models that still remain underdeveloped in the sciences of the 21st century. Yet, when Hegel's dialectics was superimposed onto Marxist ideology in the Soviet Union in the second half of the 1920s, it became a vehicle for ideological rigidity (Valsiner, 1988). In a way, an open-thought model (as dialectics is supposed to be) was turned into its opposite and made to defend the fixed rigidity of the Soviet Marxist political system. Similar phenomena can be found in our time – the axiomatic acceptance of the individualist/collectivist opposition in cross-cultural psychology has rigidified a reasonable conceptual tool. Despite analyses that point to the unity of individualism and collectivism in any society or person (Sinha & Tripathi, 2001), the classification of societies, as if those were either "collectivist" or "individualist," is rampant in psychology.

From Conceptual Tools to Rigid "-isms"

Having become a world view, a basic scientific idea begins to meet fierce resistance as its social-ideological implications become clear and its moorings to the phenomena that generated it eventually fade from the scene – perhaps to be resurrected under another name in another era, as Shep has suggested. Thus, in contemporary psychology, the *-ism-perspectives* (cognitivism, behaviorism, interactionism, etc.) have become ideological frames – akin to party slogans – that are traded in psychologists' professional discourse in terms of their positioning, rather than used to create new knowledge. Psychology suffers from fascination with some curious kind of "-ismofilia" that leads to unproductive fights – cognitivists fight behaviorists, socioculturalists fight cognitivists, etc. Most of the basic problems of science remain unsolved in the shadow of such fights.

Episodic Openings in the History of Science

At the same time that rigidification of ideas goes on in some countries, periods of social turmoil in others may lead to openness of thinking by social scientists, giving rise to new ideas. One can look at the history of ideas in psychology as being a nonmonotonic, episodic progression through "bursts of creativity" interspersed with periods of "ideological appropriation" of scientific ideas and their fixation. Thus, the social sciences in the United States developed in a "creative burst" in the 1890s – under the social stress of immigration, urbanization, and industrialization (see Valsiner & van der Veer, 2000). It is thanks to the turmoils of that decade that social sciences can appreciate the creative thought of James Mark Baldwin, John Dewey, George Herbert Mead, and others. That period was followed by the set of constraints (labeled "the progressive era") that turned U.S. psychologists away from their creative searches to follow Watson's quasi-religious creed (see Watson, 1913). In Russia and Germany in the 1920s – following the revolutions of 1917 and 1918 – the extremely uncertain economic and social conditions led to the flourishing of ideas in the sciences. In Russia, aside from the well-known heritage of Lev Vygotsky and Mikhail Bakhtin, there were many others – Mikhail Basov, Nadezhda Ladygina-Kohts, and Alexei Severtsov to name a few – who introduced true innovation in their areas of study (Valsiner, 1988). The German context was burgeoning with creative ideas in the middle of the hyperinflationary reality of the Weimar Republic. In psychology we know of the advances in *Gestalt-* and *Ganzheitspsychologie* (Ash, 1995; Diriwaechter, 2003), but aside from that it was the German natural sciences that were taking a great leap forward. All that ended in the 1930s by the "fixation" of both societies. The new "intellectual immigration" stress in the 1930s and 1940s in the United States and Mexico – due to the exodus of scientists and artists from Germany and Spain (see Tashjian, 1995) – led to a burst of creativity in the academic and artistic worlds of New York and Mexico City – despite the economic hardship left over from the Great Depression (Andrade, 1990; Pierre, 1990). The story continues close to our time – the euphoria of the fall of the Franco regime gave an impetus to the growth of socio-cultural research in Spain in the 1980s (e.g., Del Rio, Alvarez, & Wertsch, 1994).

How would our contemporary state of affairs in psychology fare in this discussion of historical fertility periods? Probably not so well, if we look at the re-surfacing of old ideas as clichés close to common sense. For example, the "nature" versus "nurture" relation depicted as "controversy" seems to recur anew in many ways – often under the aegis of new technological breakthroughs such as those currently taking place in molecular genetics and evolutionary biology. It tells us a story about the ambiguous role of technological changes in contrast to the primacy of social change. When the technology is new – but the ideas remain old – no breakthroughs can follow. Consider what we easily – under the wave of journalistic fascination in the popular press – consider as "breakthroughs" in human genome science. We are told that full description of the human genome opens vast horizons for science – and are then led to see how some old questions (e.g., "Is there a gene for schizophrenia? Or for intelligence?") are being asked, as if our science has not moved ahead from the times of phrenology. An even better parallel with phrenology is the use of fMRI high technology to answer scientifically trivial questions (such as – "Is brain area X bigger in size when homosexuals are compared with the norm?"). Such questions have been theoretically ruled out from serious science decades ago – but come back in research practice when technology is modified without the corresponding innovation in ideas.

However, when new ideas emerge in a given science and lead to the development of new technologies, the new technologies can help to streamline further growth of ideas. For example, there is no novelty guaranteed by the invention of new computers – if these computers are set up for playing games by consumers or for making the internet users open to new advertisements. In contrast, if new computers lead to the possibilities of creating new programs that solve problems previously insoluble, then we can see the role of new technology feeding forward into breakthroughs in science.

New technology at times means elimination of the discipline's original ideas all together. It may be a part of language-purification games that social sciences at times play. It is a curious phenomenon in psychology that psychologists are eager to participate in the elimination of their own domain of expertise through accepting technological "cargo" from other sciences as if that can solve their own problems. So "behaviorists" have outlawed mental terminology, "cognitivists" look askance at "behaviorists," and "socioculturalists" consider both "behaviorists" and "cognitivists" to be missing the point because of their terminology. Statistical technology has led to the use of terms like "effect" or "interaction" in ways that are far from any link with psychological reality. Ever since the "official" beginning of psychology as a separate discipline (i.e., the standard reference to the Leipzig laboratory established in 1879) the history of psychology has been filled by all kinds of efforts to reduce psychological phenomena "downward" (to elementary physiological processes) or "upward" (to complex social creations – myths, texts, etc.). It is in the effort to cope with such reductions that Shep White's contributions are central to our thinking.

Sheldon White's Historical Program

Shep White has consistently raised concerns that psychology's phobia about its own history may indicate a wider problem – with wider consequences. In "Psychology in all sorts of places" (White, 1978) Shep returns to the themes of his earlier articles, this time in the framework of George Miller's well-known call to "give psychology away." Shep begins by talking about the mythical dreamscape of psychology's past that the whole notion of giving psychology away presupposes, foreshadowing the arguments in "Proposals for a second psychology" (Cahan & White, 1992).

Having himself been drawn into the vortex of psychology "given away" to Washington policymakers, Shep offers the idea of a "three zone" social structuring of psychological research: A "core" of basic research that produces knowledge about such topics as learning, motivation, individual differences, perception, etc., a "middle layer" of "bridging disciplines" such as educational psychology that translate basic knowledge into methods of applying that knowledge in scientific ways, and finally, the practitioners (teachers, policymakers, etc.) who would use the rendered-usable knowledge in a professional matter.

Having proposed such a "basic to applied" sequence, Shep then, characteristically, deconstructs it by examining the many ways in which psychologists are creatures of their own society; the "giving" runs in more than one direction and a good deal of what is given is less "pure science" than symbols, myths, and categories that are used by society as tools of its own regeneration. He ends by asking whether

> it is possible that a psychology composed of debatable, corrigible myths might be empirical and progressive through gradual, evolutionary processes of trading in conjectures and refutations. . . . But, of course, this scientific process and its relationship to everyday activities would be badly misunderstood if one looked at it through a lens made by the mythic form of the natural sciences. (White, 1978, p. 129)

All of which sets the stage for elaborating on the notion of a "second psychology" that takes everyday practices of people as its starting point, a psychology that is no less basic or theoretical than the mythical "first psychology" modeled on the natural sciences that continues to dominate our profession.

Generality of Practice: How Can Science Deal with Everyday Life?

By developing a paper on this foundation, we seek to further Shep's project by providing additional evidence for the importance of a second psychology constructed along the lines he suggested. It would be a psychological science that

1. is both basic and applied – yet in ways that enrich our everyday life practices;
2. discounts the notion that "individual" and "society" constitute a legitimate dichotomy – and reconnect them as parts of the functioning whole;
3. takes culture and its variations to be no less central to human nature than phylogeny; and
4. seeks to replace the sectarian and ethnocentric claims of one or another "national" psychology by an international effort to understand and appreciate human diversity and its maintenance as a precondition not only for greater scientific understanding but for the survival of the human species.

Undoubtedly putting this plan into practice would entail a major change in the ways psychology is construed today. It is a general psychology that begins from centrality of culture and lives up to Kurt Lewin's saying that there is nothing more practical than a good theory.

In fact such a culture-centered psychology of human living has the generality of basic science and – because of such generality – applicability in many different social contexts. Two crucial, interconnected issues emerge from this discussion – first that of generalizing our knowledge from one setting to another and second that of applying generalized knowledge to specific settings.

Generalizing Knowledge

Forty years ago psychologists were captivated by the vision of a set of universal laws true of all humans (and animals!) regardless of time or context. Ignoring Dewey's sage advice against "either-or" thinking, contemporary social sciences have – again with remarkable historical short-sightedness – tended to turn the important recognition of context-specificity of human psychological phenomena into a total denial of general knowledge. The result threatens us with a new form of empiricism – contextual, qualitative, and situated, which is an equally blind mirror image of its older (now disparaged as "positivist") empiricism in its attempts to generate genuinely new and useful knowledge. The search for general principles remains the objective of science – and Shep's vision of a cultural-historical psychology is in this sense as basic and universal as is the theory of evolution (see LCHC, 1983, and Valsiner, 2000, for expanded discussions of this issue).

Generalizing Knowledge to Specific New Settings

General principles are not "put into practice" in their abstract forms but are translated into actions through intermediate theoretical and methodological conceptual tools as part of a program of systematic inquiry. This is the much misunderstood (and often abused) process that Marx referred to as "rising to the concrete." In modern terms, we can characterize it as the translation of abstract knowledge into concrete application contexts. Such translation requires a systematic linking of theory and method; a methodology is more than an opportunistic collection of methods (Branco & Valsiner, 1997). A "vertically consistent" conceptual system – where metatheoretical, theoretical, and phenomenological features of a research project are coordinated with methods and data – can lead to new knowledge. It is in that context that new -*isms* remain inherently (potentially) productive for our knowledge construction. The challenge is to realize that potential without falling into the traps so clearly evident in our history.

Actualizing Potentials: Proximal Advancement of the Notion of Zone of Proximal Development

In the spirit of contributing to this goal, we attempt to return to an idea both of us have covered extensively – the notion of zone of proximal development.[1] The general idea of potential for development arose from the recognition of the crisis state in psychology in the late 1920s and became crystallized in the concept of zone of proximal development in Vygotsky's last year of life. Since then, the notion has become widely popular. Certainly, since it came into common parlance following publication of a set of edited essays in *Mind and Society*, there can be little doubt that it has been used far beyond the phenomena that generated it and that it has become part of at least one world view. (A brief detour to look up "zone of proximal development" on the World Wide Web turned up 9,170 publications in 0.22 seconds.)

This evidence indicates consistent interest in the issue of movement from the past toward the future. This is a healthy interest because as long as psychology concentrates only on what already exists, it cannot deal with that side of human mentality that does not yet exist. Developmental focus on the synthesis of the remembered past and imagined future is essential if developmental science is interested in the actualization of potentialities (Cole, 1992, 1995; Josephs, 1998).

Van der Veer and Valsiner (1991, chapter 13; Valsiner & van der Veer, 1993) argued that the development of the concept of a zone of proximal development was motivated by specific practical needs (to organize instruction for an enormously diverse population with only highly-suspect IQ tests as a ready-to-hand tool when more adequate testing instruments seemed an obvious necessity). The idea of a zone of proximal development drew upon a variety of ideas present in (but not restricted to) European psychology over the preceding several decades including

- the "general law of cultural development" (Pierre Janet) – emergence of higher psychological functions of a person through transaction with the social world;
- the idea of imitation as developed by Baldwin ("persistent imitation") that provides the future-oriented, feed-forward mechanism of developmental change central to development;

[1] Vygotsky defined a zone of proximal development as "the distance between the actual developmental level as determined by independent problem solving and the level of potential development as determined through problem solving under adult guidance or in collaboration with more capable peers" (1978, p. 86).

- the centrality of the application of psychological research as the strictest test of theory and surest way to avoid sterile scientific disputes; and
- the need to study behavior over time – both in its external form and its emerging meanings.

All these are basic principles of developmental science – yet the adoption of Vygotsky's idea of a zone of proximal development in the psychology of the 1980s did not focus on developmental processes. Instead, frustrated by Piaget's emphasis on the need for development to precede learning, which restricted the possible role of the teacher, the zone of proximal development was linked with an educational ideology of restoring the role of benevolent educator in the increasingly fragile social systems of schools.[2] Then, in a manner predictable by the history of psychology, it was generalized beyond recognizable bounds.

However, we wish to argue that such a gloomy past does not determine a gloomy future. There are a variety of means open to psychologists to reconstruct both the history of the concept and its current applications to show where it may (*potentially!*) realize potentials overlooked in the rush to generalize and totalize to suit the psychological research community.

Remediating Failures of Reading Acquisition

We have chosen two examples of ways to recapture the needed specificity and applicability of a widely over-extended concept by summarizing research with children who have manifested unusual difficulty learning how to read (see Cole, 1996, chapter 9, and Maciel, Branco, & Valsiner, 2004, for fuller treatments). The problem is important practically because at present a great many children of normal intelligence fail to acquire reading skills deemed adequate for productive participation in modern societies (Miller, 1988). It is of importance theoretically because in spite of an enormous amount of

---

[2] For some unspecified reason the "more knowledgeable other" – teacher or peer – has been presented as if his/her only motivation is to help the learner to reach the next step in the educational achievement. The possibility that the "other" is a strategic actor who – aside from helping – may also try to undermine the development of the learner has been completely overlooked. Yet a tired and underpaid teacher in a classroom – terrified by the bureaucratic system of the school and unhappy in his/her personal life – may not be the epitome of educational benevolence in the teaching/learning process (Litowitz, 1997).

research (Snow et al., 1998) there remain serious disagreements about the process of reading acquisition and the most effective means for promoting it. Although differing greatly in their particulars, the following examples (which were carried out independently of each other) each seek to create conditions for learning and teaching which are atypical in ways that fit with our project of "recovering" the concept of zone of proximal development. Each assumes that teaching and learning should be interpreted and implemented as a reciprocal, two way process captured by the Russian term, *obuchenie*, which we will render as teaching/learning. This process is assumed to be bidirectional: not only the student, but also the teacher, are assumed to undergo change as a result of the activities we organized. To enable such mutual change, the power relations between teachers and learners usually present in classrooms were also modified, creating what Maciel et al. (2004) refer to as the "cocreation of mutual trust." Finally, the researchers video- and audio-taped the interactions they were analyzing in order to be able to study interactions at both a microgenetic and ontogenetic level, thereby allowing direct observation of the processes of change.

Example 1: A Small Group Remedial Reading Activity. In the early 1980s Cole and his colleagues developed an approach to the teaching/learning of reading that can be distinguished from dominant approaches in the field by its simultaneous emphasis on three inter-related points[3]:

1. Reading instruction must emphasize *both* decoding *and* comprehension in a single, integrated activity (an assumption that can be interpreted in terms of the idea that reading requires the coordination of "bottom-up" (feature – > letter – > word – > phrase – >. . . .) and "top-down" processes.
2. Under ordinary circumstances, both adults and children play an essential role in coordinating the top-down and bottom-up processes that are necessary for development of reading.
3. Successful adult efforts depend crucially on their organizing a "cultural medium for reading" that constitutes a zone of proximal development, which, in Cazden's (1981) apt phrase, makes possible the acquisition of performance before competence. That is, the activity must engage the children in the full act of reading *before* they can read independently.

---

[3] The lead in this work was taken by Peg Griffin. For a description of procedural details and the larger project of which it was a part see LCHC, 1982, and King, Diaz, Griffin, & Cole, 2000).

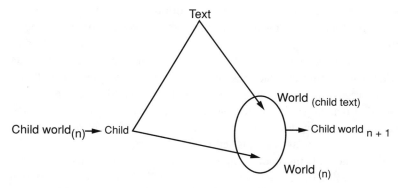

Figure 11.1. A dynamic representation of mediated action in which the child's understanding of the world at time t must be coordinated with the changes wrought by mediation of understanding through a text to arrive at a new understanding at time $t + 1$.

To see how this approach draws upon both generalized scientific knowledge and situated knowledge that is cocreated by the participants, Cole and his colleagues began by modifying slightly the common sense definition of reading as the process of decoding and interpreting text. Reading, in their theoretical framework was defined as the process of *expanding* the ability to mediate one's interactions with the environment by interpreting print. There are two significant aspects of this definition. First, learning to read and proficient reading are both subsumed in the same definition. What one learns to do is expand; what one does, having learned, is to continue expanding (see Engeström, 1987, for a general discussion of "learning by expanding"). Second, there is no dichotomy between decoding and comprehension, since comprehension is understood as the process of mediating one's interactions with the environment, including text processing (interpreting letter groups) as a condition.

Figure 11.1, which is a modified version of the classical Vygotskian mediational triangle, reminds us that reading, in the broadest sense, requires the coordination of information from "two routes" ("mediated" and "direct") that never completely coincide. Any reader must "see" the world as a mediated fashion, refracted through a text; but in order to do so, the reader's more direct access to the world, topicalized by the text, must be simultaneously engaged. Even among skilled readers, the act of coordinating the two routes may require adjustments in the representation of the "worlds" arrived at by either route singly in order to permit a new representation (expanded understanding) to emerge.

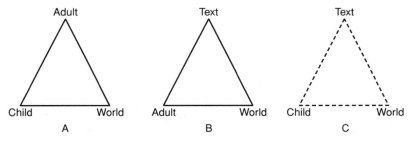

Figure 11.2. The to-be-coordinated systems of mediation that exist when a novice begins to learn to read from a literate adult. (A) The child can already mediate interactions with the world via an adult. (B) The adult can mediate interactions with the world via text. (C) The child–text–world system is the goal of instruction.

The slight discoordination depicted in Figure 11.1 acknowledges the temporality of mediation and the constant need at reconciling different sources of information. With this minimal structural apparatus in hand, we can now turn to the crucial question: Assuming that children do not begin instruction already able to read, that is expand their ability to comprehend by reading alphabetic text, how can we arrange for them to develop this ability?

Note that in attempting to answer this question, we will simultaneously be tackling the classic developmental question of how it is possible to acquire a more powerful cognitive structure unless, in some sense, it is already present to begin with. This question, called the "paradox of development" by Fodor (1983) and the "learning paradox" by Bereiter (1985), calls into doubt any developmental account of reading that fails to specify the preexisting constraints that make development possible. Bringing the endpoint "forward" to the beginning is no less relevant in developing the ability to read than in any other developmental process.

To solve these problems, we must begin by showing in what sense the endpoint of development, the ability to mediate one's comprehension of the world through print, could in principle be shown to be present in embryonic form at the outset of instruction.

Figure 11.2 displays in graphic form the fact that at the beginning of instruction there are two preexisting mediational systems that can be used as resources for creating the necessary initial structural constraints to permit the development of independent reading in the child. At the far left of the figure, we represent the common sense fact that children enter reading instruction with years of experience mediating their interactions through the world via adults. In the center of the figure, we represent the equally common sense fact

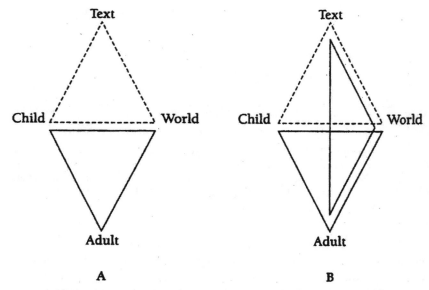

A   **B**

Figure 11.3. The juxtaposition of already-existing and to-be-formed systems of mediation that have to be coordinated. (A) The juxtaposition of the to-be-formed system involving child and text with the already-existing system of child and adult. (B) The addition of the already existing adult–text system needed to induce formation of the to-be-formed child–text–world system.

that literate adults routinely mediate their interactions through text. Finally, on the far right of the figure, we illustrate the to-be-developed system of mediation.

Figure 11.3 shows the next stage in the analytical/instructional strategy: The given and to-be-developed systems of child mediations are juxtaposed and the given adult system is then superimposed, to reveal the skeletal structure of an "interpsychological" system of mediation that, indirectly, establishes a dual system of mediation for the child. If properly coordinated in joint activity, this dual system permits the coordination of text-based and prior-world-knowledge-based information of the kind involved in the whole act of reading.

Creating the Medium: Question–Asking–Reading. The instructional/developmental task is now better specified: We must somehow create a system of interpersonal interaction such that the combined child–adult system at the right of Figure 11.3 can coordinate the child's act of reading *before the child can accomplish this activity for him/herself.* The core elements of the procedure is a scripted set of actions and a set of roles (each corresponding to a different hypothetical part of the whole act of reading) and each printed on $3'' \times 5''$ index cards. Every participant is responsible for fulfilling at least one role in the full activity of Question–Asking–Reading. These cards specify the following roles:

- The person who asks about words that are hard to say.
- The person who asks about words that are hard to understand.
- The person who asks a question about the main idea.
- The person who picks the person to answer questions asked by others.
- The person who asks about what is going to happen next.

The children chosen to participate in this study were elementary school children selected by their teachers, who identified them as having unusual difficulty learning to read that they (the teachers) were unable to deal with.

All participants including the instructor had a copy of the text to read, paper and pencil to jot down words, phrases, or notes (in order to answer questions implicit in the roles), and their card to remind them of their role. In order to move from the scripted actions and roles to an appropriate teaching/learning activity, the procedural script was embedded in a more complex, game-like social structure designed to make salient both the short-term and long-term goals of reading and to provide a means of coordinating these activities with the script. It is in this embedding process that we make the transition from a focus on the structural model of reading depicted in Figures 11.1–11.3 to a focus on the necessary transformation of the mediational structure of the group interactions with print.

Recognizing the need to create a medium rich in goals, which could be resources for organizing the transition from reading as a guided activity to independent, voluntary reading, we saturated the environment with talk and activities about growing-up and the role of reading in a grown-up's life. Question–Asking–Reading began each session with such "goal talk," discussion about the various reasons that children might have for wanting to learn to read. Joint work with the text began with a group discussion of the title or headline of the story to be read that day. Then, following the script outline which was written on the blackboard, the role-bearing cards and the first paragraph of the text were passed around.

A good deal of discussion usually ensued about who had gotten what roles; "pick the answerer" was an obvious favorite, whereas the card implicating the main idea was avoided like the plague. Once the role cards were distributed, the text for the day (usually taken from local newspapers with content that related to matters of potential interest to the children) was distributed, one paragraph at a time. The participants (the instructor and one competent reader, usually a UCSD undergraduate, and the children) then bent over their passages to engage in silent reading.

These and other procedural arrangements constituted our attempt to organize a coordinated group activity that would routinely create moments when the three mediational triangles depicted in Figure 11.3 would be coordinated to create the conditions for "re-mediating" the children's entering systems of mediation, allowing them to acquire reading as an intrapsychological process.

The Data. Our evidence for the way in which this procedure worked is derived from several sources: videotaped recordings of the instructional sessions, the children's written work on the quizzes that completed each session, and various test results. Here we will concentrate on the in situ process of coordination and discoordination around the scripted activity as a key source of evidence about individual children's ability to coordinate via the scripted roles and the points where coordination fails, resulting in selective discoordinations of the ongoing activity structure (inspired here by the early work of Alexander Luria, 1932).

In this example, two children, both of whom are failing in their reading classes, discoordinate at different moments in the publicly available scripted activity, permitting differential diagnosis of their specific difficulties. The two boys, Billy and Armandito, are starting to read the second paragraph of the day. Katie is their teacher, and Larry is an additional competent reader.

Evidence for internalization of the scripted activity is provided by instances in which the children's talk and actions presuppose a next step in the procedure with no overt provocation from the adults. For example:

(1). Katie: *OK, let's go on to the second paragraph then.*
(2). Billy: *How did they find them?*
(3). Armandito: *The Eskimos.*
(4). Katie: *I think it was an accident. (As she says this, she begins to pass out the role cards, face down.)*
(5). Billy: *(Taking a card from the stack.) How come, what kind of accident?*
(6). Billy: *(Looking at his card.) That's the same card again.*

In (2) Billy's question is an internalized version of the "what's going to happen next" role in the script that no one specifically stimulated. He takes the card handed to him, asks a relevant question about the text, and comments on the relationship between his role in the previous segment of interaction and its relationship to what he is about to do. Armandito's participation is of a different order. His comment (3) "The Eskimos" is relevant to the topic at hand, but opaque. He does not take one of the role cards and has to be stimulated by Katie while Billy continues to show evidence of coordination:

(7). Katie: *Armandito! (He looks up and takes a card.)*

(8). Billy: *We each get another one. (Referring to the cards; there are only four participants and Katie has not taken one, so someone will get an extra.)*

In a number of places in the transcript we see Armandito discoordinating within the activity which the other three participants maintain, permitting him to recoordinate from time to time. These discoordinations are of several types. The most obvious are such actions as drawing a picture instead of reading, or feigning abandonment of the activity altogether. But repeatedly, Armandito presupposes the scripted activity sufficiently to motivate quite specific analyses of his difficulties. The next example illustrates his aversion to the question about the main idea and provides information (corroborated in many examples) of his core difficulty.

(9). Larry: *(He has the card which says to pick the answerer.)*
Armandito, What's the main idea?

(10). Armandito: *I want to ask mine. I want to ask what happens next.*

(11). Larry: *No. I know what you want, but I am asking. I pick the answerer.*

(12). Armandito: *The main idea is . . . how these guys live*

In (10) Armandito is both accepting the joint task of Question–Asking–Reading ("I want to ask mine") and attempting to avoid the role that is at the heart of his problem (figuring out the main idea) by skipping that part of the scripted sequence. When Armandito accepts his role (12) and attempts to state the main idea, his answer ("The main idea is . . . how these guys live") is not only vague, it is about the *previous* paragraph.

As a consequence of an accumulation of many such examples over several sessions, Cole and his colleagues were able to obtain a consistent pattern. This pattern showed that Billy experienced great difficulty in coming "unglued" from the letter-sound correspondences when he attempted to arrive at the main idea. When asked about the main idea, he repeatedly returned to the text and sought a "copy match" in which some word from the question appeared in the text. He then read the relevant sentence aloud, and puzzled over meaning. Armandito's problem was of a quite different order: he continually lost track of the relevant context, importing information from his classroom activities that day or previous reading passages that had no relevance.

The first conclusion that we want to draw from this exercise is that the researchers were in fact successful in creating a structured medium of activity that allowed diagnostically useful information about which part of the structure depicted in Figure 11.3 was deficient in the individual children with whom we worked. However, this approach also established that the Question–Asking–Reading procedure is an effective zone of proximal development for the acquisition of reading. When engaged in the small group activity, the children were able to read and comprehend well before they could adequately do so independently. After several weeks of participation, both Billy and Armandito did in fact continue to improve their reading abilities over a period of several months, and Armandito's general behavior in the classroom changed so markedly that he won an award from the school recognizing his unusual progress.

However, such individual change could not logically be attributed to Question–Asking–Reading, both because it was part of the larger activity system of the after school program, and because Cole and his colleagues had no proper control group. Here the issue of generalization becomes prominent.

To remedy these shortcomings, King (1988) replicated the small group reading procedures in a follow-up experiment that included appropriate control conditions, had more stringently quantified pre- and post-test measures, and was conducted as the sole activity in a school prior to the start of regular classes. Her experimental study showed that Question–Asking–Reading was more effective than either a procedure called "procedural facilitation" constructed by Scardamalia and Bereiter (1985) or a no-treatment control group.

Taken together, these results, although sketchily presented here owing to limitations on space, provide support for the argument we have developed in this chapter. We used general principles derived from experimental research combined with theoretically motivated principles to create a specific form of group activity that allowed diagnosis of the process of developmental change and statements about the state of the level of understanding of each individual child. At the same time, the theoretical principles guided the design of a methodology that facilitated all the children in their efforts to overcome their reading problems. It was, in concrete form, an embodiment of the concept of zone of proximal development, no longer merely as a slogan, but as a recognized and effective form of educational practice.

Processes of Negotiation within *Obuchenie*

Operating from a similar theoretical position, Maciel, Branco, and Valsiner (2004) emphasized that the process of *obuchenie* (teaching/learning) is first and foremost a process of communication between persons based on different goal orientations. The "start-up" roles of the teacher and learner guarantee that there is some difference. For example the teacher

might assume: "I want the child to become skillful (or knowledgeable in this task, so I am going to interact with her, and move her in that direction."

while the child may assume: "That auntie is really nice, I want to have fun in the hour that I spend with her. Even though she wants me to play these odd games it is all right so long as we enjoy our time together."

Starting from such divergent communication orientations entails constant construction of the ongoing activity – by way of actions with objects as well as through importation and production of signs. Thus it is inherently a process of mutual complementarity of understanding.

Furthermore, the teaching/learning process involves gradual canalization of that understanding toward achievements in understanding that the student did not possess before, but that become appropriated after it has been achieved. This canalization is mutual – the teacher directs the student toward the goal of achievement, yet the student may succeed in avoiding such efforts through counter-effective communication strategies (as we saw in the previous example). Such mutual canalization entails constant change of participants' positions relative to the object of teaching/learning (Josephs, 1998; Rommetveit, 1992, 1998).

While communicating about specific activity issues, the participants are simultaneously involved in coordination of their mutual relations – metacommunication (Branco,1997; Branco, Neiva, Ferreira, & Pessina, 1997; Fogel & Branco, 1997). Metacommunicative processes are continuous with the flow of interaction, setting specific interpretative frames to attribute particular meanings to interactors' verbal and nonverbal behaviors. Therefore, when individuals interact with each other, metacommunication is always active as a sort of interactive background for content communication, a continuous nonverbal flux that episodically assumes a verbal format that may generate very complex or even contradictory qualitative frames for message's interpretation.

In the example of Question–Asking–Reading, Cole and his colleagues relied upon the game-like repetitive nature of the group activity and the presence of two cooperating skilled readers to ensure the operation of the metacommunicative context. In the following example, the active work of the participants to maintain the needed metacommunicative context in the face of ever-changing communicative interactions is highlighted. The example is taken from an in-depth observational study of a teacher and a 9-year-old boy (who claimed to have "learning difficulties" at school) conducted by Diva A. Maciel in Brasilia (Maciel, 1996). Full analysis of the specific communicative and metacommunicative behavior is provided elsewhere (Maciel, Branco, & Valsiner, 2004).

The child met with the experienced teacher weekly (for a year) for approximately 75 minutes for reading lessons that were videotaped to allow analysis of significant moments of co-construction of knowledge about strategies to solve problems, to develop special skills, and to deal with emotional issues important to the adult–child relationship. In the example to follow, the child's task was to choose three words (from a previous task). When he reached the second word, he hesitated, so the teacher (T) helped him by posing specific questions that guided his ideas toward one of the possible options. The general interactive atmosphere was positive and animated as indicated by nonlinguistic and paralinguistic signals such as smiles and voice intonation. The child (L) decided to choose another word. The teacher accepted his choice: the word *embroider*.

T directs attention to the organization of the student's copybook, reminding him of the right rules to write adequately (see Turn 2 in Table 11.1).

Following the interaction described above, the child notices an inconsistency in the way the sentence was constructed and says: "Oops, this is wrong!" The teacher smiles and replies: "Yes, this crochet right here!," but it seems she is referring to the *orthography* of the word, and does not notice how the sentence, the way he wrote it, did not make sense (in terms of the concatenation of meanings – "embroider" – "crochet"). As we see in Table 11.2,

Table 11.1. *Teacher does not notice*

Teacher	Student
	1- *OK, I'll choose the word embroider!*
2- *OK! Go ahead! Skip a line, otherwise it will look like a whole composition!*	
	3- (L writes down while emitting vocal sounds. When he finishes, he raises his hands enthusiastically, holding the pencil). *That's it!*
4- *Read the sentence!*	
	5- *My grandma embroiders crochet.* (He shows an amused facial expression as he says "crochet").

Table 11.2. *Teacher Lets the Child Assume the Role of Teacher*

Teacher	Student
6- *Ché cheé* (she accentuates the ending of the word and picks up the eraser).	
	7- *NO! It's not it! This is not the problem here!* (L smiles as he corrects the teacher, expressing self-confidence as he picks up the rubber from her).
8- *So, what is it, then?* (smiling).	
	9- *Embroider crochet, no way!* (his voice expresses enthusiasm).

the child is aware of that semantic misfit and announces it to the teacher – proud of being smarter than the teacher (shows confidence in his smile and voice intonation).

The episode in Table 11.1 and its aftermath gives us a minimal encounter within the complex of *obuchenie*: two people jointly construct knowledge of each other (in the given context) based on *both* the shared understanding of the communicative message (how to spell *crochet*) and the oversights each fall prey to. The latter occur all the time – the teacher may not notice something the child does, and vice versa. Each episode of divergence in attention of the one is a meaning construction opportunity for the other. If we were to generalize, we would say: the teacher can promote learning *through her own incomplete understanding* of the instructional setting. The child's detection of such incompleteness creates a space for the child to "teach the teacher" – a small-scale role reversal that skillful teachers utilize for their own goals of teaching. An experienced teacher is not afraid of "being wrong" (since any human being is that, in respect to many issues, continuously). However, such a teacher can skillfully turn one's own "being wrong" into an action strategy in the process of *obuchenie* – the discovery of the child's own competence can feed into the intrinsic motivation of the child.

The child seems happy and confident to have this opportunity to correct the teacher, who *temporarily accepts the role of student* as she lets the child "lecture" her about what is wrong here. The exchange of roles allows for the experience of reciprocity, which is very important in the co-construction of mutual trust and convergent goal orientations. The teacher is flexible enough to let the child "control the field" at that moment – and skillfully takes that "control" back at the next time.

The child bubbles with glee at his own self-competence. The teacher accepts that and helps him to continue, suggesting a way to complement the

Table 11.3. *Teacher teaches again*

Teacher	Student
10- *That's because embroider is one thing and crochet is something else!* (she says, smiling).	10- *To embroider is* . . . (he speaks at the same time as T, gesticulating with his hand)
	11- . . . *Hu hu* (he confirms what T just said, shaking his head and smiling).
12- *Does she embroider what? What does she embroider?* (she touches the table cloth), *What can she embroider?*	

sentence he started by asking oriented questions and pointing to the appropriate object – the table cloth – that would perfectly fit in the sentence (Table 11.3). She promotes the child's actions within the semiotic constraints imposed by the word *embroider*. She follows exactly those constraints that were pointed out by the child before (when he said: "To embroider crochet, no way!"). Yet that message now comes (again) authoritatively from the teacher. The skill of teaching is to move smoothly from one's own oversights (or mistakes) to making use of them as teaching tools. We observe what Rogoff designates as *transfer of responsibility* from the expert to the novice. This seems to evoke a positive attitude in both participants (Rogoff, 1990).

This microgenetic example complements the first (reading) example by showing how microtasks are created in interaction between partners in the activity of *obuchenie*. It is the modulation of the transfer of responsibility over time (and tasks) that creates the concrete setting for reaching the next nearest solution to a given problem. The "zone of proximal development" notion takes a different form here – it becomes a concrete here-and-now activity structure where one of the participants sets up the possibility for making a (small) discovery by the other. That activity is oriented toward renegotiating the boundaries of the use of meanings. This translation of the general notions of cultural-historical perspective into the activity sequences of the teacher and the learner is a microscopic illustration of a general principle – *human development takes place on the margin of what is (already) and what is not (yet)*. Hence all developmental processes are inherently nondeterministic (Fogel, Lyra, & Valsiner, 1997) and become determined in specific loci due to the use of signs in the ongoing flow of activity.

Conclusion: Ways to Actualize the Potentials of Psychology

Our major goals in this chapter have been four-fold. First, we have sought to build upon Shep White's ideas about the possibility of recovering a "second psychology," which was all but suffocated under the weight of a version of experimental psychology that treats human beings as acultural organisms whose psychological processes can be studied without taking into account the processes of development, broadly understood. In doing so, our second goal has been to provide positive examples of such research following the methods of a second psychology that follow from the tradition of Lev Vygotsky and Alexander Luria. This tradition is valuable precisely because it constituted an effort in the 1920s and 1930s to solve the major problem of psychology – that of *culturally meaningful behavior* and its *constant re-construction* by persons in activity contexts. This problem has not yet been solved – despite claims to the contrary from all kinds of -*ism*-perspectives. Third, we have tried to demonstrate that a fresh look at already existing concepts – such as zone of proximal development – and rigorous specification of those concepts can help us avoid slipping into the errors of the past which routinely create crises in psychology. Finally, in tune with Shep White's ideas about the second psychology, we have tried to show that careful observation of activity contexts can help us overcome the false dichotomy between theory and practice.

Our examples of the microstructures of the activity of *obuchenie* (teaching/learning process) show some counter-intuitive features of the actual process of communication between teachers and learners. While our folklore of teaching and learning assumes a fixed (rigid) position of teacher "giving knowledge" to the learner, the reality is quite different. Teachers create microsettings for the learners (within the wider activity context) where the learners can achieve the next moment of understanding themselves. Teachers are actors who modulate their own role in the setting all the time. At times they take full control, at others relinquish it to the learners (while, of course, keeping the control of the field as a whole). The teacher may temporarily reverse the roles with the learners and at other times pretend not to notice a mistake (hoping that the learners discover it). And, of course, the teaching/learning process is inherently filled with oversights, misinterpretations, and purposeful distortions of the images of reality. Superficially this picture may look bleak and cynical (from the viewpoint of the social ideology of "purity of education") – yet its reality allows for very creative mobilization of human potentials both in the roles of teacher and learner. The teacher is a learner who teaches. The learner is a teacher who learns.

We hasten to emphasize that neither of our examples constitutes a full exposition of a culture-inclusive, co-constructionist approach to psychology (cf. Cole, 1996; Valsiner, 2000, 2001). We have no intention of suggesting (yet) another -*ism* in psychology's already over-*ism*-ified mindscape. Rather, each is an existence proof of the kinds of teaching/learning interactions that are possible when the principles we summarized at the beginning of this article are applied in a careful and systematic way. Such existence proofs also serve to highlight the challenges of taking the next step and demonstrating that the specific examples can be used as tools to implement the forms of activity we described on a broader scale. Few classrooms or school schedules are currently arranged in a manner that could support the kind of intergenerational, group reading involved in Question–Asking–Reading. The individual teacher/learner dynamics in our second example are not applicable to settings where the teacher works simultaneously with many children. Moving the demonstrations to a next level would mean introducing this kind of activity into school classrooms on a regular basis.

Similarly, the conditions that enabled the interactions of the teachers and children in both examples point to the sort of classroom climate that is necessary for successful teaching of this kind to occur. However, creating such conditions routinely requires a great many resources currently lacking in schools including highly trained teachers and a means of moving from one-on-one to large group teaching. It also requires a society whose values allow for teachers and students to establish the conditions of mutual trust and affection that provide the metacommunicative conditions for successful teaching.

Shep White has clearly pointed out the general direction psychologists should be following. Others, including ourselves, have shown the positive benefits to be reaped by pursuing this direction. The challenge now is to move from the protected socio-ecological niches where such activities are tolerated, to making them routine within societies that are struggling for survival, a condition which all too easily degenerates into command and control, standardized procedures to achieve its goals. Even in a society oriented toward capturing large numbers of consumers, the need for which is culturally constructed, it is not possible to turn the teaching/learning process into a routine carried out from a distance through rigid robots as teachers. There is a need for promotion of the role of producers of new knowledge in any education system. Shep White's project creates a zone of proximal development for everyone's immediate futures.

Acknowledgments

We thank Diva A. Maciel for the permission to use her data. The joint work between Clark University and University of Brasilia (of which the project was a part) was funded by NSF grant # 9813720 (PI: Jaan Valsiner). The research on Question–Asking–Reading was supported by the Carnegie Corporation, and preparation of the paper was facilitated by a grant from the Spencer Foundation to Michael Cole.

References

Andrade, L. (1990). De amores y desamores: Relaciones de México con el surrealismo. *El surrealismo entre Viejo y Nouevo Mundo* (pp. 101–109). Madrid: Ediciones El Viso.

Ash, M. G. (1995). *Gestalt Psychology in German Culture 1890–1967*. New York: Cambridge University Press.

Bereiter, C. (1985). Toward a solution to the learning paradox. *Review of Educational Research 55*, 201–226.

Branco, A. U. (1997, July). *Perspectivas Teorico-Metodologicas no Estudo da Meta-comunicação*. Paper presented at the 26th Interamerican Congress of Psychology, São Paulo, Brazil.

Branco, A. U., Neiva, A., Ferreira, M., & Pessina, L. (1997, July). *Metacomunicaçao Entre Crianças: Estudo Microgenetico em Contexto Estruturado*. Paper presented at the 26th Interamerican Congress of Psychology, São Paulo, Brazil.

Branco, A. U., & Valsiner, J. (1997). Changing methodologies: A co-constructivist study of goal orientations in social interactions. *Psychology and Developing Societies 9*, 1, 35–64.

Bühler, K. (1927/1978). *Die Krise der Psychologie*. Frankfurt-am-Main: Ullsten (Original Published in 1927).

Cahan, E. D., & White, S. H. (1992). Proposals for a second psychology. *American Psychologist 47*, 2, 224–235.

Cazden, C. (1981) Performance before competence: Assistance to child discourse in the zone of proximal development. *The Quarterly Newsletter of the Laboratory of Comparative Human Cognition 3*, 5–8.

Cole, M. (1992). Context, modularity, and the cultural constitution of development. In L. T. Winegar & J. Valsiner (Eds.), *Children's Development within Social Context. Vol. 2. Research and Methodology* (pp. 5–31). Hillsdale, NJ: Erlbaum.

Cole, M. (1995). Culture and cognitive development: From cross-cultural research to creating systems of cultural mediation. *Culture and Psychology 1*, 1, 25–54.

Cole, M. (1996). *Cultural Psychology*. Cambridge, MA: Harvard University Press.

Danziger, K. (1990). *Reconstructing the Subject*. Cambridge, UK: Cambridge University Press.

Del Río, P., Alvarez, A., & Wertsch, J. (Eds). (1994). *Explorations in Socio-Cultural Studies. Vol. 1–4*. Madrid: Infancia y Aprendizaje.

Diriwächter, R. (2003, June). *What Really Matters: Keeping the Whole*. Paper presented at the 10th Biennial Conference of the International Society for Theoretical Psychology, Istanbul.

Engeström, Y. (1987). *Learning by Expanding*. Helsinki: Orienta-Konsultit.

Fodor, J. (1983). *Modularity of Mind*. Cambridge, MA: MIT Press.

Fogel, A., & Branco, A. U. (1997). Meta-communication as a source of indeterminism in relationship development. In A. Fogel, M. Lyra, & J. Valsiner (Eds.), *Dynamics and Indeterminism in Developmental and Social Processes*. Hillsdale, NJ: Lawrence Erlbaum Associates.

Fogel, A., Lyra, M. C. D. P., & Valsiner, J. (Eds.) (1997). *Dynamics and Indeterminism in Developmental and Social Processes*. Mahwah, NJ: Lawrence Erlbaum Associates.

Josephs, I. E. (1998). Constructing one's self in the city of the silence: Dialogue, symbols, and the role of "as-if" in self development. *Human Development 41*, 180–195.

King, C. (1988). *The Social Facilitation of Reading Comprehension*. Ph.D. dissertation, University of California, San Diego.

King, C., Griffin, P., Diaz, E., & Cole, M. (2000). *A Model System Approach to Reading*. http://lchc.ucsd.edu/Pubs/NEWTECHN.pdf.

Laboratory of Comparative Human Cognition (LCHC) (1982). A model system for the study of learning disabilities. *Quarterly Newsletter of the Laboratory of Comparative Human Cognition 4*, 39–66.

Laboratory of Comparative Human Cognition (LCHC) (1983). Culture and cognition. In P. Mussen (Ed.), *Handbook of Child Psychology*. 4th edition. Vol. 1. *History, Theory, and Methods*. New York: Wiley.

Litowitz, B. E. (1997). Just say no: Responsibility and resistance. In M. Cole, Y. Engestrom, & O. Vasquez (Eds.), *Mind, Culture, and Activity: Seminal Papers from the Laboratory of Comparative Human Cognition* (pp. 473–484). New York: Cambridge University Press.

Luria, A. R. (1932). *The Nature of Human Conflicts*. New York: Liveright.

Maciel, D. (1996). *Analise das Interacões Professora-Crianca em Situacão de Ensino-Aprendizagem da Leitura e Escrita*. Ph.D. dissertation, Institute of Education, University of São Paulo, Brazil.

Maciel, D. A., Branco, A., & Valsiner, J. (2004). Teacher-student interactions within learning contexts: Analysis of metacommunicative and constructive processes. In A. Branco, & J. Valsiner (Eds.), *Communication and Metacommunication in Human Development*. Westport, CT: Greenwood.

Miller, G. A. (1988). The challenge of universal literacy. *Science 241*, 1293–1299.

Pierre, J. (1990). Algunas reflexiones deshilvanadas sobre el encuentro de México y del surrealismo. In *El Surrealismo Entre Viejo y Nouevo Mundo* (pp. 110–117). Madrid: Ediciones El Viso.

Rogoff, B. (1990). *Apprenticeship in Thinking: Cognitive Development in Social Context*. New York: Oxford University Press.

Rommetveit, R. (1992). Outlines of a dialogically based social-cognitive approach to human cognition and communication. In A. H. Wold (Ed.), *The Dialogical Alternative: Towards a Theory of Language and Mind* (pp. 19–44). Oslo: Scandinavian University Press.

Rommetveit, R. (1998). On human beings, computers, and representational-computational versus hermeneutic-dialogical approaches to human cognition and communication. *Culture and Psychology 4*, 2, 213–233.

Scardamalia, M., & Bereiter, C. (1985). Fostering the development of self-regulation in children's knowledge processing. In S. F. Shipman, J. W. Segal, & R. Glaser (Eds.), *Thinking and Learning Skills: Research and Open Questions*. Hillsdale, NJ: Erlbaum.

Sinha, D., & Tripathi, R. C. (2001). Individualism in a collectivist culture: A case of coexistence of opposites. In A. K. Dalal & G. Misra (Eds), *New Directions in Indian Psychology. Vol. 1. Social Psychology* (pp. 241–256). New Delhi: Sage.

Snow, C. E., Burns, M. S., & Griffin, P. (Eds.). (1998). *Preventing Reading Difficulties in Young Children/Committee on the Prevention of Reading Difficulties in Young*

Children, Commission on Behavioral and Social Sciences and Education, National Research Council Committee on the Prevention of Reading Difficulties in Young Children. Washington, DC: National Academy Press.

Tashjian, D. (1995). *A Boatload of Madmen: Surrealism and the American Avant-garde, 1920–1950*. New York: Thames & Hudson.

van der Veer, R., & Valsiner, J. (1991). *Understanding Vygotsky: A Quest for Synthesis*. Oxford: Basil Blackwell.

Valsiner, J. (1987). *Culture and the Development of Children's Action*. Chichester, UK: Wiley.

Valsiner, J. (1988). *Developmental Psychology in the Soviet Union*. Brighton: Harvester.

Valsiner, J. (2000). *Culture and Human Development*. London: Sage.

Valsiner, J. (2001). *Comparative Study of Human Cultural Development*. Madrid: Fundacion Infancia y Aprendizaje.

Valsiner, J., & van der Veer, R. (1993). The encoding of distance: The concept of the zone of proximal development and its interpretations. In R. R. Cocking & K. A. Renninger (Eds.), *The Development and Meaning of Psychological Distance* (pp. 35–62). Hillsdale, NJ: Lawrence Erlbaum Associates.

Valsiner, J., & van der Veer, R. (2000). *The Social Mind: Construction of the Idea*. New York: Cambridge University Press.

Vygotsky, L. S. (1978). *Mind in Society*. Cambridge, MA: Harvard University Press.

Vygotsky, L. S. (1926/1982). Istoricheskii smysl psikhologicheskogo krizisa. In L. S. Vygotsky, *Sobranie sochinenii. Vol. 1* (pp. 291–346). Moscow: Pedagogika (Original published in 1926).

Watson, J. B. (1913). Psychology as the behaviorist views it. *Psychological Review 20*, 158–177.

White, S. (1976). Developmental psychology and Vico's concept of universal history. *Social Research 43*, 4, 659–671.

White, S. (1978). Psychology in all sorts of places. In R. A. Kasschau & F. Kessel (Eds.), *Psychology and Society: In Search of Synthesis* (pp. 103–131). New York: Holt, Rinehart, & Winston.

12 The Rise of a Right-Wing Culture among German Youth

The Effects of Social Transformation, Identity Construction, and Context

Wolfgang Edelstein

The Situation

In recent years the political discourse in Germany has been intensely affected by a growing awareness – in the media, the political elites and in some segments of the general public – of increasingly conspicuous neo-Nazi activity and rhetoric, especially racism, xenophobia, and anti-Semitism, and correspondingly motivated violence in young people in particular in the East of the country. The news media have reported demonstrative hostility toward foreigners, and, most spectacularly, brutal violence against those visibly different – mainly dark-skinned, but also homeless or even handicapped persons. As of September 15, 2000, the count numbered at least 93, probably 114, killed by mostly young right-wing thugs (aged 15–23) since the "transition" (Wende) in 1990. The number of 93 killed was acknowledged in September 2000 by the police, after two liberal newspapers (*Tagesspiegel* in Berlin and *Frankfurter Rundschau*) had contested the official record which had featured "a mere" 26 dead. The shift of attention, the timing and pattern of the phenomenon, the numbers, the distribution, and, most of all, the causes and explanations of the observed renascence of Nazi stereotypes and Nazi symbols are all objects of heated debates.

Nazi youth cultures are not a uniquely German phenomenon. Far-right-wing nationalist parties and racist groups are part of the political spectrum in various countries in Europe. They are voted into both national and local parliaments in France, Italy, and Austria; they play a recognizable role in Great Britain and Belgium. There are conspicuous neo-Nazi groups in Sweden and in the United States. Paradoxically the extreme right has played a lesser role in Germany's political system than in some other countries. Extreme right-wing parties such as the NPD (National Democratic Party) and, lately, the Republikaner (REPs) and the DVU (German People's Union) won some short-lived victories in a few provincial elections during the 1990s but have attracted little additional attention.

Since 1990, the year of the unification of Germany, right-wing activities have increased greatly, peaking in the early nineties in xenophobic pogroms. Activities peaked again in the late 1990s with intensified xenophobic as well as anti-Semitic violence, reaching an all-time high by 2000, with the police registering four times more violent incidences than in the early 1990s. According to the report of the Internal Secret Service (Verfassungsschutz) for the year 2000, there were about 16,000 offences of right-wing extremist nature including about 1,000 violent acts against political, racial, or other victims. These offences represent an increase of 60% compared to 1999. More than 50% were committed in the East German States, encompassing a mere 20% of the population. Although these numbers may appear large, it is in fact a low estimate of the real extent of right-wing incidents as it excludes the widespread assertion of a racist, xenophobic, or anti-Semitic cast of mind among adolescents in everyday life, for example, in East German schools, to mention but one important development (Spahn, 2001). Loosely coupled with the right-wing parties, radical youth groups produce their own prejudicial and violent programs and, aided by the internet, their own international networks, organizations, and channels. At present, the linkage between the radical groups and the NPD may be proceeding toward more densely knit organizational networks. The Secret Service has intensified the surveillance, and, in the wake of increased attention to neo-Nazi activities, and as a reaction to the many dead and the right-wing terror, the Federal Ministry of the Interior together with the Bundestag and the Länder Ministries of the Interior have initiated both legal steps to ban the NPD and programs to counteract right-wing extremism and neo-Nazi activity among young people.

In fact, the number of radical, subversive, and violent youth appears quite sizeable and, at least locally, especially in the East of Germany, possibly more representative of young people than is the case for the right-wing fringe groups in the United States, Britain, and Scandinavia who, located outside rather than inside the political spectrum, and organized more in the manner of fan groups or insider clubs, indulge in typically subversive and potentially violent neo-Nazi and racist activism. The violent skinhead core in Germany now is reported to number around 10,000 with connections both nationally and internationally.

Although, in the end, the NPD (or its potential successor organization) may come to benefit from the rise of an extremist youth culture and attract its protagonists into its fold, there is little evidence to show that the right-wing extremist movement is an outflow of the party or subject to its organization.

It is a different sociopolitical phenomenon and needs an explanation in its own right. Although by now there are considerable data from various population and youth surveys and a rapidly increasing literature (see Bromba & Edelstein, 2001), we are faced with rather heterogeneous theorizing about the nature and the origins of the expansion of right-wing movements and youthful right-wing activism. Theories are variously based on sociological, social psychological, developmental, personological, or psychoanalytical concepts. Perhaps a unitary theory would, at present, only offer misleading explanatory excuses for a multifaceted phenomenon. At this point we need to accept multiple narratives and a heterogeneous set of explanations. We shall explore a few of these and attempt to come to a provisional conclusion.

In the following, we shall leave aside more traditional interests in the social psychology of social movements and the more conventional concerns of political psychology. What is of interest here is the fact that, for the first time since the 1970s, we are confronted with a political youth movement, albeit politically contrary to the 1968 generation's. A youth movement calls for psychological explanations beyond the reach of conventional political accounts and the social psychology of political action, political arousal, and political affiliation. What is specifically needed is an account that does justice to the role of politics in adolescent life and development. Clearly, the developmental function of a political process cannot be a sufficient cause for a political movement taking hold among adolescents. Like any political movement, its causes must be primarily sought for among social, political, and social psychological factors and antecedents. A social movement that extends its sway over young people specifically needs developmental explanations as part of the configuration of causal factors that explain the movement's appeal to, and adoption by, the young. Thus, beyond the appeal of a political program or movement to the general or special public or groups that are sensitive to it, it is necessary to decipher the specific appeal to youth, and the specific developmental sensitivity, or vulnerability, that induces adolescents to embrace it.

Some Descriptive Data

The Shift of Attention

In Germany, one much debated question has long been whether there is a real increase in right-wing extremism and violence, or whether the saliency of this syndrome is a media-induced attention phenomenon (itself in need of a proper explanation). With the latest official police reports the issue seems now settled for Germany, with massive increases in xenophobic, anti-Semitic, and other unequivocally right-wing acts in the most recent years, and the most noteworthy increase around the turn of the millenium.

Disaffection with Politics

For quite a long time, interest in "mainstream politics" as measured by youth surveys has been limited in many European countries, spreading the notion of disaffection with politics (Roberts, 2000; for Germany see Gille & Krüger, 2000, the Shell Youth Studies 1997 and 2000, and the Max Planck Institute based BIJU study, Schnabel, 1993; Schnabel & Roeder, 1995; for Britain see White, Bruce & Ritchie, 2000; for a review see Wilkinson & Mulgan, 1995). However, disinterest in mainstream politics cannot be unequivocally equated with general depolitization. To express discontent, frustration about mainstream politics may lead to conscious, quasi active abstention from the usual political (and electoral) process and disinterest in the institutional structures that regulate modern politics – parliamentary institutions, procedures, and, in particular, parties and politicians (Boyte & Kari, 1996). However, it may also lead to engagement in NGOs or other fields of "new citizenship" (Rimmerman, 1998). Interest in politics and involvement in political action depends on issues, and interest in issues depends on group affiliation, gender, and level of education. The seeming contradiction between disengagement from politics and involvement in civic issues is mirrored by the question of "confidence" in the system. As in other European societies, confidence in political parties and politicians is low in Germany, compared to institutions like the courts, the universities, or even parliament itself (Deutsche Shell, 2000). The renaissance of right-wing activism and the revolt or rebellion among youth (Kovacheva & Wallace, 1994) may also testify to a political involvement of sorts. Right-wing extremists were found to be the most politically active group in a sample of South German high school students (Weiß, 2000, p. 173). Thus, while disaffection from political parties and politicians is widespread (probably reinforced by the recent and ongoing financial scandals involving high level politicians), the political attitudes and judgments of young people apparently do not reflect such basic and general distrust in "the system" as was prevalent in the 1920s and 1930s of the 20th century, undermining the Weimar republic and playing into the hands of its enemies (Torney-Purta et al., 2001, see also Frey & Rez, 2002). We should not, however, be oblivious to the fact that well into the past decade the West German Federal Republic was a fairweather community and that, with reunification on the one hand, and the globalization of the economy on the other, serious constraints have emerged that may indeed affect the loyalty to the system and its values. Nor should we forget that should the behaviors under scrutiny be a "tip of the iceberg" phenomenon, they will not be adequately represented in survey data.

Continuity or Cohort

The timing and pattern of the aggressively right-wing, neo-Nazi activity have, of course, much to do with the kind of interpretation it is possible to give the phenomenon. Thus, if we accept the theory that right-wing radicalism owes its emergence to the downfall of the GDR (a popular theory), it should be more or less confined to its territory and coincide with German unification. A number of cues do indeed support this interpretation. The data show much more neo-Nazi action in the East and a rise in frequency and radicalness beyond the threshold of social awareness with violent acts such as the pogroms in Hoyerswerda and Rostock-Lichtenhagen briefly after the "Transition." Some time ago it was disclosed that already in the final stage of the GDR some 1,000 violent neo-Nazi skinheads ("hooligans") were under continuous police observation and listed in a special file ("R" for rowdies). Moreover, according to State Security Service estimates, the extremist scene included an additional 15,000 violence-prone right-wingers (Wagner, personal communication, June 2002). However, the data also show continuity with the existence of violent groups in the West. In the late summer of 2001, the Ministry of the Interior estimates the neo-Nazi scene to number some 9,000 violent skinheads and a far greater number of fellow travelers.

Among the best data available to us are youth surveys of secondary-school-age adolescents in the State of Brandenburg, a cohort sequential study of 14–19 year olds with data waves in 1993, 1996, and 1999. The 1996 study is comparative, and includes the corresponding age ranges in the State of Northrhine-Westfalia (NRW) in the West (Sturzbecher, 1997, 2001).

The Brandenburg youth survey covers attitude indicators of extremist right-wing orientations, nationalism, authoritarianism, xenophobia, anti-Semitism, and proneness to violence. There is a certain variation between the indicators, with xenophobia running a high 30%–38% across the years, and a rather astonishing level of anti-Semitism (considering that there is practically no Jewish minority in the State; nor is there a sizeable presence of foreigners). The small number of foreign refugees seeking asylum are confined to hostels in small country towns. The face to face evidence of foreign presence mostly concerns a few isolated Turkish döner traders and elusive Vietnamese cigarette dealers. Anti-Semitism and xenophobia thus appear quite independent of the presence or absence of these objects of hate and aversion (see Ahlheim & Heger, 2000). They can be identified as social constructions, emerging from conditions and antecedents that we need to explore and understand better than we do at present. The surveys, of course, do little to cast the light of theory on their findings.

As already mentioned, Sturzbecher's survey has the advantage of a comparative data set: It was conducted both in Brandenburg in the East – the State with the highest incidence of neo-Nazi and xenophobic trouble – and Northrhine-Westfalia in the West – the most populous State of the Federal Republic. Generally, the constructs mentioned above are also represented in NRW, but their presence there is at a significantly lower level. Whereas, broadly speaking, in NRW the right-wing extremist syndrome in its more moderate expression may reach a level of 10% or maximally peak at 15%, in its more radical expression it peaks at 5%, with questionnaire items intensively affirmed at the level of 3%–5% of the respondents. (The Likert scales used range from rejection through moderate to complete assent.) In Brandenburg those percentages are generally twice as high, eliciting the assent of up to one-third of the corresponding high school population, including a small but significant hard core of right-wing xenophobic and anti-Semitic (potential) activists (ca. 5%), with a sizeable 25% or more of the population concurring at least moderately as potential fellow travelers. There is reason to give attention to important variations: age plays a role with numbers highest in early adolescence; gender, with males more affected than females, but the differences are smaller than one might expect. Level of schooling – in part a proxy for social class – plays a considerable role, with academic tracks less affected, and the lower as well as the vocational training tracks coming out much more radicalized than the former. The unsurprising implication is that working- and lower-middle-class youngsters are more amenable to the neo-Nazi culture than those attending the more demanding schools. The data may also imply that education matters, and that enlightenment about recent history and perhaps biology as it is taught in the preacademic schools may affect adolescents' political standards. That question is, of course, all important when it comes to strategies of counteraction and prevention. We know that local structures also play a role, although this is an underresearched area in representative samples. Anecdotal evidence and newspaper reports persistently point to the small towns in the East as a privileged breeding ground for neo-Nazi solidarities and rituals, such as drinking bouts in clubs and pubs and organized hangouts where violent action against foreigners often starts. These are places where unemployment looms large and job perspectives are bleak, where skinhead discos with "blood and honor" type music are organized, and where, to name a frequently invoked argument, noncontrolling ("accepting") social work seems to have played into the hands of radical groups taking over the youth club houses provided by local community administrations and establishing what the rightist groups call "nationally liberated zones" (Wagner, 1998).

As we try to assess the evidence about the changing face of neo-Nazi radicalism and racist and xenophobic action in Germany, the conclusion is that both the quantitative and the qualitative parameters have changed since 1990. In sum, there is more of it: The Eastern provinces of Germany are much more infected than is West Germany; actions are more brutal and at times more lethal; groups are more vociferous and more assertive; and, most remarkably of all, groups are better integrated in the local culture and, until recently at least, better protected against administrative and police reprisals by local structures, common acceptance or lethargy, and (accepting) social work. In short, in the Eastern provinces we are confronted with the emergence of a right-wing extremist *culture*, a densely woven carpet of local lifestyles and allegiances, including, to an extent, the adult generations in self-styled "nationally liberated zones." This view, until yesterday a minority view of a few highly committed activists (best represented by the Berlin-based Center of Democratic Culture of Anetta Kahane and Bernd Wagner), on September 28, 2000, became the official view when, in a great parliamentary debate, the president (speaker) of the Bundestag Wolfgang Thierse gave it authoritative expression.[1]

The generality question – continuity or cohort? – may receive a cautious answer to the effect that we are confronted by both. The cohort effect has been described as the post-transition emergence of right-wing radicalism, xenophobia, and racism in the East German provinces. As to the continuity aspect, best represented by right-wing orientations in the West, survey research in West Germany has always revealed a modicum of right-wing political attitudes and affiliations over the decades. It was, of course, quite

---

[1] The following is a fragment of Thierse's speech before the Bundestag: "We need to understand that something has changed to the worse. Among many people xenophobia has become an almost unquestioned part of their everyday consciousness. Right-wing extremism has become almost part of the culture. It makes use of a variety of cultural means to make itself understood. . . . In the past years I have traveled widely, in particular to places where right-wing acts of violence had been committed, to the centers of right-wing extremism. I had not been able to imagine the situation in these places, the extent of fear everywhere. I had no idea that young people don't dare to enter certain quarters, certain clubs. . . . There really exists what the extremists call "nationally liberated zones." We can give these a different name: Quarters and areas dominated by rightist thugs and right-wing ideologues . . . (from *Der Tagesspiegel*, September 28, 2000).

intensive at the beginning of the Federal Republic in the years after 1948, when Nazi activists and fellow travelers were being integrated into the republic framed within their own parties, even, for a time, as members of a political party (DRP) in a coalition government with the CDU under Chancellor Adenauer. There were bouts of activity of the right-wing fringe parties and right-wing activism in different parts of the country especially in the critical years 1992–1993 (see Hennig, 1994; Bromba & Edelstein, 2001). Rightist orientations and the distributions of the typical elements of neo-Nazi culture (xenophobia, anti-Semitism, racism, violence) among the secondary school population has been disclosed most recently by Sturzbecher's already cited study of a large sample of high school students in Brandenburg and Northrhine-Westfalia (Sturzbecher, 1997, 2001; Sturzbecher & Freytag, 2000). Their numbers long appeared limited, if not insignificant. They may have been contained by the tradition of political instruction and enlightenment in the schools of post–World War II Germany, a tradition designed to deal with the heritage and memory of Nazism to prevent it from "ever happening again." The political information and the enlightenment about the recent past transported by these social and political studies programs may have contributed to the relative immunity in Western Germany to right-wing radicalism for several decades. Recently, however, school programs delivering civic education have been criticized for dealing inadequately with the fading Nazi past. Another criticism frequently voiced is that political instruction places too much emphasis on the institutional structure of the political system which neither appeals to the young nor enjoys their trust (Deutsche Shell, 1997). Thus, in view of the data recently collected in the West, there appears to be reason to question the effectiveness of the program of civic education in the West today. All this, however, hardly goes beyond worrisome developments in comparable countries in the West.

Much more worrisome is the appearance, in the context of the post-transitional cohorts of adolescents raised in the Eastern provinces of Germany, of groups parading the insignia and characteristics of a vicious rebellion against a professedly tolerant culture and its values. Apparently these groups, in spite of signs of increasing organization especially in the violent skinhead scene, until recently have mostly been informal in structure, and they did not have to face rejection at the local level. This appears to be changing. The groups are becoming both more organized and more militant (Bundesministerium des Innern, 2000, 2001). The public has started to react, and so have the political institutions, but reactions will be blind and blunt unless guided by strategies that are informed by knowledge about the aims and motives of the participants. To paraphrase the titles of two well-known – and perhaps still relevant – descriptions of a previous generation, these young people appear to be both: "rebels with a cause" and "children of a great depression"; or perhaps rather children of euphoria turned into depression. To make sense of this statement we need to look beyond mere description.

Attempts at Explanation

Reasons for Theory Selection and Strategy of Argumentation

In the following, we shall briefly review a number of theoretical positions which may help account for the emergence of an adolescent neo-Nazi culture and neo-Nazi violence in Germany. Let us note in passing that none of the German theorizing seems to be much concerned with a comparative viewpoint or validation, in spite of the fact that, in part, we face an international phenomenon. This would warrant an attempt at understanding the observed behaviors in a broader than national perspective and include, for example, the Swedish skinhead scene or the American Nazi groups. Also, the emergent neo-Nazi movements in Eastern Europe warrant attention. It is obvious, however, that the specific sociocultural context will leave its mark on any movement that takes place within it. Thus, questions about structural generality and cultural specificity are justified. The same questions return on the intracultural level when probing for explanations of the differences found between East and West Germany. Why is it that the Brandenburg surveys yield frequencies of incidence both of anti-Semitism and xenophobia (and of their violent expression) that amount to double the numbers of militant right-wingers found in the Western State of Northrhine-Westfalia? Why does the Western Saarland feature the lowest number of violent incidents in all German States, although the economic future for the young in that State is certainly as bleak as anywhere in the East German States? (The latter comparison pre-empts the popular causal explanation referring to the bleak economic outlook and restricted job opportunities as a major cause of right-wing ascendancy.)

This is not the place to review all theorizing that may have relevance for the rise of a neo-Nazi culture. We propose to focus the discussion mainly on the aggregate level of collective behavior. Correspondingly, we select such approaches for the discussion that deal with aggregate changes in the shape and constitution of adolescence. In contradistinction, we shall give but minor space to psychological accounts of the growth and prevalence of individual dispositions that are more or less typical of members of extremist groups. We need to maintain the distinction between the attraction of radical groups for certain (e.g., violent) personalities and the structural or historical conditions under which such dispositions emerge with significantly increased frequency. In other words, we shall turn our attention most to such candidate theories which focus on the macro/micro interface and provide a plausible link between social structural change and personality or behavioral dispositions following from these changes.

We restrict ourselves to a small number of theoretical accounts of the emergence of youthful right-wing extremism, rebelliousness, and violence – markers of noncompliance with traditional standards of social integration:

(1) *Anomie theory* as formulated by Durkheim (e.g., 1968b) to account for the consequences of the transition from traditional to modern society is selected to account for consequences of the "second modernization" (reflexive modernization, Beck, 1992);

(2) Social-psychological *modernization* or *individualization theory* (Heitmeyer, 1997) purports to reconstruct the modernization of personality and the rise of individualism;

(3) *Identity theory* provides a developmental contribution to the explanation of a specific identity formation at a given socio-historical moment in time (Erikson, 1959, 1975); and

(4) *Theory of the authoritarian personality* (Adorno et al., 1950) has served to explain individual dispositions toward a fascist character on the basis of family dynamics in the parental family. In a revised version of Adorno's theory using attachment theory (Hopf, 1997; Hopf et al., 1995), certain types of family dynamics are taken to be accountable for the emergence of right-wing attitudes and behaviors.

All these theories may work in conjunction. The model underlying the selection of these accounts is that of macrostructural change producing, at the microlevel, departures from the socially integrated character upholding basic social and moral values. What these accounts attempt to explain, each in its own way, is the emergence of critical traits and dispositions of individuals. They describe changing social macrostructures from which vulnerable young people derive, or rather fail to derive, the moral, political, or interpersonal orientation characteristic of successful social integration. None of these theories, however, describe in sufficient detail the socialization practices that must be followed to bridge the gap between the collective (macro) structures and the individual (micro) dispositions and behaviors. Since what they seek to explain are complex social phenomena, different theories may plausibly account for different aspects, or they may all converge on a shared explanation. Situational factors (e.g., actual political issues and public debate, market forces, media effects, group cohesion, imitation) probably operate as contingent causes in conjunction with the major socio-historical ones. Specific conditions may be responsible for the maintenance and attractivity of engagements once contracted. Thus one set of mechanisms may affect the emergence and rise of violent, racist groups, and another set ensure their cohesion over time. In any event, it is unlikely that any one theory will be able to account for the phenomenology of neo-Nazi adolescent culture with its symbols and emblems, its music, its racism, its anti-Semitism, nationalism, biologism, its antihumanist cynicism, and its violence. And certainly any intercultural validity of such accounts will depend on serious efforts to analyze the social and psychological performance conditions provided by the individual cultural context. The present analyses are meant to apply first and foremost to the German scene, although the theories selected for the analyses reach beyond the German context.

The Structure of the Macro–Micro Argument

The strategy adopted in reasoning about the background changes in macro–micro relationships that are taken to be responsible for the emergence of the new right-wing movements and youth cultures may be summarized as follows: Macrosocial changes due to modernization give rise to changes in the familial and institutional bases of socialization (anomie) generating changes in the social psychology of child rearing and the ecology of child and adolescent experience (individualization processes). In the course of these macrosocial change processes, adolescent identity formation comes under the influence of a prolonged moratorium which generates increased vulnerability and a brittle structure subject to risk and fragility due to the combined effects of family history and the functional imperatives of the social moment. The family effects come to be sedimented in the frozen inheritance of early phases of the epigenetic cycle and brought to life again under the onslaught of adolescent identity crises. Unresolved conflicts about trust and autonomy are reactivated specifically in families whose internal structures are distorted by patterns of detached and disorganized attachment. The social moment is structured by the effects of globalization producing vulnerable individuals who are sensitive to the experiences of loss of control and of humiliation. These appear as a frequent corollary of a socially selective school system that produces a disproportionate number of losers. Thus, under unfavorable conditions the situation develops a propensity in certain adolescent groups to respond to the social psychological pressures of the social moment by constructing a negative identity. In stressful family settings disorganized attachment patterns may generate increased numbers of "authoritarian personalities" who are attracted to right-wing social formations. Such effects may be maintained and/or strengthened by local, social, or situational factors.

Anomie Theory

Durkheim's theory of anomie and of the moral consequences of the disintegration of traditional society may serve as the prototypical model of the structural and psychological consequences of transition between successive societal formations (see Durkheim, 1968a, 1968b, 1973). Durkheim's basic argument as developed in *The Division of Labor in Society* (1968a) and in *Suicide* (1968b) concerns the transition from a system of "mechanical solidarity" to an "organic" form of socio-moral order or "solidarity." Mechanical solidarity is characteristic of traditional society based on forms of cooperation using more or less unchanging rules and tools, accompanied by forms of traditional, mostly patriarchal authority that change little from generation to generation. Rights, correspondingly, are defined by hierarchy and status. The traditional structure of power in family, tribe, or state, the system of labor, and the moral and legal order give way, with the advent of industrial society, to a flexible, everchanging, and functional division of labor to rationalize the production system and maximize outcomes. This flexible economic and social organization forces the institutional order of society to increasing differentiation responding to functional necessities. It constitutes a new socio-moral order based on principles (from which rules can be deduced according to changing needs of application) and on individual rights, to which individuals refer, whatever the social organization of obligations imposed on, or chosen by, the individual.

The system of mechanical solidarity produces social cohesion of a tribal format, and calls for unconditional obedience toward the unquestioned validity of technical and moral rules. There is little differentiation, the rate of change is slow and gradual, and there is little effort at the assimilation of novelty. The same views of the world are held for successive generations, shared by parent and offspring, and children are socialized into the prevailing forms of labor and inherit the system of moral values whose authority is not contested. The scope and reach of individual action is limited by rituals, symbols, and hierarchically structured institutional orders; there is little place for the expression of doubt or the creation of individual lifestyles within this universe.

In contradistinction, the system of divided labor ideally requires simultaneous participation in functionally differentiated institutions that provide multiple channels for individual mobility predicated on success instead of hierarchy. The system rewards innovation not tradition, it responds to people's competences, self-reflexively learned and earned through self-regulated effort and reliance on the individual's own competence and efficacy. Thus individuals compete against each other for success and require rules and norms to adjudicate merit. An institution is needed that enables individuals to internalize both the criteria of performance and the structure of norms to regulate action so as to ascertain transindividual order in the differentiated system of individualistic competition. That institution of moral education, for Durkheim, is the school, and, more specifically, the classroom.

Durkheim's analysis identified demands on children who, under the regime of organic solidarity, must achieve the competence for successful action in the system of divided labor. It defined the design of the institution that successfully prepared children and adolescents for participation in that system. The modern school, ideally, is the outcome of designing education to match the requirements of a competitive system while maintaining maximum stability regarding the individual life course and the moral conduct of life.

Durkheim's depiction of the transition from traditional society to a social order characterized by the functional differentiation of labor and its cognitive and moral correlates needs updating to accommodate the transition from industrial to postindustrial society. The expectations of just rewards for individual effort (equitable returns for merit) and the stable patterns of individual lives assured by the system of institutions that provide for the regulation of the life course through the operation of schools with certified results, careers predicated on these results, and post-career security for the aged contributed to a more or less stable social equilibrium in which individual lives used to be sheltered in relative security. This equilibrium is threatened by the organizational features of post-industrial capitalism (the new "global economy"). The second ("reflexive") modernization unhinges the reliable relationship of individual effort, merit, and individual returns sustained by a welfare-oriented institutional order. Sennett (1999), among others, has painted an impressive picture of the organizational features and individual effects of the new type of digital capitalism, with hitherto unknown degrees of information management, strategic planning, local mobility, manpower flexibility, and self-inflicted exploitation as a prerequisite of an individual's success. Earlier institutional loyalties between employee and employer have yielded their place to a far reaching functionalization of the person in the organization of plant or office. Rewards, for the successful, tend to be high, while job security is low, which increases the temporal and spatial flexibility of the operation. Whereas, in Sennett's description, the price to be paid for hard-won rewards, especially in management and service positions, is increasing alienation in the now increasingly abstract, impersonal, and locally underdefined "workplace." The diminished activity and restricted fiscal power of the state leaves the compensation of increased risk to the individuals. But the chances and opportunities of individuals are restricted by an increasingly unhampered power of the markets, as justified by neoliberal theory.

Durkheim saw anomic suicide as a consequence of a radical disturbance of the social prerequisites of the activation of individual competence in purposeful action.[2] In this sense the acceleration and radicalization of social change and the profound change in the probabilities of individual success, happiness, and mastery of the future represent new and deep-felt threats. Perspectives involving joblessness and economic deprivation are complemented by predictions of ecological depletion of an endangered planet, and, restricting the perspective of an individually secure life course, the dwindling activity and the diminished financial power of the state predict the breakdown of the traditional system of social security.

For the competencies and personality structures called for by the world of work shaped by the new global capitalism, the present school system has not much to offer. The time-hallowed fit between school and work is being worn away, and with it the motivation of at least a segment of students of moderate ability to undergo the discipline needed to acquire the information and skills required to prepare for the certificates and credentials that grant access to apprenticeships, vocations, and careers. According to Sturzbecher's (2001) survey, up to 40% of the students in the lower tracks of secondary schools in Brandenburg judge neither school experience nor what is learned in school to be meaningful; nor do they trust their teachers to side with them or to act fairly in situations of difficulty or conflict. School provides them with an alienating double message: relentless pressure for achievement coupled with the subjective failure to attach meaning to what is being learned in a compulsory system with few open choices.[3] Beyond these subjective experiences looms an increasingly vague and abstract, potentially deterritorialized

---

[2] There is reason, after September 11, 2001 and faced by the suicide actors of the Palestinian intifadeh in 2002, to distinguish between the anomic suicide analyzed by Durkheim (see also Seligman, 1975, for a psychological account of hopelessness and death) and the purposefully activist suicide of the rebel whose murderous action appears to be a signal of revenge for collective humiliation. Both types of suicide, however, derive from perceptions of anomie.

[3] Note that the German secondary school system offers students fewer choices to select courses and fewer elective options than does the American system.

and inaccessible political system from which the media carry highly sim-
plified news that in turn highlight crisis, helplessness, hostility, and – with
increasing frequency – corruption. Many young people are abandoned by the
schools to their feelings of inferiority and humiliation and the rivalry and
hatred of potential competitors, especially strangers allegedly competing for
scarce jobs and the resources of the welfare system. Social and racial devaluation of the stranger in conjunction with a compensatory conception of racial
and national superiority offer themselves as strategies for maintaining self-
respect. Thus victims of the "second modernization" create their own victims –
outcasts with even lower status. Humiliation and deprivation of perspective
subvert the normative structure of mutual respect and recognition that constitutes the member of society perspective. Anomie and moral deprivation go
hand-in-hand (Edelstein, 1995, 2000; Krettenauer, 1998).

Modernization and the Rise of Individualism

A number of influential scholars have taken up Durkheim's theoretical motif
of sociomoral disintegration as a consequence of societal change, but given
it a specific modernistic twist. For Durkheim, the dissolution of collective
mentalities follows the emergence of division of labor in society, to be recon-
stituted as the morality of individuals through education; for these authors it
is the corrosion of institutional bonds or "ligatures" (Dahrendorf) that gives
rise to a new individualism with its various concomitant risks (Beck, 1992;
Beck & Beck-Gernsheim, 1993; Giddens, 1991). In a regime of weak institutions in a "society at risk" (Risikogesellschaft; Beck, 1992) the generation
shift and the socialization of the young generation constitutes a specific danger
zone. In Germany, Wilhelm Heitmeyer and his colleagues have devoted their
much cited work to this topic, and analyzed the rise of adolescent right-wing
extremism and violence as a consequence, or as an expression, of the dissolution of traditional milieus and the corrosion of inherited institutional linkages
and loyalties (Heitmeyer, 1997, 1999; Heitmeyer & Olk, 1990; Heitmeyer
et al., 1992, 1995). The central tenet of Heitmeyer's theory of individualization is that it leads to the disintegration of the collectively recognized
normative order through increasing competition and, as a consequence, to the
relative deprivation and alienation of the modernization losers. As in all conceptions that explain social change by changing macro–micro relationships,
the family, as the institution providing the link between generations, is taken
to be a major agency of social integration and, failing that, of disintegration.
Thus, the major locus of disintegration in Heitmeyer's theory is the family,
where reciprocal bonds tend to dissolve under the onslaught of market-driven

individualistic needs and interests of the individuals composing it. The dissolution of the family is double-tiered: changing form (or structure) and emotional disintegration. The change in form is borne out by data on divorce (approaching, in Germany, one marriage out of two), number of children per marriage (a number well below the reproduction rate), and the increasing number of singles, to name but a few indicators. Emotional disintegration is revealed by the increasing structural deformation of bonds, i.e., by instrumentalistic forms of interaction, expressed by laisse-faire emotional distance instead of the mutual recognition that is the essence of reciprocity. The consequences are aggravated by increasing education-related delay of autonomy and economic independence extended beyond the traditional moratorium needed for the formation of identity. The effect is increased dependency on an increasingly flawed system. The intrinsic dynamic of the system thus produces increasing discrepancy between the organizational principles of the family and those of the society, with growing tension between the principles of personal bonding and accepting relationships on the one side, and the structure of competition on the other. Competition, according to Heitmeyer, appears under various guises: the competitive nature of performance, both in the school and on the market; the competitive function of the adoption and recognition of lifestyles; and the competitive conditions of access to the increasingly identity-defining leisure markets (see Heitmeyer et al., 1995, p. 53). More and more, individuals have to sustain this dynamic on their own, deprived of the supports which the weakened institutions were formerly able to provide. Thus, with the developing modernization of socio-economic forces, individuals are exposed to the ever intensified dynamic of the individualizing dialectic.

Figure 12.1, from Nunner-Winkler (1996), graphically illustrates Heitmeyer's explanatory model of the emergence of violence-proneness in youth, with violence representing the tip-of-the-iceberg phenomenon of adolescent disaffection. Heitmeyer and his colleagues have used the same basic explanatory model for analyzing the various outcomes that interest us in similar fashion in successive publications: right-wing radicalism; political disaffection and Machiavellism; and violence (Heitmeyer et al., 1992, 1995).

Heitmeyer's predictions have not always been borne out empirically in the way he has designed the relation between family variables and incidence of adolescent deviance (political disaffection, ideology of inequality, right-wing extremism, and violence), and he has been widely criticized (see Heitmeyer et al., 1992; Nunner-Winkler, 1996; Tonn, 1998; and the various critiques of individualization theory in Friedrichs, 1998). This theory should not be understood as a predictive theory forecasting the state of certain individual variables.

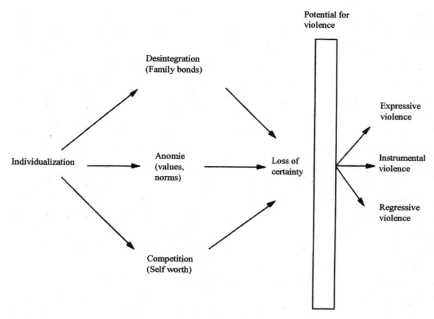

Figure 12.1. *Source:* after Nunner-Winkler, 1996, p. 406; see Heitmeyer et al., 1995, pp. 31–82, 410–420.

Rather, it should be viewed as a systemic description of the transition between generations under the pressure of modernization, deinstitutionalization, and individualization. Elements that typify the "corrosion of ligatures" characteristic of the individualization climate of modernization interact strongly with each other, thus providing positive feedback to the corrosive force of these elements. The consequence, both observed and anticipated, is a sudden change of the state of the social system. The strength of the theory, taking a Durkheimian conceptualization of anomie a step beyond Durkheim, should be seen in a convincing reconstruction of the social psychology of anomie as generated in certain types of modern families and modern institutions. It could be strengthened by adding a conception of social causality, in which strong interaction of elements within a system brings about sudden change in the system.

Identity Theory

Erik H. Erikson created the classical theory of identity formation across the lifespan in the context of historical change (Erikson, 1959, 1975). In this theory, ego identity is a feeling of trust in the reliable unity and continuity of the self, mirrored by supportive others – a feeling that provides strength and motivation for action in the present, and hope and perspective for action in the future. Basically, therefore, ego identity represents a positive cathexis of the self together with an adequate perception of and involvement in social reality (e.g., 1959, p. 94).

However, the normative process of identification both with available models and with a future enabling the person to develop a vision of a meaningful and constructive biographical project can be thwarted and turned into flawed or even negatively charged versions of the project. On the basis of clinical data, Erikson has described modalities of the family dynamic that lead to disturbances of identity formation in individuals at various levels or stages of the process.

The construction of a viable identity generally requires successful resolution of the major conflicts dominating earlier phases in childhood (trust versus mistrust in early childhood, autonomy versus shame and doubt in the toddler or play years, initiative versus guilt in the conscience-building preschool years, industry versus inferiority in the school years). Successful resolution of the conflict is followed by integration of the strengths and gains achieved in these phases with the help of supportive structures in families, preschools, and schools. But adolescence is a particularly vulnerable phase in the life cycle, and particularly dependent on the social forces, structures, and institutions in which it is embedded. Erikson has shown how a destructive family dynamic, such as an authoritarian and repressive relationship between father and son, may threaten the process of orthogenetic identity formation and put the son at risk of identity diffusion or disintegration or identification with the aggressor (Erikson, 1959, ch. 1). In his description, Erikson places the individual case expressly in the context of historical change, bringing the psychodynamic origins of the son's anti-authoritarian rebellion into the socio-historical and political focus of the present. Thus the clinically identifiable individual process serves as the base for a generalization to the socio-historic dynamic, where a group may provide an identity to its members by negatively cathecting the characteristics of a rejected ethnic group or social class and the individuals that compose it.

As adolescence sets the stage for the development of a personal identity and for a person's integration into groups that provide strength to the ego; and as adolescence, due to cognitive, social cognitive, and moral potentials, plays a decisive role in the development of a person's ideological perspective on self and society (i.e., for an answer to the questions, "Who am I?" and "Where do I belong?"), it obviously depends more than earlier phases of identity development on the social context in which a person is immersed. Beyond the family system and classroom peers who constitute the support systems and the experiential backdrop for the growth of trust, autonomy, initiative, and to an extent skillful action, the social groups, political organizations, ideological movements, and socio-historical formations that contribute one way or the other to the answer now increasingly claim their right of place. More than before, then, in adolescence a person's process of identity formation is increasingly affected, and sometimes torn, by the vectors that dominate the macro–micro interface.

Collective Identity

In the collection of essays *Life History and the Historical Moment*, Erikson (1975) published an essay on the process of collective identity formation of the protest generation of the 1960s and 1970s. The process is defined as "a critical phase marked by the reciprocal aggravation of internal conflict and of societal disorganization" (p. 195) and thus highlights the quality of macro–micro interaction. Erikson describes the changed material, social, and cultural context of the new generation, its intellectual and experiential ecology, the conditions of a new historical consciousness, a youthful awareness colored by the cognitive egocentrism that is constitutive of adolescent ideological thought ("a continuation of an egocentric narcissistic orientation determined to adapt the world to itself and a devotion to idealistic and altruistic schemes and codes, whether or not their feasibility can be proved or disproved" (p. 204). Erikson labels this adolescent mode of thinking as the "all or nothing *totalistic* (author's italics) quality of adolescence, which permits many young people to invest their loyalty in simplistically overdefined ideologies" (ibid).

The formation of identity feeds on the remains of earlier conflicts that constitute the milestones of the epigenetic sequence: conflicts about trust and mistrust, the place and power of the will, the scope of and confidence in the subjects' skill, the recognition of individual achievement. The individual equilibrium thus represents a synthesis of regressive and progressive moments from the preceding phases of the life cycle. In a cohort, these moments resonate in various and biographically specific ways with the collective motifs that express that generation's identity or social program.

In the 1960s and 1970s this program, as represented in the minds and actions of the protest generation's leadership expresses mistrust in the prevailing academic and political elites, autonomy, will, and readiness for action. Although, as in all cohorts and social movements, the collective motif is unequally represented by the participating individuals, depending on their individual psychological heritage that extends from activism and leadership to the silent acquiescence of mere fellow travelers, a feeling of collective membership and shared values is sufficient to confer legitimacy on individual judgment and action, whether in fact it is premoral, amoral, antimoral, or moral (1975, p. 207).

Negative Identity

Erikson's analysis dealt with the "humanistic protest movement" of the 1960s and 1970s that pursued progressive goals of liberation and social justice. But the terms of his theory are not limited to the analysis of "positive" group identity. An important part of his work was devoted to the clarification of identity diffusion – the psychodynamic, developmental, and social conditions that prevent, impair, or delay a positive resolution of inner conflicts that is conducive to a healthy or equilibrated identity. In his 1968 publication *Identity, Youth, and Crisis*, Erikson provides a clinical account of the structures and origins of identity diffusion as a semipathological state originating in a more or less severe regression which produces a developmental crisis in adolescence. As with the positive contributions of conflict resolutions occurring in the pre-adolescent phases of the epigenetic sequence, unresolved conflicts contribute, singly or cumulatively, to the pathography of adolescent failure to develop a stable identity, generating some variety of identity diffusion instead: negative reciprocity, based in early mistrust, guilt and weakness, anger, work paralysis, and depression.

These phenomena may lead to the choice of a negative identity – antagonistically cathecting precisely those reference persons and attributes that the ego fears most intensively to be identified with. The adolescent thus replaces the weak and ambivalent parent by a cruel and basically desperate self, a threatening exposure to a significant other's exercise of will by an excess of obedience and deference to leadership, the overwhelming pressure for activity by passive submission, and the taxing expectations of achievement by either inability to work or criminally offensive acts and norm violations. Transferring these events from the private to the public space, exclusion from normal sociability, affiliation with criminal gangs, absorption into authoritarian group structures, or the adoption of racist ideologies may provide the negative substitute for an integrated identity.

The question then arises whether "a critical phase marked by a reciprocal aggravation of internal conflict and societal organization" (Erikson, 1975, p. 195) can be identified that may provide an opportunity for an antiprogressive right-wing movement of youthful rebels to emerge in parts of German society beset by specific socio-historical vulnerabilities. We are speaking of East Germany after the downfall of socialism.

Rise of a Culture of Negative Group Identity

The pivotal concept defining a social role for a youthful cohort is spelled out by Erikson (1968): "The dominant issue ... is the assurance that the active, the selective, ego is in charge and enabled to be in charge by a social structure which grants a given age group the place it needs – and in which it is needed" (p. 246). What happens when the social situation subverts this vital condition?

As will be shown in greater detail below, following unification, for a substantive segment of the East German population, including a sizeable portion of the young generation, the outlook was anything but rosy. The expectable overthrow of the political elite had the less expected consequence of widespread, at least temporary, unemployment among the better educated who were held responsible for the practices of a police state. Similarly the bankruptcy of the erstwhile socialist economy led to extensive unemployment. This was a new and humiliating experience in many families, for mothers no less than fathers, the former being the most affected victims of the political upheavals in a country with the world's most extensive female participation in the labor force. Glen Elder, in his *Children of the Great Depression* (1974), has shown how the experience of parents' losing their employment affects their adolescent children, an experience shown to have lifelong consequences (Elder & Caspi, 1988). The teaching force was purged of its communist cadres, another authority group to suffer a humiliation witnessed by the young. All youth organizations were dissolved immediately. Although instrumentalized by the regime, these had given adolescents representative functions and opportunities for action and for leadership and now left an unfilled void. A school system planned for full employment and academic equality was unhesitatingly replaced by a system modelled after the socially selective system of the West German provinces. This led to extended disaffection among less successful students now in the lower academic tracks with little hope for apprenticeships and jobs in a crisis ridden economy. Often the consequence was an exodus, to the West, of the better qualified youth, leaving the less qualified behind without perspective in the abandoned industrial strongholds of the former planned economy. Thus, the former state and its failed socialist system became the object of shaming and devaluation and with it the biographies of those who had been responsible for running it, and were loyal to it and dependent on it. Contrary to expectation the "takeover by the West" did not produce the "flowering regions" promised by chancellor Kohl, but, compared to the West, higher rates of unemployment, lower wages and pensions, fewer economic opportunities, and a breakdown of the birth rate with long-ranging consequences for the social and educational perspectives of the entire country.

"Youth . . . is sensitive to any suggestion that it may be hopelessly determined by what went before in life histories or in history" (Erikson, 1968, p. 247). One may understand that a situation of humiliation witnessed or experienced, of opportunities unattained or foregone, of perspectives dimmed or reserved for others causes anger and resentment among those most affected by or sensitive to the threat of foreclosure of the future. Whereas the corresponding affect is often turned against those who, according to the terrible simplifications of the populists, benefit most from an allegedly unfair distribution of welfare (e.g., refugees, Jews, the handicapped), positive cathexis rebelliously targets those who both the past socialist regime and the present capitalist society unanimously identify as objects of moral and political shame and collective guilt. For example, the rebels refuse to share the public denial that is the essence of civil consensus about Germany's Nazi past. Thus what has been rejected and forbidden returns as the object of identification: the concept of the nation and chauvinistic national sentiment (against the foreigners who allegedly exploit the nation and appropriate for themselves the job opportunities illegitimately withheld); the Nazis who, according to the shared mythology, restored the pride of place to a dispossessed people; feelings and acts of violence and defiance, symbols and behaviors that confront and negate the humiliation, exclusion, and hopelessness to which they are themselves exposed. Neo-Nazi identification, anti-Semitism, and xenophobia have become the hallmark, in the German East, of the ideology of a sizeable group of dispossessed and disaffected young people who draw strength, if not comfort, from a posture of rebellion and nonalignment with the majority culture. This posture was taken, with contrary intentions by the protesters of the 1970s, and, if we may believe the testimony of Anna Seghers (1977), the fascist youth of the 1920s, and perhaps, albeit with a different justification, the suicide squads of the Palestinian Jihadis. What seems to be common to them all is a vengeful purpose: after an experience of weakness, loss of control, and deprivation of meaning, individual or collective, direct or vicarious, to obtain control over their lives and give it meaning (Skinner, 1996; Frey & Rez, 2002). This is, after all, the basic developmental function of the formation of identity in youth – a process failed at the cost of confusion, and sometimes depression and death, and sometimes won at the cost of one's life.

Authoritarian Personality and Attachment Style

Whereas Durkheim's theory of anomie focused on the sociology of collective mentalities, Heitmeyer formulated a genetic social psychology of anomie responding to Beck's theory of the rise of individualism in an at-risk society with weak institutional bonds. These theories articulate the background for an emerging identity crisis in certain groups of young people, whose family histories corroborate and strengthen the background effects. Increasingly frequent encounters with young right-wing extremists, who seemed to evidence the character dispositions described in Adorno et al.'s (1950) theory of the authoritarian personality, caused Hopf and her co-workers (Hopf 1997, Hopf et al. 1995, 1999) to return to Adorno's (1950) account of the mechanisms that generate the authoritarian personality of right-wing extremists. However, Hopf and her co-authors propose to modify Adorno's Freudian conceptualization of authoritarian submission, authoritarian aggression, and authoritarian conventionalism which he found to be characteristic of the fascist personality type. To Hopf the characteristic of aggressively right-wing adolescents today is *authoritarian dominance*, the aggressive superiority that is typical of ethnocentric contempt for others, whether Jews, foreigners, or other disempowered persons; and *anxious and submissive authoritarianism* that is characteristic of the typical followers and fellow travelers of extremist leadership.

Hopf's innovative contribution to Adorno's theory consists in a modification or substitution of the central mechanism of parent idealization, which according to Adorno is mainly responsible for the development of the authoritarian personality. Hopf proposes attachment theory (Bowlby, 1969), as it has been developed beyond Bowlby toward a theory of adult attachment (e.g., Main & Goldwyn, 1994), in order to explain the essential cathectic processes that lead to the authoritarian, ethnocentric, and aggressive dispositions of the extremist individual. To account for the psychodynamic origin of authoritarian extremism, Hopf proposes to add to the repertoire of attachment already established in attachment theory (secure, anxious-insecure, ambivalent-insecure, disorganized-insecure) the process of *detachment*, a dismissive–defensive pattern of attachment. Detached individuals disactivate their feelings and experiences with parents by repressing their memories of painful, provocative, or shaming interactions with them, by devaluation of the experience and derogation of the individuals.

This pattern places the detached individual in stark contrast to the securely attached person who is able to freely evaluate even hostile or critical relationships with the parents. Hopf found a rather close correlation between the denial of problems with parents as represented by the detached pattern of attachment and right-wing extremist attitudes including authoritarian dominance and ethnocentric aggression.

In an overview of studies of attachment and antisocial behavior, Van Ijzendoorn (1997) corroborated the relationship between a detached pattern of attachment, authoritarianism, (low) morality, and criminal behavior in adolescence and young adulthood. Similar to Hopf (Hopf et al., 1995), Van Ijzendoorn (1995), in a study of Californian undergraduates, found "dismissing" subjects to score highest on the scale of authoritarian attitudes. Attachment in this study was measured with the Adult Attachment Interview (Hesse & Van Ijzendoorn, 1997), and authoritarian attitude with the Altemeyer Inventory of Authoritarian Attitudes (1988). Insecure children, the authors conclude, have unfulfilled needs for basic trust. As a consequence, they fail to develop genuine trust and empathic concerns for others. This deficit matches Erikson's first phase of unresolved crisis in the epigenetic cycle. In serious cases, moral reasoning is absent, aggression is intensive, and deviant behavior frequent (see Van Ijzendoorn, 1997, p. 721ff). This matches Erikson's second phase, unresolved crisis of autonomy and the will. The psychological mechanism of detachment identified by Hopf at the base of authoritarian idealization (identification) would define operationally the input from family history to adolescent identity crisis, and especially the choice of negative identity. This may contribute toward explaining the uncanny violence and absence of empathy with the victims found among neo-Nazi persecutors of ethnic strangers, homeless people, and other outsiders who have been brutally kicked to death by adolescent right-wing thugs devoid of feelings of empathy or compassion.

Why should adolescents in the East of Germany be so much more prone to aggressive authoritarianism than those from the West, as the survey data show them to be? To explore the reasons, Hopf and her co-authors engaged in a subtle analysis of the social psychology of the pre- and post-transition GDR. The major thrust of their analysis is that, rather than insecurity grounded in loss of orientation due to the modernization of a conservative system (Heitmeyer's general model), the widespread hostility to strangers, even in the former GDR[4], can be traced back to the security needs and the quest for authority and guidance that appears deeply rooted in the personalities of East German xenophobes. These personality dispositions, according to Hopf et al. (1999), developed as a response to the conventionalist and conformist, rule-oriented

---

[4] In a 1990 survey of the German Youth Institute (DJI) 42% of the East German adolescent sample declared their hostility to foreigners, as against 26% of the West German adolescents.

and frequently loveless institutionalized child rearing and socialization system in the GDR, where children of working mothers – remember that most East German women were in the work force – were placed in crêches even at very young ages. Kindergartens and preschools and other full-day institutions followed. Often rearing habits in these institutions were strict and authoritarian. Experiences of early separation from parents and lack of emotional support and nuturing must have been quite frequent. Conversely, the dominant model of a happy socialist childhood was intolerant of the expression of negative moods, anger, or depressive feelings, and complaints and tantrums were suppressed. As early as 1970, an East German psychiatrist apparently identified an emotional block or inhibition ("Gefühlsstau") that could lead to aggressive or violent discharge against underdogs or strangers, once social control broke down or opportunities for venting anger arose (Maaz, 1990, 1993). To sum up, public institutions may have taken over parental functions including conflictual ones in early childhood; children in the GDR reportedly suffered more from emotional stress and repression than did children in the West; a consequence of their collective psychological heritage was the development of more vulnerable personalities (Hopf et al., 1999, pp. 84–96). The structural analogy to the lifespan effects on vulnerable children of the Great Depression is quite striking (Elder, 1974; Elder & Caspi, 1988). Consequently, with the experience of the GDR gradually running out, in the generation coming of age after the turn of the millennium this particular conflict ought to lose its force presently unless other causes and conditions ensure its continued existence.

Some Conclusions

Durkheim accentuated the function of a reliable social order for the moral stabilization of the individual. For him, the disruption of the social order in the upheavals of modernization, with the advent of industrial capitalism and its regime of divided labor and flexible institutions, made necessary a new internalized cognitive and moral competence to process the relativity and abstractness of experience and the growth and change of social reality on which experience hinges. He did not, as we do today, recognize the role that the anticipation of the future plays in the stabilization of the moral order. Major disruptions of modernization in the age of globalization are due to the threats of a future that may get out of control. No group is more vulnerable to the promises, and conversely to the threats, of the future than the adolescents who depend on its opportunities for the realization of their hopes and potentials. Conversely, no group is more amenable to anomie in the face of disorder than adolescents whose lives have not yet crystallized in the institutional patterns that society provides for the adult life course. They are doubly sensitive to disruptions that affect both the present and the future.

While Durkheim's theory sharpens our perception of the collective vulner-abilities of adolescence due to the havoc played by diminished expectations and increased insecurity in the present and future, Beck's and Heitmeyer's accounts of risk and dissolution of institutional bonds depict the more imme-diate conditions under which vulnerable individuals have to labor. The secular ascendance of individualism serves, in Heitmeyer's theory, as a backdrop for an increasing number of instrumentalistic and disaggregative families that raise egoistic, potentially extremist, and violent offspring. Following the lead of Durkheim's theory, the anomie due to the disruption of traditional patterns and institutionalizations of solidarity ("the corrosion of ligatures" described by Krettenauer, 1998) exposes adolescence to the experience of a puzzling "pluralization of options" together with a disenchanting threat of failure under the duress of individualistic competition. Erikson's theory of the adolescent identity process reconstructs the developmental conditions and inner struc-tures of adolescent vulnerability and socio-historic conflict converging in a collective crisis. To complement this account, a study of the authoritarian character in adolescents discloses the type of family relationships and repre-sentations (i.e., the patterns of detachment) that, given the secular trend and the socio-cultural situation, appear to catalyze the rise of right-wing extrem-ism, both aggressive and active and submissive and passive.

Is there a "best fit" between the phenomena and the explanatory concepts? All four theories represent plausible approaches and none contradicts the other. In effect, however, their points of attack are differentially appropriate to different aspects of the problem.

Individualization theory with its emphasis on the transformation of the family and the long-term increase of anomic loss of trust and lack of faith in the future among the losers of the modernization race has a better fit with the situation in the old Federal Republic. Perhaps other consolidated postindus-trial societies of the West, to an increasing extent, face the effects of rapid social and economic transformation and the concomitant corrosion of tradi-tion, of patterns of institutional loyalties, and of the validity claims of subjec-tively binding moral rules. There are reasons to assume that the cumulative impact of these developments may have breakthrough effects on vulnerable adolescents.

Vulnerability may be spurred by socialization in family systems that exhibit certain patterns of attachment relationships, which, under different socio-cultural conditions might have generated nonpolitical types of delinquency

(Hirschi, 1969; Sykes & Matza, 1957), as they certainly continue to do. These are families that tend to foster instrumentalistic types of relationships, coupled with strongly hedonistic needs and violence-prone behavioral strategies of self-assertion that defy integration into any socio-moral order beyond mere conventionalism. Vulnerability may also be spurred by an experience of school that combines the pressure of competition with the deprivation of meaning of curricular content.

For vulnerable individuals and groups, alienation may lead to outrage, cynicism, rebelliousness, and violent rejection of the normative expectation that others (the adult world, the representatives of society) hold for them. Action competence and self-efficacy needs may turn for satisfaction to destructive action and physical violence. Disempowerment and feelings of powerlessness, emptiness, and hopelessness may seek compensation and relief in short-lived bouts of action that turn everyone's attention on them and grant them delusions of grandeur for a while. It may lead to an amenability to ideological constructions that compensate for feelings of inferiority, seduce individuals to seek support and protection in authoritarian groups or organizations that provide a feeling of strength, and promote the adoption of racist ideologies that provide an illusion of superiority. Although we tend to think of those products of adolescent anomie that frighten and annoy us most, because they interfere disruptively with our lives and our plans, Durkheim was more concerned with the inability to live without a stable moral order. We need to extend our concern to those adolescents who respond to the moral disorder of society by hopelessness, depression, and death (Seligman, 1975). Durkheim saw them as the true victims of anomie. Perhaps more inconspicuous but hardly less worrisome than the right-wing rebels, kids suffering with depression populate the schools by the thousands.

The notion of increasing anomie among adolescents seems to fit rather well the socio-cultural situation prevailing in the East European societies and in East Germany. The former communist societies have experienced a sudden breakdown of their social and institutional order, a general devaluation of previously dominant values, among which social solidarity ranked high. Moreover, the former citizens of these states have experienced large-scale disruption of the pattern of individual lives, including the reliabilities and securities that used to protect people's lives from poverty, risk, and threats to health and survival. Everyday loyalties and trust have been jeopardized by the questioning of more or less everyone's past relationships through the disclosure of the previous regime of social and police control. These societies are characterized by the downfall of the former elites who had competed for recognition in deference to a system of criteria and assessments now rejected as unjust or dysfunctional, or both. This did away with large segments of the former academic, managerial, and political elites. An effective economic takeover by new stakeholders swiftly eliminated the previous economic system together with its protagonists.

In East Germany, and elsewhere, many parents were devalued as authorities, many fathers, and even more mothers, lost their jobs. Many teachers were eliminated for their former allegiances and loyalties. The youth organizations with their leisure activities and support systems vanished from the scene, and the internal opposition, the former dissidents, mostly disappeared in the upheavals of the transition. Unprepared after half a century of stagnation and after decades of enforcement of an authoritarian, but all things considered, widely shared political order, a deep experience of discontinuity must have produced what, to a Durkheimian view of the world, looks like anomic disruption.

Under the title "Die Quittung" ("the penalty") Franziska Augstein, in the reputed conservative newspaper *Frankfurter Allgemeine Zeitung*, described the inner relation between unification and neo-Nazi actionism (September 16, 2000). She placed her diatribe under the telling heading "the humiliated East":

> We should not be surprised at the expansion of right-wing radicalism. In their great majority, the citizens of the GDR were systematically humiliated after 1989. Not everybody is compromised politically, but almost everyone has made the experience of being cheated one way or other by the West. For 10 years East Germans have labored under the need to boost their egos, confronted with an image of dumb inferiority compared to the competent and clever West Germans. It is not adolescent unemployment that is the source of right-wing radicalism in the Eastern provinces, but the diminution experienced due to the unemployment of the parents, their loss of orientation, their resentment, the fact that they can raise no claim to the exercise of authority. An adolescent who observes that parents are deprived of dignity will look for other models and standards for his orientation. Surreptitiously, the parents approve of the misdeeds of their children.

What we have here is a description of relative deprivation as a product of the transgenerational process of anomie consecutive to the breakdown of the established social and social psychological order. Years ago the novelist Anna Seghers wrote a powerful reconstruction of the interlocking processes of collective and individual deprivation: The story of Fritz Müller's biographical trajectory through his post–World War I childhood, school experience, through his cohort's experience of unemployment and absorption into the brutal Nazi trooper organization and, finally, into the moral deprivation in Hitler's legions. No scientific description could provide a more vivid, comprehensive, and precise account of the structural constraints and biographical predicaments of a Nazi career: *Ein Mensch wird Nazi* (*A Person Turns Nazi*, Seghers, 1977).

Long Processes and Situational Factors

We have pleaded the case of interlocking systemic reasons for the rise and prevalence of right-wing extremism. There is "the long process" of reflexive modernization (Beck): individualization and dissolution of institutional stability in the West. There is the sudden post-unification breakdown in East Germany. There are the semi-universal processes of identity formation in adolescents, that, under inauspicious conditions, both historical and individual, may lead to the constitution of negative identities, and their rise to collective cultural dominance. And there are the specific family histories of authoritarian personalities active in response to opportunity structures in both social systems in Germany. As mentioned earlier, Erikson's notion of the historical moment points to the fact that processes of long duration in conjunction with the socio-cultural situation in a given present affect the vulnerabilities and motivational sensitivities of families and individuals. These causal chains generate probabilities not determinations. Individuals who might be affected are exempt, because they benefit from (social or psychological) protective factors and mechanisms. Others, vulnerable in spite of beneficial backgrounds, fall prey to a barbarous commitment: the historical moment is populated by catalytic forces that have not been mentioned yet. Whereas an entire society – but not every individual – is affected by the operation of long-term structural change, and similarly a sudden social breakdown may affect an entire cohort – but not all its members – both the change and the sudden breakdown influence individuals differentially as a function of their vulnerabilities. To gain a better understanding of these differential vulnerabilities it seems necessary to describe briefly a number of factors of limited reach that exert a collateral influence on the emergence or the crystallizing of right-wing attitudes and personality dispositions in the present socio-cultural situation.

Social Class and Situational Factors

Augstein (2000) in her piece about the humiliation of East Germans after the reunification contends that neo-Nazism is not a cause fought by the underprivileged. It has indeed been pointed out by various authors (e.g., Willems, Eckert et al., 1993) that often radical right-wing activists do have jobs or apprenticeships, normal families, and a vocational future. Augstein's point is that it is not absolute (economic) but relative (psychological) deprivation

Table 12.1. *Ethnocentrism/Xenophobia by Social Class in Percent*

	Ethnocentrism Index (High / Medium / Low)							
	High	Medium	Low	All[1]	High	Medium	Low	All[1]
Parent's SES	West Germany				East Germany			
Low	17.6	54.9	27.5	10.6	31.3	49.1	19.6	33.9
Middle	12.1	55.9	32.0	71.5	21.9	49.6	28.4	35.7
High	6.2	41.9	51.9	17.9	13.3	47.9	38.8	30.4
	11.7	53.3	35.1	100	22.5	48.9	28.6	100

[1] Percentage of SES group in total population from Hopf, 1994.

of humiliated East Germans that is causally effective in the rise of the right. As we have seen, much is to be said for this point. Yet, it must not be taken too far. Other data do disclose how the extremist syndrome, especially in its xenophobic and anti-Semitic versions is indeed typical among the underprivileged. Sturzbecher (1997, 2001; Sturzbecher & Freytag, 2000) has shown that extremist attitudes, xenophobia, and anti-Semitism is much more frequent in the lower tracks of secondary schools and in vocational schools than in preacademic tracks, both in Brandenburg (East) and in Northrhine-Westfalia (West), although twice as frequent in the East than in the West. W. Hopf (1994) has given the relation between ethnocentrism and socio-economic inequality special attention and demonstrated that, notwithstanding explanations derived from anomie, modernization and individualization theory, or from family socialization, the data show a significant contribution of social class, and thus highlight a significant part played in the process by socio-economic inequality. Using the example of ethnocentrism, the distribution across social classes for East Germany shows that xenophobia nearly doubles the frequencies in the West. With increasing status, the number of those *low* on the variable increases and of those *high* on the variable decreases, although less so in the East. Conversely, the table shows that extreme ethnocentric attitudes increase with descending class position. (See Table 12.1.)

Ethnocentrism

Xenophobia, ethnocentrism, and hate of strangers are indicators of a rightist mentality; presumably ethnocentrism constitutes the mental set within which extremist positions thrive. It has often been said that the extremist movement, with its characteristic hate of strangers, its anti-Semitism, authoritarian and nationalist orientations, and, in the extreme case, racist violence, "originates in the midst of society." Hopf's data disclose a surprising extent of at least "moderate" ethnocentrism also in the middle and upper classes which testi-fies to the truth of this assertion. Recently the government of the province of Sachsen-Anhalt (in East Germany) released a youth report corroborating that more than one third of the adolescents in the province harbor hostile feelings toward strangers. Similarly, in the IEA Civics Study just released German secondary school students (eighth graders) figure as the most hostile to foreigners of all the 28 school populations studied (Torney-Purta et al., 2001). These disheartening data are clearly in need of different or at least supplementary explanatory models than those provided by absolute or relative deprivation, anomie, or a disturbing family dynamic. All of these appear more appropriate to a tip of the iceberg than to a mainstream phenomenon. Whereas the former seems to indicate specific vulnerabilities that respond to disequilibrating processes, the latter needs explanations "from the midst of society."

What could be the nature of such explanations? There is, at present, no solid research base from which conclusions could be derived. Some conjectures may be justified, however. Various experts have argued that in the early 1990s the campaign of the Christian Democratic Party (CDU, the conservatives) aiming at the curtailment of the constitutional right to asylum for political refugees has biased the political climate against tolerance for foreigners in the country (Ahlheim & Heger, 2000; Butterwegge, 1995, 2001; Tonn, 1998). In fact, the refugees seeking asylum in the country by appeal to the constitutional right of refuge (established after World War II as a response to Nazi persecution of minorities) have long been accused of abusing their social and economic privilege. In 1999 the conservatives in the Province of Hessen won the provincial elections by staging a populist campaign against the naturalization of immigrants, a legal possibility introduced by the center-left governmental majority of the Bundestag. In a climate of apprehension about jobs and layoffs and the future of work, many voters would react to the insinuations of a "the boat is full" message and focus their anxieties on the vicarious foreign victims transforming their apprehensions about the economy and the labor market into hostility toward presumed competitors.

Anti-Semitism

Whereas the conditions of the labor market may combine working-class apprehensions and resentments in a mix of self-protective authoritarian anti-foreigner feelings, the anti-Semitic component of the extremism syndrome is in need of a different explanation. Jews, a tiny minority, are practically absent from the everyday experience of Germans. Anti-Semitism could hardly be part of socially induced resentment, unless the policy of financial compensation for persecution suffered by Jewish victims of the Nazis has added resentment to guilt. This may be a consequence of the publicity of the conjoint efforts by German industry and government to establish, 50 years after the end of the Third Reich, a funding agency to compensate Jewish as well as other slave laborers for the exploitation suffered in the German war effort. Jewish class suits in the United States, Jewish negotiators with the German government, and the fact that the political representation of German Jewry has spoken up on various issues in Germany has achieved a saliency for Jews and Jewish issues that is quite out of proportion with their numbers. The resentment may further feed on the fact of earlier restitution (Wiedergutmachung) for the persecution and dispossession of Jews by the Nazi regime and a widespread feeling that the present generation does not, in fact, owe Jews anything and that, at long last, a line (Schlussstrich) should finally be drawn. Resentments about the role played by the Jews in the politics of memory about the Nazi regime do not seem affected by the fact that many of the slave laborers to be compensated by the fund are not Jewish.[5]

Violence

Certainly, violence has a history or social psychological causality of its own, separately from the sources of resentment. The incidence of violence against strangers and other victims has increased substantively according to police reports, but schools and social workers also report increases (Melzer & Schubarth, 1995). Eckert and his coworkers (Willems, Würtz, & Eckert, 1998; Willems, Eckert et al., 1993) have studied adolescent group violence for years and pointed out the persistence of the traditional dynamic of violence in deviant groups. On the one hand the authors caution against too quick and easy acceptance of the reported increase, as the statistics may be biased by heightened awareness or by changes in the classification practices of the police. On the other hand it is difficult to ward off perceptions of increased aggressiveness in the socio-cultural environment, from soccer hooliganism to fights between members of different ethnic groups in streets or school yards.

In spite of frequent denials the case for media effects is gradually being corroborated. For one, TV viewing time has increased over the past decades, reaching an estimated average of about 18,000 hours by the end of high school in the United States, and, according to German estimates, some 14,000 hours

---

[5] Most recently there are hints that the Israeli–Palestinian conflict is contributing to a renewed anti-Semitic sentiment in Germany, but this issue has not been surveyed so far.

by age 15. According to a recent estimate, American youngsters have viewed some 200,000 violent acts by the age of 18, with TV and video games combined. With the expansive proliferation of violent video games and TV, and movies clearly featuring more violent scenes than in earlier times, a number of effects are plausible: violent conflict may be perceived as merely conventional, sensitivity to violence may be blunted, violence may be induced more easily in vulnerable or aggression-prone individuals, and lower thresholds may obtain regarding models of violent expression of hostility (Van der Voort, 1986, p. 94), or any of those effects in conjunction. In recent studies a causal relationship has been established between the viewing of violent videos and other violent media and right-wing extremist attitudes both in East and in West Germany (Weiß, 2000). The same author has adduced evidence that skinheads view violent videos three times more frequently than the average in a sample of high school students ($n = 950$) (Weiß, 2000, pp. 169–70). This suggests a complex relationship between the viewing of violent material and the mental and physical stances of these (and certainly also other) groups of viewers. Violent input, it seems, is both sought out by and influencing violent viewers. It should be noted that exposure to TV, videos, and electronic games has social, political, and moral content beyond violence as well as effects beyond violence, effects that may be more far reaching than violence. Finally, the effects of the militant, aggression-arousing music popular among right-wing adolescents should not be minimized (Eyerman, 2000; Borstel, 1998). Suffice it to merely mention the widespread disaffection with school and education especially in the lower tracks of secondary schools, discussed earlier in this paper. Dissatisfaction, alienation, and frustration provide a breeding ground for extremist attitudes, perhaps offering a compensation for the corresponding feelings of inferiority and exclusion (Edelstein, 2000).

Inadequate Countermeasures

Could there have been a protection against the surge of anomie, resentment, and hostility and the corrosion of democratic rules of conflict resolution that used to contain violent action in many cases and now tends to go uninhibited and is even justified by a vicious ideology? Whereas the consequences of the breakdown in East Germany might have been mitigated by providing attractive substitutes for the abolished youth organizations and/or by constructive programs in the schools, the scattered attempts to react to the situation were quite insufficient to counter the onslaught. At times it seems even to have helped the radicals reach their goals. Thus the Center for Democratic Culture has reported on the failure of so-called noncontrolling social work (akzeptierende Sozialarbeit) to resist the takeover, by right-wing groups, of community-owned and community-run youth clubs in East Germany. The same source reports on widespread acceptance of right-wing youth activities and even violent or criminal acts against blacks or foreign refugees among the local population of small towns, and of instances of collusion of the local administrations (Wagner, 1999; Borstel, 1998). A recent appraisal in *Psychologie heute* (the German version of *Psychology Today*) blamed the most extensive attempt at large-scale response to adolescent violence in the East, the government funded so-called AgAG program (Aktionsgemeinschaft gegen Aggression und Gewalt: Action against Aggression and Violence) for entertaining completely unreasonable notions about the causes of violence and correspondingly mistaken choices of strategies to combat it, more in line with the professional ideologies of social work than with the social and psychological realities motivating adolescent violence (Kersten, 2000).

The groundswell of collusionary "loyalty to our children," which at times seems to have tamed even police action and court decisions, has been accompanied by proclamations of "nationally liberated zones" by the organized right. The very term acknowledges the cultural permeation achieved by the right-wing activists – as recognized by the deeply worried Speaker of the German Bundestag. An openly right-wing periodical *Junge Freiheit* (*Young Freedom*), which aspires to provide an intellectually competent guidance for right-wing activity, in 1999 sported an ironic but significant reference to Gramsci's theory of cultural subversion. Together with the pervasive organizational appeal of nationalist rock music and intensive internet communication, the radical right has established a wide-ranging network of people, communications, and activities that approaches achieving something like an organizational base. In spite of a network of youth clubs sponsored, for example, by the Kinder- und Jugendstiftung (Children and Youth Foundation, a consortium raising and coordinating foundation grants and public money) and the RAAs (regional action centers for the integration of foreigners, financed mainly by private foundations), these initiatives are far from sufficient to counter the quantitative increase and the growing acceptance of right-wing activities. Clearly an overarching policy is needed that takes seriously the effects that deep and far-reaching processes of social change work on the identities, mentalities, and moral dispositions of young people.[6]

[6] Beginning in the winter of 2000–2001 a number of government initiatives have begun to fund a number of programs of protection of victims, support of participants in right-wing groups who wish to "exit," and various "alliances" for tolerance and against racism, xenophobia, and violence. A program in support of "learning democracy in schools" funded by the Federal Ministry of Education and Research and by 12 German provinces (Länder) was started in fall 2002 (Edelstein & Fauser, 2001).

References

Adorno, T. W., Frenkel-Brunswik, E., Levinson, D. J., Sanford, R. N., et al. (1950). *The Authoritarian Personality*. New York: Harper & Row.

Ahlheim, K., & Heger, B. (2000). *Der unbequeme Fremde. Fremdenfeindlichkeit in Deutschland–Empirische Befunde*. Schwalbach: Wochenschau Verlag.

Altemeyer, B. (1988). *Enemies of Freedom: Understanding Right-Wing Authoritarianism*. San Francisco: Jossey-Bass.

Augstein, F. (2000). Die Quittung (The Reciprocation). *Frankfurter Allgemeine Zeitung*, September 16, 2000.

Beck, U. (1992). *Risk Society. Towards a New Modernity*. London: Sage Publishers.

Beck, U., & Beck-Gernsheim, E. (1993). Nicht Autonomie, sondern Bastelbiographie. Anmerkungen zur Individualisierungsdiskussion am Beispiel des Aufsatzes von Günter Burkart. *Zeitschrift für Soziologie 22*, 178–187.

Borstel, D. (1998). Rechtsextreme Musik. Schriftenreihe des "Zentrum Demokratische Kultur," Berlin, Nr. 3.

Bowlby, J. (1969). *Attachment and Loss: Vol. 1: Attachment*. New York: Basic Books.

Boyte, H. C., & Kari, N. N. (1996). *Building America: The Democratic Promise of Public Work*. Philadelphia: Temple University Press.

Bromba, M., & Edelstein, W. (2001). Das anti-demokratische und rechtsextreme Potenzial unter Jugendlichen und jungen Erwachsenen in Deutschland. Expertise für das Bundesministerium für Bildung und Forschung (BMBF), Bonn.

Bundesministerium des Innern (Ed.). (2000). Verfassungsschutzbericht 1999. Bonn: BMI.

Bundesministerium des Innern (Ed.). (2001). Verfassungsschutzbericht 2000. Bonn: BMI.

Butterwegge, C. (1995). Armut, Rechtsextremismus und Sozialpolitik. *Neue Praxis 25*, 2.

Butterwegge, C. (2001). Rechtsextremismus, Rassismus und Gewalt. *Neue Sammlung 41*, 3–32.

Deutsche Shell (Ed.). (1997). *Jugend '97–Zukunftsperspektiven–Gesellschaftliches Engagement–Politische Orientierung*. Opladen: Leske & Budrich.

Deutsche Shell (Ed.). (2000). *Jugend 2000. 13. Shell Jugendstudie*. Opladen: Leske & Budrich.

Durkheim, E. (1968a). *The Division of Labor in Society*. New York: Free Press.

Durkheim, E. (1968b). *Suicide: A Study in Sociology*. London: Routledge & Kegan Paul.

Durkheim, E. (1973). *Moral Education: A Study in the Theory and Application of the Sociology of Education*. E. K. Wilson (Ed.). New York: Free Press.

Edelstein, W. (1983). Cultural constraints on development and the vicissitudes of progress. In F. S. Kessel & A. W. Siegel (Eds.), *The Child and Other Cultural Inventions* (pp. 48–81). New York: Praeger.

Edelstein, W. (1995). Krise der Jugend–Ohnmacht der Institutionen. Eine Einleitung im Anschluß an Emil Durkheims Theorie. In W. Edelstein (Ed.), *Entwicklungskrisen kompetent meistern. Der Beitrag der Selbstwirksamkeitstheorie von Albert Bandura zum pädagogischen Handeln* (pp. 13–24). Heidelberg: S. Asanger.

Edelstein, W. (2000). Lernwelt und Lebenswelt. Überlegungen zur Schulreform. *Neue Sammlung 40*, 369–382.

Edelstein, W., & Fauser, P. (2001). *Gutachten zum Programm "Demokratie lernen und leben."* Bonn: Bund-Länder-Kommission für Bildungsplanung und Forschungsförderung.

Elder, G. (1974). *Children of the Great Depression.* Chicago: University of Chicago Press.

Elder, G. H., & Caspi, A. (1988). Human development and social change: An emerging perspective on the life course. In N. Bolger, A. Caspi, G. Downey, & M. Moorehouse (Eds.), *Persons in Context: Developmental Processes* (pp. 77–113). New York: Cambridge University Press.

Erikson, E. H. (1959). *Identity and the Life Cycle. Psychological Issues, Vol. 1, No. 1.* New York: International Universities Press.

Erikson, E. H. (1968). *Identity, Youth, and Crisis.* New York: Norton.

Erikson, E. H. (1975). *Life History and the Historical Moment.* New York: Norton.

Eyerman, R. (2000). Music in movement: Cultural politics and old and new social movements. Paper presented at the conference "Adolescents into Citizens: Integrating Young People Into Political Life," Zürich.

Frey, D., & Rez, H. (2002). Population and predators: Preconditions for the Holocaust from the control-theoretical perspective. In L. S. Newman & R. Erber (Eds.), *Understanding Genocide: The Social Psychology of the Holocaust* (pp. 188–221). New York: Oxford University Press.

Friedrichs, J. (1998). *Die Individualisierungs-These.* Opladen: Leske & Budrich.

Giddens, A. (1991). *Modernity and Self-Identity: Self and Society in the Late Modern Age.* Stanford, CA: Stanford University Press.

Gille, M., & Krüger, W. (Eds.). (2000). Unzufriedene Demokraten. *Die politischen Orientierungen der 16- bis 29 jährigen im vereinigten Deutschland.* Opladen: Leske & Budrich.

Heitmeyer, W. (Ed.). (1997). Bundesrepublik Deutschland: auf dem Weg von der Konsens- zur Konfliktgesellschaft, Bd. 1 und 2. Frankfurt/M.: Suhrkamp.

Heitmeyer, W., & Olk, T. (Eds.) (1990). *Individualisierung von Jugend.* Weinheim: Juventa.

Heitmeyer, W. et al. (1992). *Die Bielefelder Rechtsextremismus-Studie: erste Langzeituntersuchung zur politischen Sozialisation.* München: Juventa.

Heitmeyer, W. et al. (1995). *Gewalt: Schattenseiten der Individualisierung bei Jugendlichen aus unterschiedlichen Milieus.* Weinheim: Juventa.

Hennig, E. (1994). Politische Unzufriedenheit. In W. Kowalsky & W. Schröder (Eds.), *Rechtsextremismus. Einführung und Forschungsbilanz.* Opladen: Westdeutscher Verlag.

Hesse, E., & van Ijzendoorn, M. H. (1997). *Attachment and politics.* Unpublished manuscript, Leiden University.

Hirschi, T. (1969). *The Causes of Delinquency.* Berkeley, CA: University of California Press.

Hopf, C. (1997). Beziehungserfahrungen und Aggressionen gegen Minderheiten. In S. Hradil (Ed.), *Differenz und Integration. Die Zukunft moderner Gesellschaften. Proceedings of the 28th Congress of the German Sociological Association, in Dresden 1996* (pp. 154–171). Frankfurt/M.: Campus, S.

Hopf, C., Rieker, P., Sanden-Marcus, M., & Schmidt, C. (1995). *Familie und Rechtsextremismus. Familiale Sozialisation und rechtsextreme Orientierungen junger Männer.* Weinheim: Juventa.

Hopf, C., Silzer, M., & Wernich, J. M.(1999). Ethnozentrismus und Sozialisation in der DDR–Überlegungen und Hypothesen zu den Bedingungen der Ausländerfeindlichkeit von Jugendlichen in den neuen Bundesländern. In P. Kalb, K. Sitte, & C. Petry (Eds.), *Rechtsextremistische Jugendliche–was tun? 5. Weinheimer Gespräch.* (pp. 80–120). Weinheim: Beltz-Verlag, S.

Hopf, W. (1994). Rechtsextremismus von Jugendlichen: Kein Deprivationsproblem? *Zeitschrift für Sozialisationsforschung und Erziehungssoziologie 14*, 194–211.

Kersten, J. (2000). Rechte Gewalt in Deutschland: "Dieser Wagon ist nur für Weiße!" *Psychologie heute 27*, 10, 46–51.

Kovacheva, S., & Wallace, C. (1994). Why do youth revolt? *Youth and Policy 44*, 7–20.

Krettenauer, T. (1998). Gerechtigkeit als Solidarität. *Entwicklungsbedingungen sozialen Engagements im Jugendalter.* Weinheim: Deutscher Studien Verlag.

Maaz, H.-J. (1990). *Der Gefühlsstau. Ein Psychogramm der DDR.* Berlin: Argon.

Maaz, H.-J. (1993). Gewalt, Rassismus und Rechtsextremismus in den östlichen Bundesländern. In H.-U. Otto & R. Merten (Eds.), *Rechtsradikale Gewalt im vereinigten Deutschland. Jugend im gesellschaftlichen Umbruch* (pp. 176–181). Opladen: Leske & Budrich, S.

Main, M., & Goldwyn, R. (1994). *Adult Attachment Scoring and Classification Systems.* Unpublished manual, University of California at Berkeley.

Melzer, W., & Schubarth, W. (1995). Das Rechtsextremismussyndrom bei Schülerinnen und Schülern in Ost- und Westdeutschland. In W. Schubarth & W. Melzer (Eds.), *Schule, Gewalt und Rechtsextremismus.* Opladen: Leske & Budrich.

Nunner-Winkler, G. (1996). Formen von Gewalt. Kommentar zu Wilhelm Heitmeyer: Gewalt bei Jugendlichen aus unterschiedlichen sozialen Milieus. In C. Honegger et al. (Eds.), *Gesellschaft im Umbau, Identitäten, Konflikte, Differenzen. Invited paper, in the Swiss Association of Social Science, Bern 1995* (pp. 405–425). Zürich: Seismo, S.

Rimmerman, C. (1998). *The New Citizenship: Unconventional Politics, Activism, and Service.* Boulder: Westview Press.

Roberts, K. (2000). How Europe's old and new democracies produce inactive citizens. Proceedings of Conference "Adolescents into Citizens: Integrating Young People into Political Life," Zürich.

Schnabel, K.-U. (1993). Ausländerfeindlichkeit bei Jugendlichen in Deutschland–eine Synopse empirischer Befunde seit 1990. *Zeitschrift für Pädagogik 39*, 799–822.

Schnabel, K.-U., & Roeder, P. M. (1995). Zum politischen Weltbild von ost- und westdeutschen Jugendlichen. In G. Trommsdorff (Ed.), Kindheit und Jugend in verschiedenen Kulturen. Entwicklung und Sozialisation in kulturvergleichender Sicht (pp. 175–210). Weinheim/München: Juventa, S.

Seghers, A. (1977). Ein Mensch wird Nazi. In *Gesammelte Werke in Einzelausgaben, Band IX Erzählungen, 1926–1944* (pp. 285–298). Berlin: Aufbau Verlag.

Seligman, M. E. P. (1975). *Helplessness: On Depression, Development, and Death.* San Francisco: Freeman.

Sennett, R. (1999). *The Corrosion of Character: The Personal Consequences of Work in the New Capitalism.* New York: Norton.

Skinner, E. A. (1996). A guide to constructs of control. *Journal of Personality and Social Psychology 71*, 549–570.

Spahn, S. (2001). Das rechte Klassenzimmer. Süddeutsche Zeitung, March 21, 2001.

Sturzbecher, D. (Ed.). (1997). *Jugend und Gewalt in Ostdeutschland*. Göttingen: Hogrefe.

Sturzbecher, D. (2001). *Jugend in Ostdeutschland: Lebenssituation und Delinquenz*. Opladen: Leske & Budrich.

Sturzbecher, D., & Freytag, R. (2000). *Antisemitismus unter Jugendlichen. Fakten, Erklärungen, Unterrichtsbausteine*. Göttingen: Hogrefe.

Sykes, G. M., & Matza, D. (1957). Techniques of neutralization: A theory of delinquency. *American Sociological Review, 22*, 664–670.

Thierse, W. Speech before the German Parliament. Reported in: Tagesspiegel, Sept 29, 2000.

Tonn, M. (1998). "Individualisierung" als Ursache rechtsradikaler Jugendgewalt? In J. Friedrichs (Ed.), *Die Individualisierungsthese* (pp. 264–297). Opladen: Leske & Budrich, S.

Torney-Purta, J., Lehmann, R., Oswald, H., & Schulz, W. (2001). *Citizenship and Education in Twenty-Eight Countries: Civic Knowledge and Engagement at Age Fourteen*. Amsterdam: The International Association for the Evaluation of Educational Achievement.

Van der Voort, T. H. A. (1986). *Television Violence: A Child's-Eye View*. Amsterdam: North-Holland.

Van Ijzendoorn, M. H. (1995). Adult attachment representations, parental responsiveness, and infant attachment: A meta-analysis of the predictive validity of the Adult Attachment Interview. *Psychological Bulletin 117*, 387–403.

Van Ijzendoorn, M. H. (1997). Attachment, emergent morality, and aggression: Toward a developmental socioemotional model of antisocial behaviour. *International Journal of Behavioral Development 21*, 703–727.

Wagner, B. (1998). "National befreite Zonen"–Vom Strategiebegriff zur Alltagserscheinung, Schriftenreihe des "Zentrum Demokratische Kultur," Berlin, Nr. 1.

Wagner, B. (1999). Zu Möglichkeiten und Grenzen der Arbeit mit rechtsextrem orientierten jungen Leuten. In P. E. Kalb, K. Sitte, & C. Petry (Eds.), *Rechtsextremistische Jugendliche–was tun?* (pp. 122–128). Weinheim: Beltz, S.

Wagner, B. Personal communication, June 2002.

Weiß, R. H. (2000). *Gewalt, Medien und Aggressivität bei Schülern*. Göttingen: Hogrefe.

White, C., Bruce, S., & Ritchie, J. (2000). *Young People's Politics. Political Interest and Engagement Amongst 14–24, Olds*. Yorkshire, UK: Joseph Rowntree.

Wilkinson, H., & Mulgan, G. (1995). *Freedom's Children. Work, Relationships and Politics for 18–34-Year-Olds in Britain Today*. London: Demos.

Willems, H., & Eckert, R., et al. (1993). *Fremdenfeindliche Gewalt: Einstellungen, Täter, Konflikteskalation*. Opladen: Leske & Budrich.

Willems, H., Würtz, S., & Eckert, R. (1998). Erklärungsmuster fremdenfeindlicher Gewalt im empirischen Test. In R. Eckert (Ed.), *Wiederkehr des "Volksgeistes"?* (pp. 195–214). Opladen: Leske & Budrich.

13   Learning Potential Assessment
Where Is the Paradigm Shift?

Alex Kozulin

Learning potential assessment (LPA) is only slightly younger than intelligence testing itself. In the early 1930s Lev Vygotsky (1934/1986) in Russia and Andre Rey (1934) in Switzerland made clear statements in favor of LPA procedures. As shown in recent reviews (Lidz, 1987; Weidl, Guthke, and Wigenfeld, 1995) even the period between the 1940s and the 1960s that appeared to be totally dominated by the psychometric approach had its share of LPA attempts. Finally in the 1960s, on the wave of widespread dissatisfaction with the existent psychometric intelligence tests, LPA approaches became operationalized (Budoff and Friedman, 1964; Feuerstein and Shalom, 1968) and started forming a field of their own (Campbell and Carlson, 1995; Kozulin and Falik, 1995). Yet at the beginning of the 21st century, 70 years since its theoretical inception and 30 years since its operationalization, LPA still remains a rather marginal form of assessment as compared to the dominant psychometric IQ approach. In terms of Kuhn's (1970) theory of scientific revolutions, the paradigm shift failed to take place. In this chapter, I will attempt to answer the question of why to the present time the LPA paradigm has not succeeded in dislodging the psychometric paradigm.

The Concept of LPA

Since its inception in the work of Binet and Simon, the concept of intelligence testing was closely connected to the task of evaluating the learning abilities of children and adults. The initial impulse for Binet's work came from the practical task of creating more appropriate educational conditions for children with different learning abilities. Moreover, Binet suggested that mental testing would be rather meaningless if it were unable to propose strategies for the improvement of children's performance.

"I have always believed that intelligence can, to some extent, be taught, can be improved in every child, and I deplore the pessimism that this question often evokes. There is a frequent prejudice against the educability of intelligence ... Some contemporary philosophers seem to have given their moral support to such lamentable verdicts, asserting that intelligence is a fixed quantity, a quantity that cannot be increased. We must protest and react against this brutal pessimism and show that it has no foundation" (Binet, 1909, quoted in Campione, 1996, p. 227).

Thus, from the very beginning, the assessment of intellectual abilities, at least in children, was undertaken not for its own sake but because it has predictive value regarding children's learning ability. It is not surprising, therefore, that the initial, and some of the later criticisms of IQ testing, focused on the wisdom of using IQ scores instead of attempting a direct assessment of the child's learning ability (see Lidz, 1987). The issue, however, becomes more complicated in the absence of commonly accepted definitions and distinctions between intelligence and learning. Intuitively we understand that a person can be a quick and efficient learner and yet a mediocre intellectual, and that a person with sharp and creative intellect can be rather slow and hesitant in learning new skills and operations. In a more general sense, if one accepts that learning is predominantly acquisition, and intellect is predominantly operation, then there is an inevitable difference between these two spheres of mental activity. In their recent review of dynamic testing Grigorenko and Sternberg (1998, p. 92) confirmed this observation concluding that "it is quite common to find children who show good cognitive test results but have a slow rate of learning and vice versa." That is why it is important to mention that many of the proponents of LPA use the term learning potential interchangeably with that of intellectual potential, and dynamic cognitive assessment as a synonym of LPA (Lidz, 1987). In both cases the assessment procedure includes a learning phase. The outcome, however, can be interpreted differently–either as a cognitive change or as a measure of learning ability. This issue will be discussed later in connection with the still ambiguous status of LPA.

For the 1920s and 1930s it would be imprecise to speak about LPA challenging the IQ testing, for the simple reason that the standard form of psychometric assessment had not yet been firmly established, at least not in Europe. One should rather speak about two different versions of mental testing. It is of interest, therefore, to examine why the IQ-type of assessment won this initial competition.

One of the more eloquent and practical suggestions in favor of LPA assessment was made by the Swiss psychologist Andre Rey (1934). He proposed basing the evaluation of learning ability on directly observable learning processes. Using as a model the task of finding one removable peg among nine pegs on the board, Rey showed that registration of the sequence of consecutive trials not only provides information about the child's learning ability but also about the change in the child's strategy. Rey thus introduced two parameters that were destined to play the central role in the LPA concepts: process orientation and experiential component within the testing situation. While IQ testing focuses on the product of the children's reasoning embodied in the number of correctly solved problems, LPA shifts emphasis on assessing the process of reaching the solution both quantitatively, i.e., the number of trials, and qualitatively, i.e., the strategy used, the type of errors, etc. Ultimately the process-oriented assessment may inform us about the type and quality of children's learning processes. The introduction of learning into the test procedure turns it from reactive into active. In the IQ assessment situation children respond to the given problem by using knowledge, strategies, and skills that they already possess. In contrast, the assessment procedure suggested by Rey allows children to develop problem-solving competence in the process of assessment. Thus children's activity, rather than children's reaction, becomes the target of assessment.

An even more far reaching version of the LPA approach was proposed by Vygotsky (1934/1986; see also Minick, 1987; van der Veer and Valsiner, 1991; Chaiklin, 2003). Vygotsky's concept of the zone of proximal development (ZPD) suggests that it is important to assess the child's problem-solving ability in the situation of cooperative activity with adults or more competent peers. Such an approach reflects Vygotsky's fundamental belief that social forms of activity form the matrix of children's development (see Kozulin, 1990, 1998). Vygotsky believed that the normal learning situation for a child is a socially meaningful cooperative activity. New psychological functions of the child originate on this interpersonal plane and only later are internalized and transformed to become the child's inner psychological processes. Thus the situation of collaborative or assisted problem solving creates conditions for the development of the new psychological functions. For a certain period of time these functions are not mature enough to be displayed by children in their independent problem-solving. However, in the testing situation that includes cooperation and help, children are capable of demonstrating the emergent functions that have not been internalized yet. The ZPD "contains" functions that are currently in a state of being formed. As to the application of the notion of ZPD to mental testing, Vygotsky suggested charting individual ZPD's for children by comparing their performance under solitary conditions with performance during the assisted problem solving. For the future discussion it is important to mention that Vygotsky suggested a wide range of interactive interventions to be used during ZPD assessment, such as asking leading questions, modeling, starting to solve the task and asking the child to continue, and so on, but he produced no standardized procedure for the ZPD assessment. Moreover, Vygotsky left open the question about the possible targets of LPA: As an illustration of the processes in ZPD he mentioned both general problem solving and school-based skills. Adherence to a spirit of LPA rather than elaboration of a set of standardized LPA procedures for a long time remained characteristic of the work done by Vygotsky's followers in Russia, e.g., Luria (1961). Thus, Vygotsky's contribution should be viewed as paradigmatic, rather than methodological.

Through his notion of ZPD Vygotsky introduced a number of important parameters of LPA: interactivity, emphasis on developing functions, and the gain-score based on the comparison of the results of aided and independent performance. If Rey suggested allowing the child to learn during the testing procedure, Vygotsky moved further forward by suggesting an active intervention on the part of adults as an integral component of the assessment procedure. The child's learning ceases to be a property of the child and, within the ZPD, becomes an expression of his or her ability to function within the socio-cultural context. In a sense the entire orientation of mental assessment is changing from that of measuring what the child is capable of doing at the present time, to what kind and what amount of interaction between the child and adults can produce the results that the child is currently incapable of producing him or herself.

Taking into account such an impressive beginning it seems puzzling that the LPA approach made little progress in the period from the 1930s through the 1960s. In the case of Vygotsky the answer seems to be rooted in very special conditions under which the field of psychological assessment found itself in Russia during this period. While in the 1920s and early 1930s Soviet psychologists and educators experimented with a wide variety of assessment techniques, in 1936 this experimentation came to a rather abrupt end. A special state decree was promulgated banning all forms of psychometric assessment – relevant courses were removed from the university curricula, books and journals on psychological assessment were locked up in special archives (see Bauer, 1968; Kozulin, 1984; van der Veer and Valsiner, 1991). This nearly total ban of all forms of psychological assessment did not prevent Vygotsky's followers from using some of his ideas about ZPD in their practice. What they were denied, however, was the professional infrastructure, i.e., public discussions, publications, and conferences. Contact with Western specialists was completely severed. Moreover, when Vygotsky's theory became acceptable again in the USSR in the 1960s, this liberalization was not extended toward the issue of psychological assessment. Thus for a long time Vygotskian psychology was denied opportunity to develop a full scale LPA program and its influence on the world psychological community was minimal.

If such a socio-political explanation seems adequate in the case of Vygotsky's version of LPA, it is obviously inapplicable to Rey's case. There was no psychological censorship in Switzerland and no state decrees against psychological assessment techniques. Yet, Rey's LPA proposal of 1934 remained unheeded. One may think of two possible reasons for this. One is that Rey himself was not particularly insistent on using the LPA procedure. He contributed to a wide range of psychological and clinical disciplines (e.g., Rey, 1969) and by no means can be called a person consistently focused on LPA. It seems symptomatic for example that when Rey (1941, 1959) introduced a new assessment technique for a study of spatial perception and planning, which eventually became popular in neuropsychology under the name of the Rey–Osterrieth Complex Figure Drawing Test, he did not include any provision for using it in the LPA format. Another possible reason for Rey's lack of success in promoting the issue of LPA as an alternative for IQ testing was its unintentional competition with Piaget's approach. The Piaget's alternative that came from the same University of Geneva was at that time much more powerful. It seemed that having two alternatives to IQ testing in a relatively limited environment of Genevan psychology was simply too much.

While the first LPA attempts remained isolated, both theoretically and what is more important, practically, the IQ testing was quickly moving in the direction of what Kuhn (1970) calls "normal science." The IQ paradigm corresponded to a wide theoretical consensus regarding intellectual abilities. First Stanford–Binet and then Wechsler batteries of tests created standard "equipment" for IQ testing. Statistical analysis of the large groups of students confirmed that on average IQ served as a good predictor of the school achievement. The paradigm was "wide" enough to accommodate for certain innovations or refinements, such as the factorial studies of intelligence (Thurstone, 1938) or a distinction between "crystallized" and "fluid" intelligence (Cattell, 1941). One also should not forget that IQ testing often replaced much more culturally- and socially-biased forms of assessment that discriminated against intellectual talent in favor of social norm and knowledge. Thus, the IQ paradigm also had a progressive social relevance.

The paradigmatic character of the psychometric approach revealed itself in the specific perception of psychological facts. Much like Kuhn's (1970) description of physical facts that were "seen" but not "recognized" by the scientists, the facts of intellectual functioning were seen exclusively in their psychometric aspect. For example, Anastasi (1954, p. 53) discusses the issue of "coaching" and clearly interprets it as a possible interference with the purity of psychometric assessment: "In so far as coaching did produce substantial rises in specific test scores, however, such studies point up the importance of safeguarding the security of test materials." In a different scientific-ideological environment studies reported by Anastasi could easily become a topic for LPA discussion. These studies focused on the differential effect of learning interventions employing either the material that was identical or only similar to that of the initial test. The sustainability of changes produced by such coaching was also addressed. Anastasi, however, attempted no analysis in the LPA direction, being apparently content with the finding that three years after the coaching experiment the difference between the performance of "coached" and "uncoached" students had disappeared.

One may conclude that in the period from the 1930s through the 1960s two conditions necessary for the paradigm shift were absent. On the one hand, the psychometric paradigm was at the height of its "normal science" phase with new testing batteries developed or older ones refined, reliability and validity of tests established, and the "rules of the game" transmitted in an institutionalized form to new generations of school psychologists. The number of what Kuhn calls "anomalies" was relatively small and anyway their presence was not acknowledged.

The First IQ Crisis and Operationalization of LPA

The first significant crisis experienced by the IQ paradigm occurred in the 1960s. It appears that an attack against the monopoly of IQ testing came from "outside" psychology and only later was reinforced from within the profession. The social rights movements of the 1960s revealed a number of "anomalies" that were previously overlooked. For example, it was "discovered" that a disproportionately large number of ethnic minority children were placed into special-education frameworks on the basis on their IQ scores alone. At the same time it was shown that many of the inter-group differences in IQ scores reflected such changeable parameters as the socio-economic status of the family. Moreover, one of the main purposes of IQ testing, i.e., selection of students for special education, came under fire from the advocates of inclusion and integration. The critical reevaluation of the societal role of IQ testing became embodied in a number of court decisions that outlawed the use of standardized ability testing by employers unless they had a manifest relationship to the specific job performance and curtailed the use of IQ tests for the purpose of excluding minority children from regular education (Elliott,

1987). Later on this attack on IQ was further amplified by the publication of popular books that questioned the scientific integrity of some proponents of the hereditary theory of IQ (Kamin, 1974; Gould, 1981).

It is during the attack on IQ that the fully operationalized versions of LPA appeared in professional literature (Budoff & Friedman, 1964; Feuerstein & Shalom, 1968). With a wisdom of hindsight, one can discern in Budoff's and Feuerstein's versions of LPA the two different directions in which the LPA approach was about to develop. Budoff viewed LPA as a procedure that supplemented the static assessment, while Feuerstein suggested replacing the static assessment by LPA. For Budoff the main aim of intelligence testing remained the same, i.e., to provide an objective basis for selecting and classifying children for special education (Budoff, 1987; Sternberg & Grigorenko, 2002). Feuerstein's position appeared to be much more radical because it dispensed with the entire philosophy of labeling and classifying students and called for an ongoing evaluation of the child's learning potential with the aim of formulating an optimal educational intervention for each individual child (Feuerstein, Feuerstein, & Gross, 1997; Feuerstein, Falik, and Feuerstein, 1998). These two directions in the study of LPA also dictated different methodologies. Budoff and many others after him (see Haywood & Tzuriel, 1992; Lidz & Elliott, 2000) adhered to the major premises of the psychometric paradigm. Not only pre- and post-tests but also the learning intervention itself was shaped in a standardized way. The issues of reliability and validity were discussed in the same terms as in standard psychometric literature (Guthke & Stein, 1996; Sternberg & Grigorenko, 2002).

Russian proponents of LPA also saw in the dynamic assessment procedure a new tool for essentially the same goal, namely to distinguish between students whose low IQ performance had a different underlying etiology, particularly between the organically mentally retarded and those with temporary developmental delays (Ivanova, 1976; see also Lidz & Gindis, 2003). Two aspects, however, distinguish the Russian version of LPA. The first is its emphasis on emotional and motivational aspects of assessment. According to the Russian studies (see Kozulin & Gindis, in press) a determining factor in the children's LPA task performance is their "emotional anticipation," which may facilitate or hinder the expression of intellectual functions. Investigation of the affective-cognitive component of children's mental activity contributed to the development of assessment instruments more sensitive to the children's learning problems. The second distinctive feature of the Russian version of LPA is its closer relation to the issue of educational intervention. For the majority of Russian Vygotskians the notion of ZPD serves as a conceptual basis for both assessment and intervention, thus techniques similar to LPA appear under the name of "diagnosis of learning aptitude" in the context of assessment and under the name "learning/teaching experiment" in the context of educational intervention (Karpov & Gindis, 2000).

Feuerstein went much further in challenging not only the static character of IQ testing, but the goals and methods of psychometric paradigm as such. If there is a need for a philosophical label, then Feuerstein's approach is close to that of existentialism. For him each individual, particularly a child or adolescent, harbors an indeterminate capacity or propensity for change. The goal of LPA is to provide an ongoing evaluation of the qualitative and quantitative discrepancy between the child's manifest functioning and his or her modifiability and to suggest appropriate intervention. There is no attempt on the part of Feuerstein to predict the future functioning of the child or to compare the child's learning potential with that of other children. The child in Feuerstein's systems serves as his or her own system of reference. In his more recent papers (Feuerstein et al., 2002) went even further claiming that individual cognitive functioning can best be described in terms of a changeable "state" and that there is no reason to try finding its more permanent traits.

Accordingly Feuerstein et al.'s (1979; 2002) learning potential assessment device (LPAD) is applied as a clinical procedure attuned to the changing performance of the child. The case studies that served as an illustration of Feuerstein's method (Feuerstein et al., 1979; Feuerstein, Rand, & Rynders, 1988) portray low-functioning children classified at best as educable mentally retarded who in the course of lengthy LPAD assessment-cum-intervention start displaying isolated instances of higher learning ability. These instances are then consolidated and at the end of the assessment period the children, themselves, as well as their teachers and psychologists change their opinion regarding the children's true abilities. The next stage includes placing these children in a new, more advanced educational setting and providing them with a remedial teaching program based on Feuerstein et al.'s (1980) Instrumental Enrichment method. Often a case study is concluded with the child successfully graduating from regular high school and acquiring gainful profession or trade.

Feuerstein's implementation of LPAD procedures was deeply imbedded into specific socio-cultural contexts. The majority of Feuerstein's case studies were written either about Holocaust survivors or immigrant children from the Third World countries. In these students the impact of psychological trauma, bi- and multi-lingualism, and the lack of formal education became firmly entangled with more standard signs of low intellectual or learning abilities. Not only the children's profiles but also those of their social and educational settings were culturally specific. Feuerstein's clients became integrated into communal settlements, kibbutz, youth villages, and other settings typical only of the Israeli scene. LPAD assessment did not stand alone but appeared as an element in the integral rehabilitation process that included remedial teaching, placement into a new socio-educational setting, and a change in the parents' and teachers' perception of the low functioning child. It is telling that the case studies that often presented the children's low IQ intake scores practically never reported their post-LPAD or post-intervention IQ. Psychologists reading these case studies were invited to "buy" the whole philosophy, rather than a specific technique.

Other versions of LPA that appeared in the 1970s and the 1980s did not try to "sell" any new philosophy, but simply offered certain assessment methods that could be used either as a complement to standard tests or as a substitute for them in some special cases (Haywood & Tzuriel, 1992; Hamers, Sijtsma, & Ruijssenaars, 1993; Carlson, 1995; Lidz & Elliott, 2000). Unlike Feuerstein's, these studies were usually conducted in more familiar educational environments of regular and special schools, with less information about and less emphasis on the overall remediation process, and more on specific pre- and post-LPA test results. Two major goals of these studies can be discerned. The first one was to provide a better tool for differential diagnosis of children with low-IQ or low achievement. For example, to differentiate between those whose low IQ scores are associated with cultural difference and/or educational deprivation and those suffering from organic cognitive deficiencies. The second goal was to show that LPA may serve as a better predictor of the child's future performance than the regular psychometric scores.

Though positive diagnostic and predictive results were obtained in a number of LPA studies conducted by different research groups, serious methodological objections have been raised (Grigorenko & Sternberg, 1998). One of them is a problem of the measurement of change. By its very nature, the test-teach-test paradigm of LPA requires repeated administration of the same test. The resultant gain score thus contains at least two different components, one of them related to the effect of the active learning and the other related to repetition effect. Some authors (Klauer, 1993) reported that a simple repetition of such standard tests as Raven's matrices produces an average gain of half a standard deviation. Because of this the validity of the LPA model became suspect. The second problem is that of a predictive value of the LPA scores. In their comprehensive review of different LPA approaches Grigorenko and Sternberg (1998, p.105) claim that "even an advocate of dynamic testing would find it difficult to argue that the empirical data, as of now, have consistently showed the higher predictive power of dynamic tests compared with static tests."

I believe that the lack of clarity regarding the nature of the processes assessed by the LPA methods contributed to the confusion regarding their predictive value. As was mentioned earlier in this paper, the concept of learning potential has often been used interchangeably with that of cognitive or intellectual potential. As a result the possible causal connections became obscured. If the true objective of LPA is to assess students' learning potential, prediction should be made regarding the students' ability to learn new material. If the objective is to assess the intellectual potential, then the prediction should be made regarding students' ability to solve certain intellectual problems. Finally, if the goal is to predict the students' classroom achievements, then LPA tasks should be shaped accordingly to this goal.

Similar doubts were expressed in Karpov's (1990) analysis of the work of Russian proponents of LPA. He observed that the number and specificity of prompting may reflect the child's previously achieved mastery of cognitive operations, while the ability to transfer the newly acquired skills to the new tasks may depend on different psychological factors unrelated to learning potential per se. Some children need more help in acquiring a skill, but are capable of transferring this skill rather easily and productively. Others may need fewer promptings in learning but are less successful in the transfer.

The potentially rich theoretical basis of LPA often remains poorly connected to practical assessment activities. For example, though many Western proponents of LPA quote Vygotsky's notion of the ZPD they hardly realized its theoretical potential. While an impressive number of studies on child-adult joint activity were generated by the concept of ZPD (see Lloyd & Feringhough, 1999), only a few of them address the issue of assessment (Brown & Ferrara, 1985). The notion of ZPD calls for an in-depth analysis of the changes occurring in the child's psychological functions in the course of joint activity. The LPA approaches typically operate with much simpler constructs such as "a gain score" or "a post-intervention score." Contemporary critics of Feuerstein's LPAD also observe that his rich theoretical schema that includes the criteria of mediated learning, the nomenclature of deficient cognitive functions, and the cognitive map has little connection to actual LPAD research. "There is a certain degree of discrepancy between the elaborateness of these theoretical speculations and the fairly meager usage of these constructs within the framework of empirical research actually conducted with the LPAD" (Grigorenko & Sternberg, 1998, p. 84).

If the anomalies in the IQ paradigm were repeatedly exposed since the 1960s, the alternative LPA model apparently failed to establish itself as a new paradigm. "Moderate" LPA approaches did not challenge the goals of psychometric assessment and did not offer a radical enough alternative to the notion of general intelligence as a stable predictor of child's learning. Feuerstein's version of LPA came closer to offering a new paradigm. It is true that LPAD has its share of internal and external problems, including its openly indeterministic ("no prediction should be made") philosophy, the problem of validity of its instruments, and high expense and effort necessary for this type of assessment. I believe, however, that the fact that in the 30 years of its existence LPAD was unable to replace static tests as a new paradigm is related not only to its own characteristics but also to the fact that the emergence in the 1980s of new assessment orientations changed the entire map of confrontation between IQ and LPA.

New Assessment Orientations

The IQ crisis of the 1960s apparently not only revealed the public dissatisfaction with the discriminatory aspects of IQ testing but also triggered reevaluation of the entire notion of cognitive and learning assessment. In a sense this response was much more far-reaching than that offered by the proponents of LPA. Being dissatisfied with static tests, the radical critics of IQ suggested dispensing entirely with the notion of controlled testing and focusing instead on such alternatives as authentic assessment and portfolio evaluation. From this new perspective even the LPA procedures and materials looked suspiciously similar to those used in the IQ tests.

For example, the rejection of psychometric tests as unsuitable for culturally different students by Valdes and Figueroa (1994) was also extended toward the LPAD. The authors claimed that the LPAD items are essentially psychometric in their appearance and, as such, are discriminatory with respect to culturally different students. They also objected to the interactive component of LPAD assessment pointing out that it requires a high degree of psycholinguistic processing and interaction carried out in the dominant language. Finally they claimed that Feuerstein's concept of deficient cognitive functions presupposes the same analysis and decomposition of children's actual performance as in the psychometric paradigm.

What is probably more important is that the LPA ceased to be the only alternative to the static psychometric approach. New conceptualizations of intelligence and learning significantly increased the number of possible alternative assessment paradigms. One of them is the information-processing paradigm that at a certain moment made a transition from its initial base in psychological laboratory to classroom assessment. Unlike the classical psychometric paradigm that attempted to evaluate the "amount" of general intelligence, the information-processing paradigm aimed at answering the question of *how* children solve problems (Das, Kirby, & Jarman, 1979; Kamphous & Reynolds, 1987). Though the majority of LPA procedures include this "how" question into their paradigm, the information-processing approaches demonstrated that one does not necessarily need a test–teach–test paradigm in order to answer this question. For example, the goals of Kaufman's K-ABC include separation of the factual knowledge from the child's ability to solve unfamiliar problems and sensitivity toward special needs of minority and exceptional children; it promises to yield scores that can be translated to educational intervention (Lichtenberger, Kaufman, & Kaufman, 1998). As such K-ABC aims at fulfilling at least some of the promises made by the LPA.

Another alternative is offered by Sternberg's (1985) triarchical theory of intelligence. Here the shift is from a search for general intelligence or general learning ability to the evaluation of the three different types of intelligence: analytical, creative, and practical. One may notice that both the standard psychometric and the LPA approaches focus predominantly on analytic intelligence. Sternberg thus changed the configuration of the field by suggesting the new targets of assessment. Like many of the IQ critics, Sternberg suggested using different content domains and different modalities and allowing students to work on the problems at their own pace.

Even further widening of the field occurred as a result of popularization of Gardner's (1983) concept of "multiple intelligences." Though one may question the appropriateness of the term intelligence in application to different abilities or inclination described by Gardner, the fact is that Gardner's work brought popularity to such alternative forms of assessment as classroom observation, examination of the products of the students creative activity, portfolio assessment, and so on. Assessment principles suggested by Gardner deliberately blurred the traditional distinction between assessment and instruction. Assessment carried out in the everyday contexts informs instruction while instruction offers new opportunities for further assessment (Chen & Gardner, 1997).

Conclusion

While the contest between IQ and LPA usually occurred around the different use of the essentially same assessment material, such as Raven's matrices, verbal analogies, Koh's cubes, and the like, the notion of multiple intelligences brought about an abundance of possible materials to be used for some form of assessment or another. The entire field of confrontation was reshaped. It was no longer an orthodox IQ paradigm versus a more or less cohesive LPA alternative, but a "post-modern" multiplicity of approaches each with its own definition of intelligence or learning and its own toolbox of assessment strategies. One may say that at this stage the IQ crisis was "resolved" not through the shift from the psychometric to the LPA paradigm, but through the radical broadening of the notion of intelligence and targets of assessment. Somewhat paradoxically this apparently strengthened the position of the standard psychometric approach. One may recall that in his description of paradigms Kuhn (1970) emphasized that a paradigm is not only a set of ideas, but also a stable form of scientific practice. Similarly, a psychometric paradigm is not only a set of ideas regarding general intelligence and methods of its measurement, but also the entire apparatus of perpetuation of this practice including university courses, textbooks, licensing exams, scientific journals, etc. Changing the psychometric paradigm does not mean offering an attractive alternative idea, but changing the entire practice of psychometric assessment. The current multiplicity of possible alternatives looks like a sign of the continuing crises rather than a sign of a paradigm shift. By moving farther and farther away from the traditional domain of intelligence testing, new approaches effectively left this field to the proponents of IQ. The latter would not aspire to measure bodily-kinesthetic, musical, or intrapersonal intelligence, but would only strengthen their dominant position in assessing verbal or logical-mathematical reasoning.

I am concluding this paper on a somewhat somber note. In spite of its early promise the LPA approach has failed so far to dislodge the predominant psychometric paradigm. Because we are discussing a subject of considerable socio-cultural importance, it is quite conceivable that a dramatic change will come not from the universities and not from educational programs but in a form of social and/or legal action that would simply outlaw current psychometric practices. Even in this case the LPA paradigm should be mature enough to step into the void created by such a hypothetical event. As mentioned earlier, one of the necessary elements of such maturity is an elaboration of the proper subject matter of LPA. In other words, the task of assessing learning potential should be distinguished from that of evaluating intellectual potential. Both tasks are equally legitimate but require different tools, methodologies, and educational implementation strategies. The transition to a new paradigm cannot be limited to a simple change of the assessment technique but will necessarily involve a more profound reformulation of the concepts of learning and intellectual development.

References

Anastasi, A. (1954). *Psychological Testing*. New York: Macmillan.

Bauer, R. (1968). *The New Man in Soviet Psychology*. Cambridge, MA: Harvard University Press.

Binet, A. (1909). *Les Idées Modernes sur les Enfants*. Paris: Flammarion.

Brown, A., & Ferrara, R. (1985). Diagnosing zones of proximal development. In J. Wertsch (Ed.), *Culture, Communication, and Cognition: Vygotskian Perspectives* (pp. 273–305). New York: Cambridge University Press.

Budoff, M. (1987). The validity of learning potential assessment. In C. Lidz (Ed.), *Dynamic Assessment* (pp. 52–81). New York: Guilford Press.

Budoff, M., & Friedman, M. (1964). "Learning potential" as an assessment approach to the adolescent mentally retarded. *Journal of Consulting Psychology 28*, 434–439.

Campbell, C., & Carlson, J. (1995). The dynamic assessment of mental abilities. In J. Carlson (Ed.), *European Contributions to Dynamic Assessment* (pp. 1–32). Greenwich, CT: JAI Press.

Campione, J. (1996). Assisted assessment: A taxonomy of approaches and an outline of strengths and weaknesses. In H. Daniels (Ed.), *An Introduction to Vygotsky* (pp. 219–250). London: Routledge.

Carlson, J. (Ed.). (1995). *European Contributions to Dynamic Assessment*. Greenwich, CT: JAI Press.

Cattell, R. B. (1941). Some theoretical issues in adult intelligence testing. *Psychological Bulletin 38*, 592.

Chaiklin, S. (2003). The zone of proximal development in Vygotsky's analysis of learning and instruction. In A. Kozulin, B. Gindis, V. Ageyev, & S. Miller (Eds.), *Vygotsky's Educational Theory in Cultural Context* (pp. 39–64). New York: Cambridge University Press.

Chen, J.-Q., & Gardner, H. (1997). Alternative assessment from a multiple intelligences theoretical perspective. In D. Flanagan, J. Genshaft, & P. Harrison (Eds.), *Contemporary Intellectual Assessment* (pp. 105–121). New York: Guildford Press.

Das, J. P., Kirby, J., & Jarman, R. (1979). *Simultaneous and Successive Cognitive Processes*. New York: Academic Press.

Grigorenko, E., & Sternberg, R. (1998). Dynamic testing. *Psychological Bulletin 124*, 75–111.

Elliott, R. (1987). *Litigating Intelligence: IQ Tests, Special Education, and Social Sciences in the Courtroom*. Dover, MA: Auburn House.

Feuerstein, R., & Shalom, H. (1968). The Learning Potential Assessment Device. In B. W. Richards (Ed.), *Proceedings of the First Congress of the International Association for the Scientific Study of Mental Deficiency*. Reigate, UK: Michael Jackson.

Feuerstein, R., Rand, Y., & Hoffman, M. (1979). *Dynamic Assessment of Retarded Performer*. Baltimore, MD: University Park Press.

Feuerstein, R., Rand, Y., Hoffman, M., & Miller, R. (1980). *Instrumental Enrichment*. Baltimore, MD: University Park Press.

Feuerstein, R., Falik, L., & Feuerstein, R. S. (1998). The learning potential assessment device. In R. Samuda (Ed.), *Advances in Cross-Cultural Assessment* (pp. 100–161). Thousand Oaks, CA: Sage Publications.

Feuerstein, R., Falik, L., Rand, Y., & Feuerstein, R. S. (2002). *Dynamic Assessment of Cognitive Modifiability*. Jerusalem: ICELP Press.

Feuerstein, R., Feuerstein, R. S., & Gross, S. (1997). The learning potential assessment device. In D. Flanagan, J. Genshaft, & P. Harrison (Eds.), *Contemporary Intellectual Assessment* (pp. 297–313). New York: Guilford Press.

Feuerstein, R., Rand, Y., & Rynders, J. (1988). *Don't Accept Me As I Am*. New York: Plenum.

Gardner, H. (1983). *Frames of Mind*. New York: Basic Books.

Gould, S. (1981). *The Mismeasure of Man*. New York: Norton.

Guthke, J., & Stein, H. (1996). Are learning tests the better version of intelligence tests? *European Journal of Psychological Assessment 12*, 1–13.

Hamers, J. H. M., Sijtsma, K., & Ruijssenaars, A. J. J. M. (Eds.). (1993). *Learning Potential Assessment*. Amsterdam: Swets and Zeitlinger.

Haywood, C., & Tzuriel, D. (Eds.). (1992). *Interactive Assessment*. New York: Springer.

Ivanova, A. Y. (1976). *Obuchaemost kak printsip otsenki ymstvennogo pazvitia u detei* (Learning ability as an approach to the assessment of the child's intellectual development). Moscow: Pedagogika.

Kamin, L. (1974). *The Science and Politics of IQ*. Hillsdale, NJ: Lawrence Erlbaum Associates.

Kamphous, R., & Reynolds, C. (1987). *Clinical and Research Applications of the K-ABC*. Circle Pines, MN: American Guidance Service.

Karpov, Y. (1990). Obuchaemost kak characteristika umstvennogo razvitia (Learning aptitude as an indicator of cognitive development). *Psikhologia 14*, 2, 3–16.

Karpov, Y., & Gindis, B. (2000). Dynamic assessment of the level of internalization of elementary school children's problem solving activity. In C. Lidz & J. Elliott (Eds.), *Dynamic Assessment: Prevailing Models and Applications* (pp. 133–154). New York: Elsevier Science.

Klauer, K. (1993). Learning potential testing: The effect of retesting. In J. H. M. Hamers, K. Sijtsma, & A. J. J. M. Ruijssenaars (Eds.), *Learning Potential Assessment* (pp. 135–152). Amsterdam: Swets and Zeitlinger.

Kozulin, A. (1984). *Psychology in Utopia*. Cambridge, MA: MIT Press.

Kozulin, A. (1990). *Vygotsky's Psychology: A Biography of Ideas*. Cambridge, MA: Harvard University Press.

Kozulin, A. (1998). *Psychological Tools: A Sociocultural Approach to Education*. Cambridge, MA: Harvard University Press.

Kozulin, A., & Falik, L. (1995). Dynamic cognitive assessment of the child. *Current Directions in Psychological Science 4*, 192–196.

Kozulin, A., & Gindis, B. (in press). Sociocultural theory and education of children with special needs. In M. Cole, H. Daniels, & J. Wertsch (Eds.), *Cambridge Companion to Vygotsky*. New York: Cambridge University Press.

Kuhn, T. (1970). *The Structure of Scientific Revolutions*. Chicago: University of Chicago Press.

Lichtenberger, E., Kaufman, A., & Kaufman, N. (1998). Kaufman assessment battery for children. In R. Samuda (Ed.), *Advances in Cross-Cultural Assessment* (pp. 20–55). Thousand Oaks, CA: Sage Publications.

Lidz, C. (Ed.). (1987). *Dynamic Assessment*. New York: Guilford Press.

Lidz, C., & Elliott, J. (Eds.). (2000). *Dynamic Assessment: Prevailing Models and Applications.* New York: Elsevier Science.

Lidz, C., & Gindis, B. (2003). Dynamic assessment of the evolving cognitive functions in children. In A. Kozulin, B. Gindis, V. Ageyev, & S. Miller (Eds.), *Vygotsky's Educational Theory in Cultural Context* (pp. 99–118). New York: Cambridge University Press.

Lloyd, P., & Feringhough, C. (Eds.). (1999). *Lev Vygotsky: Critical Assessments* (Vols. 1–4). London: Routledge.

Luria, A. (1961). An objective approach to the study of abnormal child. *American Journal of Orthopsychiatry 31*, 1–14.

Minick, N. (1987). Implications of Vygotsky's theory for dynamic assessment. In C. Lidz (Ed.), *Dynamic Assessment* (pp. 116–140). New York: Guilford Press.

Rey, A. (1934). D'un procede pour evaluer l'educabilite. *Archives de Psychologie 24*, 297–337.

Rey, A. (1941). L'examen psychologique dans les case d'encephalopathie traumatique. *Archives de Psychologie 28*, 286–340.

Rey, A. (1959). *Test de Copie et de Reproduction de Memoire de Figures Geometriques complexes.* Paris: Editions Centre de Psychologie Applique. (English translation in *Clinical Neuropsychologist 7*, 4–21, 1993).

Rey, A. (1969). *Psychologie Clinique et Neurologie.* Neuchatel: Delachaux & Niestle.

Sternberg, R. (1985). *Beyond the IQ: The Triarchical Theory of Intelligence.* New York: Cambridge University Press.

Sternberg, R., & Grigorenko, E. (2002). *Dynamic Testing.* New York: Cambridge University Press.

Thurstone, L. (1938). Primary mental abilities. *Psychological Monographs*, No. 1. Chicago: University of Chicago Press.

Valdes, G., & Figueroa, R. (1994). *Bilingualism and Testing.* Norwood, NJ: Ablex.

Van der Veer, R., & Valsiner, J. (1991). *Understanding Vygotsky.* Oxford, UK: Blackwell.

Vygotsky, L. (1934/1986). *Thought and Language* (Rev. ed.). Cambridge, MA: MIT Press.

Weidl, K. H., Guthke, J., & Wigenfeld, S. (1995). Dynamic assessment in Europe. In J. Carlson (Ed.), *European Contributions to Dynamic Assessment* (pp. 33–82). Greenwich, CT: JAI Press.

14   Teaching As a Natural Cognitive Ability
Implications for Classroom Practice and Teacher Education

Sidney Strauss

This is a chapter about why we teach. I do not ask what the best way is to teach this subject matter or that. Nor do I ask how we can assess children's learning as a result of teaching. Instead, I ask a deceptively simple question: Why do we teach in the first place? The search for answers to that question takes us to the borders between our biological, psychological, and cultural endowment as humans.

Teaching, or folk pedagogy, the social transformation of knowledge from one person to another or the attempt to engender it in others, is one of the most remarkable of human enterprises. I propose that teaching, which is central to education in the broad sense of that term, can also be seen as an essential domain of inquiry for the cognitive sciences. This is so because, as I attempt to show, teaching may be a natural cognitive ability and is essential to what it means to be a human being. Furthermore, I believe that a search for the cognitive underpinnings of teaching may lead to a description of some of the fundamental building blocks of human cognition and its development.

Learning, teaching's mirror image, has been a major focus of the cognitive sciences, to be sure, but intentional pedagogy aimed to cause learning has, by and large, been flying below the cognitive sciences' radar. Perhaps this is because teaching has been narrowly viewed as residing in the province of formal schooling that takes place in schools where adults teach youngsters. Or maybe cognitive scientists have had enough trouble defining and describing learning and the conditions that bring it about. So if there is difficulty there, the expectation might be that bringing the cognitive sciences to explore teaching, that special case of what sometimes causes learning, would be a daunting task.

These and other possible sources of reticence notwithstanding, I suggest that teaching can be added to the remarkable array of areas the cognitive sciences have studied, but it will not be just one more notch on the cognitive science's belt because teaching has the enormous power to preserve significant innovations in human society. In short, teaching can enlighten the cognitive sciences and vice versa.

As I see it, teaching can be viewed from perspectives that include phylogeny, cultural evolution, anthropology, primatology, ontogeny (child development from infancy through adulthood), nonnormative cognitive development, and functioning (as in the cases of autistic individuals, brain-damaged people, remarkably gifted teachers, those with teaching disabilities), and more. This however, gets me ahead of my story.

This chapter has seven sections. In the first, I provide different definitions of teaching. In the second section, I motivate reasons why teaching may be a natural cognitive ability. This section concludes with the point that if teaching is a natural cognitive ability, there is a need to determine the nature of the cognitive prerequisites that underlie it. The third section suggests what these cognitive building blocks might be. The fourth section addresses the cognitive conditions necessary for teaching to be learned. In the fifth section, I propose various research agendas to test for these cognitive prerequisites for teaching. In the sixth, I present some implications for teacher education. And I summarize the main points in the seventh, and concluding, section.

Definitions of Teaching

Teaching is a rather elusive concept and is quite difficult to define. Scholars and researchers from various disciplines have used different definitions of teaching and, as a consequence, have developed different calipers to measure it and its effects.

For example, Caro & Hauser (1992) studied teaching from a biological perspective. Their definition of teaching has its origins in evolutionary theory and empirical data; it is as follows:

> An individual actor A can be said to teach if it modifies its behaviors only in the presence of a naïve observer, B, at some cost or at least without obtaining an immediate benefit for itself. A's behavior thereby encourages or punishes B's behavior, or provides B with experience or sets an example for B. As a result, B acquires knowledge or learns a skill earlier in life or more rapidly or efficiently than it might otherwise do, or that it would not learn at all. (p. 153)

Importantly, Caro & Hauser (1992) argue that this definition of teaching requires neither theory of mind (ToM) nor the intention to teach on the part of the animals whose teaching they described. A few words about ToM are in order here. ToM is an area that has captured the hearts and minds of developmental psychologists over the past two decades. The main idea here is that people have an understanding that others have minds, that those minds have knowledge, beliefs, etc., and that others' behaviors can be predicted based on their beliefs.

ToM research has focused mostly on young children's social cognition, that is, whether or not young children judge situations in ways that belie their understanding that others have minds. The classic false-belief task requires children to judge if someone would behave in a particular way, a way that indicates that that person has a false belief that is different from reality, where the children being interviewed know what the reality of the situation is.

The classic false-belief task is an interview situation where the experimenter is telling a child a story that is demonstrated with puppets, a chocolate bar, hat, and a dresser. The story has two children playing ball and one of them, Sally, places her hat on the floor and puts her chocolate bar in it. When playing, Sally kicks the ball away and the other child, Mary, goes to retrieve it. While retrieving it, Sally moves her chocolate bar from her hat and places it in her dresser drawer. The child being interviewed is asked where Mary thinks the chocolate is when she returns to play with Sally. A child who says she thinks it is in Sally's hat is thought to have a ToM because he is predicting Mary's behavior based on her false belief that the chocolate is in Sally's hat. A child who says that Mary will look in the dresser does not have a ToM because he does not entertain the idea of someone else's false belief. Considerable research shows that children below age 4 do not have a ToM, as tested by the false-belief task, and children above age 5 do.

Premack (1991, 1993; Premack & Premack, 1994, 1996, 2003) argued that teaching among animals other than humans is restricted, generally related to getting food to survive, which makes it very circumscribed. In addition, Premack believes that only humans are sensitive to their young's progress. For example, the mother cheetah does not give extra time to a cub of hers who might be slow in learning how to kill prey, and she is unlikely to keep that same cub back so that she can give him "remedial lessons," at the time that his siblings are on their own.

In contrast to this biologically based definition, psychologists and educators describe teaching in nonevolutionary terms, as can be seen by the following representative quote:

> When faced with the question of determining whether an action is a teaching action, as opposed to some other action such as reciting, talking or acting in a play, it is the *intention* of bringing about learning that is the basis for distinguishing teaching from other activities. The *intention* the activity serves, then, is a part of the meaning of the concept, and not a

factual discovery one makes about the activity. (italics added) (Pearson, 1989, p. 66)

Notice that in this definition of teaching, the role of intentionality is crucial, which implicates ToM, as well. This is because the intentionality associated with teaching is to cause learning in others' minds that, in turn, involves an understanding of psychological causality.

A third definition that takes some of its cues from the cognitive sciences, in particular, ToM, involves the intentional passing on of information from one who knows more to one who knows less, i.e., at the base of teaching is a knowledge gap. The definition is that teaching is the acts a teacher performs given that teacher's beliefs about the knowledge state of the other person (the learner), where the teacher has the intention to cause an increase in the knowledge or understanding of another who lacks knowledge, has partial knowledge, possesses a false belief, or has a misunderstanding. This definition is a variant of that proposed by Frye & Ziv (in press). Other forms of teaching, such as engendering knowledge that already exists in the learner's mind, will not be included in this definition, although there is a clear need to expand this definition's generality.

What Caro & Hauser (1992), Pearson (1989), and Frye & Ziv (in press) suggest as definitions of teaching are not mutually exclusive and can be seen on a continuum, with more to be added.

That having been said, we can now turn to a comprehensive view of teaching, one that includes its phylogenetic origins, ontogenesis from its early appearance in children, and developmental course through adulthood.

Teaching As a Natural Cognitive Ability

A broad view of teaching includes at least four levels of explanation for the cognitive machinery in the mind associated with teaching: an evolutionary adaptive problem that machinery solved, the cognitive programs that solve that problem, the neurophysiological infrastructure that serves as a base for the cognitive program, and the cultural underpinnings that are designed by and support the above.

Let us all too briefly examine each and then see how they might work in concert in the case of teaching. Some claim that our neural circuitry was designed by natural selection to solve adaptive problems our ancestors faced during our species' evolutionary history that began approximately 100,000–200,000 years ago, a time when our ancestors were hunter-gatherers. It is probably the case that our brains have not changed much from that time, which is to say that encased in our modern day skull is a brain whose circuitry was selected to solve adaptive problems that existed 100–200 millennia ago.

The solution to these adaptive problems affected individuals' reproduction such that, on the average, the reproductive rate of those with a selected circuitry had more offspring than those without that circuitry.

Space limitations do not allow me to expand on this topic. Nevertheless, these ideas, after their proper exposition and justification, can serve as a partial map of the cognitive landscape of teaching, one that can guide theory and research efforts of those who might find interest in the cognition of teaching in the way I am presenting it.

Significant landmarks on this map are the need to speculate about what conferred reproductive advantage to our ancestors who could teach. A second area of importance is the need to describe the cognitive programs that produce actual teaching, that allow us to know that we are in the presence of teaching and not, say, playing a game, and that allow humans to learn to teach. A third location on the map is the neurophysiological underpinnings of teaching. One point of significance here is whether or not there is dedicated neural circuitry for teaching, as opposed to, say, deception, play, and other forms of social communication, something I doubt very much. The fourth site on our map includes the cultural expression and maintenance of teaching.

This is clearly a general map of where we might want to look, both theoretically and empirically, for the place of teaching in the cognitive sciences. It provides signposts that tell us to pay attention to certain sites. I touch on some of them in this chapter, but in order to motivate the rationale for teaching as a domain that can be studied in the areas just described, I attempt to make the case for teaching as a natural cognitive ability.

There are at least seven reasons to motivate the notion that teaching is a natural cognitive ability. None by itself leads inevitably to this conclusion; however, in concert, they suggest that teaching might just be a natural cognitive ability. In broad terms, a natural cognitive ability is universal and young children effortlessly learn the domain in question without instruction. Let us see how these and other criteria apply to the domain of teaching.

First, as mentioned, teaching with a ToM may be *species-typical*. The cognition underlying teaching among some species of animals and human beings has not been thoroughly examined. There is little controversy that chimpanzees, our closest relatives, and other primates do not teach with a theory of mind (Hauser, 2000; Povinelli & Eddy, 1996, 1997; Premack, 1984, 1991; Premack & Premack, 1994, 1996; Tomasello, 1999; Tomasello & Call, 1997). There is some convergence, then, on the idea that human beings are the only species that teaches with a ToM.

As part of this typicality in human beings, we can look at places where social interactions are rich among chimpanzees and other great apes. They have a rich social organization that includes play, fighting, roles of domination and submission, joint action to achieve a common goal, the formation of coalitions and alliances, and much more (De Waal, 1996, 1998). Yet with all this social richness, there does not seem to be teaching of the kind that takes into account others' intentions among the great apes in their natural habitats. Ethologists report very few accounts of teaching in the wild, and those that have been observed can be explained as something other than teaching.

A second motivation for teaching as a natural cognitive ability is that although other primates do not seem to teach with a ToM, it is incontrovertible that teaching with a ToM is *universal* among human beings. This means that, with few exceptions, every person in every society has taught (toddlers and some autistic individuals may be exceptions here) and has been taught by others (Kruger & Tomasello, 1996; Tomasello, Kruger, & Ratner, 1993). These are universal activities that take place in everyday life in the home, the streets, the workplace, and the fields.

There is considerable cross-cultural variation concerning the amount of teaching that takes place (from very little among the San !Kung of South Africa to very much in Europe and the Americas) and the content of what is taught (hunting techniques among the San !Kung and putting a puzzle together in Boise, Idaho).

The importance of the claim of universality is twofold. It means that everyone is exposed to teaching, which is to say that everyone has the possibility to learn to teach by virtue of that exposure, and that very universality suggests that it may be a characteristic of human's biological and cultural endowments.

Third, teaching is an *extraordinarily complex* enterprise that has much to do with mind, emotions, and motivation-reading. The richness of the kinds of knowledge needed to teach is impressive. As a miniscule sampling, consider this: In order to teach, one needs to know about others' minds, knowledge, beliefs, etc., how one can know when knowledge, beliefs, etc. are missing, incomplete, or distorted, as well as how people learn (Strauss, 1993). One also knows about others' emotions and motivation.

In addition, the number and complexity of inferences that must be made when teaching others are remarkable. As teachers, we have a representation of a problem and its potential solutions. If a student solves that problem in another fashion, we infer that he or she has a different representation of the same problem. Furthermore, we infer what that representation might be, given the nature of the student's solutions, and we infer from the student's responses to our teaching if there have been representational, emotional, and/or motivational changes. This is a miniscule part of what we do when we teach. In short, teaching has considerable complexity.

Fourth is the poverty of the stimulus argument. One of the many remarkable aspects of teaching is that so much of it is *invisible* to the eye. The visible part is the external acts of teaching. It is what we see and hear when we are being taught. It is the teachers' questions, her request for the pupils to reflect on their learning, and much, much more. It is the !Kung hunter's demonstration and explanations to a youngster of how to string a bow and the ways he checks to see if it was learned, and it is the ways master carpet weavers in Mexico teach apprentice youngsters to fashion carpets for local use.

These are but a few examples of what people do when they teach. This is what is visible to the eyes of the learner, the person to whom the teaching is directed, and, as shown, it is very complex.

However, the visible part of teaching is quite impoverished in comparison to the depth of what underlies it, the part that is not revealed to the eye, and what is invisible is the inferences teachers make and the mental processes that lead to these inferences. Furthermore, it is possible that the visible part of teaching does not reveal what gives rise to it. In other words, it might be the case that one cannot infer the invisible (what underlies teaching) from the visible (actual teaching acts). I return to this point in the section Conditions for Teaching to Be Learned.

Fifth, teaching is a *specialized social interaction*, unlike others. Yet it shares some aspects of other kinds of social interaction. For example, people have conversations, they have arguments, people collaborate with each other to achieve common goals, they play, and they engage in deception to achieve private aspirations. The differences between these social interactions and teaching are obvious when we engage in them, but they are similar, too, and what stands at the heart of these social interactions is the intentionality of the individuals involved in the social interactions.

As far as I know, there has been only one study on the development of children's play and teaching (Ziv, Strauss, & Solomon, in preparation). In that research, children ages $3\frac{1}{2}$ and $5\frac{1}{2}$ were taught a board game and were asked if they wanted to play with a friend. All did, of course, and because their friends did not know how to play the game, they had to teach it. This methodology was like that of Strauss, Ziv, & Stein (2002). After they taught their friends how to play, they then played the game together.

The results are complex and are still being analyzed, but there is a finding that bears on the point of young children being able to differentiate between the goals of teaching and playing in a competitive game. The goal of teaching is to pass on one's knowledge to someone who knows less in an attempt to close the gap in knowledge. The goal of playing the same, competitive game is to win. This difference in goals led to differences in intentions that, in turn led to differences in behaviors: There was no cheating in teaching, but there was in play.

We also found that there were two kinds of cheating (deception) in play: (a) deception about results, found mostly among the younger children, was detected when a child attempted to hide the results of a throw of the dice from the other player, and (b) deception about one's intentions, found mostly among the older children, where the child who was cheating told the other that he intended to make a move that he had not made.

Both kinds of deception involve understanding others' mental states. Deception about results involves an understanding that others can get information from the world via perception, so if one denies the other the possibility of seeing the results of a dice throw, the other cannot know what the results were. Deception about one's intentions concerns the notion that one's desires and intentions are private and cannot be known and checked by others unless one makes them public.

The point here is that at a surprisingly early age, children behave differently in two kinds of social communication situations around the same game. What differentiates them are the goals of the interactions and the intentionality of the children engaged in them.

Sixth, although teaching is *universal* among human beings, it seems to be *learned without formal education*, or even education of the informal kind. A sliver of the 6 billion inhabitants of planet earth has been taught how to teach; yet all know how to teach. All have been exposed to pedagogy; they have been taught, but, with few exceptions, they have had no instruction about how to teach.

There is sometimes a point of confusion here that I would like to clarify. The fact that people have not been taught how to teach does not mean it is not learned. Teaching *is* learned, and the section Conditions for Teaching to Be Learned picks up on this theme.

Seventh, *very young children teach*. There are two kinds of evidence that bear on this matter: Toddlers may request teaching and youngsters teach.

Toddlers May Request Teaching

Toddlers may have a sensitivity to teaching (Strauss & Ziv, 2001). Children, as young as age 2, are involved in an almost obsessive everyday activity of asking what the name of an object is. "What's this called?" is a frequent request they make. Let's look at what may be cognitively involved in this seemingly harmless question. First, they know (in using the word "know," I do not mean that this knowledge is conscious; instead, it is implicit in the situation) that objects have names. Second, they know that they do not know the name of the object they are asking about. Third, they turn to someone they believe knows the name of the object, indicating they know that there is a knowledge gap. Fourth, they know that if someone tells them the name, then they will know the name. Here is the point: their request here is for someone who they believe should know the name of the object *to teach them*, to pass on knowledge so as to close the knowledge gap. In this interpretation, although 2-year-olds do not seem capable of teaching (Ashley & Tomasello, 1998), they do seem to request it from others.

Youngsters Teach

Research shows that even $3\frac{1}{2}$-year-olds teach (Ashley & Tomasello, 1998; Astington & Pelletier, 1996; Maynard, 2002; Strauss et al., 2002; Wood, Wood, Ainsworth, & O'Malley, 1995). Their teaching shows remarkable understandings about how to bring about learning in others. As an example, Strauss et al. (2002) found that $5\frac{1}{2}$-year-olds and possibly $3\frac{1}{2}$-year-olds, who were taught a board game, could teach it to their same-age friends (pupils). Furthermore, they did not intervene when their pupils played according to the rules of a game the teacher just taught them, but they did intervene at the points when the pupil made a mistake. These two findings, among many others, indicate that very young children teach others.

The combined claims of teaching with a ToM as being typical of and universal among human beings; its phenomenal cognitive complexity; the difficulty, if not impossibility, of inferring this complexity from being exposed to the visible part of teaching; its not having been taught yet 2-year-olds implicitly request teaching; and teaching emerging among $3\frac{1}{2}$-year-olds and $5\frac{1}{2}$-year-olds teaching well, suggest a reasonableness to the idea that teaching is a natural cognitive ability.

If this claim seems acceptable, we can then ask ourselves two fundamental questions: What are the cognitive prerequisites of teaching? and What are the conditions for teaching to be learned?

Cognitive Prerequisites of Teaching

Before reading on, think for a moment about what is involved, cognitively, when we teach others. If you took time out to ponder this, you noticed that teaching is quite complex and requires many cognitive feats. I briefly present teachings' cognitive prerequisites in this section.

I restrict the conversation here to contingent teaching (Wood et al., 1995) that, by definition, has the teacher reacting to the learner's responses to her teaching. For purposes of exposition, I exclude teaching that does not require altering one's teaching based on the learner's behaviors, as in nonsynchronous teaching by television. That kind of teaching should also be analyzed in terms of its cognitive prerequisites, but that will not be presented here.

Contingent teaching situations deal with procedural knowledge, i.e., the knowledge about how to do something. In teaching, there is considerable monitoring of the self and the other. This monitoring involves entering the other's mind, in the sense of attempting to imagine what knowledge he has, what his emotional and motivational states are, and more. Mind-reading has been examined extensively over the past two decades under the rubric of ToM.

Contingent teaching almost surely requires one to have a ToM about others' minds. However, unlike what is tapped in ToM false-belief tasks, teaching requires an online ToM, one that has monitoring and an executive function that keeps teaching's complexity in line. Indeed, there is a multifaceted, mutual, and fine-tuned online monitoring in a teaching situation, where both the teacher and the learner are reading the other's mind.

I now flesh out some of these ideas where I restrict my brief exposition to the teaching feedback loop, monitoring, and executive functions from the teacher's side of the teaching dynamic.

I believe there are likely to be feedback loops between the teacher and the learner when contingent teaching occurs, as well as deep epistemological assumptions about others' minds.

As for the *feedback loops* in mutual monitoring, consider the following: A teacher is explaining or demonstrating something to a pupil. As this is going on, the teacher is looking at the child in an attempt to determine, by the pupil's facial expressions, the ranges of the learner's comfort, concentration, understanding the material, etc. This is a kind of mind- and emotions-reading that all teachers do when teaching.

As the teaching proceeds, she asks the pupil questions and from the pupil's answers, the teacher senses how much of the problem the student is grasping. If the teacher judges that the pupil understands the material quite well, she continues teaching. This seemingly trivial aspect of teaching is quite deep, and we have seen that even a 5-year-old teacher continues teaching a game to a learner when the learner plays correctly according to the rules of the game. This involves mind-reading.

However, if the teacher believes the pupil is having difficulties with the material, she generally does not continue further until the pupil has understood the material at hand. This, too, entails mind-reading. When a teacher (even a 5-year-old teacher) detects a misconception, false belief, partial knowledge, etc. on the part of the learner, this means the teacher has (a) a representation of the knowledge that is thought to be correct, (b) a representation of the learner's incorrect knowledge, and (c) the ability to detect a mismatch between those knowledge representations.

The loop part is the teacher's attempt to make midcourse teaching corrections so as to enhance understanding, but notice that this requires an online ToM because they are a result of the teacher's reading of the reasons for the learner's misunderstandings as teaching continues. In other words, the teacher changes teaching strategies based on her representation of the learner's mind.

There are different ways to make these midcourse corrections. The teacher might correct the pupil's mistake by telling him what the correct answer is and how one could get to that answer. She might change her teaching technique so as to find another way to help the pupil understand the problem and its solution. She may ask the child what is hindering his correct understanding of the problem. Then, when she has taught the material, say, in a new way she, once again, asks the learner questions so as to determine if it is now better understood, which leads to further choices and more mind-reading on the part of the teacher and so on and so forth.

All of this is very familiar and we have all engaged in it from the perspective of both the teacher and the pupil.

Let us look at some *epistemological assumptions* about the mind and learning that are implicit in teachers' teaching. Teachers have declarative knowledge that

- others have minds;
- the mind contains knowledge, beliefs, etc.;
- what is in the mind gets expressed externally veridically; that is, the pupil's knowledge, beliefs, etc. that are expressed in their words, motor behaviors, etc. accurately reflect what is in the mind;
- there is psychological causality; that is, pupils' knowledge, etc. can be changed by others; for example, by teaching, which is to say that teaching can cause learning to occur in the pupil's mind; and
- teaching that causes learning is an action-at-a-distance change; that is, teaching is conducted outside the pupil's mind but it influences changes in the mind, which are termed "learning" (Strauss, 1993, 2001).

This was a very brief and sketchy outline of some aspects of what I mean by an online ToM. Notice that, due to space limitations, I did not include the learner's ToM about the teacher's mind and her teaching and about the loops and assumptions involved in the learner's questions about the material he is being taught.

The above suggests that teaching is a remarkably complex enterprise from a cognitive perspective. The fact that very young children can carry off this complexity rather effortlessly is quite surprising. Yet there has been little theory and research development into this area on the part of cognitive scientists and educational researchers. My conceptual framework for explaining how youngsters can teach is guided by the notion of teaching as a natural cognitive ability.

Conditions for Teaching to Be Learned

I mentioned that although teaching may be a natural cognitive ability, it does not somehow magically and spontaneously come into existence. It must be learned. All children are exposed to teaching, yet it is rare that they are instructed about how to teach.

The question before us is what conditions should be met for teaching to be learned? I present a list that takes its lead from work done by Pinker (1979), where he attempted to describe the conditions that are prerequisites for language to be learned. Here I simply apply them to teaching.

First is the learnability condition. This condition is twofold. It posits that teaching can be learned in the first place. It also states that the cognitive system can adapt to any teaching it is exposed to. We need to show that the learning mechanisms are adaptive in that they allow learning of any kind of teaching. As mentioned in a previous section, although teaching is universal, it has many forms that are culture-bound. These culturally varied forms of teaching should be able to be learned by any child in his or her normative development. In other words, if we were to take an infant of French parents and, upon birth, put him in the !Kung culture and were we to take an infant born to !Kung parents and have him raised by a French family from birth, the !Kung-born child will learn to teach like the French and the French-born child will learn to teach like the !Kungs.

Second is the equipotential condition. This suggests that all kinds of teaching are possible. We touched on this in the section dealing with the many ways that people have come to teach.

Third is the cognitive constraints condition for learning to teach. The explanations we offer for how the learning of teaching occurs should be consistent with what we know about young children's basic cognitive abilities. For example, we should not suggest learning mechanisms for teaching that are beyond what we know about young children's attention, short-term memory, etc.

Fourth is the time condition. The point here is that learning to teach takes time. It is not a spontaneous, instantaneous acquisition. See Feldman (1994) for an exposition on the relations between universal and nonuniversal achievements and the place of spontaneous versus instructed conceptual acquisitions.

Fifth is the developmental condition. The learning mechanism should allow a description of the development of teaching that is consistent with data about the sequential trajectory of children's understanding of teaching and their actual teaching. For instance, were research findings to continue to find that $3\frac{1}{2}$-year-olds teach mostly through demonstration and $5\frac{1}{2}$-year-olds teach mostly through explanation with demonstrations, we would need a mechanism that could explain this developmental sequence.

The sixth condition involves constraints on input. The idea here is that the learning mechanisms must not require input that is unavailable to children. Were we to surmise that the input needed to learn to teach was not available to children, we would have a serious problem.

Teaching can now be seen as remarkably complex. Accounting for this is at the heart of our research agenda.

Research Agenda

The answers I propose for what a research agenda on teaching would look like are linked, of course, to my conceptual analysis of teaching as a natural cognitive ability. I address six areas where one can go empirically to study cognitive prerequisites.

One is research on primates and lower animals. This allows us a view of the phylogenetic emergence of teaching and what is necessary for its occurrence. We can also speculate about the reproductive advantages afforded by teaching when humans emerged as a separate species.

Second, we can shed light on the cognition of teaching via more research on young children, where we can (1) expose the ontogenesis of teaching's cognitive prerequisites that lead to the emergence of teaching and (2) describe the developmental trajectory of teaching from its emergence to its maturity. Research in this area is currently being conducted with Margalit Ziv and our students at Tel Aviv University: Noah Mor, Ayelet Solomon, and Liat Ornan.

In a third area, one can attempt to describe the nature of teaching among extremely gifted adult teachers. This would be a description of the adult end point of the full development of teachers' cognition.

Fourth, it is possible to consider teaching that has been compromised by developmental or neuropsychological problems. Were we to have hypotheses about the nature of teaching's cognitive prerequisites and were we to know what specific cognitive difficulties arise from developmental or physiological problems, we could predict nonnormative teaching.

This is analogous to knockout experiments in genetics, where a gene is knocked out and its phenotypic expression is studied. In the case of teaching, we can observe teaching in individuals who have had problems in the course of their development. We would choose developmental problems based on what we believe the cognitive prerequisites of teaching are.

I mention four groups of problems that could be studied:

- High functioning people with autism. They might not have a ToM (Happe et al., 1996).
- Brain damaged individuals; for example, those with prefrontal brain damage in the area that may be dedicated to ToM (Sabbagh & Taylor, 2000; Stone, Baron-Cohen, & Knight, 1998). Work in this area with Naama Friedmann and Noga Balaban at Tel Aviv University will begin soon on this topic, which gets at the neurological underpinnings of the cognitive machinery that leads to teaching.
- Individuals with specific language impairment, such as pragmatic deficit. Anna Gavrilov, an MA student at Tel Aviv University, is studying this, under the guidance of Naama Friedmann, Margalit Ziv, and myself.
- Teachers who have what I have coined "teaching disabilities," a term and concept that does not appear in the literature. Some teachers have enormous difficulties teaching, and it would be of interest to attempt to determine the nature of their teaching problems. This research would identify levels and kinds of teaching disabilities, something that would allow us to gain an understanding of the cognitive machinery that underpins teaching.

Fifth, one can analyze teaching using formal systems of analysis, such as artificial intelligence (AI). One could attempt to build an intelligent system that can detect teaching. One could also introduce teaching to models in an attempt to determine the roles of teaching in the evolution of artificial life systems (Parisi & Schlesinger, 2002), and one can model how an intelligent system can communicate with another intelligent system in the form of teaching (Goldman & Kearns, 1991). The use of AI and computational models can bring about rigorous definitions and descriptions of teaching that are currently virtually nonexistent.

Tzur Sayag, a student at Tel Aviv University, is doing work in these areas. In a computer environment, he is growing virtual teachers that teach virtual learners and is studying how teachers learn to teach, the importance of teachers having complete knowledge of a learner's mind (neural network) in learning how to teach that learner, and more (see Sayag & Strauss, 2004).

A sixth area that has captured the hearts (and minds) of a branch of cognitive psychology – ToM theory and research – is an excellent candidate for research on cognitive prerequisites of teaching. But, as mentioned, the classic research and theory-building will probably have to be extended because ToM research has looked at young children's social cognition about others' belief systems, whereas teaching is dynamic and interactive and requires a procedural online ToM about others' minds and how learning occurs in those minds.

Teacher Education

Making statements about teacher education when there is so little research concerning teaching as a natural cognitive ability requires more than the usual caveats and admonitions. However, I will not take that route. Instead, I throw prudence to the winds and speculate considerably beyond what discretion calls for.

Let me begin with a statement about what I do *not* want to say about teacher education. I do not believe that because children at age 2 show a sensitivity to teaching by requesting it, those at age $3\frac{1}{2}$ have the rudiments of teaching, and $5\frac{1}{2}$-year-olds are quite good teachers, there is no need to teach adult teachers to teach. On the other hand, there is no point in teaching adults to do something they were already quite good at in early childhood.

That having been said, let's see what the implications for teacher education might be, given the conceptual framework I attempted to elucidate in these pages. I discuss two: (1) a possible explanation for adult teachers' resistance to constructivist teaching methods and (2) the role of subject matter knowledge in teaching.

Adult Teachers' Resistance to Constructivist Teaching Methods

Research in science and mathematics education has discovered that most children and adults hold misconceptions about, say, the physics of objects' trajectories. These misconceptions appear early in life and seem to be quite resistant to change through teaching, although some adults overcome this resistance and become experts.

A weak analogy can be drawn to the case of teacher education. We cannot say that there is such a thing as a misconception about teaching because consensus does not exist as to what correct teaching is in the way that there is consensus about the trajectory of objects. On the other hand, teachers often seem to teach with a direct-transmission model in mind, whereas teacher education courses are often geared to teachers engaging in constructivist teaching. There might be some resistance to understanding the constructivist approach, and if that is the case, we might want to determine the nature of the model teachers hold that offers resistance to teaching via constructivism.

Constructivist teaching methods have gained contemporary currency (and many interpretations), and are based on the idea that children are active constructors and not passive recipients of knowledge they are taught. Teaching, in this view, involves the sharing and joint co-construction of knowledge. Reddy (1979) labeled this the tool-builder's metaphor, and Sfard (1998) called this the participatory metaphor. Many teacher education courses, both preservice and inservice, present instructional methods that foster this approach. My personal experience is that these courses have not had a huge success when we examine teachers' teaching when these courses end. Teachers often return to their former, direct transmission ways of teaching.

I often hear reasons for this lack of overwhelming success. One is that the school classroom is a culture that makes constructivist teaching difficult. This culture includes expectations on the parts of the principal, pupils, and parents concerning what teaching should be like.

Teachers' reticent use of constructivist teaching methods can also be explained by teachers' cognition of the teaching/learning process. In other words, one can appeal to the notion of teaching as a natural cognitive ability as a possible impediment to constructivist teaching. Research I have conducted over the past decade (Strauss, 1993; Strauss & Shilony, 1994) indicates that teachers and adults who are not teachers have a model of teaching that knowledge is directly transmitted from the source of knowledge (the teachers) to its recipient (the learner). This model resembles Reddy's (1979) conduit metaphor and Sfard's (1998) acquisition metaphor.

It is possible that adults' teaching is influenced by their natural cognition, which is to say, that at the heart of the direct transmission model of teaching is the natural cognitive ability I am elaborating in these pages. If that is the case, we might have a way of describing what stands at the core of the resistance to instruction about constructivist teaching.

The Roles of Pedagogical Content and Subject Matter Knowledge in Teaching: An Appeal to Separate Them

Shulman and his co-workers (Shulman, 1986; Wilson, Shulman, & Richert, 1987) proposed a taxonomy of the kinds of knowledge teachers employ.

Among the kinds of teacher knowledge Shulman proposes are pedagogical content knowledge (PCK) and subject matter knowledge (SMK).

In broad strokes, PCK refers to teachers' professional knowledge about how to make subject matter understandable to children. It includes teachers' knowledge of students' preconceptions about subject matter, which concepts and skills are particularly difficult for children to learn, what makes them difficult, ways to make these difficult concepts and skills easier, and how these are different at different ages. In shorthand form, it is the knowledge teachers have about children's minds, how their minds work when learning takes place, and the roles of instruction in fostering learning.

The area of teachers' SMK has many aspects, only two of which are briefly discussed here: definitions of what subject matter (SM) of disciplines is and how that subject matter is organized mentally by teachers (i.e., what their SMK is).

Definitions of Subject Matter of Disciplines

The psychological description of the SM of disciplines, and its related pedagogy, has a century-long history. Among the most influential contemporary scholars to study these issues is Schwab (1962). The core of his ideas includes two main aspects of the structure of SM in disciplines: its syntactic and substantive structure.

The syntactic structure of disciplines concerns the ways researchers obtain data, interpret it, and draw conclusions. In short, it deals with ways people in a field come to know and understand it. The ways one knows and understands a discipline are discipline-dependent: Knowing and understanding music are not the same as knowing and understanding physics or literature or psychology. Those special ways of knowing that characterize each discipline are part of teachers' SMK and their understandings of it should influence how they teach.

The substantive structure of SM in a discipline pertains to the main concepts of a discipline and their relations. As an example, the main concepts in cognitive developmental psychology, from the structuralist viewpoint, are logico-mathematical structures as the psychological entities that interpret the world and guide behaviors; assimilation and accommodation as invariant psychological functioning; disequilibrium as a mechanism of structural change, etc. For information processing adherents, among the main concepts are knowledge organizations as the principal psychological entities that influence the interpretation of environmental data and that guides behaviors; attention mechanisms that influence which environmental information gets acted on; encoding, maturation, and automatization as mechanisms that foster learning, etc.

Substantive structures influence researchers' views of their discipline and lead them to ways they choose to obtain the data they interested in, interpret that data, and draw conclusions. In other words, substantive structures influence syntactic structures, and vice versa.

What constitutes a discipline or field has been a subject of intense investigation in the history and philosophy of science and the social sciences. What teachers understand to be the syntactic and substantive knowledge of disciplines comprise most of teachers' SMK.

Research and theory development led me to appeal to keep SMK and PCK separate, rather than see them as inextricably intertwined, as Shulman (1986) suggested. The main idea is that *how* we teach is related to our understandings of the mind and how learning takes place in others' minds. *What* we teach is related to our SMK.

Let me give an example of what I mean. Many teachers believe that complex material is difficult to learn, and one way to make that complex material easier is to break it up into its component parts. This teaching strategy is guided by a view of the mind and learning. In contrast, the places where teachers break up the material into its parts are connected to their SMK.

My theoretical work suggests and my research shows that teachers with considerable and deeply organized SMK and those whose SMK is impoverished and organized in a shallow manner *teach the same way*, a way guided by their conception of others' minds and learning (Strauss, Ravid, Magen, & Berliner, 1998; Strauss, Ravid, Zelcer, & Berliner, 1999; Haim, Strauss, & Ravid, in press).

In contrast, these same studies found that *what* these teachers taught was very different. Teachers who broke up complex material did so at the places where they thought that the subject matter could be broken. And because they had different SMK, due to their different knowledge organizations, the subject matter they taught was different.

In contrast to Shulman's (1986) suggestion that PCK and SMK are inextricably intertwined, my work indicates that teachers' SMK should be kept conceptually separated from their understandings of how it is learned (PCK).

An implication from my view is that we should not have illusions that teacher education courses about how to teach difficult concepts in, say, history (i.e., teaching PCK) should influence their SMK about history. Similarly, there is no reason to believe that teaching teachers about history (SMK) will influence the ways they will teach history.

Summary

I sketched a brief position about how teaching has the possibility of shedding light on the cognitive sciences and vice versa. As far as I know, some of the areas mentioned above have not been studied at all, and the others that have been studied have had little research conducted in them. And when that research was conducted, it was not motivated by the conceptual account I have been giving here about teaching as a natural cognitive ability.

I believe the positions outlined here* have the possibility of opening up research on teaching so that it could include the nexus where humans' biological, psychological, and cultural endowments are examined. And in so doing, we may be exploring an area that is fundamental to what it means to be human.

References

Ashley, J., & Tomasello, M. (1998). Cooperative problem-solving and teaching in preschoolers. *Social Development 7*, 143–163.

Astington, J. W., & Pelletier, J. (1996). The language of mind: Its role in teaching and learning. In D. R. Olson & N. Torrance (Eds.), *The Handbook of Education and Human Development* (pp. 593–620). Oxford: Blackwell.

Caro, T. M., & Hauser, M. (1992). Is there teaching in nonhuman animals. *The Quarterly Review of Biology 67*, 151–174.

Chomsky, N. (1965). *Aspects of the Theory of Syntax*. Cambridge, MA: MIT Press.

De Waal, F. (1996). *Good Natured: The Origins of Right and Wrong in Humans and Other Animals*. Cambridge, MA: Harvard University Press.

De Waal, F. (1998). *Chimpanzee Politics: Power and Sex Among Apes*. Baltimore, MD: Johns Hopkins University Press.

Feldman, D. H. (1994). *Beyond Universals in Cognitive Development*. (2nd ed.). Norwood, NJ: Ablex.

Fodor, J. (2000). *The Mind Doesn't Work That Way: The Scope and Limits of Computational Psychology*. Cambridge, MA: MIT Press.

Frye, D., & Ziv, M. (in press). Teaching and learning as intentional activities. In S. Strauss (Ed.), *Theories of Mind and Teaching*. Oxford: Oxford University Press.

Goldman, S. A., & Kearns, M. J. (1991). *On the Complexity of Teaching*. Paper presented at the Twenty-Eighth Annual Symposium on Foundations of Computer Science.

* Much of what appears here is inspired by many ideas I got from Shep, both in his written pieces and through memorable conversations. He has been a steadfast encourager of my work, and I am indebted to him for that and much more. But indebtedness is in the eyes of the beholder. He never encouraged that feeling in me. This chapter is written with him in mind. Some of the ideas here resulted from research that was supported by the Israel Science Foundation (grant number 797/02).

Haim, O., Strauss, S., & Ravid, D. (in press). Relations between EFL teachers' formal knowledge of grammar and their in-action mental models of children's minds and learning. *Teaching and Teacher Education.*

Happe, F., Ehlers, S., Fletcher, P., Frith, U., Johansson, M., Gillberg, C., Dolan, R., Frackowiak, R., & Furth, C. (1996). "Theory of mind" in the brain. Evidence from a PET scan study of Asperger syndrome. *NeuroReport 8,* 197–210.

Hauser, M. (2000). *Wild Minds: What Animals Really Think.* New York: Henry Holt.

Kruger, A. C., & Tomasello, M. (1996). Cultural learning and learning culture. In D. Olson & N. Torrance (Eds.), *The Handbook of Human Development and Education* (pp. 369–387). Oxford: Blackwell.

Maynard, A. E. (2002). Cultural teaching: The development of teaching skills in Maya sibling interactions. *Child Development 73,* 969–982.

Parisi, D., & Schlesinger, M. (2002). Artificial life and Piaget. *Cognitive Development 17,* 1301–1321.

Pearson, A. T. (1989). *The Teacher: Theory and Practice in Teacher Education.* New York: Routledge.

Pinker, S. (1979). Formal models of language learning. *Cognition 8,* 217–283.

Povinelli, D. J., & Eddy, T. J. (1996). What young chimpanzees know about seeing. *Monographs of the Society for Research in Child Development 61,* 2 (Serial no. 247).

Povinelli, D. J., & Eddy, T. J. (1997). Specificity of gaze-following in young chimpanzees. *British Journal of Developmental Psychology 15,* 213–222.

Premack, D. (1984). Pedagogy and aesthetics as sources of culture. In M. Gazzaniga (Ed.), *Handbook of Cognitive Neuroscience* (pp. 15–35). New York: Plenum.

Premack, D. (1991). The aesthetic basis of pedagogy. In R. R. Hoffman & D. S. Palermo (Eds.), *Cognition and the Symbolic Processes: Applied and Ecological Perspectives* (pp. 303–325). Hillsdale, NJ: Lawrence Erlbaum.

Premack, D. (1993). Prolegomenon to evolution of cognition. In T. A. Poggio & D. A. Glaser (Eds.), *Exploring Brain Functions: Models in Neuroscience* (pp. 269–290). New York: Wiley.

Premack, D., & Premack, A. J. (1994). Why animals have neither culture nor history. In T. Ingold (Ed.), *Companion Encyclopedia of Anthropology: Humanity, Culture and Social Life* (pp. 350–365). London: Routledge.

Premack, D., & Premack, A. J. (1996). Why animals lack pedagogy and some cultures have more of it than others. In D. R. Olson & N. Torrance (Eds.), *The Handbook of Human Development and Education* (pp. 302–344). Oxford: Blackwell.

Premack, D., & Premack, A. J. (2003). *Original Intelligence: Unlocking the Mystery of Who We Are.* New York: McGraw Hill.

Reddy, M. (1979). The conduit metaphor: A case of frame conflict in language about language. In A. Ortony (Ed.), *Metaphor and Thought* (2nd ed., pp. 164–201). Cambridge, UK: Cambridge University Press.

Sabbagh, M. A., & Taylor, M. (2000). Neural correlates of theory-of-mind reasoning: An event-related potential study. *Psychological Science 11,* 46–50.

Sayag, T., & Strauss, S. (2004). Teaching & artificial life. In D. Ravid & H. Bat-Zeev Shyldkrot (Eds.), *Perspectives on Language and Language Development: Essays in Honor of Ruth A. Berman* (pp. 159–171). Dodrecht, Holland: Kluwer.

Sfard, A. (1998). On two metaphors for learning and the dangers of choosing just one. *Educational Researcher 27,* 4–13.

Shulman, L. S. (1986). Those who understand: Knowledge growth in teaching. *Educational Researcher 15*, 4–14.

Stone, V. E., Baron-Cohen, S., & Knight, R. T. (1998). Frontal lobe contributions to theory of mind. *Journal of Cognitive Neuroscience 10*, 640–656.

Strauss, S. (1993). Theories of learning and development for academics and educators. *Educational Psychologist 28*, 191–203.

Strauss, S. (2001). Folk psychology, folk pedagogy and their relations to subject matter knowledge. In B. Torff & R. J. Sternberg (Eds.), *Understanding and Teaching the Intuitive Mind* (pp. 217–242). Mahwah, NJ: Lawrence Erlbaum.

Strauss, S., Ravid, D., Magen, N., & Berliner, D. C. (1998). Relations between teachers' subject matter knowledge, teaching experience and their mental models of children's minds and learning. *Teaching and Teacher Education 14*, 579–595.

Strauss S., Ravid, D., Zelcer, H., & Berliner, D. C. (1999). Teachers' subject matter knowledge and their belief systems about children's learning. In T. Nunes (Ed.), *Learning to Read: An Integrated View from Research and Practice* (pp. 259–282). London: Kluwer.

Strauss, S., & Shilony, T. (1994). Teachers' models of children's minds and learning. In L. Hirschfeld and S. Gelman (Eds.), *Mapping the Mind: Domain-Specificity in Cognition and Culture* (pp. 455–473). Cambridge, UK: Cambridge University Press.

Strauss, S., & Ziv, M. (2001). Requests for words are a request for teaching. *Behavioral and Brain Sciences 24*, 1118–1119.

Strauss, S., Ziv, M., & Stein, A. (2002). Teaching as a natural cognition and its relations to preschoolers' developing theory of mind. *Cognitive Development 17*, 1473–1487.

Tomasello, M. (1999). *The Cultural Origins of Human Cognition*. Cambridge, MA: Harvard University Press.

Tomasello, M., & Call, J. (1997). *Primate Cognition*. Oxford: Oxford University Press.

Tomasello, M., Kruger, A. C., & Ratner, H. (1993). Cultural learning. *Behavioral and Brain Sciences 16*, 495–511.

Wilson, S. M., Shulman, L. S., & Richert, E. (1987). '150 ways of knowing': Representations of knowledge in teaching. In J. Calderhead (Ed.), *Exploring Teachers' Thinking* (pp. 104–124). London: Cassell.

Wood, D., Wood, H., Ainsworth, S., & O'Malley, C. (1995). On becoming a tutor: Toward an ontogenetic model. *Cognition and Instruction 13*, 565–581.

Ziv, M., Strauss, S., & Porat, A. (in preparation). *Developmental Differences in Early Childhood Concerning Children's Understanding of Teaching, Play, and Theory of Mind.*

Index